Best Places
to Stay
in Florida

THE BEST PLACES TO STAY SERIES

Best Places to Stay in America's Cities
Kenneth Hale-Wehmann, Editor

Best Places to Stay in Asia
Jerome E. Klein

Best Places to Stay in California
Third Edition, Marilyn McFarlane

Best Places to Stay in the Caribbean
Third Edition, Bill Jamison and Cheryl Alters Jamison

Best Places to Stay in Florida
Third Edition, Christine Davidson

Best Places to Stay in Hawaii
Third Edition/Bill Jamison and Cheryl Alters Jamison

Best Places to Stay in the Mid-Atlantic States
Second Edition, Dana Nadel-Foley

Best Places to Stay in the Midwest
John Monaghan

Best Places to Stay in New England
Fifth Edition, Christina Tree and Kimberly Grant

Best Places to Stay in the Pacific Northwest
Third Edition, Marilyn McFarlane

Best Places to Stay in the Rocky Mountain States
Second Edition, Roger Cox

Best Places to Stay in the South
Second Edition, Carol Timblin

Best Places to Stay in the Southwest
Third Edition/Anne E. Wright

Best Places to Stay in Florida

THIRD EDITION

Christine Davidson

Bruce Shaw, Editorial Director

HOUGHTON MIFFLIN COMPANY
BOSTON • NEW YORK

For information about permission to reproduce selections from
this book, write to Permissions, Houghton Mifflin Company,
215 Park Avenue South, New York, New York 10003.

Third Edition

ISSN: 1048-5430
ISBN: 0-395-66615-5

Printed in the United States of America

Illustrations prepared by Eric Walker
Maps by Charles Bahne
Design by Robert Overholtzer

This book was prepared in conjunction
with Harvard Common Press.

VB 10 9 8 7 6 5 4 3 2

To my favorite traveling companions:
Chip, Mike, and Jen

Acknowledgments

Books are not just the result of the author's research and writing, but also the reflection of the aid and encouragement of a number of people. This has been particularly true of *Best Places to Stay in Florida*, which depended on the interest of so many.

My thanks first to researchers who visited places included in the first and second editions, most of which are also in this third edition: Jeff Bernstein, Ruth and Bob Davidson, Corbie Morrison, Helen and Chuck Moxley, Mary and Linda Prior, and Suzan Helgerson Pruiett. Many thanks to the various tourism and visitors' bureaus of Florida counties, the Florida Department of Natural Resources, Inn Route, Marcella Schaible of Bed and Breakfast Company: Tropical Florida, Al and Donna Blaustein, and Linda Durgin. My greatest appreciation goes to my family for their support and encouragement during the long weeks of travel and revision.

Contents

Introduction   1
State map   4
Planning for Florida   5
Finding the Real Florida   13

Best Places to Stay in Florida
    The Northeast Coast   25
    The Panhandle   126
    Central Florida   161
    The Southeast Coast   221
    The Keys   295
    The West Coast   365

Recommended Guidebooks   453
What's What   457
    *A cross-reference of accommodations by type
    and special interests*
Index   469

Introduction

Best Places to Stay in Florida is a gleaning of the best Florida has to offer out of hundreds of motels, hotels, inns, B&Bs, condos, and resorts.

This book includes a map showing the regions into which we've broken the state, some travel tips, and a brief history on the early development of Florida as a resort. At the beginning of each regional chapter is a brief description of the history, geography, and attractions of that section of the state. Notice, too, that there is a listing of the "best" of several specific types of accommodations, such as Beachside, Budget Finds, Eclectic Finds, etc. These designations are for those who wish to stay in a place that has a particular ambience or location.

In describing the various accommodations in this book, we have tried to describe objectively the intentions and successes of a place. Obviously, the criteria for judging a "best" Budget Find will differ from those for a "best" Spa. The primary standards are distinct atmosphere, cleanliness, and the palpable presence of outstanding management. In some cases, the latter may be a hotel corporation with high standards; in others, it may be a retired school principal running a B&B who lends her books out to guests to read at night. Under no circumstances can anyone pay to be included in *Best Places to Stay*.

The majority of accommodations in *Best Places to Stay in Florida* were seen personally by the author. A few inns and hotels were initially seen or rechecked by a researcher, and some establishments were seen twice, once by a researcher and a few months later by the author. The researchers were charged with the task of viewing places — usually anonymously — with the same criteria that the author used. In addition, the opinions and experiences of relatives and friends living in a particular area of Florida were often solicited. While there's always an attempt to keep personal values and interests out of the selections, some biases have certainly crept in. We are not exactly ashamed of these biases and believe that many other modern travelers share them.

No doubt there have been some oversights, either for lack

of time or because an excellent resort or inn was new. This is particularly true of some resorts on islands accessible only by boat and a few recently restored inns in small towns. If you know of a "great place" that you think we may not be aware of, please write. On the last page of this book you'll find information about sending in a Best Places Report.

All accommodations listed in the book have air conditioning — not an unimportant consideration in Florida. With only occasional exceptions, all guest rooms described also have private baths. The few exceptions are in B&Bs and Budget Finds where most rooms have private baths but a few share a bath — ideal for those on a tight budget. Some historic B&Bs have bathrooms with old clawfoot tubs; a shower head and metal shower curtain surround are rigged up above. Some of these work pretty well and some do not. If it's important for you to have a bathroom with a real shower stall or fixed enclosure, ask about bathroom choices when making reservations. Some of the larger B&Bs and inns have both an old-fashioned tub for soaking and a new shower stall in a modern tile bathroom.

Few places described in this book are overpriced, crowded with tour groups, across a busy road from the water or an attraction for children, or decorated with plastic furniture. Very few chain hotels or high-rises are included. The most important criterion for all who researched accommodations was, Would I want to stay here?

Our one regret is that a good many of the recommendations are expensive. As everywhere in the world, you get what you pay for, and in Florida you pay quite a bit, especially during the winter season. But there are ways to get around this — you might consider visiting a plush resort in November, when skies are gloomy in Cleveland or New York, but gorgeous in Naples or Boca Raton. Or choose to come to South Florida during the height of the winter season, but stay at a Victorian B&B instead of a costly resort. Or rent a condo that may initially appear expensive but will offer savings in meals prepared in the kitchen. There are also methods of saving on air travel during certain seasons and times of the week, which a good travel agent can advise you on.

Best Places to Stay is not just for people with a great deal of disposable income, who can take a vacation whenever they feel the need. In fact, it is because most travelers to Florida are not in this lucky elite that a book like this is so important. One way or another, traveling to Florida from another part of the country and staying for a long weekend or several days is costly. Each year thousands of people come back from Florida after a honeymoon, getaway golf weekend, or trip to Disney World with disappointment or disillusionment. The hotel was glitzy and overpriced. The beach was half a mile away across a hot asphalt highway. The motel was an hour from Disney World. . . . Such experiences can sour even the good times on a Florida vacation.

Most of these too-typical experiences are undergone by travelers who have saved for months to go to Florida. When they finally do, they enjoy splurging a little. But no one enjoys wasting money, even those who have a lot of it. Vacationers to Florida want to feel good about the environment they're staying in, to get their money's worth, and to come as close as possible to the kind of vacation they've fantasized about. Therefore, our final criterion was, Is this place worth it? The answer was a definite "yes" for those accommodations described in this book, qualified as the "yes" may sometimes be.

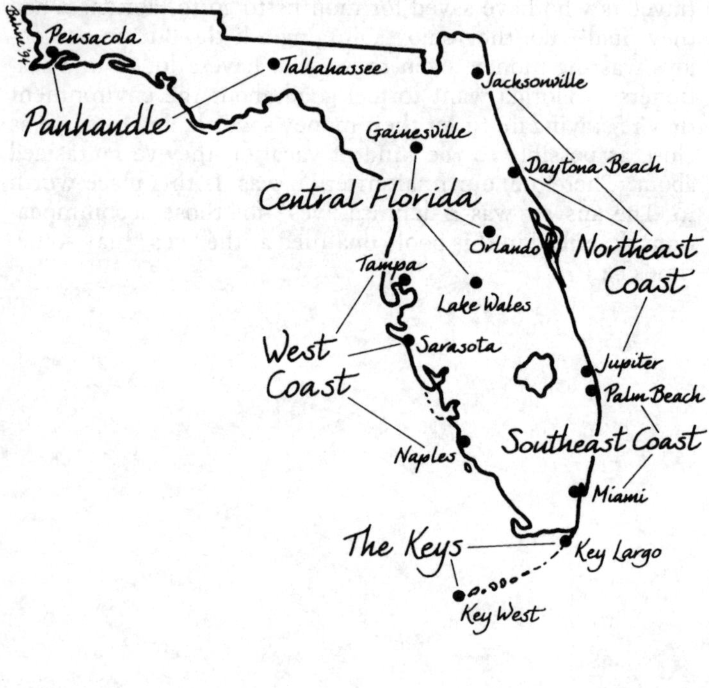

Pensacola

Tallahassee

Jacksonville

Panhandle

Gainesville

Daytona Beach

Central Florida

Orlando

Tampa

Lake Wales

Northeast Coast

West Coast

Sarasota

Jupiter

Palm Beach

Naples

Southeast Coast

Miami

The Keys

Key Largo

Key West

Planning for Florida

Getting There

It is possible to drive from the Northeast or the Midwest and arrive in Florida within 24 hours. College students do it all the time on spring breaks. But unless you've got the endurance of a college kid, it's unwise to start a Florida holiday this way. The alternatives are to drive and stay at hotels along the way, take a series of buses or trains, or fly. The latter choice is preferred by most vacationers, who have limited time in Florida and want to get there as soon and painlessly as possible.

A travel agent is the best source of information on what flights are the least expensive. Buying tickets several weeks in advance or flying in the middle of the week can lead to substantial savings. Agents can consult computer listings to find the best deals.

Organizations such as group travel clubs, AAA, AARP, and American Express also have some very good deals. These organizations charge a fee for membership. If you belong to an airline's frequent flyer club, have senior citizen "getaway" tickets, or belong to a college alumni group that can obtain group fares, you can also save.

The quality of airports varies in Florida, although most are very good. The most crowded is Miami International Airport, largely because of all the people who come through on their way somewhere else: a Caribbean cruise or a flight to South America or the islands. If you're planning on a vacation to southeast Florida or the Keys, consider flying to Fort Lauderdale's airport 40 minutes north of Miami and then driving to your destination. The 40 extra minutes is worth it; besides, you could be delayed at the Miami airport for at least 40 minutes just because of the crowds or a lost bag.

Driving in Florida

Many of the larger hotels in Florida either offer shuttle service to and from the airport or have agents for rental companies working out of their hotels. Some vacationers prefer to take the shuttle to their accommodation and, after a couple days of enjoying their hotel's amenities, rent a car from an agent for the remainder of their stay. Rates vary depending on the season in Florida. Winter rates are higher throughout the state, even in the north, where winter is actually the low season. It's always best to reserve a car in advance, particularly in southern Florida in winter.

There are a number of rental agencies in Florida. Whichever you choose, be certain it has road service. A couple of the bargain companies don't provide this service and may not tell you that — until you call from a roadside phone for help. All agencies provide minimal insurance and optional collision insurance that they urge you to get. The latter is quite costly and is necessary only if your own insurance policy doesn't cover you for collision in a rental car. Be advised, however, that you will usually be responsible for the deductible portion on your policy and will probably have to pay for any damages immediately, with your insurance company reimbursing you later.

It's important to remember several things when driving in Florida. The state is full of tourists — many of them driving in unfamiliar rental cars and not knowing exactly where they're going. Many drivers travel in the left lane at snail-slow speeds, particularly in the Orlando/Disney World area, and on roads where there is no median strip or there are frequent crossways on the median strip. This is because there are so many attractions and accommodations on the left side of the street. With only a name or street number to go by, people will inch along until they figure out where to cross.

The situation is complicated by the number of elderly drivers in the state. Many of them haven't been in Florida for long either, and may be forgetful. They, like tourists, will often drive at extremely slow speeds in the left-hand lane — or any lane — of a major highway. They may also slow down nearly to a stop before making a right or left-hand turn. For some reason, drivers in Florida, old and young, use directional signals sparingly. Or they turn on a directional signal to go left and then, after turning left, leave the signal on for miles and miles — what Jerry Seinfeld calls "the eventual left." In short, you have to drive defensively, purchase clearly marked street maps, and get precise directions for any destination so you don't contribute to the problem or become involved in an accident.

For the most part, Florida's roads are well maintained and well marked. In some areas, there seems to be construction all the time, and the roadwork causes delays. But the state makes an effort to have most of the work done by the start of the winter season.

The most heavily traveled highways run from north to south. Old Route 1, constructed on the roadbed of Flagler's railway, runs along the Atlantic coast. This is a great highway for sightseeing, especially from Boca Raton to Palm Beach. Often only one lane wide, it's congested in the Miami area and has almost a rural feel to it north of St. Augustine and Ponte Vedra.

Interstate 95 runs almost parallel to Route 1 and is a faster road. It, too, can get congested, particularly from Miami to Fort Lauderdale. It is often better to pay the toll and take the Florida Turnpike, which runs from Florida City, just south of Miami, to the junction with Interstate 75 northwest of Orlando.

The west coast equivalent of I-95 is I-75; it is usually less traveled than 95. Florida's other interstate highway is I-10, which runs from Jacksonville to the Alabama border and beyond. A huge network of state highways crisscrosses the middle of the state from 10 south. A few, like Highways 27 and 41 (the Tamiami Trail), are narrow and old but are favored by many for their lack of congestion and the interesting sights along the way.

Rates

Many hotels in Florida have high and low seasons and in-between periods called shoulder season or value season; the range of rates in one year can be enormous due to the season. Often, the person who sees the rates for a resort in a fall magazine article is in for a shock when making reservations for the same place in February. Almost all of the resorts and hotels in this book have group rates and special packages. Hotels in cities sometimes have discount rates on the weekends, while places in tourist spots may have lower rates during the week.

Unless money is no object, always ask for detailed information about the range of rates. Many hotel reservationists will initially quote you a price for a superior or deluxe room. You may have to request specifically the price of a standard room.

You probably will have to ask for information about any packages or specials, too. But once you begin to ask questions and establish your interest in "values," as the industry calls them, you'll find that most personnel taking reservations will be extremely helpful in giving you the information you need to save money.

Unless a hotel has only one type of room and one standard rate for that room year-round, *Best Places to Stay in Florida* lists a range of rates, from high to low, for each accommodation. In other words, we give the lowest seasonal rate for the lowest-priced room available and the highest seasonal rate for the highest-priced room. If suites, apartments, or cottages are available, we do the same for each of those. Rates usually go up about $10 each year for a room and a little higher for suites. Some B&Bs and inns may not raise prices for two or three years.

With the exception of a few urban hotels, rates listed are for double occupancy. Some city hotels that cater to corporate executives traveling alone list only single rates and then add a charge for "extra person" when a couple occupies the room. Many hotels that do not list corporate rates in the data do, in fact, have them. Deciphering the rates for spas may be tricky because the spa may quote a rate as "double occupancy," but the rate is still "per person." Some spas include nearly all treatments in the per-person rate, while others charge separately for them.

Taxes and Other Added Charges

Visitors to Florida sometimes are confused by the room and meal taxes in Florida, particularly when resorts in the same town quote different taxes. The state has a sales tax on all hotel rooms. Sometimes this is figured into the price of a room, sometimes it isn't. In many cases, various local and county taxes are added onto the basic state tax. We have made every effort to provide you with all tax charges in the data above each entry. But because taxes keep going up and the reporting of taxes can be inconsistent from hotel to hotel, the information we provide may not be the total tax liability. When making reservations, be certain to ask what the total tax charges will be in addition to the basic room rate.

Most hotels and resorts also have a fee for any "extra person" or "extra adult" in the room above its stated capacity. In other words, if you are a family of four and have a grandparent traveling with you who plans to sleep on a roll-away in a room with two double beds, there will be a charge. In some hotels, the "extra person" would have to be in a separate accommodation or the hotel may advise you to book a suite with a capacity for six people. Every place is different, so it is wise to ask ahead when making reservations.

Most hotels and resorts in Florida do not take pets. A few family vacation cottages and B&Bs have a tradition of allowing small animals for a fee. Even these are beginning to change former policies and are simply pointing guests to the nearest boarding kennel. The few places in the book that will take pets are listed at the end of the rate data in the beginning of each write-up.

Some resorts have a no-tipping policy; gratuities are figured into the room rate. At others, a service charge is added to your bill. Again, be sure to inquire about all fees and charges, especially if you're on a tight budget.

Payment

Payment is almost always by credit card in Florida, though some hotels will accept a personal check with proper identification (one or two major credit cards). Many hotels also require credit card identification with traveler's checks. One way or the other, it's difficult to vacation in Florida without plastic of some sort. The exceptions to this are a few small inns and B&Bs that will not take credit cards and prefer a check or cash.

Traveler's checks are usually a solid standby, and almost all of the accommodations in this book will take traveler's checks with proper identification. Some hotels in the Art Deco district of Miami Beach don't accept them, though, because they are operating on a shoestring and simply do not have the cash on hand. It's best to discuss payment when making reservations.

Late Check-out

Be sure you know check-in and check-out times and the policy on extended check-out. Some hotels have a liberal policy about using their pool and changing rooms; others do not.

Policies sometimes change according to season even in the most laid-back resorts.

Traveling with Children

Florida is a great place to vacation with kids. Most hotels and resorts allow children to stay with parents at no charge. The ages at which they allow this vary, however, so it's important to take note of this in the information at the beginning of each entry in this book.

The personnel at the hotels, resorts, and various attractions in Walt Disney World bend over backwards to accommodate families. If you have young or handicapped children, inquire about high chairs, strollers, cribs, or wheelchairs, so you can avoid having to bring them along. If you stay at a hotel or resort owned by Disney World, ask about the various Family Plans — these combine the price of accommodations, attraction tickets, and meals (including tip), making for a more carefree vacation in Disney World.

Bugs and Other Florida Wildlife

It goes without saying that anyone traveling to Florida should bring lots of suntan lotion and maybe a wide-brimmed hat. But many people forget to bring insect repellent, and even in beautiful Florida there are plenty of insects that bite and sting. Many of the least populated regions of Florida are so lovely you may want to sit and take it all in — you can sit for hours watching a troop of ducks or the pelicans diving for fish. If you do, you're a sitting duck yourself. Insect repellent is imperative. Stop at a drug store and buy some if you've forgotten to bring it with you. In areas that have biting ants, spiders, or sand fleas, you should keep repellent on your feet at all times.

In some coastal regions of Florida, signs are posted warning of sea lice. These are small critters in the ocean who love to hide in the elastic bands of swimsuits. They are not a big problem as long as you do not sit around in a wet suit. You should take off bathing apparel immediately after getting back to your hotel and rinse it a couple of times in tap water.

Many jokes circulate outside of Florida about golfers seeing alligators lounging on a golf course green or waddling onto a resort's front lawn. These cases are rare. Alligators tend to be shy. However, their protection by the law has resulted in some overpopulation and aggressiveness over food sources. What they consider a "food source" can be pretty disturbing. There have been incidents in recent years of hungry alligators going after pet dogs and children in Boynton Beach and along the Loxahatchee River. Anyone who wants to play Crocodile Dundee should forget it in Florida. Alligators are magnificent creatures, but they should be avoided except in supervised tours.

General Safety

There has been some concern in recent years regarding human predators and the safety of tourists in Florida, especially in Miami. As in any large city, it is wise not to be an easy mark. Avoid driving in unfamiliar or poorly lighted areas at any time of day or night. If you are at an airport parking lot late at night, pay the extra money to get a burly porter for your luggage or, if available, ask for security. Always stay in well-lighted areas near people, and pay attention to any intuitive negative feelings about groups of kids hanging around or a lone stranger who is loitering.

When renting a car, be sure you know exactly where you are going before leaving the airport. In general, it is best to stop driving shortly after sundown and to bring enough money so that you can stay in a secure hotel, rather than sleeping by the side of the road or at a rest stop. After the murder of a tourist who had been sleeping at a rest stop near Tallahassee, 24-hour security was mandated at all highway rest stops, which has made Floridians and out-of-state visitors feel safer. But it is uncertain how long this will continue.

Always keep one credit card, a few dollars, and a quarter in a skirt or pant pocket just in case you are parted from your wallet. Don't be obvious about using a map when you are sightseeing — this identifies you as a stranger, especially if you get out of the car to make a phone call at a public phone by the side of the road; there have been instances of purse snatching or pocket picking while tourists were distracted making a call. There have also been some "smash and grab" robberies, in which the robber smashes the window of a rental car and then grabs a purse or briefcase from the seat or floor of the car.

People who would watch their wallet on a crowded city street or be suspicious of a stranger following them in New York or Washington, D.C., often unwind so thoroughly on a Florida vacation that they forget to be careful in the state's large urban areas. Taking standard precautions should be enough to avoid robbery or injury.

Things to Do

There's an enormous range of things to do and see in Florida. Most towns have visitor centers and tourism associations with lots of information on area attractions, and many hotels have racks of promotional materials. The number of offerings can be so overwhelming that first-time visitors may see the well-advertised attractions that don't appeal to them and miss the places that would genuinely interest them.

The concierge or someone at the front desk will usually recommend area attractions, beaches, and parks. The innkeepers at B&Bs are usually great resources for what to see in a particular area. You may want to do a little reading ahead of time and ask friends who've been to Florida for suggestions. Many cities and towns have tourist bureaus and chambers of commerce that are more than happy to send you free information before a trip.

Finding the Real Florida

The Early Development of Florida

At the end of the 19th century, Henry Flagler, John D. Rockefeller's partner in Standard Oil, retired early from the oil business and began to develop the east coast of Florida as a resort mecca via railroad. He, of course, would own it, and perhaps grow rich. He never became wealthy from his hotel and railroad building, but he did do a great service to Floridians then struggling to survive — and to the millions living elsewhere in the nation who would enjoy the sunshine and beauty of this state.

Initially, Flagler improved only the existing railroad to St. Augustine, the settlement he had earlier visited with an invalid wife and found grossly lacking in civilized amenities. Besides the unpleasant hotel he and his family stayed in, there were only a few public buildings, some huts made of scrub palm, and the salt-weathered farmhouses of struggling settlers. So Flagler built a spectacular hostelry in St. Augustine, the Ponce de Leon; and a less imposing one across the street to accommodate the spillover. Eventually, Flagler erected hotels up and down his Atlantic Ocean rail route that offered the luxury his wealthy friends and colleagues were accustomed to.

However, once guests arrived, there was little to do, save fish or swim or change clothes three times a day and promenade the hotel verandahs. This could become a bore a few weeks into the season. So Flagler created resorts around a number of recreation activities: shuffleboard, swimming, croquet, and golf — a game imported from Scotland played for the first time in Florida on a course Flagler built in 1897. Thus was born the tradition of the Florida "destination resort" and the "golf resort."

By 1912, Flagler's railroad and string of resort hotels reached from St. Augustine to Key West, an incredible achievement at the time, since much of Florida was jungle and swamp. The railroad bridges to Key West, one of them traversing a seven-mile-long expanse of water, were considered in their day an engineering marvel to rival the Panama Canal.

Flagler's arena of development was principally the east coast, with a few forays into agricultural central Florida. On the west coast, Henry Plant, a wealthy rival of Flagler's, was also building a railroad system. He had first come to Florida as a land speculator, and he returned after the Civil War to purchase several narrow-gauge railroads that ran from Savannah, Georgia, to Jacksonville. From Jacksonville he turned to Tampa and the west coast.

Like Flagler, he had his triumphs. Plant's engineers created the port of Tampa by constructing a causeway and piers in the deep waters of the bay. During the Spanish-American War, the U.S. War and Navy departments moved troops and supplies through Tampa — rather than Flagler's Miami — because the harbor could accommodate larger ships. Though the west coast did not offer quite the challenge that the keys did, building a railroad was not easy here, either, for the west coast was also swampy, with dense jungle and a plethora of mosquitos and other stinging, biting wildlife. Tampa became Plant's base, and it was here that he built in 1891 what many consider his greatest achievement: the Tampa Bay Hotel, a fantastical gingerbread and Moorish brick palace that is now part of the University of Tampa. Rooms went for the unheard-of price of $75 a night. When the hotel was completed, Plant invited Flagler to the grand opening. Flagler wired back asking how he would find Tampa. Plant is reputed to have wired back, "Just follow the crowd, Henry."

As the years passed, the west coast towns of Naples and St. Petersburg were developed and became popular. F. Scott Fitzgerald and his family frequented the Don CeSar, a pink stucco palace majestically sited on St. Petersburg Beach and the Gulf of Mexico. Writers and artists journeyed on the railroad to the Casa Marina in Key West, Flagler's last grand resort. The Vanderbilts, du Ponts, Colliers, and Lindberghs preferred the serenity of the barrier islands of the west coast, then accessible only by boat.

In the early days of Florida development, few people owned winter homes, so most stayed at one of the elegant watering holes. Many of these were made of wood, and some of the most elegant eventually burned down. In their place, Spanish-style hotels were built in the 1920s of shellstone and stucco. Some of the fantastic hotels built by Flagler and Plant and a 1920s visionary, Addison Mizner, have fortunately survived. The Ponce de Leon in St. Augustine and the Tampa Bay Hotel in Tampa now house colleges. The Boca Raton, an eclectic stucco palace built by self-taught architect Mizner, is still thriving as a resort hotel, as is the Breakers, which was originally built as an annex to the Royal Poinciana but thrived on its own.

Of all the resort towns that Flagler created along his railroad, Palm Beach became the most exclusive and the most desirable. The oceanfront Royal Poinciania Hotel, which opened in 1894, was the largest resort hotel in the world and became the place for the powerful and wealthy to spend the season. Later, beautiful mansions and "cottages" were built in Palm Beach in lavish but exquisite taste.

Many showed an appreciation for Florida's Spanish heritage and for the building materials native to the area, most notably coquina and coral stone. Coquina is a shellstone made of thousands of tiny shells that congeal over the centuries with sand and are harvested, then cut into masonry blocks that are enduring and beautiful. The best examples of coquina buildings are in St. Augustine, where there was a ready supply of stone from nearby Anastasia Island. The shellstone was used by itself or as a basic building material to be plastered over with stucco. But it is most arresting when the stone is left in its natural state.

Coral stone, or key stone, is even more lovely. When cut, the pores and wavy tendrils of the once-live coral become visible; often little spiral shells are perfectly preserved in cavities of the coral. Addison Mizner used a great deal of coral stone as embellishment for archways and window frames in his buildings. Some of the mansions this eccentric designed can still be seen on Palm Beach's Worth Avenue residential area and shopping district.

For all its natural beauty and exciting architecture, Palm Beach was considered unbearably snobby in the 1920s and 1930s, and people who didn't have the right last name were often frozen out socially in the balmiest of weather. Miami was initially developed as an orange-growing region, but it soon became the common man's answer to Palm Beach. It was created in the 1890s by Flagler and a young widow from Cleveland named Julia Tuttle, who hoped to make a fortune for herself and her children. She died at 49 before this could happen, and in the last years of her life gave Flagler more than a hundred acres to build a hotel on, along with half of her other land holdings, figuring that a railroad and hotel would greatly increase the value of her property. In Miami, Flagler built the Royal Palm, the first of many hotels in Miami.

The vegetation in Miami and its barrier islands across Biscayne Bay grew so luxuriantly that, in the 1890s and for years after, no one thought too much of cutting down trees and shrubs. Some of these trees were coconut palms that had been imported by the Spanish and Americans; others were oranges, limes, bananas, and guavas. There were also various palm trees and thickets of mangroves. Miami Beach was mostly swamp in the 1890s, filled with biting insects, snakes, cabbage palm, and Spanish bayonet, a vicious form of yucca.

Miami Beach Development in the Twentieth Century

By the 1920s, Miami was a civilized and exciting city that was more open and welcoming than Palm Beach had ever been. A sandbar and marshy area in Biscayne Bay that had been filled in when the Miami River was dredged to create a canal was now called Miami Beach, and it was becoming a resort playground. The principal area developed for tourists and retirees during the first half of the century was South Beach: lower Collins Avenue, Ocean Drive, and neighborhoods just east of Biscayne Bay. Some of the most innovative development occurred during the 1930s and 1940s, resulting in what is now known as the Art Deco district.

Though it is difficult to devise an all-encompassing description of this architectural and decorative style, the buildings were usually of stucco, with smooth, streamlined exteriors on corners and entryways. Art Deco architects used their fancy in devising decorative plaster ornaments on these buildings, and often introduced modernistic decorative friezes and borders on the exteriors. The hotels and apartment buildings were painted in bright pinks, lemon yellows, and sherbet pastels. Contrasting colors were used to accentuate different sculpted decorative lines and protrusions.

At the time, Art Deco was considered up-to-date and chic. Elegant shops and restaurants were built and the entire area became fashionable. Soon this area became the playground of the wealthy upper middle class of New York and other northern cities, particularly of Jews and others who had been denied access to Palm Beach. Many people retired and lived here permanently in elegant apartment buildings.

But in the 1950s and 1960s, Art Deco began to look silly. Flat, utilitarian buildings came into vogue and lower Collins

Avenue, which had been so fashionable, began to decline. Developers moved to upper Collins Avenue to build new hotels and residential apartment buildings, and the South Beach neighborhood deteriorated still further (see description of Art Deco on page 22).

The developers on upper Collins Avenue maximized profits on their expensive plots of oceanfront land by packing as many people into the hotels as possible. The high-rise hotels that they built were much bigger than anything the lower Collins section of Miami Beach had ever seen. Looking at this congested forest of hotels today, it appears as if someone from midtown Manhattan came to the beach and got homesick. To many, this area is still considered quite fashionable, but it has a decidedly urban feel to it except when you are actually on the beach.

Preserving natural areas or sharing the beach was the last thing developers were thinking about. The high-rises obliterate any view of the beautiful beach unless you're inside one of the overpriced rooms or suites. In the South Miami Beach neighborhood you can get to the beach from Ocean Drive, which runs parallel to lower Collins Avenue, but on upper Collins Avenue, unless you're staying at a Collins Avenue hotel, you cannot get to the beach without walking down a side street. Collins Avenue north of 44th Street is wall-to-wall hotels and condos — the beach is behind the lobbies and boutiques of the concrete and glass buildings. Fortunately, there are still some public beaches just north and south of the high-rise stretch, at the side streets of 21st, 46th, 65th, 75th, and 81st.

In fairness to the developers, it must be said that many tourists coming to Florida from the North were used to skyscrapers and concrete and didn't demand anything better of the hoteliers. The sunshine and the ocean were enough to make them feel they were on vacation. There were restaurants and jazz clubs and other nightlife nearby or across the bay in Miami, one of the most beautiful cities in the United States. So thousands of people found — and still find — their experience in a high-rise on Miami Beach perfectly satisfactory. But others have taken their honeymoon or family vacation in Miami Beach and have been greatly disappointed.

The beach behind the big hotels on upper Collins Avenue is lovely, with wide sweeps of pale sand and good-sized waves. There's a pleasant raised boardwalk on the beach with railings and good lighting that's safe to walk even in the evening. Biscayne Bay, on the other side of Collins Avenue, is also a lovely stretch of water, but the high-rises of upper Collins Avenue are most unbeachlike. There are some notable exceptions (see "Best Beachside Accommodations" and "Best Eclectic Finds" in the chapter *What's What*). In general, Miami Beach is best for people who want the specific combination of urban development and beach.

Central Florida and Disney

After World War II, the average worker began to earn enough to afford a modest winter vacation in Florida, and the state opened up to the average traveler rather than the average millionaire. In response, hundreds of hotels and motels opened their doors. The ability of many older people to sell their homes after retirement and buy one in Florida also spurred the tourist boom. Most of these retirees had children and grandchildren who would want to take a break from chill northern winds to visit. There wasn't always room for them with Mom and Dad, so more motels and hotels were built.

The majority of these families, as well as the wealthy who had come for decades, still came only for the winter. They stayed mainly on the east and west coasts of south Florida that Flagler and Plant had tamed. Tallahassee, in the middle of northern Florida, was chilly in the winter and concentrated on passing the laws of the state and educating its young people. The rest of northern Florida had more in common with the Georgia countryside than it did with Palm Beach. Central Florida was given over primarily to agriculture, especially the growing of citrus fruits. For decades, citrus growing was the region's economic mainstay, rather than tourism and winter residency.

One exception to this was the Orlando area, southwest of Daytona Beach. In the middle of this century, the city of Orlando was still a sleepy Southern town. Prosperous families and elderly widows who preferred the beautiful lakes and fragrance of orange blossoms to the faster-paced activity of the coasts would come to Orlando and nearby Winter Park and Mount Dora every winter. Mansions and more modest bungalows curved around the lakes, and the pace of life beneath moss-draped oaks was very slow. But some developers from Anaheim, California, changed all that.

For many years, farmers in the central Florida region had

had to deal with the devastating effects of frosts in the winter that could destroy a citrus crop. Some farmers found that they could do much better financially by selling their groves to large developers for housing. When farmers in Kissimmee and Lake Buena Vista, just south of Orlando, were approached by anonymous developers from Disney, most sold their land.

Since the opening of Disney World in 1971, the Orlando area hasn't been the same. There are still the lovely lakes in and around Orlando and some stately old homes and oak-lined streets. Certainly, the purchase and development by the Disney people of agricultural land in Lake Buena Vista and Kissimmee helped the area economically. But it also created a boom that still continues — and that the highways of Orlando and surrounding towns cannot always handle.

The Magic Kingdom, patterned after California's Disneyland, opened first, followed by EPCOT, an Experimental Prototype Community Of Tomorrow, and Disney-MGM Studios. Although these attractions are several miles south of Orlando, the city and surrounding communities have experienced enormous growth in the last two decades. An amazing number of shopping centers, housing developments, hotels, and motels have mushroomed near Disney World, as well as many secondary tourist attractions: Flea World, Xanadu, Sea World, Fort Liberty, King Henry's Feast, Mardi Gras, Water Mania, Citrus Circus, Great American Fun Factory, Shell World, Jungle Falls, and the Elvis Presley Museum. Some of these, such as Sea World, are wonderful; others are tacky and tasteless. None has a low admission price.

The Other Florida

One result of Disney World and the subsequent development of Orlando is that people now come to Florida throughout the year, rather than just in winter. Today, more people come to central Florida than to the coasts. The Orlando area has changed from an agricultural economy to a thriving metropolis where large corporations have their national headquarters and distribution centers.

But for all the prosperity, the growth has created some problems of congestion and a strain on services and highways. The growth has also made Orlando and Disney World almost synonymous with the word Florida. Not everyone is happy about this, especially old-timers and jaded travel writers. Disney World, EPCOT, and Sea World are wonderful places to visit, and it is to the credit of their developers that they are beautifully landscaped and maintained. Orlando is an exciting city with restaurants, clubs, museums, cultural events, and commerce. But Orlando and the east coast of Florida have been overdeveloped, and they certainly don't represent all that is Florida.

Comfortable accommodations and modern transportation were never meant to destroy the natural beauty, character, or heritage of Florida. But in the last four decades, development and overdevelopment on both coasts have nearly succeeded in doing that. In the 1950s and 1960s, the gracious lines of Spanish-style architecture, as well as the traditional tin roofs and bungalow styles of the Old Florida domestic architecture, were replaced by a modern style that reflected none of Florida's heritage. Florida became the sort of place where finding wooden furniture rather than plastic in a hotel room was unusual. Rooms that had ceiling fans and windows and doors for cross-ventilation were replaced by sealed, air-conditioned boxes where you couldn't open a window to get a sea breeze. Native trees were destroyed and many species of wildlife threatened. Novelist Joy Williams describes with fitting anguish what has happened to the state in her guidebook, *The Florida Keys:* "Florida, that splendid, subtle, once fabulous state, has been exploited, miscomprehended and misused, drained and diked, filled in and paved over. The values of man have been imposed with a vengeance."

Anyone with a little knowledge of the state's history and wildlife is apt to ask, where is the real Florida? Where are the natural white beaches, the hammocks of Florida hardwoods, the haunts of pirates and conquistadors? Where are the Cuban cigar factories, the streets of canopied oaks draped with Spanish moss, the wood-framed Victorian homes and Southern mansions, the old train depots? It is all still here. One purpose of this book is to present some of what is best and rarest in the state, and to enable visitors to see the diversity, uniqueness, and wild beauty that is Florida.

Florida's Intracoastal Waterway

The series of channels, inlets, lakes, and rivers between the mainland shore of Florida and its barrier islands is a region unto itself, the Intracoastal Waterway. Some vacationers have never navigated the Intracoastal until coming to Florida, but it is not unique to the state. It runs from northern Maine down the Atlantic coast, past the Carolinas and Georgia, around southern Florida, up the west coast between the mainland and gulf islands, and ends in Brownsville, Texas. In Florida, an inland route crosses the mainland. Most boaters start this route north of Palm Beach at the St. Lucie River, navigating the river canal west to Lake Okeechobee, crossing the lake to the Caloosahatchee River, then following the river west to the Gulf of Mexico. Along the route of both the inland and coastal Waterway are some state parks where it's pleasant to stop and picnic.

If you are lucky, you may see dolphins dipping in and out of the water or manatees (sea cows) lumbering through the Intracoastal and its canals. Manatee protection zones are marked by white signs along the Waterway, particularly in Fort Lauderdale. In these areas, boaters must run dead slow from mid-November to mid-March.

You can sometimes swim with manatees in canals off the Intracoastal and on the keys if your boating party has stopped for a while. They're gentle mammals who eat marine plants and are found in fresh water as well as salt. In fact, they are the state freshwater mammal, while dolphins are the state saltwater mammal. If there's a garden hose handy, you can turn it on to make an arc over where the manatees are swimming, and they'll raise their heads to get a swallow. Manatees do not have teeth and will not hurt you. However, you can hurt them, so do not swim on their backs or play rough. If you see plastic netting on an adult or baby, swim with them to get their confidence and then take the net off. This plastic netting has been responsible for the killing and maiming of many manatees and other marine animals.

Like manatees, dolphins are willing to swim with humans, but this is not as easy to do in the wild as it is with manatees, who move a good deal more slowly. If you should have the opportunity to swim with a dolphin, do so gently. They love humans, and some swimmers try to do tricks with them, play piggyback, or hold onto their fins for a ride. These stunts, done in shows with trained animals, can hurt dolphins outside of a controlled environment. It's better just to pat them gently or swim close by.

The Real Florida

Finding the real Florida is, of course, a rather personal quest. To the families who flock to Seaside on the Emerald Coast, it may mean an old-style clapboard cottage on the Gulf of

Mexico. To a retired couple looking for a winter retreat, it may mean sharing a duplex with friends for a few days on Palm Island or staying at a grand old resort, with the ghost of F. Scott Fitzgerald walking the elegant corridors. To others, the real Florida may be a secluded fishing shack on a canal in the keys, with herons and pelicans the only rivals for the fish.

For most travelers who develop an interest in finding the real Florida, a vacation means seeing Florida's native wildlife and rich vegetation, learning about the state's Native American and Latin heritage, and discovering an architecture influenced by many elements in the state's history. To offer what is genuine in *Best Places to Stay in Florida*, an effort has been made to choose accommodations for their authenticity and integrity. As often as possible, places have been selected for their natural beauty and for a sense of intimacy and quiet. The beach, destination, and golf and tennis resorts have been chosen with an eye to their respect for the environment and success in making a large resort seem small. Even in the cities that Flagler and Plant first developed, there are still owners and managers of urban hostelries who maintain a respect for Florida's exotic greenery, lovely beaches, and eclectic mix of cultures.

At the beginning of each regional section is a list of the best accommodations in each category, for example, "Best B&Bs" or "Best Island Getaways." These categories are a help to people who want to focus on a specific *type* of place to stay, satisfying a particular recreational, business, atmospheric, or budgetary preference.

Definitions

Art Deco: A style of architecture and interior design popular in Miami Beach in the 1930s and '40s that was streamlined, decorative, and modernistic. Most examples are in the South Miami Beach neighborhood of Ocean Drive and Collins Avenue. See the information on Art Deco hotels in "Finding the Real Florida."

chikee hut: A shelter with a roof of thatched palm fronds built by Florida Indians and the early Spanish and American settlers. Adaptations are used throughout Florida today to serve as everything from beach shelters to bars. Some of the best examples are found at Seminole Indian villages.

conch: Pronounced "conk." A marine mollusk with a sweet, flavorful meat used in chowders, fritters, and other Florida dishes. At one time, the spiral, pink shells were used by Native Americans to call people home or announce a celebration. *Slang:* a native of the Florida Keys.

Conch Republic: A nickname for Key West.

coquina: Spanish for shellstone; a white stone made up of congealed marine shells cut to form masonry blocks.

coral stone: Cut coral, used as a decorative veneer or in blocks. Sometimes called key stone or coquina. The most beautiful is composed of fan-shaped coral, with small shells or fragments of shells trapped in the crevices of the coral.

Florida room: A screened or glassed-in porch, usually on the back of a house.

hammock: A hardwood forest or thicket of native trees and shrub.

key lime: A small, round yellow lime used in key lime pie and other Florida desserts and dishes.

Old Florida: A style of architecture popular in the 1920s in domestic or public buildings that includes crimped tin roofs, wooden clapboards, double-hung windows, and porches with overhangs. The term sometimes refers to an eclectic mix of architecture that includes Mediterranean, Italian, Moorish, Victorian, and Old South styles. It can also refer to an interior design typical of Old Florida buildings.

tabby: Concrete made from sand, lime, and shellstone dust or chips.

The
Northeast Coast

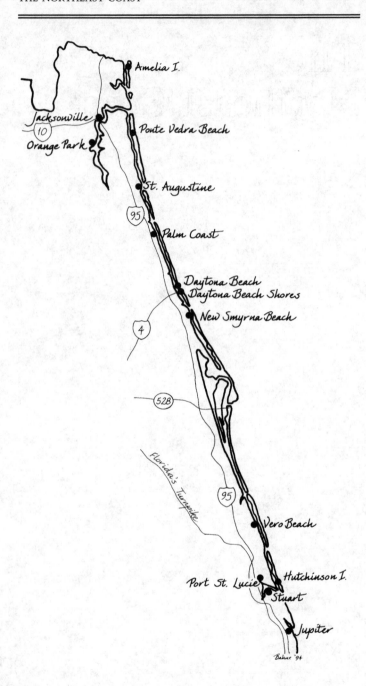

Amelia Island
Amelia Island Plantation, 33
Elizabeth Point Lodge, 36
Florida House Inn, 39
Phoenix' Nest, 42
Ritz-Carlton, Amelia Island, 45
1735 House, 47
Daytona Beach
Coquina Inn B&B, 50
Indigo Lakes Resort, 52
Live Oak Inn and Restaurant, 54
Perry's Ocean-Edge, 56
Daytona Beach Shores
Sunny Shore Motel, 59
Hutchinson Island
Indian River Plantation Resort, 60
Jacksonville
House on Cherry Street, 64
Omni Jacksonville Hotel, 66
Plantation Manor Inn, 68
Jupiter
Comfort Suites, 70
Jupiter Beach Resort, 73
New Smyrna Beach
Riverview Hotel, 75
Orange Park
The Club Continental, 77

Palm Coast
Sheraton Palm Coast Resort, 81
Ponte Vedra Beach
The Lodge and Bath Club at Ponte Vedra Beach , 82
Ponte Vedra Inn & Club, 87
Marriott at Sawgrass Resort, 85
Port St. Lucie
Club Med-Sandpiper, 89
St. Augustine
Carriage Way B & B, 92
Casa de la Paz, 94
Casa de Solana, 96
Castle Garden, 99
The Kenwood Inn, 100
Old City House Inn, 103
The Old Powder House Inn, 105
St. Francis Inn, 107
Southern Wind, 109
Victorian House, 111
Westcott House, 113
Stuart
HarborFront, 115
The Homeplace, 118
Vero Beach
The Driftwood, 121

Best B&Bs

Daytona Beach
  Coquina Inn B&B
Fernandina Beach
  Phoenix' Nest
Jacksonville
  House on Cherry Street
  Plantation Manor Inn
New Smyrna Beach
  Riverview Hotel
St. Augustine
  Carriage Way
  Casa de la Paz
  Casa de Solana
  Castle Garden
  The Kenwood Inn
  Old Powder House Inn
  St. Francis Inn
  Southern Wind
  Victorian House
  Westcott House
Stuart
  Harborfront
  The Homeplace

Best Beachside Accommodations

Amelia Island
  Elizabeth Pointe Lodge
  1735 House
Jupiter
  Jupiter Beach Resort
Ponte Vedra Beach
  The Lodge and Bath Club at Ponte Vedra Beach
  Ponte Vedra Inn and Club

Best Budget Finds

Jupiter
  Comfort Suites-Intercoastal Marina

Daytona Beach
   Perry's Ocean-Edge
   Sunny Shores Motel

Best City Stops

Jacksonville
   Omni Jacksonville Hotel

Best Eclectic Finds

Vero Beach
   The Driftwood Resort

Best Island Getaways

Stuart
   Indian River Plantation

Best Resorts and Spas

Amelia Island
   Amelia Island Plantation Resort
   Ritz-Carlton, Amelia Island
Daytona Beach
   Indigo Lakes Golf and Tennis
Palm Coast
   Sheraton Palm Coast Resort
Ponte Vedra Beach
   Marriott at Sawgrass

Best Small Hotels, Inns, and Motels

Amelia Island
   Florida House Inn
Daytona Beach
   Live Oak Inn and Restaurant
New Smyrna Beach
   Riverview Hotel

Orange Park
  The Club Continental
St. Augustine
  Old City House Inn

The northeasternmost corner of Florida is whistling distance from Georgia. Not surprisingly, the summer resorts of **Amelia Island** attract many people from Atlanta and other southern cities and towns. The island, named after the daughter of King George II has both an Old South and a beachside ambience. The island has a varied heritage and is the only place in the United States to have been under eight different flags, among them the "Amelia Island Patriots," a ragtag American group. Amelia Island was fought over for years by nations and pirates for its strategic location until it found stability under the U.S. flag. During the late 19th and early 20th centuries it enjoyed prosperity as a resort, and it's becoming popular again for its charm and natural beauty. There are some interesting B&Bs here, as well as Amelia Island Plantation, a large coastal resort.

In making reservations, bear in mind that in April some large resorts have tennis tournaments that can drive the rates up almost to the summer high. Other hotels and B&Bs in northern Florida offer the same rate year-round. When making reservations, it's best to check on rates for the precise period you'll be staying. During April tennis tournament season, especially, a day or two can make a difference.

The largest town on Amelia is **Fernandina Beach.** The old section of Fernandina, developed in the late 19th century, has a neighborhood of Victorian homes and turn-of-the-century public buildings that can be seen on a self-directed walking tour. Fernandina's Historic District is listed in the National Register of Historic Places and should not be missed. There are some interesting pubs, restaurants, and boutiques in the fine old buildings that line meandering Centre Street, which ends at the historic shrimp docks on the Intracoastal Waterway.

The largest city in Northeast Florida is **Jacksonville.** Approximately 30 miles west from the coast, it is a lively river city that has enjoyed a recent cultural and economic revival. This area has both a coastal atmosphere and, especially just outside the city proper, a Panhandle country feel. The Riverside-Avondale section of town has a variety of historic properties, some of which have recently been made into B&Bs.

Northeast Florida, like Central Florida has real *towns*. Getting excited about this is something that people from New England and the Midwest — with their town squares and Main Streets — cannot entirely understand. Most municipalities in Florida are unfortunately just a a grid of highways with shopping centers, mobile home parks, and housing developments strung out along that grid — no real town center and not much community spirit.

So, when a town is a real, recognizable *town*, it's a big deal. Such places are often referred to as "historic" and yet, when an outsider rolls into town he may see just a bunch of old clapboard or Spanish style dwellings and some businesses with 1920s architecture. This is not a big deal to outsiders, but to Floridians, a piece of the state's heritage has actually been preserved instead of being torn down to make room for something bigger and flashier with no connection to the past. The state actually has an extremely interesting and varied heritage dating back to Spanish explorers, and the architecture in some Old Florida towns reflects this, with a mix of Spanish, Victorian, Bahamian, and even Moorish styles.

The oldest town in the state and the oldest continuously settled city in the United States is **St. Augustine,** located on Matanzas Bay, part of the Intracoastal Waterway. Most of the city's fine old buildings, some dating from Spanish possession, have been lovingly preserved. East of the city proper, on a sandbar accessible by St. Augustine's graceful Bridge of Lions, is a nice beach.

To find out about the history of the town and get oriented, most first-time visitors take advantage of the Information Center on San Marco Avenue. In addition, there are sightseeing trolleys and horse-drawn carriage tours — which are more expensive than the trolleys but the most fun. There *are* some tourist traps, but for most visitors, it is enough simply to walk the narrow streets and take in a few of the attractions in a self-guided walking tour after going on a trolley ride.

Most people start at the fort, Castillo San Marcos, and the Spanish Quarter, and then explore the side streets off King Street. Be certain to get a look at King Street's Flagler College, the former Ponce de Leon Hotel built in 1887 by Henry Flagler, with early stained-glass windows by Louis Tiffany. Across the street is the Lightner Museum, which was once the other Flagler hotel in town, the Alcazar. The oldest house in the United States, a few streets southeast of the Alcazar, is also worth seeing.

There are many more interesting sights along the east coast. Just south of the white beaches of **Daytona** is Cape Canaveral. It may not seem that there's much going on here, particularly if a shuttle isn't due to go up, but there are some space exhibits and a national wildlife refuge that should not be missed. Most of the accommodations are motel and hotel chains, though some people venture farther south to stay in **Stuart.**

South of Cape Canaveral and the John F. Kennedy Space Center are beaches, state recreational areas, and the attractive Old Florida town of Melbourne. Just off the coast of Stuart is beautiful **Hutchinson Island,** accessible by bridges over the Indian River. Strict zoning laws here protect the wonderful mangrove swamps along the water. The House of Refuge, built in 1875 as a rescue station for sailors, is now a historical museum and the site of green sea turtle research and preservation work.

Residents of the island and nearby Stuart are mindful of the delicate ecology of the area. Each year in late spring and early summer, the turtles migrate to the beach to lay their eggs. During the nesting season, there are expeditions to nearby beaches to see the wild turtles. After the eggs are laid, the sites of the buried eggs are labeled with a small wooden sign-post so beachcombers can avoid damaging the nests. Also on Hutchinson Island, the Elliott Museum commemorates the life of inventor Sterling Elliott and includes displays of Indian artifacts, a typical Victorian parlor and dining room, a smithy, antique automobiles and motorcycles, and a number of Elliott's own inventions.

Farther south are fashionable **Vero Beach** and the quiet town of **Jupiter,** which home-boy Burt Reynolds has put on the map with his dinner theater (now under new ownership) and acting institute. Nineteen-fifties songster Perry Como lives here, as do a number of wealthy, influential people who prefer to live a serene life on the Intracoastal in Jupiter rather than in the limelight of Palm Beach or Miami.

AMELIA ISLAND

Amelia Island Plantation

Fernandina Beach
Amelia Island, FL 32034
904-261-6161
800-874-6878
800-342-6841 in Florida

A resort and residential community on 1,200 acres

General Manager: John West.
Accommodations: 600 rooms and villas. **Rates:** $114–$459 (varies according to season); Packages and group rates available; midweek package discounts. **Minimum stay:** With some packages and during holidays. **Added:** 8.5% tax. **Payment:** Visa, MasterCard, Discover. **Children:** Free in room with parents; some charges with recreational packages. **Smoking:** Nonsmoking rooms available. **Open:** Year-round.

It is understandable why people come back to Amelia Island Plantation year after year. In fact, there is so much to do and see here that some people give up trying after twenty years or so, and simply buy a house or villa on the property and move in. There have been recent complaints, however, that the sales pitch is a little heavy for those who only want to come here to relax and use resort or conference facilities, rather than buy a summer place.

Amelia Island is only 30 minutes from the Jacksonville airport, but when you come through the security gates you enter a world of lush forests of myrtle, live oak, magnolia, and pine; acres and acres of undulating marsh grass; exotic tropical birds that stalk the lagoons; and long stretches of white beach with sand dunes rising beyond.

It takes the sound of someone laughing or whacking a tennis ball to recall that this is also a busy resort. Amelia Island Plantation has a staggering array of activities: tennis, golf, swimming, biking, jogging, working out, hiking, fishing, and boating, as well as horseback riding and historic sightseeing.

The resort is probably most famous for golf and tennis. The challenging Amelia Links, designed by Pete Dye, has 27 holes that break down into three distinctive "nines": Oceanside, bordering the Atlantic and the dunes; Oakmarsh, featuring challenging holes near the edge of the marsh; and Oysterbay, with marsh hazards and twisting fairways. Amelia Island's newest course, designed by Tom Fazio and opened in 1987, is Long Point. The natural beauty of the marshland, dunes, and woods has been masterfully incorporated.

The tennis settings are just as impressive. There are 25 tennis courts: 19 clay, four Omni (grass), and two Deco-Turf hard courts. Three are lighted. There is a well-supplied pro shop and excellent instruction for both adults and children. Activity centers around Racquet Park, a beautiful facility nestled among live oak trees dripping with Spanish moss. Racquet Park also houses a fitness center and a glass-enclosed pool. On a cool spring or fall day, swimming in this large heated pool feels like being in a big glass house in the jungle.

Racquet Park also has a well-appointed conference center, refurbished in 1991. This is a 6,000-square-foot meeting space with four rooms that hold up to 125 people. The center has its own restaurant, hotel rooms, and suites.

A larger facility is the 22,500-square-foot Executive Meeting Center, with five seminar rooms and a 6,000-square-foot ballroom that can be divided into smaller rooms. The Amelia Inn, just a few yards away, has soundproof meeting rooms that can accommodate groups of 100 or more. Services offered include a message and copy center, call-service buttons in each meeting room, round-the-clock conference planning, a banquet kitchen, audiovisual assistance, multimedia presentation equipment, and secretarial service. Executives can sign up for "management communications adventures," outdoor expeditions that foster team planning.

There is a tremendous variety of accommodations for families, groups, and couples, including full-size houses in the rental pool. The newest accommodations are in Sea Dunes, Turtle Dunes, and Piper Dunes, four-story stucco buildings with barrel-tile roofs and small balconies overlooking the island. Inquire about the intricacies of seasonal rates and the Plantation's special packages and group rates when making reservations. Rooms and villas on the ocean, while expensive, often have dramatic views of the rolling dunes and the Atlantic.

All of the accommodations are attractively decorated and well furnished. Each rental villa is rated every year; any villa that falls below the resort's high standards is taken out of the rental pool.

> **The sense of timelessness at Amelia Island Plantation is nowhere more evident than on the boardwalk in the salt marsh. You look out over acres of marsh grass and quiet water. Far out on a point of land, you may see a solitary white heron standing still as a statue.**

All villas have well-equipped kitchens, but there is a variety of restaurants at the resort. The most romantic is the Dune Side Club at the Amelia Inn, overlooking the oceanside golf links and the dunes. Excellent French and American cuisine is served here. The wine cellar is commendable, and recommendations for appropriate wines are graciously made.

Seafood dinners are served at the Verandah, in the Racquet Park Center. This is an airy, easygoing restaurant with lots of wood and big windows, ideal for families. The Beach Club Bar & Grill serves grilled seafood and steaks for lunch and dinner. For breakfast, lunch, and snacks, there are a number of other restaurants throughout the property. Three lounges serve drinks, and the informal Scoop serves ice cream concoctions.

Although Amelia Island is a great place for family togetherness, the resort makes it easy for parents to get away from their children and vice versa. A babysitting service is available, and there is also a wonderful children's program for ages three to twelve. Available during the spring and summer and for special holidays, it includes supervised recreation on the playgrounds, including one on its own little island; field trips and special projects; hikes and sports; and games. There is swimming instruction at the kiddie pool, and tennis instruction for older children. The Beach Club has an unobtrusive electronic game arcade. The Club also rents out body boards, beach chairs and umbrellas, rubber rafts, and boats. Paddle-boats are available for exploring the Plantation's natural lagoons and narrow tributaries.

Both kids and adults enjoy fishing for bass, redfish, and bream at the stocked lagoons on the property. There is also fishing and crabbing in the Intracoastal Waterway. Farther out in the Atlantic are tarpon, marlin, and kingfish. The Amelia Angler, at the Beach Club, will arrange deep-sea charter boats for guests.

The Plantation itself is worth exploring, starting with the Sunken Forest Trail, actually a boardwalk through a ravine of ancient myrtle and oak. Some of the smaller myrtle trees are reminiscent of the twisted, ancient olive trees that grow on Tuscan hillsides — and they are just as old, if not older.

A stay at Amelia Island Plantation inspires many guests to take an interest in the island and its history. The area was home to the Timuquan Indians for centuries until the Spanish and the English discovered it. From then on, it had a rather bloody and unstable history, until well into the 19th century. Altogether, Amelia Island has been under the flags of five different nations on eight separate occasions and has had many names. The name that finally stuck was that of the winsome, never-married daughter of George II.

Elizabeth Pointe Lodge

98 S. Fletcher Avenue
Amelia Island, FL 32034
904-277-4851

A brand new inn with old-fashioned appeal

Innkeepers: David and Susan Caples. **Accommodations:** 20 rooms. **Rates:** Rooms $75–$115, suites vary; ask for quote. **Included:** Full breakfast and morning newspaper; afternoon lemonade. **Minimum stay:** For special events. **Added:** 8.5% tax; $15 additional person. **Payment:** Major credit cards; personel check. **Children:** Welcome; children 5 and under free in room with parent. **Pets:** Not allowed. **Smoking:** On the porch only. **Open:** Year-round.

Innkeepers David and Susan Caples built Elizabeth Pointe Lodge in 1991 after successfully operating another B&B on Amelia Island, the 1735 House, in addition to a rental business. Susan had spent childhood summers on the New Jersey shore and both loved the look and the feel of old-fashioned summer places. They envisioned a shingled, Nantucket-style cottage on the beach with furnishings that would look as if they'd been there "forever" and where people would walk in and think, "I'm home." With cleverness and professionalism (both studied at the Cornell's hotel management school), as well as thoughtfulness for their guests' comfort, they succeeded admirably.

The lodge they created with architect David Beer has the best of both the old and new. Although there are none of the disadvantages of a genuinely old inn — no water stains on the ceiling or whistling drafts from oceanfront windows — there is the lazy *comfortableness* of an old place.

The center of activity is the lounge in the middle of the house, called the library. A rough stone fireplace dominates one wall, while a cushioned window seat runs beneath a long row of small-paned windows. In the corner is a bay window with a round oak table where people play cards or visit. Floor to ceiling bookcases are along two walls and the Caples encourage guests to read whatever they fancy sitting on the library's plaid-cushioned wicker sofa. This is a place where guests can really settle in.

Outside is a wrap-around porch with white wicker rockers. Near the bay window, the porch widens enough to hold two tables with chairs where guests can take meals or just read. The view here is wonderful, with softly sloping sand dunes covered with flowering vines and sea oats and the sea roaring in on the harder sand below. The Caples have chaises here for guests to use. Bicycles are also available for those who wish to ride into the historic village of Fernandina Beach.

In the afternoon, the staff always sets out fresh lemonade, and in the evening there is complimentary wine. Limited but delicious menus are available for lunch and dinner for those who don't wish to go out. Guests can also buy homemade muffins and cookies throughout the day and scrumptious desserts in the evening. They can eat on the porch, in the library, or in the big dining room or Sun Room, where breakfast is served each morning.

The staff is efficient and patient, there to help anyone who needs it. They are a very good group, made up of old-timers who have been with the Caples family for years, energetic young people in their twenties, and members of the Caples' B&B seminars who learn innkeeping by serving in various roles at Elizabeth Pointe Lodge. In the summer, the Caples' daughers, Katie and Beth (for whom the inn was named), devise activities for the kids staying at the lodge.

The full breakfasts are worth writing home about, largely thanks to the skills of the Caples's longtime cook, Ona. Most northerners don't like grits, but they like Ona's. Her biscuits are oversized and fluffy, and her fruit muffins are loaded with fruit. A typical breakfast starts with three kinds of cold juice dispensed from old-fashioned glass milk bottles,

> Staff members seem to genuinely enjoy themselves, in spite of their often hectic pace, and there is a sense of everyone being part of one big, happy, hard-working family.

a choice of packaged cereals, creamy grits, an egg dish such as scrambled eggs with dill, muffins or biscuits (or both), fresh fruit salad, brewed coffee, and an assortment of teas. Everything is laid out at 7:30 A.M. on a long buffet from which guests help themselves till 9:00 or 9:30. Most people sit together at big oak tables, but honeymooners sometimes sit out on the romantic back porch.

The dining room doubles as a conference room for seminars the Caples hold on B&B management and marketing for potential B&B owners. The couple also have what are called "empowerment" retreats for high-level executives, who meet at the lodge and at a newly renovated house next door, Miller Cottage. The cottage is part of another Caples enterprise, Lodging Resources, which rents out Miller Cottage and other houses and condos. Among these is Katie's Light, a replica of a Cheasepeake Bay lighthouse named after the couple's older daughter.

Even with all they have going on, Susan and David have found time to gradually individualize the guestrooms at Elizabeth Pointe Lodge. All rooms have pine woodwork and floors, and windows overlooking the ocean or island. Furnishings are simple, with reproduction sleigh beds and four-posters, wicker rockers, armoires, and oak or pine bedstands.

Number 9, on the second floor, has white curtains at the oceanfront windows and a hand-stitched quilt on the brass bed. Number 8 has rose touches, with lace curtains and a white eyelet spread. The pillows are oversized, covered in lace or embroidered linen. Another special room is number

13, which has a wedding ring quilt on the four-poster bed and pretty blue and cream striped wallpaper.

All bathrooms have oversize faux marble tub-showers (a few with Jacuzzis) and brass fixtures that look a hundred years old. A brass and glass shelf above the sink holds a small vase of sea heather and wild asters, and there's another in the bedroom. The oceanfront kings and queens are the most desirable accommodations at the lodge, although decorative touches in the other rooms compensate for their less dramatic views. Fourth-floor rooms have lots of interesting angles — and there's an elevator. All rooms contribute to the quiet rejuvenation of the spirit that is part of being a guest at Elizabeth Pointe Lodge.

Florida House Inn

20–22 South Third Street
Amelia Island, FL 32034
904-261-3300
800-258-3301

A rambling inn and restaurant in a historic district

Innkeepers: Karen and Bob Warner.
Accommodations: 11 rooms. **Rates:** Rooms $65–$115, suites $125. **Included:** Full breakfast. **Minimum stay:** 2–3 nights for weekends. **Added:** 8.5% tax. **Payment:** Major credit cards; personal checks. **Children:** Allowed. **Smoking:** Only on verandah and in pub. **Open:** Year-round.

The Florida House Inn looks just the way the state's oldest extant hotel should: a turn-of-the-century clapboard structure painted deep green, with louvered shutters, white-railed verandahs, gingerbread brackets upstairs and down, a big oak tree in the back yard, and a picket fence out front.

But it wasn't always like this. Innkeepers Bob and Karen Warner spent a year restoring the Florida House after decades of neglect had left it a town eyesore. Now listed on the National Register of Historic Places, the inn looks just right — the heart-of-pine floors, plaster walls, and fireplaces have all been brought to life. While the restoration focused on bringing back the original whenever possible, there was also a sensible response to 20th-century guests' needs for modern bathrooms and amenities.

Guests enter the inn by the front verandah and a paneled wood door. Inside is a typical 19th-century entryway with a stairway in the middle of the hall, a front parlor to the left, and a room on the right that's been made into a pub with plaid wallpaper, a fine old fireplace, and a British feel. The parlor is small and has a lovely wood-paneled fireplace, a sofa, and a table with magazines.

At the back of the long hallway is a door to a large brick courtyard and the entrance to the restuarant. Here, guests eat a full breakfast at long pine tables, boarding-house style: freshly squeezed orange juice, fruit, eggs, and breakfast meats. Every day it's a little different. Afterwards, guests can linger at the table and talk with others, rock on the verandah, or sit out in the courtyard among the camellias.

The nine charming rooms and two suites are individually decorated, with quilts and ruffled shams and pillows on the four-poster beds, handmade rugs on the pine floors, armoires, and — another nod to the 20th century — TVs and telephones. Room 2 is especially nice, with a queen bed and large tile bath with shower as well as a spacious porch. Room 9 has a king bed covered in plaid and a tub against one wall that has the same plaid in a valance above. A toilet and tiny corner sink are in a closet-size room at the other end of the wall. Another standout is number 10, with a queen-size bed, a wood-paneled fireplace that was diligently stripped and refinished to reveal the old wood, and a tile bath that has a whirlpool.

Guests often spend a good deal of time just relaxing at the inn, but there is certainly a great deal to do in Fernandina Beach and elsewhere on Amelia Island. The Florida House Inn is just off the main street of town, called Centre. Numbered streets run perpendicular to Centre and streets with tree names run parallel, so it's quite easy to find one's way around. The historic district covers about 30 blocks, running from the Intracoastal Waterway and the shrimp docks at the foot of Centre to the edge of the town proper. On the edge of town is Fort Clinch, a state park and popular beach.

Most of the buildings on Centre Street are brick or masonry and include the turn-of-the-century Nassau Courthouse and a Greek Revival Methodist church where the bells play a carillon every afternoon at four o'clock. The residential homes fanning out from Centre Street are mostly clapboard Victorians with gingerbread details. Trolley tours leave from the shrimp dock, but it's also fun to take a self-directed walking tour of old homes, using the map for sale at the Chamber of Commerce, located in the old depot near the docks.

Fernandina Beach calls itself the "Birthplace of the Shrimping Industry." It's interesting to sit on a bench on the dock and watch the shrimp boats with their wide wings of nets go out each day or to see people coming back with their catches after a day of fishing. Charter fishing boats do a brisk business here. Rental boats are available for a pleasure cruise up the Intracoastal. Brett's Waterway Café, next to the shrimp dock, is an excellent restaurant for seafood for either lunch or dinner.

> **The restaurant at the Florida House serves lunch and dinner and is open every day except Monday. The boarding house tables encourage folks to get to know each other. Sunday brunch is popular with island residents as well as hotel guests and includes fried chicken, eggs, ham, butter beans or black-eyed peas, sausage gravy, and cornbread.**

When meals are not being served, the dining room can double as a conference room for businesses that hold retreats or meetings here.

Guests have access to most of the verandahs at Florida House, which are furnished with comfortable chairs and rockers. There's also room to spread out in the beautifully landscaped courtyard, where white iron lawn chairs are arranged around tables on the brick pavement. This courtyard, shaded by a 200-year-old oak tree, has become a favorite place for wedding receptions in Fernandina.

The Phoenix' Nest

619 S. Fletcher Avenue
Fernandina Beach, FL 32034
904-277-2129

*A whimsical B&B
with better-than-
average privacy*

Innkeeper: Harriett Fortenberry.
Accommodations: 5 suites. **Rates:**
$65–$85; weekly rates available,
7th night free. **Included:** Continental breakfast; use of bicycles and boogie boards. **Minimum stay:** None. **Added:** 8.5%
tax. **Payment:** Major credit cards; personal checks. **Children:**
Not appropriate. **Pets:** Not allowed. **Smoking:** On the porches
only. **Open:** Year-round.

When you drive into the dusty parking lot of the Phoenix'
Nest, you might first ask, "Is this really the place?" The
Phoenix' Nest is an eclectic mix of styles and relaxing ambience that seems serendipitous — as if no one else has ever
been lucky or clever enough to find and appreciate the place.
Later, it's a little puzzling. What was it about that place that
made it so special? The funky, crazy decor? The sight of the
ocean each morning? The artistry and kindness of the host-
ess? The feeling of escape?

The Phoenix' Nest is special; but it is not for everyone.
This B&B is right on A1A/Fletcher Avenue, the main drag
along the Atlantic at the northern end of the island. The New
England–style house, built in the 1930s, is of gray clapboards,
and it's hard to tell if they're *painted* gray or *weathered* gray.
One of the louvered shutters may be slightly askew. There is
no tennis court or swimming pool. The front yard is less a
lawn than a happy assortment of orange and yellow wildflowers and wild grasses. Those who expect social interaction
with other B&B guests will find that there's no breakfast
room or sitting area where everyone gathers. This is a place,
as owner Harriet Fortenberry puts it, "Where you can be with
the person you came with."

Each of Ms. Fortenberry's five suites has a private entrance
and a view of the beach across the street (a small slice of
which she owns and guests may use). When making reservations, Harriet gives the advantages and disadvantages of each
accommodation with winning candor, trying to determine
the best available room for her guests. Each has a distinct per-
sonality.

The first-floor Manatee has an unusual kitchen with a low antique ice chest with a Grecian bust sitting on it and an elegant mirror above. The kitchen itself is well-equipped with a wall of cabinets, ceramic tile counter, and basic appliances. In the bedroom, the king bed has a vivid floral comforter and is decorated with fine color photographs by the owner's son. The lower price of the Manatee reflects the fact that the view of the ocean here is somewhat obstructed by the staircase that goes up to the suite above.

> **Harriet delivers tomorrow's Continental breakfast of pastries and fruit in a special basket every evening while everyone is out at dinner. She will also cook dinner if requested and leave it in the room for guests to reheat in the microwave.**

Another suite, Gaillardia, is named after the wildflowers that grow profusely in the front yard. It is quite elegant and has three windows overlooking the water. There is no full kitchen, but a deep green parson's table is decorated with maidenhair ferns and azaleas and set with china and crystal.

The Dolphin is a three-room suite, with walls of creamy painted horizontal wooden siding, deep red carpeting, and a queen bed. There's a narrow closet of a bathroom and a small kitchen. All suites at the Phoenix' Nest have cassette players, and this one is in an antique secretary. The collection of cassettes includes everything from Rampal to Belafonte.

An upstairs front suite, the Pelican, has its own deck and a seabird's-eye view of the ocean. Natural wood French doors lead into a small bedroom with a wicker double bed and seafoam carpet. The kitchenette is really just a closet, and the pretty papered bathroom is also small. Behind the bath is a room with twin beds. In typical Fortenberry fashion, this peaceful back bedroom "makes up" for the fact that the bed is not a king or queen and the kitchenette and bathroom small. It's an interesting room with dark grasspaper walls and window cornices made from a dhurrie rug. Harriet says everyone gasped at the idea of cutting up a lovely rug to make cornices, but she simply liked the color and texture and thought it would make a distinctive window treatment. And so it does.

The Coconut Hut is a nutty place. It looks rather like a cinder block garage and at one time was used for storage. The walls are rough stucco and enclose a long bed–sitting room, small bathroom, and, behind a screen of louvered shutters and doors, a full kitchen. The king bed and sofa are covered in vibrant colors. Chairs are a mix of Art Deco and traditional, but it is the decorative touches that amaze: a hat rack with old hats, a chain of shells around the bathroom door, a feather boa, a hula skirt draped over a louvered shutter. It's like a big garage sale where Harriet encourages guests to try on all the stuff. "It brings out a sense of play in people."

The drawers in a 1930s china cabinet almost spill over with her collection of old records and magazines. Harriet's magazine collection goes back to the 1700s. As Harriet says, "When you read about a problem of 1889, no one could expect *you* to solve it. *You* can *relax.*"

All five suites have paddle fans, ocean views, a kitchen or kitchenette, private bath, TV and VCR, books, artwork, and a feeling of both peace and zaniness. Harriet has a great collection of videos, too — everything from Gracie Allen comedies to *Casablanca.* Guests also have the use of boogie boards and bicycles and, best of all, access to Harriet's slice of the Atlantic across the street from the house. She has two white Adirondack chairs on the sand among the sea oats.

Ultimately, the uniqueness of the Phoenix' Nest comes down to the uniqueness of Harriet Fortenberry. Originally from the Carolinas, she came to Amelia Island at a time when her life had changed dramatically and she had to make a new life for herself. Obviously, she found refuge and refreshment here — and a chance to express her philosophy of not just surviving, but truly relishing life. Harriet values her privacy, just as she respects the privacy of her guests, so she does not always spend time talking with guests or sharing her philosophy; but she doesn't need to — the place is permeated with it. Most people who stay here come away with an acceptance and celebration of the craziness of life.

Ritz-Carlton, Amelia Island

4750 Amelia Island Parkway
Amelia Island, FL 32034
904-277-1100
800-241-3333
Fax: 904-261-9063

*A sophisticated
island retreat*

General Manager: Michael Carsch. **Accommodations:** 404
rooms, 45 suites. **Rates:** Rooms $145–$315, suites $415–$675;
$2400 for presidential suite; packages available. **Minimum
stay:** With some packages. **Added:** 8.5% tax. **Payment:** Major
credit cards. **Children:** 18 and under free in room with parents. **Smoking:** Nonsmoking rooms available. **Open:** Year-
round.

The Ritz-Carlton on Amelia Island provides an escape to
beauty and luxury. The beach is lovely here, with sea oats and
flowering vines growing on the gentle slopes. Nearby are
thick woods and quiet marshes that serve as sanctuaries for
waterfowl and other animals. There's also a golf course, serpentine swimming pool, and a hotel of towers and porticoes
filled with marble and brocade. It may seem a little showy,
but perhaps because Amelia Island has been a family vacation
spot for so long, it's also a place where you can relax and enjoy
yourself — largely because the patrons who come here
haven't forgotten that this is the beach.

   This particular beach is part of the Summer Beach Resort
and Country Club. It is obvious that the Ritz is part of a country club as soon as you turn into the landscaped drive. To the
left is the Summer Beach Clubhouse, golf shop, and the golf
course. Beyond it is the seven-story Ritz, its ornate Victorian
fountain spraying water in front of the porte cochere and uni-
formed bellmen at the door. Inside are patterned marble

floors, fine antiques of inlaid wood, oil paintings, Audubon prints, brocade wall hangings, and, as always, a highly trained staff to satisfy a guest's every need and whim.

The hotel is designed in a big U shape. The conference facilities and tennis center are in one wing, a fitness center and indoor pool are in the other. The lobby, a lounge and bar, and the reception and concierge desks are in the main area connecting the wings. The far end of the lounge forms a semicircle overlooking the ocean. Planters filled with bromeliads, orchids, and tropical greenery divide the large room into three spaces. On one side is a long marble bar and a small lounge; at the other is a cozy sitting room with a fireplace. In between is the main lounge, where the traditional Ritz afternoon tea is served.

> **The outdoor pool is shaped like a lagoon with landscaped islands of palms and tropical greenery; the elegant indoor pool has floor-to-ceiling windows and looks out over the outdoor pool and the sand dunes.**

The Grill Room and Dining Room serve dinner only, while the more informal Café serves three meals a day. Though service is occasionally on the slow side at the Café, the food is excellent, as it is at all the restaurants. You can choose an asparagus-crab omelette with hollandaise sauce at breakfast, chilled seafood salad at lunch, and grilled tarragon-lemon prawns or lamb chops in a rosemary bordelaise sauce at dinner. And Florida's traditional Key lime pie is an event in itself: no simple wedge of pie here, but a small individual pie swimming in a pool of vanilla custard, edged with loops of raspberry and apricot syrup and garnished with fresh mint leaves. It's a good thing so much recreation is available.

Apart from the obvious choice of golf on the Summer Beach course, there is tennis on 11 lighted courts, including a banked court for spectators and both hard and clay surfaces. Swimming is a special pleasure at the Ritz: the Atlantic is only a few yards from the back door, and there are two swimming pools. The fitness club and spa are near the indoor pool.

Horseback riding is offered at the other end of the island at Seahorse Stables. The stables are near the bridge to Little Talbot Island, where locals often fish. Amelia Island is unusual in that it allows riding on the beach. Boats can be chartered at the shrimp docks in Fernandina Beach.

Spend some time exploring the charming, historic town of Fernandina Beach. The Chamber of Commerce, in a railroad depot near the docks on Front Street, sells maps that can be used as a guide for a walking tour. There are wonderful examples of Victoriana in the houses and public buildings of the 30-block historic district; ornate embellishments show the influence of Moorish, Queen Anne, Chippendale, and Carpenter styles, which combined make one grand architectural statement. Especially fun is the "C House" on the corner of Beech and 8th streets and Fairbanks Folly on 7th Street.

During a stay, one is struck by the contrasts on Amelia Island. The Parkway just off A1A is rather wooded, with ancient myrtle and live oak trees draped with Spanish moss. It's hard to believe that the city of Jacksonville is only 25 minutes away; this could be rural Georgia. The turnoff into the Summer Beach Resort has a much tamer, landscaped look, with wedges of green lawn and flower beds planted along the road. The manicured golf course and Mediterranean-style Ritz loom beyond.

Although northerners often think of all of Florida as a winter resort, Amelia Island is at its best in summer and in the temperate months of fall and spring. In July and August, the Ritz-Carlton attracts southerners who come to the northeast Florida coast to escape the heat. In the winter months, the Ritz hosts a number of business meetings in its conference center. Although it's easy to get to the island from the airport and I–95, there's also a ferry from Mayport, which is fun to take, especially if you have children along.

1735 House and Amelia Island Lodging Systems

584 S. Fletcher
Amelia Island, FL 32034
904-261-5878 (1735 House)
904-261-4148 (reservations for
   other island rentals)
800-872-8531

A nautical-themed B&B

Innkeepers: Emily and Gary Grable. **Accommodations:** 5 suites. **Rates:** $85–$95. **Included:** Continental breakfast. **Minimum stay:** None. **Added:** 8.5% tax; $5 extra person (child or adult). **Payment:** Major credit cards; personal checks. **Chil-

dren: No children under 6. **Smoking:** Only on porches. **Open:** Year-round.

The 1735 House, built in 1928, was the first B&B to open on Amelia Island. Because it is right on the ocean, is reasonably priced, and has charming rooms, it is still one of the most popular B&Bs on the island.

In 1735, Englishman James Oglethorpe, governor of Georgia, "discovered" Amelia Island and named it after the daughter of George II. Amelia Island soon became a pirates' hideout, and there are still many local legends of buried treasure. In keeping with local history, the suites resemble ship captains' quarters — small, with an efficient use of space. Each has an attractive bath, a compact master bedroom, and a narrow room with bunk

> The sand here is very fine, and the green-blue surf is warm. There's usually a nice Atlantic breeze to cool the air. The days are made for lying on the beach or taking long walks along the dunes.

beds. Furnishings are in wicker, wood, or rattan. Oceanfront suites have a living/dining area with a table and chairs. Three suites have kitchenettes, and all have color TVs. Walls are of knotty pine, with various nautical brass fittings and antiques for decoration.

Breakfast is a generous meal of pastries, fresh fruit and juice, and coffee or tea, which comes to your room in a wicker basket with the morning newspaper. There is no dining room here, but there are lots of places for lunch and dinner in the nearby seaport town of Fernandina Beach. Ice, juice, and tea are available in the galley.

Amenities include beach towels, mini-lines for drying clothes, and plastic bags for storing wet swimsuits. Although there are no telephones in the rooms, you can use the galley telephone for free local calls or credit card long-distance calls.

The front of the 1735 House faces South Fletcher, or Route A1A, the beach's main road. The house is not set back from the road, which might bother light sleepers. Another minor drawback for country inn perfectionists is that, despite its charming interior, the facade of the 1735 House is unprepossessing. The inn is a squarish, New England–style house with white vinyl clapboard siding and black aluminium shutters and awnings. The reason for the vinyl and aluminum exterior is practical: the house is right on the shore and exposed to the elements. Parking is at the front door.

A brick patio overlooking the ocean runs the length of the back of the house. It's furnished with chairs and tables and, although it's for everybody to enjoy, is directly accessible from the first-floor Captain's Suite — ideal for a family with children who love the beach.

The Grables and their staff also operate Amelia Island Lodging Systems, a reservations service listing a variety of vacation accommodations, from a large log cabin to a bungalow in the woods to a large resort with more than 100 rooms and villas.

One favorite is the lighthouse at 736 South Fletcher, owned and operated by the Grables themselves. It has four stories: a bedroom and sunken shower bath on the first floor, a galley and living room on the second, a master bedroom with a queen-size captain's bed on the third, and an observation deck on the top floor. A reproduction of the original Amelia Island Lighthouse, its wooden floors and ceilings and old brass fixtures give it an authentic feel.

Also offered by Lodging Systems is a newly renovated four-bedroom home right on the ocean. It has a dining room table that seats 10, a full kitchen, a utility room, a covered breezeway with a Ping-Pong table, and a screened-in porch overlooking the water.

There is tremendous variety in price and style in the Grables' listings; write for a brochure or call for a rundown on the places that would suit you best. It's a good idea to keep in mind the dynamics of the island when renting a place. The narrow southern end, near the Ritz-Carlton and Amelia Island Plantation Resort, is the trendier, wealthier end of the island, where private residences are usually large and well-kept. Farther north, the houses are smaller and don't have the manicured landscaping that houses near the Ritz have. These are real Florida summer places, where you can come in from the beach with a little sand on your feet and not feel that you'll destroy the decor. Most families with young children would probably be more relaxed in these imperfect little houses on or near the beach.

DAYTONA BEACH

Coquina Inn B&B

544 S. Palmetto
Daytona Beach, FL 32114
904-254-4969

> *Early 20th-century*
> *Florida architecture*

Innkeepers: Jerry and Susan Jerzykowski. **Accommodations:** 4 rooms; 1 suite. **Rates:** Rooms $75–$105, suite $195; special packages available. **Included:** Full breakfast; afternoon tea or cordial; shuttle service from Halifax Harbor and Daytona Marina when requested; bicycles. **Minimum stay:** Five nights during Race and Bike Week. **Added:** 10% tax. **Payment:** MasterCard, Visa; personal checks. **Children:** Older children allowed. **Smoking:** Only on verandah. **Open:** Year-round except Christmas.

Coquina Inn's Daytona Beach address might lead one to associate this inn with all the negative connotations of the Daytona area. Although the Coquina Inn is on a main thoroughfare of Daytona and is just minutes from Halifax Harbor Marina and the ocean, the atmosphere is residential and quiet here. The Coquina Inn is in the historic district of Daytona Beach, where fine old homes line streets with names like Magnolia, Orange, and Cedar. This inn is one of the finest examples of Florida architecture in this gracious neighborhood, and it has been meticulously restored by the talented owners, Susan and Jerry Jerzykowski.

Built in 1912, the inn derives its name from the coquina shellstone on its facade and distinctive fireplaces. It is a beautifully proportioned house, with arched windows on the front of the house and in the sun porch, a Spanish tile roof, and casement windows. The house was neglected for years, so there were no remodeling jobs from the 1950s to encumber Jerry and Susan's restoration efforts. This is not to say that refurbishing the place was an easy job. The Jerzykowskis spent many months repainting, redecorating, and updating the heating and cooling systems and plumbing.

> **Breakfast is spectacular: the best china and silver are set out in the dining room and, in the winter, candles are lit. A typical meal might be homemade bread and fruits from the local farmer's market followed by thick slices of French toast filled with strawberries and cream cheese, or egg soufflé elegantly presented with fruit and fresh mint.**

The oak floors in the drawing room and the Mexican tiles in the sun porch are original. Brass sconces on the walls and ceiling fans on the high ceilings complete the gracious mood of these two rooms, joined by French doors. The dining room is formal, with salmon walls and built-in cupboards. The graceful windows here and throughout the house are made more beautiful by gauzy curtains above narrow wooden shutters or richly draped curtains.

The four guest rooms are on the second floor and are named for Florida flowers: Azalea, Magnolia, Hibiscus, and Jasmine. The latter was originally the master bedroom. It has a mahogany queen bed, an original coquina fireplace, and soft peach plaster walls. The bathroom has the original old tub and an oak floor. The Jasmine can be joined with the Hibiscus for a family. Hibiscus has a sitting area, a large bath, and an outdoor deck where breakfast may be served.

Magnolia has an old double bedstead and a twin daybed. The adjoining bathroom has a clawfoot tub and old brass and porcelain fixtures. The beautifully decorated Azalea is papered in green floral stripes and has lots of fancy pillows on the bed. Azalea has a bathroom at the end of a quirky little hallway within the room. The Sweet Suite, the most expensive accommodation at the Coquina, has two adjoining bedrooms, two baths, and a fireplace and sunporch.

All of the rooms have small decorative touches like antique dolls, beribboned baskets, or old oval mirrors. Most have sitting areas and spacious mirrored closets. The original oak floors are accented with Oriental rugs. Jerry and Susan have made a great effort to create early-20th-century graciousness.

This ambience carries over to the marvelous breakfasts, which can be brought to your room for a small extra charge or enjoyed on the new patio among the pink oleander.

Susan and Jerry enjoy creating personalized "packages" for guests for only a little more than the usual rate. If they're informed in advance, they can make arrangements for an anniversary, honeymoon, or Valentine stay, with champagne and fresh flowers in the room, breakfast in bed, and an evening cruise. They like telling people about local attractions and provide bicycles free to guests, as well as shuttle service from Halifax Harbor Marina for those who arrive by boat. Susan and Jerry run a catering business as well as the B&B and will prepare picnic lunches for a small additional charge. They will try to provide any service that will make a guest's stay more memorable.

Indigo Lakes Golf & Tennis

2620 W. International Speedway
   Blvd.
Daytona Beach, FL 32114
904-258-6333
800-223-4161 in Florida
800-874-9918 in U.S./Canada
Fax: 904-254-3698

> *A quiet retreat near the speedway*

General Manager: Lon Yaeger. **Accommodations:** 211 rooms and suites. **Rates:** Rooms $75–$95, suites $85–$115; packages available; higher rates during Daytona Race Week. **Minimum stay:** With some packages. **Added:** 10% tax; $10 extra adult. **Payment:** Major credit cards; personal checks. **Children:** Under 12 free in room with parents. **Smoking:** Nonsmoking rooms available. **Open:** Year-round.

It's hard to believe that Indigo Lakes, with its 4,000 acres of woodlands, ponds, marshlands, and lagoons, is just five minutes from Daytona Regional Airport and the International Speedway. There are several acres of beautifully landscaped lawns and gardens surrounding the main buildings and great herons standing guard in the marshes. An effort is made throughout to bring the outside indoors, with rich wood paneling and large windows overlooking the woods and greenery.

Accommodations include rooms and suites in the inn and villa-style suites at the "village." The best overlook the pool and golf course. All inn rooms are attractively decorated and have a patio or balcony, cable TV, bedside television and light controls, in-room safes, direct-dial phones, and study areas. Rooms are furnished with king-size beds or two doubles. A few suites have parlors and kitchenettes.

> **The conference facilities are among the best in Florida. The 22,000 square feet of meeting space can accommodate up to 300 people and was designed for small meetings; there is none of the crowded, impersonal feeling of large convention hotels.**

The inn has a handsome reception area and lobby, where it's pleasant to read or watch the passing scene. A brass and glass chandelier hangs above the stairway, which is paneled in rich woods. The carpet of deep indigo follows a color scheme carried out in many of the common rooms.

Standard accommodations in the main hotel buildings are spacious and include a small refrigerator and coffeemaker. Views are of landscaped areas and the pool or of the parking lot, so ask about the view when making reservations. A short walk or ride from the main building are the deluxe accommodations of the "village," a cluster of low-rise, shake-roofed buildings. Executive king suites offer a king-size bed, a spacious study area, a screened-in patio, and a whirlpool. Executive doubles have two double beds, a dining/study area, a living room, a well-equipped kitchen, and screened-in patio with a washer and dryer. Suite 7111 is particularly nice, with a view of a pond. Double and king suites can be combined to form spacious two-bedroom suites.

The conference center is made up of three interconnected conical buildings with shake roofs. The landscaping is attractive and conscientiously maintained. All meeting rooms have individually controlled sound and air-conditioning systems, music, lights, teleconferencing installations, state-of-the-art video, and audiovisual equipment with rear-screen projection. The adjacent banquet center can cater receptions or sit-down meals. There is courtesy transportation throughout the resort, and airport transportation is free with 24 hours' notice.

The facilities include a fully equipped fitness club and health spa with a Parcourse fitness trail, a six-lane Olympic-size pool, and excellent golf and tennis. Indigo Lakes has a full-service golf shop, putting and chipping greens with a practice sand trap, and a 400-yard driving range.

The attractive tennis center has 10 all-weather courts lighted for night play and a pro shop. Pros are available for group clinics and private lessons, and the tennis center will match guests with appropriate partners. Racquetball is also available.

Indigo Lakes has its own restaurant, Major Moultrie's, with good gourmet food in a setting that has almost a rural feel to it. There are also a number of restaurants on the mainland in Old Daytona and in Daytona Beach. However, once you come to the self-contained Indigo Lakes, you really need not go anywhere else.

Live Oak Inn and Restaurant

448 S. Beach Street
Daytona Beach, FL 32114
904-252-4667
Fax: 904-255-1871

A historic inn in Old Daytona

Innkeeper: Vinton Day Fisher. **Accommodations:** 4 rooms. **Rates:** $95 on weekends, $70 Monday–Thursday; reduced rates for packages and longer stays. **Included:** Beverage on arrival, extended Continental breakfast. **Minimum stay:** 5-night minimum during special events. **Added:** 10% tax; $10 extra person. **Payment:** Major credit cards, personal checks. **Children:** Young children discouraged because of antiques. **Smoking:** On porch and verandah only. **Open:** Year-round.

The Live Oak Inn is not part of the Daytona beach scene, although that famous strip of sand is quite easily accessible. The inn harks back to a gentler time in this part of the world. Old Daytona is on the mainland, while Daytona Beach and Daytona Beach Shores are on a barrier island across the Intracoastal Waterway. (Guests arriving by boat can dock at the marina and simply walk across the street.) Built in the late 1800s, the Live Oak is one of the oldest houses in the county and is reputed to be the site of the founding of Daytona by Mathias Day.

The main house sits impressively on the corner, surrounded by attractive gardens and a picket fence. Ancient oak trees, festooned with Spanish moss, shade the old clapboard building. An old-fashioned wrap-around porch is furnished with rockers. As one would ex-

> **The spirit of the early Daytona era has been beautifully preserved here in the choice of antiques and other appointments, but also in the atmosphere the innkeeper has created.**

pect at a "real Florida inn," many guests sit out here reading or gazing out at the marina and Intracoastal across the street. A heavy wood door leads into a formal 19th-century entryway and the reception area. Throughout the inn, there are lots of windows that let the sun shine in. Tables and chairs are set up in the front parlors for restaurant guests. There is also outside dining on one side of the porch.

A typical dinner begins with an appetizer of oysters sautéed in Creole butter or escargot Dijonnaise, followed by fresh seafood or a fine cut of beef in a mustard shallot wine sauce. A typical dessert is white chocolate raspberry cheesecake or a delicate flan. The gourmet breakfast, for inn guests only, can be eaten on the restaurant's porch or in the dining rooms. A typical morning meal includes orange juice, homemade muffins, summer sausage, cheese, fresh fruit, and hot beverages. Innkeeper Vin Fisher calls this a German or European breakfast — it's not exactly a full American breakfast, but it can hardly be called a simple Continental either. The restaurant is wheelchair accessible.

In the evening, the restaurant's lounge and bar provides a pleasant gathering place — more neighborhood pub than bar. It's in the back of the house, a 1920s addition. It looks squarish and a bit awkward from the outside, but inside, it blends beautifully with the rest of the place. The entire room is paneled in cathedral-like gothic wainscoting in a dark-stained wood. Above are small windows of wavy old glass that run the length of the walls.

The four upstairs bedrooms are decorated with late 19th-century antiques, iron bedsteads, and period color schemes.

Bathrooms are small to moderate-size but are equipped with Jacuzzis. Two of the rooms have enclosed porches, and a third has a balcony — all overlooking the waterway and the marina, which is Florida's largest.

The Foster Room is especially appealing, with sky blue plaster walls, a white iron bedstead, and a balcony. The Rogers Room — named after Dr. Josie Rogers, Daytona's first woman doctor and its only woman mayor — has polished maple floors, period antique furnishings, and a black iron bedstead. The bathroom has the original black and white floor tiles.

An effort is made to educate guests with a light hand about the history of Old Daytona. In only a few years, the Live Oak Inn has become well known in the area for delicious food and as a good place to put up visiting friends and relatives who are wary of the honky-tonk beach scene across the bridge.

Perry's Ocean-Edge

2209 S. Atlantic Avenue
  (Route A1A)
Daytona Beach, FL 32018
800-447-0002
In Florida:
904-255-0581
800-342-0102

*A budget standby
on the ocean*

Owners: The Perry family. **Accommodations:** 204 rooms, suites, and efficiencies. **Rates:** Rooms $45–$103, efficiencies $55–$113, suites $124–$206; weekly rates available. **Included:**

Continental breakfast. **Minimum stay:** 2 nights with packages. **Added:** 10% tax; $10 extra person; $3 extra for ground-floor rooms. **Payment:** Major credit cards. **Children:** Under 16 free in room with parents; no students not accompanied by adult. **Smoking:** Allowed. **Open:** Year-round.

Ninety percent of the families, couples, and retirees who stay at Perry's Ocean-Edge return. Two major reasons are the beach and the enclosed atrium swimming pool. But perhaps most important is that guests feel at home at Perry's. The resort has been owned by the Perry family for more than 50 years, and they have some unbeatable traditions. Mornings begin with the fragrance of doughnuts cooking in the big kitchen. These are served at a Continental breakfast buffet in one of the resort's 1950s-style lounges.

Although Perry's is located right on the Daytona Beach hotel/motel strip, once inside, most guests feel removed from the noise and crowds because the activity here focuses on the resort's indoor pool and the beach. The white concrete and glass hotel, with its aquamarine trim and vinyl additions, is classic '50s style, adding to the feeling that Perry's Ocean-Edge has been here for years and will continue its traditions of hospitality and service for many more.

Behind its big twin towers are two large pools, shuffleboard courts, a putting green, a kiddie pool, and lots of green lawn — 700 feet of it. This is unusual on the east coast of Florida, where a lawn demands a great deal of maintenance. It's great for children to romp on and gives a backyard homeyness to the entire recreational area. Chairs and tables with umbrellas are placed here and there on the lawn. Well-swept cement paths connect the pool and recreational areas to the beach and the ocean beyond. Daytona Beach is wide and sandy — a favorite of kids who like to make sand castles or bury little brothers. But it should be enjoyed with caution, as driving is allowed on the beach and cars can appear suddenly.

If it gets cloudy or rains, no problem; it's a wonderful excuse to use the indoor pool, covered by a Plexiglas and redwood enclosure. Asparagus ferns spill out of planters hanging from the ceiling. On the patio underneath, circular brick planters hold tropical trees and flowers. A gazebo encloses the whirlpool. Lawn chairs and chaise longues surround the pool, and there are little tables with yellow canvas umbrellas for enjoying a drink or talking with friends. At one end of the atrium is a series of tiered goldfish ponds with waterfalls.

Kids love this pool, and because it's enclosed, parents and grandparents can feel safe having children play and swim any time of day. Although parental supervision is certainly expected at Perry's, the staff seem genuinely to enjoy having kids around. The Perrys have done a good job of training their young personnel and they, too, keep coming back year after year.

For those who want something more exciting than sun and surf, there are of course the car and motorcycle races at Daytona Beach International Speedway. The Daytona Beach Kennel Club offers greyhound racing; there's also golf, tennis, river cruises, deep-sea fishing, and big-name nighttime entertainment in Daytona.

Although some rooms overlook the indoor pool in the original motel, these are older and can be noisy. Better choices are the suites in the South Tower or the larger North Tower suites. These are well designed, with two double beds in the front of the suite and, tucked behind a half-wall, a third double backed with bolster cushions that serves as a sofa during the day. Opposite is the dining area with a table and chairs and an adjacent L-shaped kitchenette, which can be used for a small fee. When not in use, this can be closed off with a woven-wood curtain. The bathrooms have two vanities, a hair dryer, and ample closet space.

The decor in the suites is a bit dull, and the Perrys seem reluctant to spend much on refurbishment. They are slowly whitewashing the furniture and replacing bedspreads and torn curtains. But with the competition of a new Marriott up the street, it is surprising they are not redecorating with greater speed. Outside the rooms, indoor-outdoor carpeting is buckled and stained in some areas. To some extent, Perry's Ocean-Edge is resting on its laurels, apparently relying on the loyal old customers to return, and perhaps losing younger customers who prefer the freshness of new resorts on the strip.

The informal restaurant, Perry's Smokehouse, serves breakfast and lunch. Those who wish to eat in can buy relatively inexpensive groceries at the supermarket across the street.

Sunny Shore Motel

2037 S. Atlantic Avenue
Daytona Beach Shores, FL 32118
904-252-4569
800-874-2854

A well-maintained budget motel on the beach

Owner: Vicki Ogle. **Accommodations:** 34 rooms, suites, and efficiencies. **Rates:** Rooms $36–$54, suites $68–$97, efficiencies $40–$61; weekly rates available. **Minimum stay:** 5 nights. **Payment:** Discover, MasterCard, Visa. **Added:** 10% tax; $5 extra adult; $3 for cribs and roll-aways. **Children:** Under 12 free in room with parents; no students not accompanied by adult. **Smoking:** Allowed. **Open:** Year-round.

Daytona Beach has been overrun in the past few years by wild college crowds in winter and spring. If you're planning a vacation on this famous — and infamous — beach, it's important to choose accommodations carefully. Families and adult couples are usually happiest at places like the Sunny Shore, which doesn't allow college-age students without their parents. Though Sunny Shore is oriented to vacationing families, groups and couples are welcome, as long as they are quiet and turn out the lights early.

All the rooms have recently been redecorated and have blue wall-to-wall carpeting and new vinyl kitchen floors.

Sunny Shore is immaculate, inside and out. Rooms have modern furniture and are designed with the vacationing family in mind. Baths have a separate vanity area, which eases morning crowding. Most families choose an efficiency with two double beds and a small kitchen.

The best rooms are at the back of the motel, especially 211 and 212, which have small balconies overlooking the ocean. Although the motel is on busy Atlantic Avenue, guests are here for the beach and the reasonable prices. They can park their cars in front of their rooms and usually leave them there all day. From the parking lot, it's just a few steps to the pool and the beach beyond. Groceries are available at the supermarket just down the street.

Daytona Beach is wide and gorgeous, and the surf is warm, with a variety of wave heights that depend on the time of day, the weather, and the season. You can bodysurf or swim or just wade along the shore.

Watch out for cars on the beach. Residents and visitors are still allowed to drive right on the beach, so parents of small children cannot go to sleep in the sun, no matter how far from the surf their children are playing.

Summer is the high season here, so a family can get a very good rate in the winter, fall and spring — except for Race Week, when the place is extremely crowded.

HUTCHINSON ISLAND

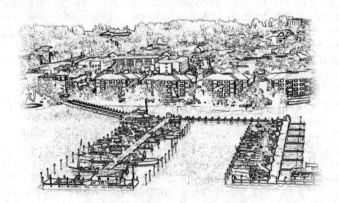

Indian River Plantation

555 N.E. Ocean Boulevard
Hutchinson Island
Stuart, FL 34996
407-225-3700
800-444-3389

> *A true
> destination resort*

General Manager: Jeff Johnsen. **Accommodations:** 200 hotel rooms, 70 1-bedroom suites and studios; 53 1- and 2-bedroom oceanfront condos. **Rates:** Hotel rooms $130–$195, 1-bedroom suites $210–$395, studio $160–$245; packages available. **Minimum stay:** 2 or 3 nights with some packages. **Added:** 6% tax. **Payment:** Major credit cards. **Children:** Under 17 free in room with parents. **Smoking:** Nonsmoking rooms available. **Open:** Year-round.

Stuart, Florida, is a city of inlets and rivers, with the Atlantic Ocean surging just beyond the Indian River and Hutchinson Island. Indian River Plantation Resort is easily accessible by bridges, but with its location on quiet A1A, the resort has an insular feeling.

The resort's marina is located two miles north of the St. Lucie Inlet on the Indian River stretch of the Intracoastal Waterway. The land along the marina is rimmed by mangroves. Guests walk from their boats down a wooden pier and through a small forest of these trees to reach the plantation's hotel. Those arriving by car cross picturesque bridges over the Indian River to the island. In the lobby, white ceiling fans revolve lazily and a cool peach marble floor is underfoot. On a platform in the center of the lobby guests can sit surrounded by large planters of green plants. Just outside is a waterfall.

> **The marina is one of the most beautiful in Florida — a full-service, 77-slip facility. Along with a fuel dock and utility and telephone hook-ups, there are washers and dryers, showers, lockers, and a well-equipped ship's store. The marina staff are cordial and helpful. Mariners should make reservations well in advance of arrival time, especially in season.**

After registering, hotel guests take the elevator to rooms above the lobby or walk across a courtyard under huge white latticework archways to the accommodations in the other wing. (Larger villa accommodations are at the other end of the resort.) There are 200 hotel guest rooms, all of them a bit larger than the average standard hotel room, with thick carpeting and quilted spreads. Amenities include hair dryers, remote control cable TV, private balconies, and nightly turndown service.

The hotel is adapted from the Old Florida style: gray roof and clapboards, white trim and latticework, and touches of pale peach on the terraces. Although the style is carried out not with the traditional tin and wood but in sturdy vinyl and other practical materials, none of it looks cheap or flimsy.

In addition to the standard rooms at the resort's new hotel, there are also spacious suites and one- and two-bedroom villas. Located in mid-rise buildings, these accommodations are particularly sought after by families and those here for longer stays. They have fully equipped kitchens and attractively furnished bedrooms and living/dining areas. Most have spectacular views of the ocean and dunes. From the top floors of the open-air hallways in some of the villas, you can look out at the Atlantic on one side and the Indian River on the other.

Apart from ocean swimming and beaching, there is an impressive array of recreation at Indian River Plantation. There are 13 tennis courts, seven of them lighted for night games. The tennis center provides excellent instruction, clinics, and tournaments for guests and club members of all ages, as well as equipment rentals and an excellent pro shop. The Porch, an informal restaurant serving three meals a day, overlooks the courts, and is ideal for lunch after a vigorous game.

Golf is on an 18-hole, par 61 course that includes a challenging driving range and a putting green. You might lose a lot of balls in the water on the driving range, but it's a lot of fun. There are three swimming pools, and water sports like Jet Skiing and water skiing. The marina rents boats and arranges deep-sea fishing excursions and sunset cruises along the Intracoastal Waterway. The resort also has bicycling and jogging trails and a fitness facility.

For a change of pace, the county beach is just a few minutes away, with very warm water, lovely natural vegetation, and just enough shells to be interesting.

Indian River Plantation has a convention center that includes an impressive grand ballroom and a number of breakout rooms and hospitality suites. The Elliott Amphitheater has a modern stage, a floor-to-ceiling projection screen, an audiovisual system, and cushioned armchairs arranged in tiers, with individual lighting and writing space for each conference participant. These facilities, coupled with the resort's natural beauty and recreation, make it popular with business, professional, and environmental groups.

The resort's restaurants, lounges, and bars must take some of the credit for its popularity. Of the four restaurants, Scalawags is the largest and most elegant, with both indoor and terrace dining. All the delicious pastries and pies are made from scratch at the plantation. The Inlet is the resort's small, formal restaurant and serves only dinner. The Porch, overlooking the tennis courts, serves three meals daily. The Emporium, with its old-fashioned decor, serves meals throughout the day and has an ice cream parlor. Although the food is not up to the standards of the other three restaurants, its informality and proximity to the gift shop and marine store make it a good place for families with children.

Families will enjoy the area's nearby attractions; these are not glitzy commercial lures. The House of Refuge, for example, built in 1875 as one of seven coastal rescue stations, is now a museum of marine artifacts and

> **A year-round supervised activities program for kids includes snorkeling, bike rides, movies, parties, and lots of time on the beach. A camp program in the summer offers children tennis, golf, and swimming lessons, fishing trips, arts and crafts sessions, and field trips to nearby attractions.**

19th-century living quarters, and a research facility for the study of the life cycle of green sea turtles. They say that when the resort was being built, a turtle's nest was found on the property and all construction was halted on that site until the nesting season was over. This is typical of the attitude at the plantation and in the town of Stuart. Guests at the resort have the privilege of enjoying carefully preserved natural beauty while indulging their love of recreation and sport.

JACKSONVILLE

House on Cherry Street

1844 Cherry Street
Jacksonville, FL 32205
904-384-1999

*A B&B that feels
like a friend's home*

Innkeepers: Carol and Merrill Anderson. **Accommodations:** 4 rooms. **Rates:** $65–$80. **Included:** Full breakfast; hors d'oeuvres and wine in evening. **Minimum stay:** 2 nights during special events. **Added:** 10.5% tax. **Payment:** MasterCard, Visa; personal checks. **Children:** 10 and older welcome. **Smoking:** Only in common room and on porches. **Open:** Year-round; occasionally closed for two or three days.

Carol and Merrill Anderson are extremely congenial hosts who seem to truly enjoy all those who stay with them. Their house looks more New England than Florida, with square-rigger architecture and small-paned lights on each side of the sturdy-looking door. The street the B&B is named after ends at a little neighborhood park and the St. Johns River. Cherry Street is part of the Avondale/Riverdale historic district, one of the most desirable sections of Jacksonville. This "reservations only" inn is a wonderful place to rest and feel at home, and it is also within easy driving distance of many area attractions.

A large grandfather clock stands by the entryway. In the spacious foyer, the Andersons display some of their old wooden decoys; most of the collection is in the living room.

The guest rooms are decorated with more decoys, four-poster beds, and antiques. Though some of the wonderful bedsteads are antiques, the queen mattresses are firm and new. The rooms are carpeted or have area rugs on the light pine floors. Windows afford views of the St. Johns River or of gardens. Baths are modern, though one or two are on the small side.

The Andersons' only first-floor room is popular with small families. It has a sunny sitting room with a couch and a pair of twin beds. As always, there are wooden ducks on the shelves.

In the morning, it's best to plan an active day of sightseeing in town so that you can work off the delicious breakfast. A typical morning meal includes croissants and fruit followed by something hearty like eggs Benedict. If you have dietary restrictions or prefer low-calorie food, Carol will accommodate you. Still, it's a mistake to miss out on a real Anderson breakfast. Guests can enjoy an extra cup of coffee on the screened-in porch overlooking the backyard and the St. Johns River.

> **In the evening, Carol and Merrill offer guests wine and two or three of Carol's superlative hors d'oeuvres, served on the porch or in the living room. This is a beautifully appointed front parlor with pale aqua walls and brocade wing chairs. To keep the room from looking too elegant, the Andersons have covered almost every available surface with some variety of duck decoy.**

Omni Jacksonville Hotel

245 Water Street
Jacksonville, FL 32202
904-355-OMNI
800-THE-OMNI

> *A downtown hotel near trendy Jacksonville Landing*

General Manager: Peter Austin. **Accommodations:** 354 rooms. **Rates:** Rooms $79–$160, Omni Club rooms: $164; Packages and discount weekend rates available. **Minimum stay:** With some packages. **Added:** 10.5% tax. **Payment:** Major credit cards. **Children:** Under 18 free in room with parents. **Smoking:** Nonsmoking rooms available. **Open:** Year-round.

The Omni Jacksonville is one of the few top-notch hotels in downtown Jacksonville. Why they're so scarce in a town that has recently had a major urban renewal is hard to say; perhaps the hotel business just hasn't caught up with the resurgent city.

The Omni is near Jacksonville Landing, an urban harbor development with dozens of trendy shops and some lively restaurants. The St. Johns River and Intracoastal Waterway are adjacent, so guests can take river-taxi rides, cruise on a big replica paddlewheeler, and stroll along the Riverwalk.

The Omni is a popular convention hotel for companies

from out of town and is also a meeting place for smaller Jacksonville-area businesses. The entrance off busy Water Street is impressive, with light marble floors, massive veneered pillars, and Oriental art. The reception area is spacious enough to handle registering convention groups, and the staff remains polite and unruffled even when working with large groups.

> **The Omni is a convenient business hotel and also a wonderful place to mix business with pleasure: the entire Jacksonville Landing area is hopping day and night.**

The second-floor conference rooms include the Florida Ballroom, which can be subdivided. Just off the ballroom is a big sitting area for taking a break between meetings or lingering for informal discussions.

Juliette's, the hotel's restaurant, is named after Juliette DuBois, a 19th-century city resident who was famous as a cook on her father's riverboat. Juliette's has a clubby atmosphere; the food is not great, but it's certainly acceptable. The Atrium offers terrace dining in a four-story botanical garden. A comfortable lounge on the first floor is popular with both the Jacksonville business community and visitors from out of town.

Rooms are a bit larger than the average standard accommodation. Some of the rooms overlook city streets and parking lots, but the best expose a slice of the busy St. Johns River. The rooms are spanking new, with thick wall-to-wall carpeting and light oak furniture. The baths have ceramic tile and marble sinks.

Nearby are the beaches of the northeast Florida coast, just as wide and beautiful as Daytona but less crowded.

St. Augustine, the oldest established city in the United States, and Fort Caroline, the first European colony, are both within easy driving distance. Marineland, one of Florida's oldest and most worthwhile attractions, is an hour away.

Residents of Jacksonville fondly refer to their city as "Jax" — there is a feeling of vitality and strong community pride here. After a stay at the Omni, you may find that the mood of "Jax" is catching.

Plantation Manor Inn

1630 Copeland Street
Jacksonville, FL 32204
904-384-4630

*A B&B with Old
South hospitality*

Innkeepers: Jerry and Kathy Ray.
Accommodations: 8 rooms. **Rates:**
Rooms $75–$135, suites: $100. **Included:** Full breakfast; afternoon cocktails. **Minimum stay:** None. **Added:** 10.5% tax. **Payment:** MasterCard, Visa; personal checks. **Children:** 12 and over welcome. **Smoking:** Only on porches. **Open:** Year-round.

Carolinans Jerry and Kathy Ray were not exaggerating when they named their B&B Plantation Manor. The three-story house is very southern, very much the manor. It sits on a slight rise on a corner lot in the city's most attractive historic neighborhood. The two Doric columns that support the overhang above the entryway are massive. Slightly smaller columns support the second-floor verandah that wraps around the imposing house. Built in 1905 and occupied by a number of successful Jacksonville citizens, it began to deteriorate by the middle of the century. After the Rays bought the place, Jerry and a team of workers undertook the arduous task of renovating the house. It took a year to complete the new roof and four-foot overhangs outside, and eight months to strip the cypress woodwork of layers of paint in the interior, to say nothing of spackling and painting and decorating — Kathy's domain.

The finished house has high ceilings, patterned pine floors, plastered or papered walls, and an elegant wooden banister. Furnishings are a mix of 19th-century antiques, gilded French provincial reproductions, and contemporary pieces. Guests enter the wide formal entry and first see the ornate living room, which has a semicircular sofa before a paneled and tiled fireplace.

On the opposite side of the entry hall is a room that was probably a formal dining room in the original house and is now an attractive boardroom for businesspeople who conduct executive retreats and conferences at Plantation Manor. A large table has space to spread out, and large double doors close off the room from the rest of the Manor. A fax machine sits in the corner.

> **All the rooms on the second and third floors have access from the second-floor hallway to the verandah. This is furnished with white iron lawn furniture cushioned with big pillows and is shaded by large old trees.**

In the middle of the house is what was probably a back parlor in 1905 and is now a dining room. Here Kathy serves breakfast at whatever time guests request it. A typical morning meal might consist of a ham omelette, homemade breads and pastries, fresh fruit and juice, coffee and tea.

A side door leads to a small porch and several steps down to a brick-paved patio and a swimming pool. The area is surrounded by flower beds and has become a favorite for weddings and receptions in Jacksonville. It would be easy to feel like a southern belle in such a setting.

Not surprisingly, a favorite bedroom at the Manor is the Honeymoon Suite, which has bright green walls, a four-poster bed, tiled fireplace, walk-in closet, a loveseat in the sitting area, and Oriental rug on the natural pine floors. The bathroom has a pedestal sink, brass and porcelain fixtures, built-in drawers original to the house, and a spanking new shower as well as an old tub. The large bathroom also has a bay window with a padded window seat decorated with white embroidered pillows. The one very modern note in the Honeymoon Suite is the 52-inch TV opposite the four-poster, which the Rays seem to feel guests expect today.

The Louie Room, down the second-floor hallway from the

Honeymoon Suite, is furnished with a full bedstead in tiger maple, an armoire with a beveled glass mirror, and an Oriental rug on the natural wood floor. Bouquets of false flowers decorate some surfaces, evidence of a slight fussiness in the house that is perhaps part of the southern Victorian look.

The third floor has a private suite called the Pewter Room where Kathy has made the most of the interesting angles created by the eaves. Here, the original matchstick paneling has been painted pale green, and the focus of the room is a curving pewter and brass bedstead. A daybed opposite has a pretty Battenberg lace coverlet. Plush green wall-to-wall carpeting covers the floor.

All the suites and rooms have private bathrooms that nicely combine new and old features, as well as telephones and TVs — usually large-screen models.

Though Kathy and Jerry could play the role of lord and lady of the manor, they are down-to-earth southerners who came late to the pleasures of antique collecting and historic homes. They stand ready to make a visit as pleasurable and, for their business clients, as efficient, as possible.

JUPITER

Comfort Suites – Intercoastal Marina

18903 S.E. Federal Highway
Jupiter, FL 33469
407-747-9085

A budget suite motel on the Intracoastal

Owner: Lou Gatti. **Accommodations:** 36 rooms. **Rates:** Jacuzzi room $69–$125, 2-queens room $59–$125; weekly and monthly rates available. **Included:** Continental breakfast. **Minimum stay:** None. **Added:** 6% tax; $5–$20 extra adult depending on season and day of week. **Payment:** MasterCard, Visa. **Children:** 19 and under free in room with parents. **Smoking:** Nonsmoking rooms available. **Open:** Year-round.

The Comfort Suites motel is located just off Route 1, also called Federal Highway. Although Route 1 is congested and lined with dozens of gas stations and shopping malls farther south, the stores and the traffic thin significantly in Jupiter. By the time the highway winds up the coast to the Comfort Suites, there are only trees and dunes on the west side of the road and houses and marinas on the east side. The Comfort Suites motel fits right in, with its gray-stained siding and Florida-style tin roof. The motel is set back a bit and, in spite of being on a highway, there is little noise this far from the town center.

> **For water sports and boating, there are marinas just down the road where visitors can also get information about the best places for fishing.**

Guest rooms face the Intracoastal and a landscaped patio and pool. A wooden pier stretches out over the water, with stairs at the front of the pier leading down to a small beach (though most guests swim in the pool only). A tiled Jacuzzi wreathed in green plants is built a few feet above the pool so that guests have a slightly elevated view of the waterway while they soak. Each room has a small patio or balcony furnished with vinyl outdoor furniture.

It's pleasant to sit out here night or day. This stretch of the Intracoastal is especially beautiful. The view stretches out over a wide strip of water, a small island, then more water and Jupiter Island, and finally the Atlantic. It's not heavily populated, and manatees and many waterfowl come to feed here. There are boats and Jet Skis on the water, especially on the weekends, so it would be inaccurate to say this is a remote, untouched area, but it is peaceful in spite of the recreational activity.

In addition to the outdoor Jacuzzi available for all guests to use, several of the suites have Jacuzzis right in the room. These accommodations are about $10 more than the regular two-queen suite during off-season but are the same price during high season. Therefore, it's worth it to call early for reservations and specifically request a Jacuzzi suite. Further reductions in the room rates are available for extended stays during high season if you call two or more months in advance. The Jacuzzi suites all have a sitting area with a foldout couch, coffee table, a small square table, and sliders to a small patio or balcony with a water view. The bedroom area has a queen- or king-size bed.

A small kitchenette has a Formica countertop and sink with a little refrigerator beneath. A tiny closet is in the entryway near the bathroom. Except for the Jacuzzi, there is no tub, but the shower is oversize and includes a little seat. Furniture in the guest rooms looks like blond oak but is actually a good imitation in Formica. Families with older children or couples traveling together can request rooms with connecting doors.

The regular or "Queen" suites are similar in decor to the Jacuzzi suites but have two beds instead of one and are therefore more economical for a family. The bathrooms have a tub shower. One or two more kids can be bedded down on a foldout couch in the sitting area overlooking the patio, though you'd want to spend a lot of time outside to avoid feeling too cramped. These suites also have a small countertop and a sink with cupboards beneath, although there is no fridge. There's also a small square table with two chairs.

On the patio near the pool is a small barbeque grill. Simple meals can be prepared if you're in a Jacuzzi suite with a refrigerator, but most guests eat in Jupiter or nearby Tequesta, where there are several reasonably priced restaurants and pizza places. In the morning, Comfort Suites has a complimentary Continental breakfast of coffee, tea, muffins, and pastries. These are served at a long counter in the reception center where there are two round kitchen tables. Some folks take breakfast back to their rooms or eat on their patio.

There is a small laundry room by the reception area, and dry-cleaning establishments and supermarkets in Jupiter and Tequesta.

Nearby attractions include the Jupiter Lighthouse, Burt Reynolds Dinner Theatre, and the peaceful Jonathan Dickenson State Park. Hobe Sound, just up the highway, has a nice walking beach.

For those who wish to drive 40 minutes farther up the coast, there's the town of Stuart, which looks just like any other overdeveloped Florida town until you get to the northern end. Just east of Federal Highway, there's a small regional theater and some interesting little shops and restaurants in the historic district — a real town, a rarity in modern Florida. A visit here is of greater interest to adults than kids, though there is a wonderful shop called Rare Earth Pottery where the potters will make stoneware plates from the clay impressions of small hands.

The Jupiter Beach Resort

5 North A1A
Jupiter, FL 33477
800-228-8810
407-746-2511
Fax: 407-744-1741

> *A sophisticated retreat on uncrowded Jupiter Beach*

General Manager: Alan Wieme. **Accommodations:** 197 rooms and suites. **Rates:** Rooms $101–$365, suites $179–$325, penthouse $400–$1,000; packages available; no charge for roll-away or crib. **Minimum stay:** With some packages and high-season weekends. **Added:** 10% tax. **Payment:** Major credit cards. **Children:** 17 and under free in room with parent. **Smoking:** Nonsmoking rooms available. **Open:** Open year-round.

Compared to other towns in Palm Beach County, Jupiter is little known. Once a small fishing village, the town has grown enormously in the last 25 years. Jupiter Inlet Colony and Jupiter Island have now become more exclusive than the town of Palm Beach. There is still an uncrowded, nautical feel to the area, and it's possible to find a place to park your car near the beach even on the weekends.

At the Jupiter Beach Resort, however, you need not worry about parking. You can do it yourself or ask the valet. The hotel is luxurious but also informal. The decor and atmosphere often remind visitors of a U.S. Caribbean island resort. Staff make you feel at home, and their name tags, with their hometown included, remind you that lots of people here are from someplace else.

A variety of accommodations are available, from Sunset rooms (lower floors overlook the parking lot, but higher floors have good views) to Deluxe Oceanfronts. The best deal here is an Oceanview room. These have a good view of the ocean, especially if you are high up. No matter what the location or price, rooms are furnished with wicker and bamboo furniture. Bed choices are two doubles, a queen, or a king. The color scheme is Caribbean — lots of sea green, melon, and coral. Gauzy mosquito netting hangs above the bed. Hallways to the guest rooms have reed floor coverings, which fit the West Indies theme of the resort but can be tough to walk on for anyone arriving in business shoes or high heels.

Bathrooms all have ceramic tile and Corian sinks, and the

usual bath amenities are blessed with the helpful addition of beach-tar remover. One small drawback is that balconies on even the expensive Oceanview rooms are tiny, with just enough room for two wicker chairs in the narrow space. But the views are super — Jupiter Inlet and Jupiter Island, the Intracoastal Waterway, and the Atlantic beyond.

> **An elevated boardwalk meanders from the pool patio down to the breezy beach. Sea oats, sea grapes, and many wildflowers and vines grow on the dunes.**

Most people eat at festive Sinclair's American Grill or on the patio outside overlooking the pool. Food is more than adequate, and the Sunday brunch is especially good. The one jarring note is that a "dune dog" is apparently the mascot for the resort. Thus, an adult in a large animal suit (looking more like an overgrown rat) ambles through the lobby and restaurant trying to talk to the guests. The clientele, including most of the children, are too sophisticated (and too far from Disney World) for this to be anything but intrusive and embarrassing.

Other restaurants include the Dune Dog Cafe and an ice cream parlor. Bananas is a friendly bar by the lobby where you can get anything from healthful fruit drinks to rum drinks to hearty meals. Service is friendly and efficient. Those on an extended stay who wish to venture out to area restaurants might try Ruth's Chris Steakhouse in North Palm Beach, or Nick's Tomato Pie for Italian cuisine.

Jupiter Beach Resort is the site of a number of meetings and conferences for area businesses. The conference staff have the reputation in the county for "trying harder" than most area hotels to make such business events productive and pleasant. Meeting rooms are at the far end of the resort, away from the beach and Sinclair's Grill. In between are the spacious lobby and lounge. Both resort guests and residents of nearby communities enjoy relaxing here. The lounge is decorated in bright Caribbean colors, and soft music is played on a polished grand piano.

The back of the resort is organized around the beach and the patio and pool. There's also tennis, a game room, and a fitness center. At nearby marinas, sailing, windsurfing, snorkeling, boating, and fishing are available by the hour or by the day.

NEW SMYRNA

Riverview Hotel

103 Flagler Avenue
New Smyrna Beach, FL 32069
904-428-5858

*A historic B&B
with old-fashioned
comfort*

Owners: Christa and Jim Kelsey. **Accommodations:** 18 rooms and suites. **Rates:** Rooms $63–$78, suites: $90–$150; corporate rates available Sunday through Thursday. **Included:** Expanded Continental breakfast. **Minimum stay:** None. **Added:** 10% tax; $10 extra person. **Payment:** Major credit cards. **Children:** Well-behaved children welcome. **Smoking:** Discouraged. **Open:** Year-round.

The completely renovated Riverview Hotel stands near a bridge over the Indian River, part of the Intracoastal Waterway. The house is architecturally Old Florida, with a gray tin roof, pink wood clapboards, and lots of railed verandahs. The house is two stories in some sections, three in the older sections. Old-fashioned cloth awnings in a deep burgundy cover the verandahs on the second and third floors.

Originally the home of the bridge-tender, the Riverview was built in 1886 and was restored in the 1980s by Cissie and John Spang, who earlier refurbished the Park Plaza Hotel in Winter Park. They did an excellent job here, restoring the old pine floors and covering them with fine Oriental rugs. Much of the furniture in common rooms and guest rooms is natural or painted wicker. There are good reproductions and some authentic antiques. In the large common room by the reception area, French doors open onto a brick patio and deck with a covered walkway that leads to the restaurant next door.

Nightly turndown service includes chocolates on the pillow, scented oil on the light bulb, dimmed lights, and white terrycloth robes placed at the corners of the bed. In the morning, guests are given breakfast in bed: warm pastries, bowls of fresh fruit, cereal, juice, and coffee, along with a newspaper. Many guests enjoy their breakfast on their private patio or balcony.

The guest rooms have wood ceilings and paddle fans, wicker and oak furniture, wooden Venetian blinds, and antique embellishments. Bathrooms are modern but have an old-fashioned feel.

French doors on the first floor open to the patio and pool. Balconies on the second floor overlook the pool; these rooms are very romantic. The patio is pretty, with wicker baskets and clay pots of flowers on the brick pavement and an ivy-covered fence offering a screen from the street and bridge. The pool itself is kept very clean and has a colorful Italian ceramic tile border along the top. Brown Jordan chaises and slant-back lawn chairs are placed around the pool.

The poolside rooms and the verandah rooms have wicker chairs or loveseats just outside the French doors. Guests can have their breakfast served here or in their rooms. There is no dining room in the hotel, so most guests have lunch at one of the little places on the beach. Riverview Charlie's, the restaurant next door, is great for seafood at dinner. Built of 100-year-old brick and old beams, Riverview Charlie's has docking facilities and a wide deck overlooking the river that's wonderful for promenading after a big meal.

The Riverview is on Flagler Avenue, with just a narrow brick sidewalk in front of it, but the owners have seen to it that there is ample parking. New Smyrna Beach is similar to Daytona (a little tacky but with a wide sandy beach), and the shops and boutiques in the old part of the town are fun to poke around in. Many guests love staying in the middle of this old town, with the sound of cars bumping over the Indian River Bridge and the clang of the alarm as the drawbridge is raised. But if you're a light sleeper, request one of the rooms at the far end of the hotel.

ORANGE PARK

The Club Continental on the St. Johns

2143 Astor Street
P.O. Box 7059
Orange Park, FL 32073
904-264-6070
Fax: 904-264-7441

Luxury Italian Renaissance accommodations at a budget price

Owners: The Massee family. **Accommodations:** 22 suites. **Rates:** Rooms $55–65, 1-room suites $75–$120, 2-room suites $135, king efficiency $400/week, tower apartment $450/week; weekly, monthly, and midweek rates; other discounts available. **Included:** Continental breakfast. **Added:** 9% tax. **Payment:** Major credit cards. **Children:** Welcome. **Smoking:** Non-smoking rooms available. **Open:** Year-round.

The Club Continental was built as a private summer home in 1923 by Caleb Johnson, heir to the Johnson (later Palmolive) Soap Company fortune. At the time, Orange Park had no electricity or paved streets. Johnson and his family loved the remoteness of the country and named their Mediterranean estate Miro Rio. (Today, the Club is an easy 15 miles south of the metropolitan city of Jacksonville.) Eventually, the estate came down to Margaret Johnson Massee's son, Jon, who had the idea of making the estate into a private club in the 1960s. Renamed Club Continental, the place became synonymous with fine dining, Mediterranean elegance, and southern graciousness. Jon's son, Caleb Massee, his sisters Karrie and Jeanne, and mother, Frederica, now manage the club. It is a combination private dining and country club, a resort, and an inn with surprisingly reasonable rates.

Guests turn off busy Orange Park streets into residential

Astor Street and then enter the lacy iron gates of the Continental Club into what seems like a different era and perhaps a different country. Magnolias and huge live oaks shade the parklike grounds. A circular drive winds its way to the iron gates and a fountained courtyard, and then to the arched doorway of the vine-covered mansion. The architecture and interior decor are Mediterranean, with ornate columns, coffered ceilings, leaded windows, carved stone reliefs, wrought-iron filigreed lamps, and lovely archways.

For all its elegance, the place has a lived-in feel to it. The stucco in the original building is a bit stained. The walls of the foyer have never been painted and have a mellow patina. Leaves that fall in the courtyard are not swept away immediately by an overly efficient gardener. Flowers that begin to fade are not always replaced right away — all part of the relaxed Continental ambience. This is not an immaculately manicured resort but a family home and club still lovingly cared for by the Massees. Karrie or Jon Massee is often at the reception desk, and Frieka, the elder Mrs. Massee, is often on hand to describe the history of the place or to help with checkout.

Just beyond the elegant staircase is the club lounge, originally the mansion's morning room, now decorated with family photos. Archways lead to what was once the drawing room, now frequently used for dining and for wedding receptions. Ornate black wrought-iron rods hold the drapes at the French windows that lead to a vine-covered loggia. Leaded-glass windows flank a carved stone fireplace. At the other end of the house is another loggia that Jon Massee enclosed to create a club dining room overlooking the garden and the St. Johns River. Another smaller room in the back is furnished with pieces that Frieka Massee found in the attic: an antique European tapestry and an old marble table with intricate iron and brass embellishments.

The dining room, open to club members and overnight guests only, is well known in the area for its Continental and American cuisine. A typical dinner might begin with Parmesan oysters or a creamy onion soup flavored with white wine and ginger, and then proceed to Norwegian salmon or a rich veal Continental, followed by pecan torte. It may be difficult to get dinner reservations on a Saturday night if there is a wedding reception scheduled, but this is almost made up for by the excellent Sunday brunch, which includes offerings such as creamy shrimp and artichoke soup, eggs Benedict, and soft-shell crabs. There is also a complimentary Continental breakfast for guests every morning that usually includes homemade pastries, an assortment of cereals, and fruit.

Overlooking the river outside the dining room loggia is a landscaped terrace that wraps around the side of the house to the swimming pools and kids' wading pool. Just beyond the drive are the tennis courts. The tennis pro is quite popular here, and the facilities include seven courts, two of which are lighted for night play. On a sandy spot under the oaks just in front of the tennis courts is a volleyball net for pickup games. A few hundred feet away is a marina with 85 slips

> **The peaceful waters of the St. Johns River are a presence everywhere at the Club Continental. The estate is located on the widest part of the river, so it is almost like looking out over a small lake. A romantic stone balustrade that runs along the river is a lovely place to walk in the evening.**

available for guests' boats, with advance request. The club can also arrange for sailboat charters.

Expansive river views are part of the experience in most of the guest rooms. The original mansion has four rooms and two suites on the second floor and an apartment on the third, called the Inn at Club Continental. Room names like the Mexican Room or the English Room reflect the origin of furnishings brought back from the Massees' travels. The tower apartment has been recently refurbished and has a well-equipped kitchen, a living room with cushioned bamboo sofas, French doors to a newly tiled balcony, a king-size bed and a daybed, and a private bathroom with the original ceramic tile still intact. The apartment is a good choice for a family or for anyone planning a long stay.

Also appropriate for extended stays are the suites in the Winterbourne, another mansion on the grounds, which was built in 1870 and restored by Mrs. Massee in the 1950s. There is no maid service here, so these accommodations are really like renting a small home. All have period furnishings and private baths. Most suites have views of the water, though any view of the grounds is attractive. The spacious drawing room is often the site of weddings and receptions. A pillared porch runs along the front of the house, and a wide lawn sweeps down to the river.

The newest accommodations are in a two-story, balustraded building that beautifully matches the Mediterranean architecture of the club, down to the texture and color of the stucco. These rooms, called Continental suites, have a king-size or double bed, spacious private baths (some with Jacuzzis), tiled balconies, and river views. Room 201 is a wheelchair-accessible room and one of three rooms that have two double beds. Room 204 has an antique fireplace, a king bed, a spacious sitting area, reproduction and antique furniture, and a hand-painted mural in the large bathroom. The fireplace and Jacuzzi suites here are an amazing bargain: $120 in the winter on weekends, even less during the week or off-season.

Next door to the Continental Suites is the River House Pub, an Old Florida–style cottage with white clapboards and a tin roof that could be straight out of Key West. Used as a golf clubhouse after the Civil War, it is reputed to be the oldest clubhouse in Florida. It was destined for demolition until Frederica Massee bought the old place and had it moved here by the river. Now a smoky little game club and pub, the River House is popular with a mix of blue-collar workers and wealthy sages who love to come here to shoot the breeze, listen to the live entertainment, and play poker. Jeanne Massee Patterson and her husband, Bill, run the place as an informal complement to the Continental's formal dining club. Outback is a wonderful multilevel deck that has a pool table, subtropical plantings, wood swings, plenty of room for parties, and a superlative view of the St. Johns.

The Massees are a resourceful and interesting family, and they run the Club as a labor of love. If there is a disadvantage to having the third and fourth generations of a family run such an enterprise, it is that occasionally there seems to be some confusion as to the division of labor among the Massees; perhaps the place is too much like home. For example, sometimes no one is at the reception desk when a guest wants to check in or out, and it is unclear who was supposed to be there. However, this is a small price to pay for old-world ambience, excellent dining, and bargain suites.

PALM COAST

Sheraton Palm Coast Resort

300 Clubhouse Drive
Palm Coast, FL 32037
904-445-3000
800-325-3535

> *A large, lush
> resort complex on
> the Intracoastal*

General Manager: Fred Corso.
Accommodations: 154 rooms.
Rates: Rooms $90–$150; packages available. **Minimum stay:**
With some packages. **Added:** 9% tax. **Payment:** Major credit
cards. **Children:** Under 17 free in room with parents. **Smoking:** Nonsmoking rooms available. **Open:** Year-round.

All guest rooms at the Palm Coast Resort overlook the
water — either the Intracoastal or the resort's marina. The
Sheraton resort is part of a residential resort community
sculpted out of 42,000
acres of scrub palm and
pine forests by ITT a few
years ago. It has become
a popular place for golf,
tennis, and boating and
has received Sheraton's
Resort of the Year award.

> **The big draws here are the
> views and the sporting
> activities. The beach and
> the resort's beach club are
> just a few minutes away by
> free shuttle. The ocean is
> warm, and the waves are
> big enough for some body-
> surfing but not so big that
> they overwhelm children.**

Guest rooms have king-
size beds or two doubles,
and rooms are spacious
enough for a family. The
appointments are Shera-
ton's basic light oak hotel
furniture, but the bed-
spreads and coordinating
drapes are attractive and the carpets are thick underfoot.

For freshwater swimming, there are two pools as well as
whirlpool spas. Fishing rods, boats, and bicycles, including
tandems, can be rented. The resort has a miniature golf
course and volleyball and badminton nets set up in the recreational center.

Golf is excellent, with three different 18-hole courses.
Arnold Palmer designed the challenging Matanzas Woods and

Pine Lakes, a long course with lots of water and sand hazards. Pretty Palm Harbor has native oaks and palms and fairways that pros describe as "testy."

Tennis here is world-class, with three surfaces: clay, hard, and grass. There are 16 courts, with some lit for night play. The Players Club tennis complex includes a clubhouse restaurant and a pro shop.

Many companies hold small meetings and conferences here. The resort's seven meeting and banquet rooms can accommodate groups from 10 to 300. An open-air, waterfront pavilion of natural wood is pleasant for outdoor parties. A conference staff attends to the details, from banquets to audiovisual needs to transportation.

The resort's restaurant serves breakfast, lunch, and dinner, and a generous buffet on Sundays. Cocktails and after-dinner drinks are served in Henry's Lounge, where there is live entertainment. Like the restaurant, Henry's has a lovely view of the pool and marina at night. The marina (at Marker 803 on the Intracoastal Waterway) has 80 slips — enough to accommodate you if you call ahead and small enough to be friendly.

PONTE VEDRA BEACH

The Lodge and Bath Club at Ponte Vedra Beach

607 Ponte Vedra Boulevard
Ponte Vedra Beach, FL 32082
904-273-9500
800-243-4304

A Mediterranean-style beach and fitness club

General Manager: Laurence P. Magor. **Accommodations:** 42 rooms, 24 suites. **Rates:** Rooms $149–$209, suites $209–$239; packages available; daily service charge in lieu of gratuities. **Included:** Bath Club facilities and exercise classes. **Minimum stay:** Two nights with packages. **Added:** 9% tax. **Payment:** Major credit cards. **Children:** Under 17 free in room with parents. **Smoking:** Nonsmoking rooms available. **Open:** Year-round.

The town of Ponte Vedra is rather upscale; the oceanside homes north and south of the lodge are some of the most attractive in Florida. The Lodge and Bath Club at Ponte Vedra Beach reflects both the exclusive clubbiness of the area and its sporting informality. Those who know the Bath Club consider it a special place. The rates are far more reasonable than they are at points farther south, and the crowds are thinner.

> **The patio, paved with brick and tabby, has a beautifully tiled Mediterranean-style fountain and courtyard. Tiered flower beds, bordered in tiles with a shell motif, rise above the main swimming pool, which overlooks Ponte Vedra Beach.**

The low-rise buildings of the lodge are buff-colored stucco. The arched windows sport blue-green awnings. The Mediterranean details and Spanish red-tile roofs give it the aura of a 1920s country club. Guests enter the resort through leaded-glass double doors to a terra cotta–tiled entryway. Upstairs, there's a lounge and bar with lots of windows looking out over the ocean.

Conference rooms are found in this upstairs area and also downstairs. The meeting space includes 2,500 square feet indoors and 4,000 square feet outside, ideal for outdoor banquets and receptions. All of the meeting space overlooks the ocean. One reason the club is so successful for meetings as well as vacations is the service. There is a great sensitivity to guests' needs here. A maid quietly sweeps the terra cotta tiles outside a conference room while a meeting takes place, rather than vacuuming. Staff members pride themselves on having "five-star spirit."

The rooms also deserve five stars. Every accommodation has at least one balcony — many have two. The furniture is bleached oak. All bathrooms are very large and have a long vanity counter, Jacuzzi, shower, and terrycloth robes.

The oceanfront suite is the lodge's most expensive accommodation. It features a full kitchen with aqua tile counters and bleached oak cabinets. The living room has a balcony and a fireplace flanked by comfortable sofas. Another balcony is just off the bedroom. All accommodations have a cushioned window seat and a king or queen bed. The bathroom has a small TV and a makeup mirror in addition to the standard luxuries. The Superior Corner rooms, with two queen beds and two balconies, are the best value for a family. These are actually the lodge's standard rooms, but they are a cut above the usual hotel standard.

The decor throughout the hotel includes lovely artwork. Many of the public areas have vaulted wooden ceilings and detailed stonework. The attention to design is found in all the outdoor recreational areas, too. Masonry walls around the fitness center and pool area are bordered with aqua tiles. Windows have little wells beneath them for flowers and Mediterranean detailing above.

The lodge has a children's pool, an adult pool that is heated year-round, and a big whirlpool partially enclosed by a tiled wall — a lion's head at its center spouts water. From the pool, one can look out to the Atlantic. Rates at the lodge also include privileges at the fitness center across the boulevard at the Bath Club. A renovation in 1993 created an expanded aerobics room, a larger exercise room with additional Nautilus equipment, and direct access to the lap pool from these rooms

The beach is accessible via a wooden stairway that goes over the low sand dunes and vegetation at the back of the property. In the summer, especially, the beach is a favorite gathering place for adults and children of all ages. The water is warm, and there's always a cool breeze. For those who seek other activity, there are several excellent tennis courts and golf courses nearby.

Most guests dine at the lodge's restaurant, the Mediterranean Room, which has a well-stocked wine cellar and some outstanding offerings in local seafood and Black Angus beef. Large, Palladian-style windows overlook the water. Guests may also choose to eat at the Ponte Vedra Inn and Club, just up the boulevard.

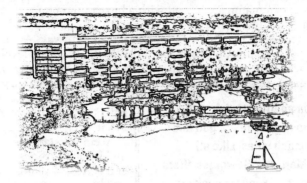

Marriott at Sawgrass Resort

1000 TPC Boulevard (Route A1A)
Ponte Vedra, FL 32082
904-285-7777
800-228-9290

> *A conference and sports resort with 99 holes of golf*

Accommodations: 327 rooms, 23 suites, 180 villas. **Rates:** Rooms $100–$185, suites $149–$195, villas $225–$500; packages available; lower rates on some weekends; $20 for extra adult in room. **Minimum stay:** With some packages. **Added:** 9% tax. **Payment:** Major credit cards. **Children:** 17 and under free in room with parents. **Smoking:** Nonsmoking rooms available. **Open:** Year-round.

As they say at Sawgrass, you can play golf here for nearly a week and never play the same hole twice. The five descriptively named courses are Marsh Landing, Oak Bridge, Valley, Sawgrass Country Club, and the PGA Tournament Players Club Stadium course. The latter includes a 17th hole in the middle of a lagoon.

Golf is the focus, but tennis is also excellent. Four of the ten Har-Tru courts are lighted at night, and instruction is available for both adults and children. In addition, Sawgrass offers croquet and croquet clinics. Swimming is at three beautiful pools. The resort's health club has a steam room and sauna, Universal weight equipment, and exercise classes. Off the property, there is horseback riding, deep-sea fishing, and swimming on Ponte Vedra Beach.

The view through floor-to-ceiling windows in the reception

area is of a manmade lagoon with a huge outcropping of rocks from which water tumbles back into the lagoon. Beyond that is a free-form swimming pool and a green fairway. A curved stairway from the reception area leads down a level to the Cascade Lounge, which has little waterfalls and tropical beds that are planted with ferns, banana trees, and palms. It sounds corny, but it's very restful.

> **In addition to the hotel rooms, there are golf and beach villas. Like all Marriotts, Sawgrass offers some excellent packages.**

Accommodations are divided into "series." Several series 34 rooms overlook this lagoon and the swimming pool. They and series 100 corner suites are worth requesting if you can afford them. All rooms are luxurious, with thick carpeting, designer fabrics, and large tile baths.

Formal dining is in the critically acclaimed Augustine Room, a softly lit space with dark walls, scallop-backed leather banquettes, and old prints on the walls. The nouvelle American cuisine is expensive but excellent.

More casual is the Café on the Green, overlooking the TPC Course and serving breakfast, lunch, and dinner. Four of the golf clubs have their own dining rooms for lunch and dinner. Cascades, just off the hotel lobby, is good for a sundowner. Champs is a larger, clubbier lounge with a spectacular view of the lagoon and waterfalls. Service is courteous and faster than in many hotels in Florida.

The high-rise architecture of the hotel is a bit institutional, with green-tinted windows and metal grills. But the accommodations and staff at Sawgrass make guests feel a warm welcome, and the rooms and excellent recreation make up for the somewhat dull exterior.

Ponte Vedra Inn and Club

200 Ponte Vedra Boulevard
Ponte Vedra Beach, FL 32082
904-285-1111
800-234-7842

> *A gracious club with luxury accommodations on the ocean*

General Manager: Dale Haney. **Accommodations:** 202 rooms and suites. **Rates:** Rooms $89–$209, suites $209–$289; meal plans and packages available. **Minimum stay:** 2 or 3 nights with some packages. **Added:** 9% tax. **Payment:** Major credit cards. **Children:** Under 16 free in room with parents. **Smoking:** Nonsmoking rooms available. **Open:** Year-round.

The Ponte Vedra Inn and Club was founded in 1928 as a private club. The rooms in the original inn have been converted into executive offices, so guests no longer stay in the old building, but the new buildings are some of the most tastefully decorated accommodations in Florida. They are directly on the beach, along with the fitness center and spa. The various club amenities — the original inn, the golf course, the tennis courts and racquet club, the conference center, the restaurants — are on the other side of Ponte Vedra Boulevard beside a subtropical lagoon.

The rooms and suites are tucked into low-rise stucco buildings with names like Beach House, Ocean House, and Summer House. These are set back a bit from the boulevard, with a lawn and parking out front and the ocean and beach in the back. There is a range of accommodations, including presidential suites, standard suites, superior oceanside suites, and large and small deluxe suites.

Although winter is the low season, only one or two days (or no days) of a week's stay may see rain or overcast skies, so it's worthwhile to consider coming then. The resort also offers golf, tennis, spa, and holiday packages. A standard suite, $170 during the low season, has a terrace and large windows overlooking the ocean, a living/dining area, and a charming kitchen with a breakfast bar.

> **There is plenty to do here besides swimming and sunbathing. It is a delight simply to walk the grounds: there are several varieties of palms, massive beds of bright annuals, and lush green lawns. A lagoon meanders through the area, with a golf island in the middle and a small dock.**

Some bedrooms have padded bentwood bedsteads. Others have four-poster beds. Sliding glass doors call attention to the ocean view. Step outside and you're on a beach of bright, clean sand. The water is deep blue and pleasantly warm. There are usually couples walking along the beach and lots of kids and their parents swimming or playing in the sand. Just a few minutes away on Route A1A is a more dramatic beach with high dunes that sweep down to the ocean. It is worth hiking up to see them, though visitors should stay off the fragile dunes.

For golfers, there's the Golf Club, a pro shop, the Golf Club Restaurant, and two spectacular championship courses — the Lagoon Course and the Ocean Course. Both have enough bunkers and water hazards to keep you busy. Tennis is just as exciting, with 15 Har-Tru courts overlooking the lagoon, all lighted for night play. Individual instruction is hardly inexpensive here, but the group rate (for a minimum of six players) is affordable at $10 per hour. The resort offers some good tennis packages. There is also a spa and fitness center near the beach with a swimming pool and a whirlpool.

The buildings that make up the spa are the original Ponte Vedra Inn cottages built in the 1930s. They have white shingles, gray shutters, and decks overlooking the sand dunes and ocean outside; inside are fireplaces and pine floors. The spa package includes specially prepared lunches upon request, such as grilled chicken with asparagus and tomato salad or a fruit plate with raspberry sorbet. The menu changes daily. The fitness center has a complete Nautilus circuit, treadmills, stationary bikes, and free weights. Aerobics classes are held throughout the day, and there's a steam room and sauna to relax in. The spa offers a complete program of herbal wraps, nutrition analysis, skin care and facial treatments, manicures, pedicures, and massages.

The Ponte Vedra staff members, some of whom have worked here for years, take seriously the beauty of the resort and its tradition of hospitality. They'll go out of their way, literally, to help you find a lost sweater or a stray tennis racket.

The spa and fitness center could do a brisk business just from guests who've overindulged at the resort's five restaurants. The same executive chef has run the culinary operations for 15 years. Pastries and breads are made at Ponte Vedra's own bakery. The restaurants take pride in providing interesting entrées and offering a wide range of choices, from Continental to Old Southern. Service is warm and gracious, in the southern tradition.

PORT ST. LUCIE

Club Med-Sandpiper

3500 Morningside Boulevard
Port St. Lucie, FL 34952
407-335-4400
Reservations:
800-CLUB MED (800-258-2633)

A family Club Med with a European clientele

Accommodations: 270 rooms.
Rates: $160–$225 per person; $1,050–$1,450 weekly; $685 per child; rates slightly higher for holidays; 2- and 3-week pack-

ages available. **Included:** All meals, water sports equipment, activities. **Minimum stay:** Varies with season. **Added:** $50 membership fee per adult; $30 initiation fee for families new to Club Med. **Payment:** Major credit cards. **Children:** 5 and under free during special promotions. **Smoking:** Nonsmoking rooms available. **Open:** Year-round.

Club Med still has the reputation of being a singles club, but the organization has changed in the decades since it was founded in Europe. The Sandpiper Club Med, 45 minutes north of Palm Beach International Airport, is activity-oriented, as all Club Med resorts are. It's also family-oriented and very European — 80 percent of the guests are European, and 70 percent of those are French.

The Sandpiper sits on 1,000 acres in a residential neighborhood of Port St. Lucie, facing the mile-wide St. Lucie River. The resort consists of shake-roofed pavilions for activities that are both enclosed and open, and clusters of low-rise hotel accommodations.

Rooms are carpeted, modern, and comfortable, with either a patio or balcony furnished in white wicker. The best rooms face the river and are 10 percent more expensive than those that do not. However, a number of second-floor garden-view rooms do provide a view of a generous slice of the river from the wide windows.

Rooms have two doubles or a king bed, with no telephones or TVs. Toddlers can bed down on the pull-down couch or on a roll-away. Children over age five must be in a separate room; you can reserve adjoining rooms. The rooms are plain, but nobody spends a lot of time inside anyway. Activity and socializing in the sun are what it's all about at Club Med.

The staff organizing the fun and games are exuberant and mostly European, and always changing. Called *gentils organisateurs* ("nice organizers"), the average G.O. stays at the Sandpiper for less than a year. Although G.O.s are polite enough to leave you alone if all you want to do is sit on the beach and read a book, this really isn't the place for loners. G.O.s make every effort to get everybody staying at the Sandpiper —whether alone, with a spouse or lover, with another single friend, or with a family — involved in the activities.

The G.O.s organize a rich variety for their G.M.s (*gentils membres*), also called G.E.M.s. On property, there are pedal boats, rowboats, and sailboats, with free instruction. There's also waterskiing, swimming in the river or in one of five pools, tennis, 45 holes of golf, a trampoline for high-flyers, a fitness center, a pitch-and-putt course, and pick-up games of basketball and volleyball. Guests are encouraged to mingle during activities: young and old, European and American, related and unrelated.

The same spirit of togetherness is evident at meals. G.O.s eat with G.E.M.s, and meals are a lot of fun. Breakfast is served from 7:00 to 10:00 A.M., but people linger as late as 11:30. Lunch is a festive time, when the G.O.s and G.E.M.s plan afternoon games. Dinner is from 7:30 to 9:00 P.M., with dancing afterwards.

Once a week there's an after-dinner show in the auditorium put on by G.O.s for the guests, though guests often get involved in the show, too. These shows are not amateurish; the auditorium is well equipped and the staff includes a professional set designer and a costume designer.

There is an impressive program for children of all ages, and friendly, attentive G.O.s and babysitters take care of the kids. "Baby Med," for infants four months to one year, is available Monday to Friday between 8 A.M. and 6 P.M. The Baby Med center is well equipped and brightly decorated. The babies and toddlers play outside and nap inside under close supervision. Food is prepared by a baby-food specialist. For parents who need a babysitter at night, local babysitters may be hired through the G.O.s.

For children aged two to eleven, the resort's Mini Club meets Monday through Friday, 9 A.M. to 9 P.M. The G.O.s organize arts and crafts activities, start volleyball and other court games, take the kids to the mini-pool, and give instruction in sailing and water skiing. For teenagers, there are water sports and rollerblading — even a Rollerblade instructor.

With so many organized activities for all ages, family members can spend as much time together or apart as they wish. Sometimes it is enough simply to sit under a palm tree near the beach and gaze out at the beautiful St. Lucie River.

ST. AUGUSTINE

Carriage Way B&B

70 Cuna Street
St. Augustine, FL 32084
904-829-2467

*A budget B&B
in America's
oldest city*

Innkeepers: Diane and Bill Johnson. **Accommodations:** 7 rooms, all
with private bath. **Rates:** $69–$105
weekend nights; $49–$95 weeknights. **Included:** Full breakfast; complimentary beverages and desserts; complimentary
bicycles. **Minimum stay:** 2 nights with Saturday stay. **Added:**
9% tax; $10 extra adult or child. **Payment:** Discover, Master-
Card, Visa; personal checks. **Children:** 8 and older welcome.
Smoking: On verandahs only. **Open:** Year-round.

Carriage Way B&B is in Old St. Augustine, on a small corner
lot at Cuna and Cordova Streets. It's a Victorian-style clapboard house painted a smooth cream with country blue trim.
It looks like somebody's grandmother's house, and right away
you feel at home. Indeed, the Carriage Way is run by congenial grandparents Diane and Bill Johnson, who recently
bought the inn and have added their special way of doing
things.

The verandahs are among the most appealing features of
the house. The verandah on the ground floor, open to everyone, is a nice place to watch the world go by — or at least
one's fellow tourists. The upstairs verandahs are only for
those who are lucky enough to get rooms opening onto them;
ask for rooms 1 or 3 to take advantage of these lookouts.

All the rooms have dark wood furniture from the turn of
the century. Most pieces are simply old; some are real antiques. All give a homey, genuine feeling to the place. Most of
the rooms have wall-to-wall carpeting in rose or deep green
and small-print wallpapers. Some bathrooms have tubs, others have showers. There are telephones but no TVs or radios
in the rooms. There is a TV in the parlor.

Guests can use the downstairs parlor and the dining room
at any time. There are homemade desserts, cold beverages,
and hot tea and coffee in the dining room all day. The complimentary breakfast usually consists of fruit and orange juice,

homemade white bread for toast, fruit bread or muffins, an entrée such as waffles, pancakes, or eggs with sausage or bacon, and tea or coffee. Although no lunches or dinners are served, there is a sweet snack in the afternoon, and guests can order special drinks or request a picnic basket for a small additional charge.

After breakfast, most guests go for a walk in the historic neighborhood. If you can do without 20th-century inventions like television at the Carriage Way, you can probably get along without a car in St. Augustine, even for eating out. It's more pleasant to walk through the narrow streets of this oldest of American cities than to struggle through in a car, trying to remember which streets run which way. Walking back and forth to this B&B, you'll pass the shops, taverns, and restaurants of the historic Spanish Quarter.

> **A fine old Spanish fort, Castillo de San Marcos is just a few minutes' walk from the Carriage Way. The Spanish Quarter has a number of other interesting structures, many of them presenting the crafts and small industries of earlier eras. On a typical day you might happen upon a blacksmith at work or a young woman selling candles or herbs.**

Many people take a horse-drawn carriage tour through the old city. These are all a bit different, with some drivers dressing the part in old-fashioned livery and others wearing simple pants and T-shirts. As the carriages thread through the old streets, the drivers give lively lectures on historic lore and points of interest. Many of the streets in the old section of town are brick, and the clip-clop sound of the horses' hooves is very pleasant. There are also sightseeing tours on small trolleys, and you can pick up a map for a do-it-yourself walking tour from the Visitor Information Center, which has an orientation movie.

Casa de la Paz

22 Avenida Menendez
St. Augustine, FL 32084
904-829-2915

*Views of the
water and
Old St. Augustine*

Innkeeper: Jan Maki. **Accommodations:** 4 rooms, 2 suites. **Rates:** $70–$100; midweek discounts. **Included:** Full breakfast. **Added:** 9% tax. **Payment:** Major credit cards; personal checks. **Children:** 17 and older welcome. **Smoking:** Only on verandahs and in courtyard. **Open:** Year-round.

Avenida Menendez, named after Admiral Don Pedro Menendez de Aviles, the Spanish founder of St. Augustine, is the main thoroughfare of the city's historic district. Many of the rooms in the Casa de la Paz have beautiful views of lovely Matanzas Bay, directly across the street.

Walk out the arched door of the Casa de la Paz and turn left to explore the Castillo de San Marcos, the Spanish fortress constructed in the 1670s to protect the town against the British and other marauding enemies. The Spanish Quarter, starting on San Marco Avenue and winding through Charlotte, Cuna, and other narrow streets, is just adjacent to the fort. The little streets are lined with Victorian and turn-of-the-century houses and interesting shops. This area is commercialized and even cute at times, but still historically interesting. La Parisienne, on Spanish Street, makes a fine lunch stop.

Or turn right and stroll down to another part of St. Augustine's old town. The oldest house in America is located off Avenida Menendez on St. Francis Street. The house is built largely of coquina and has a patio where you can rest your feet after you'd had your fill of history.

Though Casa de la Paz has a wonderful location for those interested in sightseeing, it is also a find in itself. Built in a Mediterranean revival style, the house has white stucco, brown trim, and exposed timbers under a tile roof. The many windows offer lots of light and much archi-

> **The location of this charming B&B is perfect for exploring the nation's oldest established city.**

tectural interest. Some are covered with ornate Spanish grills, and small ones on the side of the house are leaded and diamond-paned.

A courtyard in the back of the house, where innkeeper Jan Maki plans to do extensive landscaping, has a feeling of both openness and seclusion. The little courtyard patio has mature trees and low-growing plants outlined by brick walkways.

All of the rooms in the back of the house look out over the yard, so if you can't get one of the waterview rooms in the front of the house, not to worry. Some rooms have private verandahs. Each room is a little different — one might have a little alcove, another a big bookcase loaded with books, and still another two odd little windows overlooking the water. All are decorated with antiques.

The Captain's Suite, with its third-floor dormer windows overlooking the bay and the old town, is most in demand. One room is quite a bit smaller than the other, but fun, with two tiny windows and a shelf between — perhaps for your elbows as you gaze out at the bay. The bath in the hallway between the rooms, like all the bathrooms, is bright and fresh looking.

Casa de la Paz is a traditional, homey B&B, so if you have no interest in sightseeing, you can simply stay here, reading and relaxing. The lounge in the front of the house is furnished with small tables where guests gather for breakfast and at other times of the day. Originally the living room of the house, it has big windows that look out over the avenue and the bay, and a fireplace flanked with bookshelves.

The formal dining room is furnished with an Oriental rug and Chippendale furniture. Throughout the house there are elaborate moldings and chair rails, which are accented with period wallpapers and clean plaster walls. Most of the floors downstairs are pine — recently refinished, well polished, and graced with fine rugs.

The breakfast is full: pancakes and baked apples or a baked egg dish, croissants, homemade muffins or bread, fresh fruit, juice, tea, and coffee. If you prefer, you may have breakfast in your room, but guests are encouraged to linger after breakfast and chat with other guests.

Casa de Solana

21 Aviles Street
St. Augustine, FL 32084
904-824-3555

One of the most distinctive historic inns in St. Augustine

Owners: Jim and Faye McMurry. **Accommodations:** 4 suites. **Rates:** $125; $10 for extra adult. **Included:** Full breakfast; admission to Oldest House museum; use of bicycles. **Minimum stay:** 2 nights on weekends, holidays. **Added:** 9% tax. **Payment:** Major credit cards; personal checks. **Children:** 13 and older welcome. **Smoking:** Only on verandah.

The Casa was completed in 1763 for Don Manuel Solana, a Spanish military official. St. Augustine at the time had fewer than a thousand houses and was shortly taken over by the British. Today, Casa de Solana is the fourteenth-oldest house in the town. When horse-drawn carriage tours clip-clop down Aviles Street and pass the corner on which the Casa majestically stands, the drivers point out the house to tourists. So many history buffs and curiosity seekers want to see the house (without staying there as paying guests) that Faye and Jim McMurry finally had to put up a polite sign on the door explaining that the house is not a museum and is not open except to inn guests. That should be reason enough to become one.

The main house stands squarely on the generous city lot, with an attached carriage house. At one time, there were also slave quarters. Although the McMurrys have had city approval to rebuild these on the side of the house for extra rooms to rent, they have decided against it, preferring to keep the Casa small. The house is made of blocks of coquina, a popular 18th-century building material of native shells that has proved enduring. At the

> **The butter at breakfast isn't just a soft slab put on a plate; Faye and her assistant use butter molds to form flowers, swirls, pumpkins, or even Santas, depending on the season and their whim.**

Casa de Solana, the coquina surface has been covered with a thick coat of plaster and painted with a pale pink wash. The verandah pillars and trim are painted brown, which accentuates the Spanish feel of the house. There are lots of small-paned windows in the house and graceful fanlights above those in the first-floor entryway.

Surrounding the house and garden is a thick stucco wall, painted pink like the house and covered with ivy, giving a secluded, Mediterranean feel to the garden. The front of the house faces Charlotte Street, but house and garden encompass the entire narrow block from Charlotte to Aviles; you enter Casa de Solana through the back gate on Aviles Street. The garden and big lawn (well, big for an old St. Augustine place) are the first things you see. A tiny goldfish pond and a fountain are tucked in the corner by a raised brick patio where the McMurrys have placed a table and chairs. A neat brick path leads to the entry door.

Inside are polished oak floors and one of the finest collections of antiques and Oriental rugs in St. Augustine. Casa de Solana was built as a grand house, and Faye and Jim have been sensitive stewards of the fine old place, adding some of their own southern elegance.

Guest rooms here are all suites. The British Suite, on the third floor, has a sitting area with a comfortable couch and two wing chairs. Though Casa de Solana might seem too Old St. Augustine to have a TV in any of the rooms, the British

Suite does, with HBO. The bedroom has dormers and a brick chimney in the middle of the room. An antique Eastlake upholstered chair adds grace.

The Confederacy Room has a private first-floor entrance. Walls are of clean, white plaster, and interesting touches include decorations in a Confederate theme. There's an Oriental carpet in the bedroom, mahogany furniture, a queen-size bed, and an impressive fireplace.

The Colonial Suite on the second floor has a brass double bed, a sitting room with sofa and velvet chairs, and a little vine-shrouded balcony overlooking both lawn and garden.

The Minorcan Suite features a sitting room with a fireplace and cushioned wicker chairs and sofa. The bedroom has a king-size bed in a beautiful mahogany frame. Here the bathtub is right in the middle of the bedroom, behind ruffled curtains; the sink and toilet are in a separate small bathroom. The windows overlook the garden and the brick courtyard.

Most of the antiques in the sitting areas and bedrooms are valuables, not just old furniture. On the coffee table in each sitting room you'll find candy, a cut glass decanter of sherry, and two glasses. There's also complimentary cheese and wine in the downstairs common room each evening.

The dining room of Casa de Solana is elegant, with a grand piano, a long, highly polished mahogany table, old chairs upholstered in fine needlepoint, and small crystal chandeliers. The room itself is large and airy, with deep windowsills filled with plants, elaborate blue swags above the windows, exposed rafters, and a handsome marble fireplace. A generous breakfast is served here at 8:30, usually something like egg and sausage casserole, muffins, and banana nut, pumpkin, or sweet potato bread.

Faye serves whatever fruit is in season, often canteloupe with strawberries. Orange juice is freshly squeezed, and the coffee and tea are hot. In keeping with southern tradition (St. Augustine is, after all, part of the South), Faye serves grits with all her egg dishes. Though Faye is not the sort of innkeeper who sits and chats with guests for hours, she is very knowledgeable about St. Augustine history and heritage and is a wonderful source of information on museums, old buildings, and good places to eat.

Castle Garden

15 Shenandoah Street
St. Augustine, FL 32084
904-829-3839

A play-castle with elegant rooms

Proprietor: Bruce L. Kloeckner.
Accommodations: 6 rooms and suites. **Rates:** $55–$150; discounts for extended stays and senior citizens. **Included:** Full breakfast. **Minimum stay:** None. **Added:** 9% tax. **Payment:** Major credit cards; personal checks if approved in advance. **Children:** No infants. **Smoking:** Only on sun porch. **Open:** Year-round.

The easiest way to find Castle Garden is to head for Ripley's Believe It or Not on the corner of A1A and Shenandoah Street. Although close to the center of activity, Shenandoah Street, which ends at the bay, is a quiet side street in an upscale neighborhood. Yet this B&B is within walking distance of the old Spanish part of town — an ideal location for anyone who wants to both rest and sightsee.

Castle Garden is a whimsical design constructed of blocks of shellstone and shaped like a medieval castle.

The Castle Garden was built as a carriage house for one of Henry Flagler's partners. He lived in the garish mansion that is now Ripley's Believe It Or Not and had 17 children. Behind the carriage house was a smithy — the blacksmith chimney is still visible in the back garden.

Admittedly, the building looks a bit odd from the outside, almost like a miniature Moorish castle that could be one of the local tourist attractions. But it has recently been restored and is a delight. The entrance is on the side of the house via a pleasant screened-in porch. The hallways are painted a soft peach, and the polished floors are original pine or new oak.

On the first floor is a front parlor with a breakfast room and the manager's kitchen behind it. One of the best guest rooms is also on the first floor: a honeymoon suite. This has a queen-size bed, a cathedral ceiling, and a large Jacuzzi gussied up with a swagged bath curtain. The room is decorated in florals and rose. Castle Garden has one other lavishly decorated honeymoon suite and prides itself on its skill in pampering honeymoon couples. Several weddings have taken place in the back garden, where Spanish moss drapes the old trees.

All the rooms have queen-size beds except for one, which is furnished with a king or two twins, depending on the guests' preference. All guest rooms have private baths, but a couple of them are detached — the bath is across the hallway or downstairs and through the kitchen. These rooms are good budget accommodations.

Breakfast is full and varied. The cereal is homemade granola, and there's always a gourmet egg dish and fresh fruit. All guests receive complimentary wine and chocolates on their pillow at night during their stay. Those staying in a suite receive a complimentary fruit basket and bottle of wine or champagne and a newspaper each morning.

While the logical choice for entertainment might be Ripley's or the old section of St. Augustine, it's pleasant just to stroll through Castle Garden's neighborhood. Head down to the quiet end of Water Street and enjoy the marshes and bay — it's a wonderful way to get a feel for the residential section of St. Augustine.

The Kenwood Inn

38 Marine Street
St. Augustine, FL 32084
904-824-2116

One of St. Augustine's oldest B&Bs

Innkeepers: Mark and Kerrianne Constant. **Accommodations:** 14 rooms and suites. **Rates:** $65–$95, $10 extra person. **Included:** Expanded Continental breakfast;

Added: 9% tax. **Payment:** Visa, MasterCard. **Children:** 8 and older allowed. **Smoking:** Only on verandah. **Open:** Year-round.

The Kenwood Inn was already a wonderful B&B before Mark and Kerrianne Constant took over, and they have done much to improve this fine Victorian house. They've painted the clapboards pink with clean white trim and, according to Mark, "generally spruced up the place." But not so much that it's lost its Old World charm. The Constants are experts at caring for historic lodgings, having redone the Inn at Strawbery Banke in Portsmouth, New Hampshire, before moving to St. Augustine's historic district in 1988.

One of their loveliest achievements is the Country Shaker Suite. This has deep blue wall-to-wall carpeting, white-washed plaster walls, a pine bedstead with a handmade quilt, maple rockers, and old-fashioned ceiling fans. Running along the length of the sitting-room wall is a wooden Shaker peg board, from which hang antique dolls and household imple-ments like iron rug beaters. There is some imaginative furni-ture, like a coffee table fashioned from a half-collapsed an-tique ironing board.

All the guest rooms are fresh and comfortable. The three-room bridal suite on the third floor is particularly desirable, despite the climb, and has views of the water and most of St. Augustine's historic district. Since the Constants moved out of the inn into a house nearby, their former living quarters are available for guests. Their daughter's former bedroom is quite ruffly, with painted wood paneling, a rose and white bed-spread, and an adjacent sitting room furnished in wicker. Both the bedroom and the sitting room have bathrooms.

Mark and Kerrianne's former bedroom has a queen-size bed set against a backdrop of stenciled white walls and dusty rose trim. The windows have both curtains and shutters with fab-ric panels. This room also has a sitting room furnished in wicker, and is quite spacious.

The common rooms downstairs are elegant and warm, with well-polished floors of natural pine. Coffee and tea are available all day on the downstairs landing, and there's an honor fridge for those who wish to keep wine or their own snacks cold. Guests take a generous Continental breakfast of homemade coffee cakes and fruit in the sunny enclosed porch or at the handsome dining room table in the adjacent sitting room. This common room is light and comfortable, with deep-cushioned chairs, a white brick fireplace, and lace curtains at the large bay window that looks out over the front porch.

The other sitting room, near the front entrance, is more formal, with an ivory and gold brocade Chinese sofa, a Chinese rug, and some fine antiques. A door behind the sitting room leads to the courtyard and garden.

> **Hallways to the guest rooms are carpeted and have handmade touches such as dried-flower arrangements or quilted wall hangings. Bathrooms are immaculate, with decor that coordinates well with the pretty bedrooms.**

Unlike most St. Augustine B&Bs, the Kenwood Inn has a swimming pool. A thick stucco wall and heavy wooden gate on the street side make the oval, tiled pool and the patio area very private. The garden beyond has mature trees, including an old pecan, some bright annuals, and wisteria. There's also a little goldfish pond.

From the pool you can look up at the inn and get a sense of how it grew. The original house is a solid, squarish building, almost like a New England captain's home. The second-floor verandah, built between 1865 and 1885, has intricate gingerbread ornamentation. By 1886, the Kenwood was a boarding house. A wing added in 1911 doesn't have the gingerbread charm of the original but serves to screen the garden.

The porch on the Marine Street side of the house has been enclosed, so there isn't much room for rocking outside, but there's enough space near the front door for two cushioned wicker chairs and two rockers. An old-fashioned paneled door with two oval panes of etched glass and a brass pineapple knocker complete the Victorian picture. Sometimes you have to share the love seat with the family cat.

Old City House Inn and Restaurant

115 Cordova Street
St. Augustine, FL 32084
904-826-0113

> *An inn and restaurant run by a family with exacting standards*

Innkeepers: Alice and Bob Compton. **Accommodations:** 5 rooms. **Rates:** $60–$100 weekends and holidays; $50–$80 Sunday–Thursday. **Included:** Full breakfast; free parking. **Minimum stay:** 2 nights with Saturday stay. **Added:** 9% tax. **Payment:** Major credit cards; personal checks with credit card. **Children:** Allowed; limits on some rooms; extra charge for breakfast for more than double occupancy. **Smoking:** Only on verandahs. **Open:** Year-round. **Pets:** Some arrangements for pets.

In its first year of operation, the Old City House Restaurant won several four- and five-star ratings from Florida and national food critcs. Lucky guests sample the wonderful fare for breakfast, when the restaurant is closed to the public every day but Sunday. A typical breakfast might be quiche, strawberry pancakes, or a vegetable cheese crêpe, served with a breakfast meat or seafood, and a variety of fresh fruits, muffins, and juice. The kitchen will try to accommodate dietary restrictions. The dining room is airy and well lighted, with off-white plaster walls, tile-topped tables, and oak chairs. Service bustles, and the attractive presentations make all meals even more appetizing.

The inn itself is no less an achievement. Each room has a private entrance and is individual in decor and dimensions.

The five rooms are all above the first-floor restaurant and, like many St. Augustine B&Bs, are less expensive on weekdays. Most have light plaster walls, new wall-to-wall carpeting, and pretty floral or eyelet spreads on the queen-size beds.

> **The Inn was built in 1873 as a stable for a mansion and was renovated as a rental cottage in the 1890s; it has also served as an antique store and a millinery.**

Bathrooms are spanking new but blend well with the old-fashioned rooms. Each room or suite has something that makes it special: an alcove with a pretty love seat, lacy pillows on the bed, or a small private balcony.

The large deck on the second floor is for inn guests' use only. It's furnished with lawn chairs and tables with umbrellas and is perfect for reading and relaxing any time of the day. Below the deck is a patio with seating for the restaurant that has an arched wood and plaster gateway to the street.

This is a city house — it's right in the middle of St. Augustine and opposite the old courthouse. The big deck overlooks the courthouse's parking lot, quite a busy place during the day. The downtown location is an ideal starting place for any tour of St. Augustine. The Lightner Museum, Henry Flagler's first hotel in town (now a college), the old Spanish fort, the brick streets, the park, and the craft shops are all within walking distance of the Old City House Inn.

The building was restored in 1990. Its first-floor facade is of coquina, and the other exterior walls are plaster, now painted a buttery yellow. Green and brick-red paint accent the Palladian and small-paned windows. The red tile roof and railed balconies give the house a Spanish look.

This is the type of inn guests like to come home to after a day of sightseeing. Alice and Bob Compton, a retired couple, keep the atmosphere congenial. The Comptons' son, John, is the chef, and he runs the restaurant with his wife, Darcy. The elder Comptons serve wine and cheese upon guests' arrival and lend them bicycles for touring the old city.

The Old Powder House Inn

38 Cordova Street
St. Augustine, FL 32084
904-824-4149
800-447-4149

*A Victorian built
on the site of a gun-
powder storehouse*

Innkeepers: Al and Eunice Howes. **Accommodations:** 9 rooms.
Rates: $59–$109 weekends; $45–$99 Monday through Thursday. **Included:** Full breakfast; afternoon coffee, tea, and pastry; evening wine and hors d'oeuvres. **Minimum stay:** 2 nights on weekends. **Added:** 9% tax. **Payment:** MasterCard, Visa; personal checks. **Children:** Age 8 and older welcome. **Smoking:** Only on verandahs. **Open:** Year-round.

Cordova Street seems to be the place to open a B&B in St. Augustine; there are now several on this street. But it's certainly an ideal spot. The old Spanish part of town, the busy bay, Flagler College, the park, the fort, and the courthouse are all are within easy walking distance. Yet this end of the street is quite peaceful at night.

The hallways and common rooms are gracious and airy. The breezy verandahs upstairs and down have Victorian spindle railings and are furnished with wicker chairs and swings.

Each of the nine rooms is decorated with a theme. A cozy first-floor front room where a collection of antique clocks is displayed is called Splendid Time. Gauzy lace curtains hang at the windows.

Upstairs, Queen Anne's is a good deal larger and has a more spacious bathroom. The high old-fashioned bedstead has a new queen-size mattress and lacy fabric draped above the white headboard creating a canopy effect. Grandma's Attic, at the top of the stairs, is decorated in floral wallpaper and has a bathroom a little smaller than Queen Anne's. East Point, in front on the second-floor, has a verandah and a rather small kitchenette with a microwave and sink. This little suite is a good choice for a week's stay.

> **The Old Powder House Inn is a real painted lady, a big clapboard house painted in shades of mauve, purple, raspberry, green, blue, and white, with gold leaf on some of the Victorian detailing.**

All of the rooms at the Old Powder House Inn have private, modern bathrooms and are fresh and clean. The small-paned windows let in a lot of light and provide views of mature trees and other Victorian homes in the neighborhood.

The house was restored in 1989 by the previous owners. The new owners, Al and Eunice Howes, who live on the premises, have done a splendid job of upgrading even more. They love to entertain and to tailor guests' visits to their own particular needs, essentially creating custom packages for honeymooners and others. Fresh flowers are in every room, and at breakfast there's fine china and elegant stemware on the tables.

Guests can spend as much time as they want in the backyard, in the 10-person Jacuzzi, or on the screened-in porch at the front of the house, where they may help themselves to coffee and tea throughout the day. Just inside is a sitting room with a fireplace that has New England country decor and a comfortable sofa to sink into after a day of sightseeing.

A full breakfast is served in courses in two quaint tea rooms on the other side of the sitting room. Each table is set for two, providing an intimate breakfast for a couple — and a little relief for parents traveling with children, who get their own table. However, the Howes are happy to put two tables together if it's requested. In the afternoon, specialty coffees and tea are set out with homemade pastries and, in the evening, a soothing glass of wine and hors d'oeuvres.

St. Francis Inn

279 St. George Street
St. Augustine, FL 32084
904-824-6068

> *A budget find in
> St. Augustine's
> historic district*

Innkeepers: Capt. Stanley and Regina Reynolds. **Accommodations:** 11 rooms and suites, 2 apartments, 1 2-bedroom cottage. **Rates:** Rooms $49–$70, suites $75–89, apartments $75–97, cottage $140. **Included:** Continental breakfast and admission to Oldest House. **Minimum stay:** None. **Added:** 9% tax; $10 extra adult in room. **Payment:** MasterCard, Visa; personal checks. **Children:** 12 and older allowed in apartments and cottage. **Smoking:** Not allowed except on verandah and in garden. **Open:** Year-round.

The St. Francis Inn is just down the street from "the Oldest House in America" as well as many of the other important sites of Old St. Augustine. Located across the street from a little park, it is a good place for both adults and their school-age children. A few of the suites have kitchenettes, and there is a cottage near the pool appropriate for groups and families.

The St. Francis attracts mainly an adult clientele wishing to soak up the Old World ambience and spend quiet evenings in the antique-filled common rooms. The innkeepers therefore prefer that only children 12 and older visit the inn and generally rent out only the apartments and cottage to families.

The public rooms have white stucco walls and fine Spanish arches leading into the lobby area. There are several fine old fireplaces, all of which work, and plenty of well-worn Oriental rugs and antiques.

The apartment and the rooms with kitchenettes are convenient for those who want to fix some of their own meals. A couple of rooms open onto the second-floor verandah overlooking the brick street and St. Francis Park.

The five-room cottage, ideal for a group of friends or a family, was once slave quarters for the main house. It has a full kitchen, bedrooms upstairs, and a sitting room that opens onto the small pool. The pool seems spartan compared to the spectacular ones at other Florida accommodations, but it is quite adequate.

The guest rooms have recently been updated with new carpeting and painted woodwork. Some of the old furniture is not quite antique, but it fits with the inn's unpretentious quality. The inn's staff regard its oddities with humor: "Ya gotta like old here!"

Even nicer is the brick courtyard that both the cottage and the back side of the inn overlook. Here there is a little goldfish pond surrounded with lush plants, a banana tree, and, closer to the street, a group of wrought-iron lawn chairs with a table. The trunk of a tree has grown over the old walkway, which gives an idea how long this little garden has been here.

The St. Francis Inn is the oldest established guest house in St. Augustine. The original home was built for Gaspar Garcia in 1791. The Spanish influence is obvious, with a stucco exterior over coquina, brown wooden timbers, and a second-floor verandah overhanging the street. Third-floor dormers and a mansard roof were added later. After trading hands several times — Spanish, British, and American — the house was converted to a boarding house in the mid-19th century and has remained a guest house since then.

Southern Wind

18 Cordova Street
St. Augustine, FL 32084
904-825-3623

> *A Victorian B&B, a cottage, and a yacht*

Innkeepers: The Dern family. **Accommodations:** 8 rooms and suites, 6 cottage rooms and suites. **Rates:** $60–$129 weekends; $50–$79 Monday through Thursday off-season. **Included:** Full breakfast; champagne for weekend honeymoon or anniversary couples. **Minimum stay:** None. **Added:** 9% tax. **Payment:** Major credit cards. **Children:** Children under 6 free in room with parents; adults only in Southern Wind East. **Smoking:** Prohibited except on verandahs. **Open:** Year-round.

Southern Wind is owned by a family originally from California. Their first venture in hostelry was their B&B on Cordova Street, a buff-colored Victorian called Southern Wind East, managed primarily by their son. Cottage accommodations are available in Southern Wind West, around the corner. The Derns also have function rooms on a yacht nearby, the *Southern Wind.*

On the first floor at Southern Wind East is a formal dining room where breakfast is served and, opposite that, a parlor with a fireplace and a large bay that has a second dining room table for guests. A polished wood banister leads upstairs to the guest rooms and a slightly shabby hallway.

The rooms are lavishly decorated — Mrs. Dern worked as a

decorator before opening this B&B and makes generous use of rich fabrics. One room worth noting is the Crystal Suite, which has a dormered ceiling, a sunny enclosed porch with a daybed, and a queen-size bed with a white quilted bedspread. The original pine floor is warmed by a blue Oriental rug. The blue and white Porcelain Room has a spacious bath with a clawfoot tub and a marble counter. The Honeymoon Suite has a bay window and a small but attractive bathroom. The queen-size bed is elaborately draped. A fringed rug in rosy shades completes the romantic, old-fashioned room.

> **Out front is a comfortably furnished wraparound porch with hanging baskets of ferns. The pillars and balustrade are decorated with tiles made by guests to commemorate an anniversary or other special event. The Derns will furnish you with plain white tiles and paints; when they have a number of finished tiles, they send them off to be fired.**

Breakfast is served in the formal dining room from the mahogany buffet, which stands in front of an exquisite tapestry. The full breakfast includes fruit, cereal, juice, homemade breads, a baked egg dish, and a choice of gourmet coffees, tea, or hot chocolate. Guests eat at the large dining room table or at two smaller tables. On weekends when the inn is full, guests may also take breakfast at the big mahogany table in the parlor.

Just around the corner is the Derns' pink and white bungalow called Southern Wind West, the Family B&B. The decor and furnishings are less elaborate than those of the suites and rooms at the B&B on Cordova Street. Each has a kitchen or kitchenette with microwave. One of the front units has a tile fireplace and a queen-size sofabed in the living room and a double bed in a sleeping alcove. Another unit has double beds with a dining room and kitchenette. The two units share a front porch furnished with a bench and table and chairs.

In the back of the house is a deck leading to a unit called the Raspberry Room. This has a queen-size bed and small corner kitchenette. The Garden Room, also in the back, has a queen-size bed and a daybed; this room is attractively decorated in peach and blue. It has the bungalow's original kitchen, with a big old porcelain sink and drain board. All the bathrooms have new plumbing and were recently repainted and redecorated.

The Derns' yacht, *Southern Wind,* is docked just half a mile away. It is available for weddings and other celebrations and is always stocked with champagne.

Victorian House

11 Cadiz Street
St. Augustine, FL 32084
904-824-5214

A B&B with an easy informality

Innkeeper: Daisy Morden. **Accommodations:** 4 rooms and 4 suites. **Rates:** Rooms $60–$85, suites $65–95; 7th night free. **Included:** Continental breakfast. **Minimum stay:** 2 nights on weekends. **Added:** 9% tax; $10 extra person. **Payment:** Major credit cards; personal checks; cash. **Smoking:** Allowed only on verandahs. **Open:** Year-round.

This cream-colored house with blue trim is true to its name, with several gingerbread dormers, a railed front porch, blue-shuttered windows, and a picket fence around the garden.

Some of the rooms have small-patterned country wallpapers, and windows have light, ruffled curtains. Area rugs give warmth to the wood floors. All guest rooms have handsome private baths. There are four rooms in the main house and two suites in an adjacent carriage house.

The generous breakfast includes homemade breads and muffins, granola, fresh fruit, juice, herbal teas, and coffee. After breakfast, guests can sit on the front porch and watch the scene on narrow Cadiz Street. The little garden and brick courtyard look neat and well cared for. The wicker chairs on the front porch are a bit worn, and the comfortable cushions a bit faded, but like everything at the Victorian House, they have a homey feel, as if life were too full to stop and make everything picture-perfect. The staff at the Victorian House are very friendly and accommodating. At "the meagerest encouragement," manager Holly Mulkey will sing to guests on birthdays and other special occasions.

> **On the front porch, a rocker cushion is hand-stenciled, a hint of what visitors will find inside. Daisy Morden has stenciled this old place to give the interior a fresh country feel. Her favorite motif, a willow with a bird, shows up on curtain trim, plaster walls, and even the floor.**

At the Victorian House, you're right in the middle of the historic district. Aviles Street is narrow as an alley, with tightly packed houses, some only a few feet from the pavement. Walk east toward the waterfront and you're on the Avenida Menendez, a main thoroughfare, and Matanzas Bay. Walk north, south, or west and you'll pass some of St. Augustine's most famous attractions. On St. Francis Street is "the Oldest House in America"; the museum, bookstore, and old brick courtyard are well worth a visit. As a fan of historic St. Augustine and one of the first people to restore an old house here, Daisy can tell you some of the best sights to see.

From the Victorian House you're within walking distance of the Oldest Store (free to Victorian House guests), the Lightner Museum in the Flagler-built Alcazar Hotel, and Plaza de la Constitucion, a parklike gathering spot off King Street. A bit farther are the Castillo de San Marcos and the Spanish Quarter, which is almost like an open-air museum. After you've taken it all in, you can rest your tired feet on the porch of the Victorian House.

Westcott House

146 Avenida Menendez
St. Augustine, FL 32084
904-824-4301

A lovingly restored Victorian over-looking the bay

Owners: Sharon and David Denni-son. **Accommodations:** 8 rooms. **Rates:** $95–$135; lower rates Sunday through Thursday except holidays. **Included:** Continental breakfast. **Minimum stay:** None. **Added:** 9% tax. **Payment:** MasterCard, Visa; personal checks. **Children:** Free in room with parents. **Smoking:** Only on verandahs. **Open:** Year-round.

Westcott House is one of the prettiest Victorian B&Bs in all of Florida. This is partly due to the house itself: the three verandahs and Italianate gingerbread details on the exterior and the fireplaces, fine banisters, and old pine floors of the interior. But it is due also to the painstaking year-round maintenance bestowed on both the house and grounds. Westcott House is a home that is well loved.

This has not always been the case. The house was built in the late 19th century by Dr. John Westcott, a prominent St. Augustine citizen. Among his many achievements was the development of the part of the Intracoastal Waterway that links the St. Johns River to Miami. After his death, the house fell into disrepair. When the Dennisons took over the house, the place was in such decay that it was questionable whether it could ever be brought back.

The eight guest rooms are all beautifully decorated and appointed. Harbour View, in the front of the house on the first floor, is decorated in rich blues. Rosalind is decorated in shades of pink and rose, with ponderous Victorian furniture. Anastasia has an incredible mahogany vanity with triptych mirrors. Esmeralda is white and green, with green curtains. Other guest rooms have lace curtains or elaborate swags, and queen- or king-size beds. The private baths off the rooms are immaculate, and a few have claw-foot tubs.

> **Standing in the Victorian parlor today, it's easy to appreciate the Dennisons' hard work. The room is graced by a blue and gold carved fireplace, polished wooden floors, a beautifully upholstered settee, and ornate swags at the bright windows. The Victorian furniture is dark and heavy. Everywhere, a vivid imagination, concern for authenticity, and a bit of whimsy are apparent.**

Outside, the same attention to detail is obvious. The clapboards are painted a delicate salmon, and the long, louvered shutters are Williamsburg blue. On the front porch are wicker furniture and hanging ferns. The porch overlooks a small lawn running to a flower bed at the foot of a low coquina wall.

At the side of the house is another first-floor verandah. There's a smooth lawn and more flowers and greenery in the side garden, as well as a small fountain. The pretty back garden overlooks the quiet, well-to-do residential neighborhood of Marine Street. The backyard has a bricked-in courtyard with groupings of white-iron lawn tables and chairs. Many guests take breakfast here, or they can have breakfast on the side verandah, in the parlor, on the front porch, or in the privacy of their room. The innkeeper serves fresh fruit, cereal, pastries, juice, and coffee.

Guests are treated to a complimentary bottle of wine on arrival, and most feel quite pampered here. Turndown service includes a snifter of brandy and fine chocolates waiting by the bed. Terrycloth bathrobes are available if you request them. At any time, you can count on the staff to assist you.

But it's the sunny location on Matanzas Bay — part of the Intracoastal that Dr. Westcott helped develop — that makes this restored Victorian so special. From the lawn and garden, you look directly across Avenida Menendez to the water. You can hear seagulls overhead, halyards rattling against masts, people laughing and joking from their boats, and the clopping of hooves as horse-drawn carriages pass.

Westcott House is close to everything that people come to St. Augustine for. The city's yacht pier is a half-block down the avenue. There are restaurants, boutiques, carriage and trolley tours, museums, and historical sites within walking distance. The beach is a short drive across the beautiful Bridge of Lions. If the weather's fine, you can go sightseeing or spend the day at the beach. If not, there's always the pleasure of staying inside.

STUART

HarborFront Inn B&B

310 Atlanta Avenue
Stuart, FL 43994
407-288-7289
Fax: 407-221-0474

> *An eclectic river-front B&B near Stuart's old town*

Hosts: John, JoAyne, and Amy El-bert. **Accommodations:** 2 rooms, 3 suites, 1 cottage, 1 apartment. **Rates:** Rooms $65–$90, suites $80–$100, cottage $75, apartment $115, *Silver Lady* yacht $85; 10% discounts Sunday–Thursday and by the week; $10 for extra adults. **Included:** Full breakfast for those in rooms and suites; breakfast $5 per person for cottage and apartment;

free dockage on a first-come, first-served basis and advance notice. **Minimum stay:** 3 nights in cottage and apartment. **Added:** 6% tax. **Payment:** No credit cards; personal checks; cash. **Children:** 12 and older welcome. **Smoking:** Outside only. **Open:** Year-round.

This hideaway B&B is located on a narrow back road bordering the St. Lucie River, just off Route 1 near the historic section of Stuart. Originally built in 1908, it was once accessible only by water. The house almost looks like a vacation cottage, with an exterior of natural shingles and lots of porch and deck space overlooking the water. The deep blue trim and crimped tin roof are typical of houses built at this time in Florida. The additions to the main house, as well as the guest house suites that are a part of the B&B, all have been built in keeping with this style.

The inside of the HarborFront is an interesting mix of summer-camp informality, 1920s interior decor, and custom-made contemporary cabinetry. A few years ago, an expert woodcarver redid the dining room and bar, carving fantastic shapes and creating unusual curved handles on the bar cupboards. The dining area extends into the living room where there is a large fireplace and a comfortable sofa. The furniture is a mix of modern, traditional, and funky.

The longer one explores the house and grounds, the more quiet surprises one finds. Decks sprout everywhere on the sides and back of the house and cottages, providing lots of space for sitting and gazing out at the river. In the center of the house is a small atrium, where the Elberts' pet parrot judiciously looks over guests from his large cage.

A large tree growing near the suite cottage at first seems like just a pleasant shade tree until one realizes that the shiny green orbs hanging from the branches are real avocadoes — and the next day, there are avocadoes on the menu. A hammock is strung between two banyan trees, and wonderful little sitting areas have been created here and there in the large backyard. The focus is on the river and total relaxation.

Although HarborFront is small and informal, there are several accommodation options. The largest is the Cottage. This has a small bedroom with a queen-size bed, cable TV, sitting room, a well-equipped kitchen, and small bath with shower. The furniture is a mix of 1950s Formica and traditional. Most people staying in the Cottage cook for themselves, but breakfast is available for an extra charge.

HarborFront also has a riverfront apartment with a private deck, living room with cable TV, bedroom with two double beds, and large bath with a shower and double sinks. A small library separated from the living room by French doors will sleep two more. Another building, called the Guest House, has two more suites, both of which have private entrances and sliders to decks. The Garden Suite has a queen-size bed, wicker sofa, and a modern bath with shower.

> **A breezy porch stretches the width of the back of the house. Guests eat breakfast out here and often linger to talk with other guests or read.**

The Riverfront Suite is larger, with a living room with an impressive water view, a separate bedroom with two double beds, and a bath with two sinks and an oversize shower. With its pleasant deck, this suite is especially nice for a honeymoon couple.

In the main house, all the guest rooms are on the first floor. The nicest of these is the Sun Room, which has a full riverfront view, a private deck, queen-size bed, sitting room, and bathroom with a shower. As the name suggests, it is very sunny and furnished mostly in white. The Master Bedroom Suite is also attractive and includes a queen-size bed, sleep sofa, and full bath. The master suite can be joined with the Guest Room, which has a queen bed, a sofa and desk, and a large bath with a tub and shower.

Still another option is an overnight stay on the *Silver Lady*, the HarborFront's yacht. It is moored at the B&B's backyard dock and is also available for half-day or full-day cruises.

Breakfast is generous, and different every day. One morning it might be waffles, another time an egg dish. Fresh fruits from the garden are used as much as possible. Guests usually eat on the porch overlooking the river or in the atrium. On Friday nights, there's a fish barbeque at the HarborFront that includes appetizers, seasonal vegetables, fresh salads, homemade dessert, wine and beer.

Just a few blocks away are the boutiques and craft shops of Stuart's historic district as well as quite respectable live theater. (Guests do have to cross a busy street to get there, so it's easier to drive the short distance.) Sailing and fishing are available at nearby marinas. Good places for dinner are Luna's for Italian food and Flagler's Grill in the historic district.

The Homeplace

501 Akron Avenue
Stuart, FL 34994
407-220-9148

A homey retreat built by one of historic Stuart's town fathers

Innkeeper: Jean Bell. **Accommodations:** 3 rooms. **Rates:** $65–$80. **Included:** Full breakfast; snacks and juices. **Minimum stay:** None. **Added:** 6% tax. **Payment:** MasterCard, Visa; personal checks. **Children:** Young children discouraged because of antiques. **Smoking:** Only on porches. **Open:** Year-round.

The Homeplace was originally the home of one of Stuart's most important residents, self-made architect Sam Matthews. Innkeeper Jean Bell consulted his daughter and only child after Bell and her husband bought the house with the idea of restoring it and turning it into a B&B. It seems the Matthews family referred to the house as "the homeplace." It is indeed a place to come home to, thanks to Jean's thoughtfulness and vibrancy, as well as the authenticity of her restoration.

Sam Matthews was born on Prince Edward Island, grew up in New England, and moved to Florida as a young man to help build one of Henry Flagler's famous hotels. He stayed on to build a number of buildings in Stuart and other parts of Martin County and to become a highly respected member of the fledgling Stuart community in the early part of this century. With both New England and Florida details, the home he built for his family reflects his origins. After years of neglect and near-demolition, Jean Bell and her husband had the house moved from its former site to a curve of Akron Avenue in the historic district of Stuart.

Built in 1913, the house is a traditional New England style with wood clapboards and shingles and white trim. The generous eaves are typical of houses built in Florida before air conditioning. The front porch has gingerbread detail and a fanciful carved screen door. The porch steps are stenciled with a pineapple, the traditional symbol of hospitality.

Guests enter a small foyer with a tin ceiling and wood floors. A large living room is furnished with Victorian parlor antiques, and the formal dining room has a large table and buffet. The kitchen is, as Jean says, a "play kitchen," full of early-20th-century metal utensils, a wood-burning stove, and a wooden butter churner. Jean actually does all the food preparation at her kitchen at home, just across the street. There is always wine and soda in the refrigerator, as well as a fruit basket and sweet breads for guests to snack on in the afternoon and evening.

Through French doors in the sitting room at the back of the house are the pretty garden patio and pool. Furnished in cushioned white wicker, the sitting room has matchstick-paneled walls and an oak floor. Here, Jean has some of her "Victorian Hangups" for sale, which she creates in a happily disheveled sewing room. The Victoriana include frilly "dream bags," hankie/bonnets, baby bibs, flower girl gloves and baskets, padded satin hangers, and beribboned wreaths. These same Victorian mementos decorate hallways and guest rooms.

> **The town dates from the early 20th century and has been revived recently so that there are now some interesting shops and galleries, a bakery, a couple of good restaurants, and live theater.**

Each of the three guest rooms has a history. Opal's Room is airy, with five windows framed by white Battenberg lace curtains and balloon shades. The double oak bedstead is carved with leaves and covered with a chenille spread and embroidered pillows. An old washbasin sewing table, floral carpet, and a rose velvet side chair complement the old-fashioned room. The sepia photos and dusty diary belonged to Opal, an opera singer in Europe during the early 20th century.

The small bathroom has an oval tub, with exposed brass pipes and shower surround. There's more of the matchstick paneling popular in this era on the bathroom walls and the bedroom ceiling.

Prissy's Porch overlooks the pool patio and the old-fashioned tin roof of the house. The room *is* prissy: lots of satin and lace pillows on the bed and "Victorian Lady" furnishings. The iron bedstead has a verdigris finish and a floral spread. Overhead is a white paddle fan. The bureau is made of inlaid woods, and the dressing table has an old mirror. The Victorian look is completed by lace balloon shades, ferns, and a washstand with porcelain basin and pitcher. Jean got creative in the small period bathroom, which has matchstick paneling on the ceiling and walls. A faded green shawl serves as a curtain for a stained glass window set low in the wall. Jean rigged a brass showerhead and surround above the old porcelain tub for those who wish to shower rather than soak, and she painted the belly of the tub a soft peach. An antique potty chair sits in the corner. Only the vinyl floor and the toilet are new.

The Captain's Quarters across the hall is far from prissy. The queen bedstead here is brass and has a navy blue bedspread. A mahogany easy chair is upholstered in maroon velvet. There's natural matchstick paneling on the walls and a maroon rug on the pine floors. The bathroom for this room was the original family bath for the Matthews. The nautical theme of the Captain's Quarters is accentuated by a reproduction masthead from the *Mystic Belle.* Jean did the reupholstering and refinishing for all the furniture in the Homeplace, as well as hunting down the antiques in the place and special touches like the masthead.

Jean is very accommodating and will serve breakfast in bed for honeymooners, but most guests prefer to eat in the formal dining room downstairs. Usually, she has juice, a selection of muffins and sweet breads, seasonal fruits, and then a gourmet egg dish, with tea or coffee. Everyone sits around the dining table to talk, and sometimes guests move into the Victorian front parlor or the sitting room.

Afternoon actvities for most guests include a dip in the pool or a trip to the old section of Stuart. Jean also has bicycles and a tandem bicycle to loan. The town has a number of boatyards and marinas and the opportunity for water sports and boating on the Intracoastal Waterway.

VERO BEACH

The Driftwood Resort

3150 Ocean Drive
Vero Beach, FL 32963
407-231-0550
Fax: 407- 234-1918

> *A whimsical, funky place with excellent accommodations*

Accommodations: Number of accommodations varies depending on rental pool. **Rates:** Hotel rooms $55–80, oceanfront rooms $110–$160, 2-bedroom villas $140–$190. **Minimum stay:** None. **Added:** 10% tax. **Payment:** Major credit cards; cash; checks. **Children:** Welcome in most accommodations. **Smoking:** Permitted. **Open:** Year-round.

The Driftwood Resort has a long history in pretty Vero Beach. In fact, at one time, it *was* Vero Beach, here before anyone thought of this small settlement as a vacation resort. Its first owner, Waldo Sexton, one of the few settlers here in the early part of this century, was a man of few financial resources and much imagination. He built his beachside home out of driftwood that washed up on the beach and began taking in overnight visitors simply because there was no other place for them to stay in the area. As the years went by, he decorated the place with whimsical finds, most of them also swept in by the ocean: old bricks, brass odds and ends, ornate wrought iron bedsteads, decorative pieces from shipwrecks, broken ceramic tiles, and later, artifacts from his travels around the world.

> **The Driftwood prides itself on being a place where guests can get a suite for what they would pay for a room anywhere else. This is a good place for families and the budget-conscious.**

Today's visitors take Ocean Drive along the beach and turn into the resort's driveway beneath two stone columns that are topped by whimsical iron birds that look as if they may have been constructed out of an old automobile heater. Just inside the "gates" is a rather perfunctory parking lot. The small reception center is furnished with antiques and photos of the Driftwood and Vero Beach in the old days. Extending from the reception center is a row of funky-looking units that have brightly colored carved wooden doors and an odd assortment of decorations out front: ornate iron railings that may have once been bedsteads, terra cotta Italianate friezes, worm-eaten wooden mastheads, and iron bells.

Inside, these units are very attractive, with Italian ceramic tiles on the floor and comfortable cushioned furniture in bamboo or bleached hardwood. The suites typically have an open layout with a sitting area and well-equipped kitchen, a small bedroom with a king or queen bed, and one or two tile bathrooms. Parking for both the resort and the restaurant, which is open to the public, are practically on the front steps of these accommodations, so they can be a little noisy.

On the other side of the parking lot are slightly newer accommodations with brick and driftwood exteriors and marvelous Italian ceramic tiles embedded in the walls. Inside are nicely furnished suites that seem a bit quieter than their counterparts across the parking lot.

The newest accommodations at the Driftwood are four-story villas approached by winding brick pathways that give a secluded feeling. These villas have interesting details such as brick archways in the kitchen area, Italian tiles, or stained glass windows. There are large terra cotta tiles on the floor and wall-to-wall carpeting in the bedrooms. Some of these villas, such as 123A and 124A, can be combined to make a two-bedroom, two-bathroom suite, ideal for couples traveling together or families with older children.

Still other units at the resort have a 1950s beachy feel, with wood floors and compact kitchen appliances, and long plank kitchen tables. All have a separate bedroom and at least one tiled bathroom.

The accommodations are packed pretty tightly on this oceanfront lot, so no matter where guests stay, they are close to the pool and the wooden stairs down to the beach. Kitchens and kitchenettes in all the accommodations allow guests to cook for themselves, but there is also a lively restaurant. Waldo Sexton really let himself go here, with stained glass windows, pecky cypress walls, and crazy artifacts from all over the world.

There are those who believe that the quirky ambience of the Driftwood has been "ruined forever" now that it's become a time-share resort, mostly occupied by time-sharers who've bought a perennial week in the sun in addition to weekenders. It is true that the feeling is not as homey as it once was. The people behind the desk are certainly not as cordial as they could be — welcoming guests to the Driftwood is just another job to them. But for those who have no past experience with the Driftwood and minimal expectations, the caliber of the welcome is insignificant. The breezy location on the beach, the comfortable accommodations, the exuberant atmosphere of the resort's bar and restaurant, and the crazy collection of art and shipwrecked treasures make this place a treat.

The Panhandle

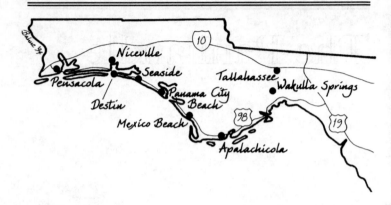

Apalachicola
Gibson Inn, 131
Destin
Sandestin Beach Resort, 133
Mexico Beach
Driftwood Inn, 136
Niceville
Bluewater Bay, 137
Panama City Beach
Marriott's Bay Point Resort, 139
Pensacola
Leichty's Homestead Inn, 143
New World Inn, 145
Pensacola Grand Hotel, 146
Seaside
Seaside, 148
Tallahassee
The Cabot Lodge, 152
Governors Inn, 154
Wakulla Springs
Wakulla Springs Lodge, 156

Best Beachside Accommodations

Mexico Beach
  Driftwood Inn
Seaside
  Seaside

Best City Stops

Tallahassee
  Cabot Lodge
  Governors Inn
Pensacola
  Pensacola Grand Hotel

Best Eclectic Finds

Wakulla Springs
  Wakulla Springs Lodge

Best Resorts and Spas

Niceville
  Bluewater Bay
Panama City Beach
  Marriott's Bay Point
Destin
  Sandestin Beach Resort

Best Small Hotels, Inns, and Motels

Apalachicola
  Gibson Inn
Pensacola
  Leichty's Homestead Inn
  New World Inn

The farther north you go in Florida, the more southern the state becomes. The soil looks like the coppery earth of Georgia and the vegetation is similar to that of other southern states, with magnolias, camellias, azaleas, and loblolly and other pines growing in abundance. Spanish moss hangs from big live oaks and old, twisted myrtle trees.

Food is also different. In north Florida you can get hush puppies, cornbread deep-fried like a doughnut, sometimes with herbs or green peppers chopped into them. You also find biscuits and grits, sometimes with gravy, and black-eyed peas. Iced tea is served in the restaurants year-round; you need to specify hot tea when you want that instead. Fried chicken is done the right way here — deep-fried and flaky. You can get fresh okra in the supermarkets.

Culturally, too, northern Florida is more southern. You can spend a week or more in Key West without ever hearing a southern accent, but not in **Tallahassee** or **Pensacola.** People are friendly and take time for conversation. There are many fundamentalist churches, and country music is popular. Lots of Georgians, Louisianans, and Alabamans come to the northeast or Panhandle coast to vacation or retire, as the breezes are cooler than back home. All the major cities have airports and offer basic accommodations in chain hotels or motels, but some charming inns and cottages have opened in recent years, particularly in the harbor section of Pensacola and along the Gulf of Mexico, also known as the Emerald Coast. The waters of the gulf have a dozen shades of blue and green and the white sand has a fine, powdery consistency. In some areas, it is possible to hire a boatman for a ride through the bayous and other backwaters near the gulf.

In the fall, the region is warm and pleasant, but it's at its best in the spring, when the flowering trees and shrubs are in bloom. No garden-lover visiting Tallahassee should miss the Maclay State Gardens — broad pathways of bricks salvaged from Tampa streets lead to formal, informal, and woodland gardens. The azaleas and dogwoods of March give the gardens their most spectacular color, but tree-high camellias in the late winter are also showy. Other attractions in the Tallahassee region are the Museum of History and Natural Science and Bradley's Country Store. There are few distinctive accommodations here, though inns are beginning to catch on.

Most hotels and B&Bs in northern Florida offer the same rate year-round, but when making reservations, it's best to check on rates for the precise period you'll be staying. On the gulf coast of the Panhandle, the high season and the highest prices are in summer. The lowest rates are in winter, when the area is apt to be damp and chilly. Spring and fall are considered "shoulder" seasons by some resorts. In Tallahassee, rates at some hotels change according to whether or not the legislature is in session.

Partly because of the rather run-down nature of some of the towns bordering the gulf, the Emerald Coast has been called the "Redneck Riviera." Because it is a summer, not a winter, destination, the coast has not been extensively developed, and it is less prosperous than other areas of Florida. The towns tend to be nondescript places with more convenience stores and bait shops than anything else. But lack of development has become a plus in Florida, and the area is becoming increasingly popular, particularly with Midwesterners. Both out-of-staters and Floridians consider the Panhandle curve of the gulf a "find" in all but the coldest months.

The dip in the Panhandle into the Gulf of Mexico is marked by the historic town of **Apalachicola.** Apalach, as local residents refer to it, is a fascinating place. Before the Civil War, steamships traveled the Apalachicola River carrying cotton from Georgia to be shipped to Europe and New England mills. Later, Apalach became a major lumber port. In the early 1800s, a strategically positioned fort on the river's banks was fought over by the Spanish, Americans, British, runaway slaves, and Choctaw Indians.

In the 20th century, the area fell on hard times, and its beautiful coastline was ignored by developers who were essentially ravaging the natural beauty of the southeast coast. This neglect has been something to be grateful for; but now, ironically, there is an effort to attract tourist dollars by advertising the area as "Florida's Forgotten Coast." St. George Island, a barrier island a few miles from Apalachicola, was recently named one of the top ten beaches in the United States, partly because there are no hordes of people lying on the sand. In Florida, especially on the southeast coast, an uncrowded beach is an exciting thing.

West of Apalachicola is **Panama City,** a somewhat depressed factory town. South of the city is **Panama City Beach,** characterized by motels and high-rises along the admittedly pretty beach and some commercial attractions that probably wouldn't survive as secondary attractions in the Disney World region. One lovely area here that should never be missed is Shell Beach and St. Andrews State Park.

There is great fishing along the coast, both in rivers and in the Atlantic. Hundreds of years ago, the Indians of the gulf lived peacefully along these shores, largely because the plentiful fish and game made fighting unnecessary. Basically nomadic, the Indians roamed up and down the coast. They swam and partied a lot, and during celebrations would roast the catches of the day over hickory campfires along the beach.

Between Panama City Beach and Pensacola, there are a number of impressive beaches, Fort Walton being one of the most beautiful. The most notable resort town along this stretch is **Seaside,** a planned community patterned after New England and Old South beach towns. At the entrance to Seaside, signs are posted for motorists to slow down for the pedestrians who walk back and forth across the road, but there's little need for a sign. People driving by for the first time are so amazed at the 19th century buildings and the absence of cars on the brick-paved streets that they automatically slow down and rubberneck during the whole four minutes it takes to drive past the town.

North of Seaside is DeFuniak Springs, a planned community of the 1880s, created as a winter home for intellectuals and visionaries from Chatauqua, New York. Turn-of-the-century brick buildings line up opposite the town depot and railroad tracks, looking almost like a movie set. But the prettiest part of DeFuniak Springs is around the lake, a few hundred yards from the depot where Victorian houses, Old South mansions, and small bungalows encircle the water. Also sited on the lake is a small library in a white clapboard building, reputedly the state's oldest public library.

The principal city near the border with Alabama is Pensacola, an old harbor town that has experienced quite a revival in recent years. The most interesting area here for out-of-town visitors is the historic waterfront area, which looks almost like the French Quarter in New Orleans. Many of the buildings are brick and have wrought-iron balustrades on their second-floor verandahs. The community is proud of its revitalization and has some sidewalk and seafood fairs during the year, which they stage as much for their own enjoyment as for the tourists'. Pensacola is sited on a large bay so there are water views from many parts of the city.

APALACHICOLA

Gibson Inn

U.S. Highway 98 and Avenue C
P.O. Box 221
Apalachicola, FL 32320
904-653-2191

> *One of Florida's
> oldest inns*

Owner and general manager: Mich-
ael Koun. **Accommodations:** 29 rooms, 1 suite. **Rates:** Rooms
$55–$85, suite $780–$110; $5 discount on weekdays; pack-
ages available. **Minimum stay:** With some packages. **Added:**
6% tax; $5 extra person. **Payment:** Major credit cards. **Chil-
dren:** Free in room with parents. **Smoking:** Restricted. **Pets:**
$5 fee. **Open:** Year-round.

Apalachicola is a hard word to pronounce, but the town itself
is an easy place to get used to, particularly with the Gibson
Inn as a base. It's a slow-paced town, but anyone who asks,
"What's there to do here?" is not looking hard enough.

In 1907, at the height of Apalachicola's prosperity, a South
Carolinian named James Fulton Buck built the Franklin, the
town's first inn. In the late 1920s, when the cypress trees had
died out and the town had become a center for oystering, the
Gibson sisters — Sunshine and Annie — bought the place
and changed its name.

Shortly after the Second World War, when army officers were billeted in the Gibson, it began to deteriorate, and by the time the present owners bought it in 1983, it was a refuge for derelicts. Fortunately, though, no one had ever "modernized" the interior. Beneath layers of paint and filth were the original black cypress and heart-of-pine banisters, railings, wainscoting, and paneling, all remarkably well preserved. The exterior of the inn is squarish and solid-looking, with a tin roof, a widow's walk, and wrap-around veran-

> **Narrow hallways lead to lots of nooks and crannies and to second-floor and third-floor guest rooms, all decorated in a 19th-century Old Florida style, with paddle fans and wood slat blinds.**

dahs on the first and second floors. Painted deep blue, the inn has white latticework, windows, and verandah railings.

The Gibson's restaurant has a wide following. Fashioned after a steamboat dining room (steamships once plied the Apalachicola River), it has the original solid post and beam construction. Matchstick paneling runs halfway up the walls, with cream-colored plaster and old photographs above. Globe lanterns of brass and green glass hang from the ceiling. The seafood here is excellent, though service can be a bit slow.

The guest rooms at the Gibson Inn have white-iron or mahogany four-poster beds, woven rugs on the polished pine floors, camelback sofas, antique armoires and side tables, white ceiling fans, and pedestal washbasins with porcelain or brass fixtures. At the same time, there are all the modern amenities: air conditioning, cable TV, and private telephones.

Room 208, on the second floor, is one of the inn's best. It has white-painted paneled walls, deep green trim, and a small-print paper in cranberry and green. The king bed has a crocheted canopy top, and a dhurrie rug is on the pine floor. Although other rooms have access to the verandah from the hallway, this is the only guest room with direct access to this breezy spot, through French doors in both the bedroom and sitting room. Some furnishings here look a bit tired.

Although the Gibson Inn is the sort of place where you could spend half the day reading in your room or rocking on the verandah, there are some interesting things to do on the water and in the town. Just off the coast of Apalach are four pretty barrier islands that provide miles of beaches and excellent fishing. These islands were the source of Apalachicola's fame as an oystering center during an earlier era. Many guests set out on a walking tour that stops at the John Gorrie Museum and two historic Greek Revival structures, the Trinity Episcopal Church and the Raney House. These are on the National Register of Historic Places — as is the Gibson Inn.

It's important to note that Apalachicola does not have the polished antique look of St. Augustine or Fernandina Beach in Florida's northeast. Many of the historic brick buildings here are run down and even abandoned, and the waterfront is a working harbor, not a tourist spot.

DESTIN

Sandestin Beach Resort

Emerald Coast Highway (Route 98)
Destin, FL 32541
904-267-8000
Reservations:
904-267-8150
800-277-0800
Reservations for Sandestin Beach
  Hilton Golf & Tennis Resort:
  800-HILTONS

> *A huge resort on one of Florida's lesser-known beaches*

General manager: Wayne Olcott. **Accommodations:** 545 rooms, suites, and villas. **Rates:** Inn rooms $55–$119, suites $82–$173; 1-bedroom villas $102–$223, 2-bedroom villas $106–$323, 3-bedroom villas $131–$473; discounts; packages and weekly rates available. **Added:** 8% tax. **Minimum stay:** 3 nights on major holidays and some packages. **Payment:** Major credit cards, except American Express. **Children:** Free in room with parents. **Smoking:** Some nonsmoking rooms available. **Open:** Year-round.

Sandestin sits on 2,600 acres of land off the Emerald Coast Highway. There are seven and a half miles of beach on the property, pretty lagoons, and acres and acres of white sand dunes. Sandestin Beach Resort offers a great deal of recreation and, in some cases, accommodations directly on the ocean. In an area of mediocre motels and fast food restaurants, Sandestin offers a sense of insularity.

Sandestin is split by the highway, with some villas, a new Hilton hotel, tennis courts, and a golf course on one side; and another golf course, the inn, the conference center, and more villas on the other side. This poses fewer problems than one would think; trams pick up guests at stops scattered about the property.

> It is enough simply to enjoy the beach and water at Sandestin, but there is more to do. In addition to several swimming pools, golf, and tennis, there are catamaran sailing lessons, sailboat and motorboat rentals, bicycle rentals, fishing, Jet Skis, volleyball on the beach, a fitness center, a children's activities program, and a number of water sports. There's also a marina and a yacht club.

The Beachside Tower suites are in two high-rise buildings a few steps (and an elevator ride) from the sugary sands of the gulf. These have small terraces on the parking lot side of the building and generous ones on the ocean side. The views from the top floors are breathtaking and, because the architects incorporated so much glass into the building, you almost feel as if you're still outdoors. The towers have spacious executive suites on the low end of the price range, and four-bedroom apartments on the high end. There are also one- and two-bedroom suites.

The clustered Bayside Villas, more spacious and more expensive, are a better choice for those who don't like high-rise buildings. Also desirable are the two- and three-bedroom Gulfwalk Villas near the beach, the rustic Fairways overlooking the golf course, and the Linkside units, which back up to a canal or golf course. The new Villas at Vantage Point are rather gaudy, with a pink stucco exterior, a too-blue barrel tile roof, and a two-story floor plan that's a little impractical for families.

Although the villas and other accommodations are privately owned, many are in a rental pool and available by the day, week, or longer. All suites and villas have fully equipped kitchens and are well cared for. Owners compete to provide the most attractive furnishings and decor on the rationale that the more elegant the surroundings, the more likely the accommodation will find a steady stream of renters. All property owners in the rental pool have to abide by high decorating and maintenance standards set by management.

Most convention-goers and vacationing couples stay at the resort's inn, on the bay side of Emerald Coast Highway, next to the conference center. These also have kitchenettes, with a small refrigerator, stovetop, coffeemaker, and toaster. A small balcony looks out over the resort or the bay, though by Gulf Coast standards the water is a bit disappointing — a dull green that gets brown close to shore, with none of the little islands and sandbars that dot other parts of the coast. However, the inn is a center of activity: grass and clay tennis courts, a swimming pool and golf course, the brightly tiled Sunset Bay Cafe, and the conference center are all here.

A new Hilton on the gulf side of the resort has 400 additional suites. Standard suites have bunkbeds in an entryway, a king-size bed, sofa, dining area and refreshment center with a fridge and stovetop. The bathroom has a tub shower, toilet, mini-television, hair dryer, and telephone, and there's another sink and vanity in the dressing area, easing the bathroom bottleneck in the morning. Decor is fresh and pretty.

The lobby and meeting rooms downstairs are open and airy, with comfortable new furnishings. The Hilton has its own restaurant and lounge, Sandcastles, and a snack grill by the pool. Across the dunes is the resort's Elephant Walk restaurant. Its three interconnecting buildings have Old Florida green metal roofs, with conical towers and cupolas, barn-red wooden clapboards, and lots of walkways overlooking the water for after-dinner strolls.

Because this is a residential community with many year-rounders, there are also some special pleasures not available at impersonal hotels — like an informal group who get together every morning to jog. Guests can keep abreast of special events on the Sandestin Information Station, channel 10.

Within the complex are tennis and golf shops. There is also excellent shopping at the Market just outside the security gate. The Market is architecturally Old Florida, in stucco with conical towers on the gray metal roofs. Covered walkways join the various shops and an informal restaurant. The tropical landscaping includes lagoons, fountains, and small islands frequented by watchful blue herons.

MEXICO BEACH

Driftwood Inn

2105 Highway 98
P.O. Box 13447
Mexico Beach, Fl 32410
904-648-5126
Fax: 904-648-8505

> *A budget find
> on the
> Emerald Coast*

Owner: Peggy Wood. **Accommodations:** 30 rooms, suites, and houses. **Rates:** Rooms $55–$65, suites $65–$75, 2-bedroom/2-bath Victorian houses $75–$120, apartments $125–$180/week; monthly rates available. **Included:** Complimentary coffee and pastry. **Minimum stay:** In some units. **Added:** 8% tax; $6 for extra adult. **Payment:** Discover, MasterCard, Visa; cash; check. **Children:** Welcome. **Smoking:** Allowed. **Open:** Year-round.

The Driftwood looks so small and unassuming on the outside, but it has a good deal of variety in its accommodations, with rooms in the inn that sleep from two to six, beach cottages, and two-bedroom, two-bath Victorian houses located just across the street. The architecture of the original inn is Old Florida: tin roof, gray clapboards, white latticework and trim, and gingerbread detailing on the broad, overhanging eaves. It's basically an expanded motel, but a motel with much charm. The office and gift shop in the front of the inn look almost like an old-time depot. Subtropical gardens and small fountains are on each side of the entrance.

Inn units are located on the two floors of the main building. They are extremely compact, with an efficient little kitchen and a bed–sitting room. A porch is furnished with a table and chairs. Furnishings are traditional and a cut above the usual motel appointments.

The conical beach cottages, next to the main inn, have attractive, balustraded verandahs overlooking the gulf. With two units in one building and four in another, these are more spacious and have a bit more privacy than the inn. The two-bedroom "Victorian houses" are just across the street. They also have the Old Florida architecture of tin roofs, verandahs, and pastel clapboards. The houses have an open, airy feeling and are furnished with 1920s- and '30s-style furniture.

With advance notice, pets are allowed at the Driftwood — unusual for Florida. All accommodations have cable TV and a telephone. In the morning, staff put out coffee and sweet rolls.

Mexico Beach is little known even in Florida. Clapboard and stucco cottages line the main road

In the back of the inn are gardens with Greek statuary, windmills, a tiny waterfall, and other whimsical decorations. Lawn chairs under a thatched pavilion give shelter from the noonday sun. A wooden walkway leads to sand dunes and the pristine beach.

and spread out onto little side streets. There are a few eateries and stores, but for the most part, this is not a highly populated — or commercial — area. The inn is located directly on Highway 98, but 98 has only two lanes and no rush hour.

NICEVILLE

Bluewater Bay

1950 Bluewater Boulevard
P.O. Box 247
Niceville, FL 32588-9981
904-897-3613
800-874-2128

A resort, marina, and golf club overlooking a bay

President: Conchita Yates. **Accommodations:** 120 rooms, suites, villas. **Rates:** Studios and efficiencies $85–$120, 1-bedroom villas $105–$150, 2-bedroom villas $135–$185, 3-bedroom villas $155–$205; weekly and monthly rates; discounts; packages. **Minimum stay:** 2 nights with packages. **Added:** 6% tax. **Payment:** Major credit cards. **Children:** Free in room with parents. **Smoking:** Some nonsmoking rooms available. **Open:** Year-round.

Bluewater Bay sits on 2,000 acres just outside Niceville, a quiet Panhandle town. Much of the land overlooks the Choctawhatchee Bay. The various accommodations are well sited in the pine forests, and within the complex is a large residential area of executive homes. There are jogging and bicycle trails along the roads and lots of kids playing basketball in their driveways.

> The water of the bay is a deep cobalt blue that invites swimming and boating as well as gazing from a chaise longue. On the private beach, guests can rent catamarans, Sunfish, and Windsurfers.

At the resort, the feeling is either nautical or golf-oriented. Hotel-style accommodations consisting of one-bedroom studios and efficiencies are at the marina. The two-bedroom suites overlook the bay, and many three-bedroom units overlook the golf course.

The marina is full service, with 120 permanent slips and a launch ramp. Captained charter boats are available. At the end of a wooden walkway next to the marina is a small bay-side beach with gentle waves and a sheltered picnic area.

There are some outstanding villas in the pine and deciduous woods around the beautiful golf courses. Gleneagles Green's two- and three-bedroom accommodations are stucco with shake roofs. The handsome Villas of St. Andrews are stone and stucco with one or two levels. Attractively decorated and ideal for a small family or two vacationing couples, these are the first choice of many guests. On the bay are the Bay Villa Condominiums, with efficiencies, one- and two-bedroom units, and two- and three-bedroom multilevel townhouses. All two- and three-bedroom accommodations have washers and dryers. There is also a laundromat at the marina.

The casual Greenhouse restaurant, at the tenth tee, is popular for lunch. Flags, overlooking the marina, is a bit more formal, specializing in seafood. There is also a snack bar at the tennis shop, and a lounge. Many guests cook for themselves, and there are supermarkets close by. If you are staying at a daily rate or have a tennis or golf package, daily maid service is provided, which includes light kitchen cleaning.

There are 21 tennis courts: ten Rubico, nine hard, and two CalGrass. Twelve are lighted. The pro shop has stringing service, ball machine rental, and video analysis equipment available. Tennis is free on the hard surfaces, and the charge for other surfaces and night play is minimal.

Golf is on four 9-hole courses where guests can play a short game or combine two for an 18-hole game. The courses, designed by Tom Fazio, are ranked among the best in the state.

In the summer, the recreation center has activities for kids: field trips, arts and crafts, and tennis and golf instruction. The center has a video game room, bike rentals, and mini-golf. Babysitting service is available. The resort publishes "Out of the Blue," a newsletter that lists current activities for both kids and adults.

PANAMA CITY BEACH

Marriott's Bay Point Resort

4200 Marriott Drive
Bay Point
Panama City Beach, FL 32408
904-234-3307
800-874-7105

> *A beautiful*
> *resort on a*
> *picturesque bay*

General manager: Robert Mercer.
Accommodations: 199 rooms, 170 villas. **Rates:** Rooms $105–

$165, suites $165–$290; packages available. **Minimum stay:** On holidays and special weekends. **Added:** 9% tax. **Payment:** Major credit cards. **Children:** Under 18 free in room with parents. **Smoking:** Nonsmoking. **Open:** Year-round.

Technically, Bay Point is on a mainland lagoon and a quiet bay, but it feels like an island resort. Once you arrive at Bay Point, you won't want, or need, to leave. There is everything here in the way of sports, recreation, dining, even shopping. Service is marked by the informality you would expect at a resort and the courtesy and graciousness you would find at a fine southern hotel.

The resort is near Panama City, one of the most depressed cities of Florida's struggling Panhandle. The ride from the regional airport past miles of shopping malls and fast-food restaurants is unappealing, but once you drive through the security gates of Bay Point you leave it all behind.

Guest accomodations are in Bay Point's pink and gray Old Florida–style hotel. Built in 1987, it is five stories tall, with a gray tile roof and recessed balconies overlooking the water and the golf courses. The grounds are beautifully landscaped, with large beds of annuals, thousands of azaleas, tall loblolly pines and native magnolias, and a few palm trees and tropical ferns.

Magnolia Court, a few steps up from the lobby and reception area, is like an enormous and friendly living room. On one wall is a marble and brass fireplace. Club chairs and bridge tables are grouped around the room. Every afternoon, free refreshments are served, and the big piano in the corner plays old favorites. French doors lead onto a terrace overlooking the lagoon.

Guest rooms at Bay Point are roomy, with a choice of a king bed or two doubles, good traditional furniture, and reading lamps on the bedside wall. The rooms are equipped with mini-bars and coffeemakers and have good closet space. Upstairs rooms have small balconies, while first-floor lanai rooms have patios with a table and lawn chairs. Bathrooms have timed heat lights and a retractable drying line.

Those who wish larger accommodations can rent villas through a rental pool. Bay Point Resort, like all Marriotts, has some great packages, too. There are additional reductions for small groups and conventions, and much can be said for staying at Bay Point during the off-season; October and November are especially beautiful.

The back of the hotel faces a natural lagoon fronting on St. Andrews Bay and the St. Andrews State Park. Still farther out are the beach and the Gulf of Mexico. At Bay Point's marina, you can rent sailboats, Windsurfers, or snorkeling equipment, and charter boats for excellent deep-water fishing. With 145 slips, this is the largest private marina on the Gulf Coast.

Bay Point is famous for golf. Its Lagoon Legend course is one of the toughest in the South. On this 7,080-yard, par 72 course (nicknamed "the Monster"), 16 of the 18 holes have water hazards, and there are lots of berms and sand traps. But golfers play it with humor and compare games over a drink at the Lagoon Legend Clubhouse afterwards. Lowest

A short ride on the resort's Mississippi paddlewheeler takes you to Shell Beach, one of the most beautiful in Florida, with seven miles of fine, pale sand and gentle surf.

score of the day gets a free dinner at Fiddler's Green restaurant. Club Meadows, designed by William Byrd, is a flatter, easier course with fewer water hazards. It still offers a challenging game on its open fairways, with some difficult sand and water hazards.

Tennis is also outstanding at Bay Point. There are 12 Har-Tru courts, four lighted at night. The pro shop rents and re-strings racquets. Tennis instruction is available, and the pros can match you with other players. The resort hosts a number of competitions during the year.

There are several swimming pools, including a heated indoor pool; indoor and outdoor whirlpools; and a small but well-equipped fitness room. Free bicycles are available. With 10 miles of paved roads and paths, Bay Point Resort is an ideal place for walking as well as bicycling. Its 1,100 acres are beautifully landscaped and maintained, and security is excellent. In March, its 5,000 azaleas bloom in a spectacular display of color. One favorite stroll is the boardwalk across the Grand Lagoon to Teddy Tucker's, a weathered boathouse that serves drinks and snacks.

The resort has a variety of restaurants, and the food and libations are excellent. One of the most popular restaurants, particularly with conventioneers, is Fiddler's Green. A buffet area serves large groups. Typical selections include broiled steaks and seafood specialties with delicate sauces. Service is courteous and a good deal speedier than in most Florida restaurants. Windows overlook the flowers and plants of the terrace outside and the Grand Lagoon and Bay beyond.

Another popular restaurant is the Greenhouse, at the Bay Point Yacht and Country Club. Overlooking the harbor and clubhouse pool, the Greenhouse is perfect for a romantic dinner. It is indeed a greenhouse, though a posh one, and has Italian tile floors, hanging baskets of lush tropical plants, white tables and chairs, and tiny Tivoli lights outlining the windows. The Greenhouse is open only on Friday and Saturday afternoons and evenings.

Two thirds of Bay Point's business is with convention groups. There are two conference areas to choose from — in the country club's conference center, which is across the parking lot, and in the hotel proper — with a total of 20,000 square feet of meeting space. The hotel's Grand Lagoon Ballroom can be divided into eight rooms. The smaller conference rooms across from the ballroom have a combination blackboard/movie screen behind oak doors. Conference banquets are lavish.

Convention participants and their families can enjoy all the facilities of the resort. In the summer months, this includes an excellent children's program, the Alligator Point Gang. Named after the lagoon where the group's clubhouse is located, the program is a bit like summer camp and includes a wide range of activities and lunch at Teddy Tucker's. Staffed by teachers, the program sometimes includes discussion of the area's history.

The Panhandle was once the home of Indian tribes who fished and crabbed. Their feasts are reenacted at Marriott's Indian fish roast every Friday and Saturday on the verandah of Fiddler's Green. Part of the resort was at one time an Indian "junkyard," where native women would toss cracked or broken pots.

Contributing to the self-contained island atmosphere is Bay Town, the small shopping center with an upscale women's clothing boutique, a wine shop, a bank, a dry cleaner and laundry, a hair salon, a gift shop, and a deli. Bay Town is one more reason you won't want to leave this gracious "island" until you have to.

PENSACOLA

Liechty's Homestead Inn

7830 Pine Forest Road
Pensacola, FL 32526
904-944-8800

> *A small B&B with down-home friendliness and comfort*

Owners: Neil and Jeanne Liechty. **Accommodations:** 6 rooms and suites. **Rates:** $69–$79; discounts available; $5–$10 for extra person in room, depending on age. **Included:** Breakfast voucher equaling $3.49 for adults, $1.99 for children; complimentary dessert night of check-in. **Added:** 10% tax. **Payment:** American Express, MasterCard, Visa; personal checks. **Children:** Allowed. **Smoking:** Prohibited. **Open:** Year-round.

Jeanne and Neil Liechty built their inn in 1986 on Route 397 near I-10, 10 minutes from downtown Pensacola. They have worked hard to make it inviting and restful. In the last few years, they have added the Victorian Restaurant and Bakery and expanded their gift shop and banquet business.

With the piney woods that once stood behind the Homestead removed to make way for residential development, a garish sign announcing the inn, and a new strip mall across the highway, the Homestead's setting has become less than peaceful. But the Homestead is still one of the best places to stay in the Panhandle because of its charming guest rooms.

With its slate blue vinyl siding, the Homestead Inn does not pretend to be a real turn-of-the-century farmhouse. Yet the place has some authentic touches: small-paned windows, a railed, gingerbread porch, and double front doors with Victorian oval windows. The inn's country decor is enhanced by antiques, Orientals and braided rugs, quilts, and homey crafts decorating the walls.

Each of the six rooms at the Homestead bears the name of a patriot or historic figure, like Betsy Ross or Robert E. Lee, and holds a collection of books in the room about that figure. The George Washington Room is appropriate for honeymooning couples, with its fireplace, pine-framed king-size bed, braided rugs, and brass ceiling fan. A blue easy chair accents the deep blue of the mantel and woodwork.

The Abraham Lincoln Room has a double bed and a daybed appropriate for a child. The tub is unusually large, a place to luxuriate.

The first-floor guest room has a private courtyard and hot tub. A ramp from the parking lot makes it wheelchair-accessible. Other rooms are equipped with skylights and fireplaces. All are well decorated with antiques or good reproductions, telephones, and TVs. The new heating and air-conditioning systems are excellent.

> **The Homestead has been a favorite of local honeymooners since its opening.**

Though honeymoon guests can have their breakfast in bed, most have the breakfast buffet at the Victorian Restaurant next door. Neil Liechty is from Indiana Mennonite country, and he believes in having his guests rest easy from their labors and eat their fill of wholesome Amish cooking. His restaurant serves classic American and southern dishes in a large dining room that has a mix of Victorian and early American country furnishings.

The country breakfast usually includes eggs and grits, ham or sausage, quiche, pancakes, fresh fruits and juices, homemade pastries, Amish waffles, and freshly brewed coffee. B&B guests receive a voucher to be used at the restaurant. Those who don't wish to have the breakfast can apply the voucher toward the cost of lunch. On the evening of check-in, guests receive a homemade dessert. Honeymooners receive a bottle of champagne.

The Liechtys have added a garden behind their inn and restaurant with romantic gazebos and shelters for receptions and outdoor weddings. One pavilion has a huge grill for barbecue feasts. The Liechtys have also converted what was once the B&B's kitchen into an indoor banquet room for local parties and weddings.

Admittedly, there is nothing in particular to do on the property other than relax in the romantic back garden: no swimming pool, no golf, no horseback riding. The living room on the first floor has been made into an office for the banquet business, so there is no longer an indoor sitting area. Thus, the Homestead Inn is a place to enjoy your room, food "made from scratch," and the person you're with.

New World Inn

600 S. Palafox Street
Pensacola, FL 32501
904-432-4111

Once a harborfront warehouse, now a Pensacola landmark

Manager: Janice Sheehan. **Accommodations:** 14 rooms and 2 suites. **Rates:** Rooms $80, suites $100; various discounts available; $10 for extra person. **Included:** Continental breakfast. **Minimum stay:** None. **Added:** 10% tax. **Payment:** Major credit cards. **Children:** Welcome; 18 and under free in room with parent. **Smoking:** Allowed. **Open:** Year-round.

New World Landing was originally a box factory. Today it's a popular inn, restaurant, and convention center. Restored and previously owned by Pensacola preservationists Kay and Arden Anderson, New World Landing was renovated with an eye towards luxury as well as history. Throughout the inn, the look of a 19th-century factory blends with Victorian opulence. Outside, a bow of windows dresses up the exterior of the restaurant, and a scalloped awning embellishes the brick-paved inn entrance. Beside the inn is a small city garden.

The oak floor of the entryway and check-in area is a dark parquet — not the original factory floor, but elegant and fitting for this hotel. The red brick ceiling supports have been left standing and give character to the lobby. The wooden check-in counter looks as if it were salvaged from either an old hotel or a 19th-century dry goods store. A small sitting area just opposite check-in has wing chairs and a camelback sofa. Here and throughout the hotel, the walls are decorated with 19th-century etchings and photographs.

A wide oak staircase takes guests to the second floor, where 14 guest rooms, two suites, another sitting room, and a spacious hallway have been created out of the original huge open space. All of the accommodations have been furnished with ceiling fans, four-poster beds, and deep carpets. The furniture is a mix of good reproductions, mostly in Queen Anne and Chippendale styles, and genuine antiques. The bathrooms have old brass fixtures, oak toilet seats, and Corian sinks. There are telephones in both the bedroom and bath.

The restaurant at New World Landing is made up of three separate and individually decorated dining rooms. The main dining room is the Barcelona Room, which has Spanish decor and overlooks the garden at the entrance. The Marseilles Room, most often used for banquets, is very French, with mirrored walls, fine wall paneling, brass and crystal chandeliers, and ornate window treatments. The Pensacola Room, another banquet facility, is more down-to-earth, with large photographs of waterfront and city activity in the 19th century. The food here is quite good and leans toward the Continental. Also popular is the inn's Liverpool Pub, an old-style bar with lots of brass and wood.

> The waterfront district and South Palafox are great for poking around in, with charming boutiques and antique shops selling silver, brass, Belgian lace, furniture, and art work. A few blocks away is a park and Pensacola's Museum of Art.

Though the interiors of both the inn and the restaurant are intimate, full-scale gatherings are easily handled in New World Hall. The convention center can accommodate up to 1,000 for meetings, 800 for dining, and 600 for dancing. The hall can also be partitioned for smaller meetings.

New World Inn is a good jumping-off place from which to explore the Pensacola's history. You can ride one of the inn's bikes or walk to a number of interesting buildings in the historic district overlooking the bay. Because the town escaped urban renewal in the 1950s and 1960s, many distinctively southern buildings remain. The Quayside Market, across the back parking lot, is a brick shopping complex with New Orleans–style wrought-iron balconies.

The Pensacola Grand Hotel

200 E. Gregory Street
Pensacola, FL 32501
904-433-3336
Fax: 904-432-7572
Reservations: 800-348-3336

> *A restored train depot*

General manager: Nancy Halford. **Accommodations:** 212 rooms and suites. **Rates:** Rooms $90–$100, suites $204; honeymoon package available. **Minimum stay:** None. **Added:** 10% tax. **Payment:** Major credit cards. **Children:** Free in room with parents. **Smoking:** Nonsmoking rooms available. **Open:** Year-round.

Pensacola's recent revitalization is reflected in the Grand Hotel's blend of old and new. The historic Louisville and Nashville Depot has been painstakingly restored. The stained and leaded glass, mosaic floors, and golden oak of the old station are all here. That's the "old"; the "new" is the glass and steel high-rise addition behind it.

> **Guests can wander through the elegantly refurbished waiting room of the old train station or relax with a drink in the L & N Lobby Bar, then enjoy the comfort of a modern hotel room.**

The three-story 1912 depot is a boxy structure of light brick. A wing that once stretched out along the railroad tracks has been cleverly converted into retail shops, an old-fashioned barber shop, meeting space, and an audiovisual center. There's also a restaurant, the 1912, which has excellent seafood and a festive Sunday brunch.

Throughout the old depot, the original details and furnishings have been preserved and restored. In the waiting room lobby, an elaborate stained-glass lamp hangs above an exquisite green marble table. In the waiting room lobby, the original mosaic floors are partially covered with area rugs. The adjacent picturesque bar has an equally captivating atmosphere.

The new building begins in the back of the reception area. The transition is marked by a change from mosaic floor to carpet, where the train tracks once ran. Here the walls are of modern black and green marble, and the new elevators have elegant brass doors. Curving up from the middle of this lobby and reception area is a brass and Plexiglas spiral staircase that takes guests up to the second-floor meeting space.

The old depot is a lot of fun, and the guest rooms in the modern glass tower rising behind it are quite comfortable. Some of the nicest are the bi-level suites with Jacuzzi. Other suites are luxurious one- or two-bedroom accommodations. Some rooms look out at Highway 110 and areas of the city that are still somewhat dilapidated, so ask about the view when making reservations.

SEASIDE

Seaside

Route 30A
P.O. Box 4730
Seaside, FL 32459
904-231-1320
800-277-TOWN
Fax: 904-231-2219

> *A beachside
> resort of cottages
> encircling a new
> town center*

Owner: Robert Davis. **Accommodations:** 184 suites, cottages, and B&B rooms. **Rates:** Dreamland Heights hotel suites $105–$195, honeymoon cottages $285–$305, motor court $115–$130, B&B rooms $135–$175, B&B suites $175–$195, Ruskin Place apartments $411–$500, vacation cottages $110–$363/night, $595–$1,447/week; off-season midweek packages. **Included:** Continental breakfast. **Minimum stay:** 3 nights in vacation cottages during summer and holidays. **Added:** 8% tax. **Payment:** Major credit cards; personal checks. **Children:** No children in hotel or honeymoon cottages; children free in vacation cottages. **Smoking:** Nonsmoking cottages available. **Open:** Year-round.

Located on 80 acres of the Panhandle's Emerald Coast between Panama City and Pensacola, Seaside is a planned community patterned after a 19th-century beach town. The developers took the best from American beachside towns, threw in a little Disney fantasy, and added their own caprice.
Seaside was originally a parcel of beachfront property, cov-

ered with palmetto and other scrub vegetation, that developer Robert Davis inherited from his grandfather. With sandy soil, bordered by wet marshes and dense woods of myrtle and oak, the land was unfit for agriculture. But several acres were right on the water, and the rest were accessible to the water by the narrow secondary highway that bisected the property. Davis built Seaside, a remarkable collection of Victorian and early 20th-century beach cottages with a town center and resort amenities.

Although Seaside was initially a summer destination for Floridians and other southerners, it is becoming popular for fall and spring vacationers and it has become famous throughout the country for its town planning. A few people live here year-round.

Guests stay in the privately owned cottages in the resort's rental pool, which are available at weekend, weekly, monthly, and seasonal rates. The Dreamland Heights Hotel, the Motor Court, and Josephine's B&B appeal to those staying for a short period.

Architectural styles in the cottages for rent remind one of Key West, Nantucket, Cape May, Savannah, Charleston. The cottages have crimped tin roofs and clapboards painted in blues, grays, and ice cream colors like raspberry and lemon. Although all houses have heating and cooling systems, simple cross-ventilation through open doors and windows works well at Seaside. The cottages have porches in a variety of styles: front porches, back porches, side porches, widows' walks, screened towers, and cupolas. Latticework and gingerbread are everywhere.

The interiors are well planned, with efficient, fully equipped kitchens; antique furnishings (or good reproductions); comfortable beds; washers and dryers; and homey touches like rocking chairs and handmade quilts. Guests are welcomed with a wicker basket of Perrier, gourmet coffee, a bottle of chilled wine, and fresh flowers.

Groceries are available at the community's excellent but expensive produce and meat market. Both Destin and Panama City have large supermarkets, and most families buy supplies on their way to Seaside. A fish market next door sells seafood — fresh and cooked — in an informal atmosphere.

There is a variety of restaurants in Seaside and nearby towns.

A wide range of accommodations is available. In addition to dozens of cottages, there are apartments on the third and fourth floors of the Dreamland Heights Hotel, an award-winning contemporary building (too contemporary for some tastes) by architect Steven Holl. These apartments have two floors, high ceilings, dramatic decor, roof terraces, and great views of the gulf. These accommodations are for adults only; children under twelve are not permitted.

The new Motor Court accommodations, behind the resort's Central Square, are the most modest and the least expensive at Seaside. What they lack in water views they make up for in price and in their accessibility to Seaside activities. These accommodations are not for the claustrophobic, but they are cleverly designed and compact, with many built-ins. In only a few hundred square feet, there is a bedroom with queen bed, kitchenette, and sitting room with TV and VCR. Furnishings and decorative touches are circa 1950: Formica tables and Naugahyde chairs, movie posters, and Art Deco memorabilia.

The honeymoon cottages, right on the beach facing the gulf, are ideal for couples. Tall and narrow, they have a bedroom and bath on the first floor and a kitchen and sitting room on the second. They are small but well designed, with Scandanavian-style fireplaces in the sitting rooms, efficient kitchens, and ceramic tile baths. Offering special honeymoon packages, these accommodations are operated like a small luxury hotel, with bathrobes, nightly turndown service and refreshments, and room service. Each evening a breakfast basket is delivered to the cottage. Both floors of the honeymoon cottages have back porches that look out over the gulf and the sand dunes. The downstairs porch behind the bedroom has a deck and a Jacuzzi for two. Heavy canvas curtains can be drawn across the screens for privacy. When it's breezy on the beach, the curtains billow out like sails.

Ruskin Place, Seaside's arts center, has some apartments above its galleries and boutiques rented by artists and shop owners. These accommodatons are in buildings that look like row houses in an Old South or New England city and overlook the promenade and gardens of the artists' colony. Apartments are rented for the long term, mostly by artists and shop owners, though one or two can usually be rented by visitors.

The oldest looking accommodations in Seaside are actually the newest: Josephine's B&B Inn. This was built in the style of a plantation home, with imposing white pillars, a crimped tin roof and widow's walk on its third floor, chimneys at either end, verandahs on the first and second floors, and a rose garden and white picket fence out front.

The floor plan is that of a traditional plantation house: a formal foyer (with grandfather clock), a front parlor on one side of the house and a dining room on the other, kitchen in the back, and a long hallway leading to a couple of back bedrooms. The dining room is an intimate restaurant; a fire crackles in the green marble fireplace on all but the warmest months.

The B&B rooms all have antique and reproduction furnishings, brass light fixtures, pine floors, and fireplaces, where most guests enjoy the brunch that's delivered to them each day. Each room has a kitchen alcove with a mircrowave, small sink, coffeemaker, half-size fridge, and small-screen television.

> The beach pavilions on the dunes have become a symbol of Seaside and the relaxed style of life it promotes. Each brick street at Seaside has its own pavilion, and recent additions have been extremely imaginative. They're particularly pleasant for drinks in the late afternoon when the sun is going down over the Gulf of Mexico.

Other accommodations under the wing of Josephine's B&B include a guest house behind the main house, with two one-bedroom suites. These are often used as honeymoon suites, and are similar to a young couple's "first apartment."

Seaside's wide sweep of beach is surely one of the most beautiful in Florida. The sand is white and fine; the dunes have gentle contours and are covered with palmetto, catbrier vine, and sea oats. At times the water turns a dark indigo near the horizon and, because the sand beneath the water is so white, a pale aquamarine on the sandbars near the shore.

Although many people at Seaside cook in their cottages, there are a number of restaurants. Basmati's restaurant serves Asian cuisine. Bud and Alley's has seafood, pasta, steak, and snacks. Shades, opposite the beach, has a popular bar and a dinner menu that includes barbecued ribs and shrimp, crab cakes, and hamburgers. Josephine's Dining Room, at the B&B, serves roast duck and lamb, grilled steaks, and chicken dishes complemented by good wines. Pickles, Dawson's Yogurt, the Silver Bucket cafe, Modica Market deli, and the Sip and Dip have takeout for sandwiches, pretzels, hot dogs, ice cream and yogurt, homemade desserts, and drinks. Catering services are available through the Silver Bucket.

Days at Seaside can be lazy or packed with activity. It's easy to start a game of volleyball on the beach behind Bud and Alley's restaurant. You can rent sailboats, catamarans, boogie boards, and "aqua trikes," and arrange for lessons in sailing and windsurfing at the Cabana Man. Large sailboats and deep-sea fishing craft can be chartered in nearby Destin. Kite flying is very popular at Seaside because of the steady breezes. The resort has three swimming pools, six tennis courts, and world-class croquet. Bicycling is a favorite pastime at Seaside, and bikes can be rented at Seaside's open-air market. And everybody at Seaside is a great walker — the best kind of exercise, because you can stop and chat with neighbors.

Those who planned Seaside have done everything possible to promote neighborliness. For example, every house at Seaside must have a white picket fence, but the fences don't join at property lines, creating walking paths between houses. The very layout of the town is friendly: clustered around a town center, Seaside has its own post office, shopping area, town hall, and a recreational area with two pools, six tennis courts, shuffleboard, and a croquet course. Cars are discouraged on the brick thoroughfares; most people bicycle or walk on the streets and oyster-shell paths. There is a sense of community here that is unusual and precious.

TALLAHASSEE

Cabot Lodge

2735 N. Monroe Street
Tallahassee, FL 32303
904-386-8880
800-223-1964 in U.S.

A chain with exceptional hospitality

General manager: Mickey Brady.
Accommodations: 160 rooms.
Rates: $56–$60. **Included:** Continental breakfast and cock-

tails. **Minimum stay:** 2 nights for football weekends. **Added:** 10% tax. **Payment:** Major credit cards; personal checks with Diners or American Express credit card. **Children:** Under 12 free in room with parent. **Smoking:** Nonsmoking rooms available. **Open:** Year-round.

Tallahassee has dozens of modern chain motels, but very few go beyond the ordinary and the boring. Cabot Lodge stands out as a rare property. It's not authentic Old Florida; construction is fairly recent, and the widow's walks on the roofs are just for show. But Cabot Lodge is very clean and neat, with chain-hotel efficiency, and the Old South hospitality is genuine.

> **Several separate buildings house the guest rooms, but there are only two floors to each, so the place seems small and innlike.**

The accommodations are standard motel rooms but are attractively decorated. Rooms have either one king-size bed or two doubles. Although there are no suites, families and couples traveling together can take connecting double rooms.

The main building, like all the guest-room units, is a plantation-style structure of yellow clapboards with green trim and white-railed balconies. Its common room sets the Cabot Lodge apart from the other places on Route 27 — this spacious room looks and feels like a living room, with comfortable wing chairs and sofas. Guests can come anytime to sit and talk with friends, enjoy the apple juice and coffee that are always available, or borrow a book from the library.

Every evening from 5:30 to 7:30, complimentary cocktails are served at the small bar in the living room. Kids get free soda, and there's popcorn for everyone, popped on an old-fashioned popper. Guests really enjoy this, and according to one member of the staff, "If people linger past 7:30, it's okay. This is the South."

Continental breakfast is laid out here, too, with fresh orange juice, croissants or some other pastry, and tea and coffee. Guests can eat in the living room or on the back porch, which runs the width of the building. The old green and white rockers and white tables and chairs give Cabot Lodge a homey feeling. The porch overlooks an oblong pool and a sunning area with lawn chairs and chaise longues.

The young staff members — often college students — are polite and accommodating. They'll turn the porch into a reception area for a wedding or family reunion, take your child over to the electronic game room while you finish your coffee in the living room, or direct you to the lodge's jogging trail by walking you all the way there. This is real southern hospitality, proffered without pretension.

Cabot Lodge is near the intersection of Route 27 and I-10, a short drive from the airport and downtown. Most people staying at Cabot Lodge are in Florida's capital city on professional or government business. The lodge caters to these busy people, but it is also appropriate for vacationing couples and families. Since 1993, there has been a second Cabot Lodge just off I-10 on Thomasville Road. Though it is a high-rise and lacks the charm of the original, it has the same high standards.

Governors Inn

209 S. Adams Street
Tallahassee, FL 32301
904-681-6855
800-342-7717

A city hotel with southern ambience and service

General manager: Charles Orr. **Accommodations:** 40 rooms and suites. **Rates:** Rooms $119, suites $149–$219; corporate and monthly rates available; packages. **Included:** Continental breakfast and cocktails. **Minimum stay:** 2 nights on some football weekends. **Added:** 10% tax; $10 for extra adult. **Payment:** Major credit cards; personal checks. **Children:** Under 12 free in room with parents. **Smoking:** Nonsmoking rooms available. **Open:** Year-round.

The Governors Inn is outstanding for service, imaginative guest rooms, sensitively restored architecture, and a location convenient to the capitol district. The inn is the achievement of Bud Chiles, the son of Florida's governor, Lawton Chiles, Bud's wife, Kitty, and some fellow visionaries. The group bought abandoned downtown property a few hundred feet from state government buildings on the lower end of Adams Street. Now referred to as Adams Street Commons, this area has since been rehabilitated as part of Tallahassee's historic district. It has cobblestone streets and charming brick and stucco buildings that house everything from boutiques to dentist's offices. The Chiles' work in opening the Governors Inn in 1984 was instrumental in the revitalization of the area.

A stucco building with awnings, the inn stands at the corner of Adams and College Park. It occupies two narrow warehouselike buildings that were 19th-century hardware stores. The interior of Governors Inn is elegant, but nonetheless retains hints of its humble warehouse origins. At the top of a winding stairway is a second-floor corridor that links the two storefronts. The original stores had very high ceilings on both the first and second floors. The architect has

There are several rooms for business meetings, conferences, and parties, including the Caucus Room, popular for small gatherings. Because the Governors Inn is close to state government buildings, conference rooms are in demand. Reserve well ahead of time, especially if the legislature is in session.

made three floors of this space, creating some very interesting loft guest rooms.

No two rooms are alike. They differ not only in their decor, but also in shape, height, the use of sky lights, and the odd angles of their ceilings. All rooms are named after a governor and have a framed drawing of him, with a biographical sketch hanging on the wall. The furnishings are either antique or good reproductions in cherry, mahogany, or oak.

Many of the guest rooms are duplexes. The most popular for businesspeople, legislators, and lobbyists are the loft suites, with at least one couch, upholstered chairs, and a desk or table or both. The bedroom is in a loft accessible by a spiral staircase. The junior suites have a small work area with a desk or table and a double bed. Even these smaller, lower-priced rooms are elegantly decorated.

The largest suite, and one of the most luxurious, is the Governor Holland. It has an armoire hiding the TV and a large sitting area. The couch opens into a bed, as do all couches in the suites. The bath is extra large, with a whirlpool tub. The Governor Holland has one of the best views, overlooking Adams Court. Other views at this city inn overlook brick buildings or a College Park street scene.

Many businesspeople like to spend time in the Florida Room, the lounge off the lobby that manages to have the atmosphere of both a British club and a southern parlor. Inn guests meet here for complimentary cocktails from 4:30 till about 8:00. In the morning, a Continental breakfast of fresh, seasonal fruit, croissants, freshly squeezed orange juice, and coffee and tea is served here on fine china and silver.

The staff at the Governors Inn try to ensure that the atmosphere is restful and gracious. Many amenities here make life easier for busy people: free valet parking, shoeshine service, complimentary morning newspaper, room service, free limousine service within the capitol district, several phone jacks in the rooms, secretarial and translation service, copiers, and a small library. Babysitting and a message center are also available.

WAKULLA SPRINGS

Wakulla Springs Lodge and Conference Center

Edward Ball Wakulla Springs
  State Park
One Springs Drive
Wakulla Springs, FL 32305
904/224-5950
Fax: 904-561-7251

> *A state park, lodge, and conference center*

Accommodations: 27 rooms. **Rates:** Rooms $60–$65, suite $85–$250. **Minimum stay:** 3 nights for package. **Added:** 10%

tax; $6 crib; $6 roll-away. **Payment:** MasterCard, Visa. **Children:** 11 and under free in room with parents. **Smoking:** Non-smoking rooms available. **Open:** Year-round.

Less than 15 miles south of Tallahassee, in the midst of pine forest and marshland, Wakulla Springs is one of the world's largest and deepest freshwater springs, with water so clear you can look down and see the bottom over a hundred feet below. The water from the spring — thousands of gallons gushing forth each second — forms the Wakulla River. The state park system operates wildlife observation and glass-bottom boat tours on the river so that visitors can observe the spectacular wildlife that has found a haven here.

Since the 1940s, public access to the springs has been controlled. No private boating or fishing is allowed, and only one area is designated for swimming. As a result, the wildlife here is allowed to thrive in its "primal density," as the state's brochure says. Primal is right: vultures brood on cypress trees, dozens of baby alligators sun themselves on the bank next to their mothers, brown snakes slither up branches overhanging the river, long-legged egrets stand stock-still waiting to catch fish, and anhingas dive underwater and emerge, then stand drying their wings on a stump in the river.

This is just during the summer, when the bird population is relatively low for the park and some of the other animals are too hot to be out. In fall and winter, the numbers of waterfowl swell, with the arrival of thousands of migratory birds, which rarely fly away when the tour boats come by.

The numbers and variety of deer, turkeys, snakes, alligators, rare snails, and jumping fish are breathtaking. They thrive in river, riverbank, and marsh, and in forests of wild magnolia, hickory, oak, and pine. Eerie cypress trees — always draped with Spanish moss — stand above the swamps and river. Nurturing it all is the spring — deep, ancient, amazingly clear.

Although Wakulla Springs has been a wildlife refuge for years, the state acquired the park in 1986, renaming it the Edward Ball Wakulla Springs State Park. Ball was a financier related by marriage to the DuPonts, who initially owned the land. In the late 1930s he developed it — or sensitively underdeveloped it — as a vacation refuge for his wealthy friends. From the beginning, it was not a sybaritic resort but a place for those who wanted a simple place to observe wildlife in a natural state.

Edward Ball built the two-story lodge in 1937. The architecture is Spanish Mission, with a red tile roof, a stucco exterior, generous archways, and, in some cases, ornate grilles over the windows. This looks just the way a lodge ought to, with a big stone fireplace, comfortable sofas and chairs, and high, beamed ceilings. These beams are intricately hand-painted with Aztec and Toltec symbols, as well as river scenes, wildflowers, waterfowl, Spanish galleons, and geometric designs. These were painted by a German immigrant who left his work unsigned. Most visitors to the lodge spend a good deal of time craning their necks to see the painted beams.

> **Swimming is popular at Wakulla Springs, with locals who come for the day as well as lodge guests. The deep river basin is clear and cold, and serves as one big swimming hole — but mainly for the ducks and alligators. There is one designated area that is safe for two-legged swimmers and has a 33-foot diving tower.**

Guests entering the lodge from the back garden come into a glass-enclosed porch that is part of an arched loggia. The ceiling here is of pecky cypress and the walls are of adobe. Small bamboo tables and chairs make the porch a good place for playing cards or talking with friends, and it can be set up for conference groups and wedding parties. The terrace overlooks the back lawn and the wide paths that slope down to the springs and swimming area.

Marble is used extensively inside. Some of it is from France and Italy, but most is from Tennessee, brought here by train in the 1930s. The beautiful stone — gray and white or pink-veined — is used on the stairs and floors everywhere, and runs halfway up the high walls.

The dining room, just off the lobby, is lent a warmer ambience by many arched windows overlooking the yard and a large bird feeder. The food served is one of the best-kept secrets of Florida: hearty, healthful, cheap, and, in some cases, very southern. Breakfast can be as large or small as you wish, with à la carte offerings and a "real southern breakfast" of ham or fried chicken, grits, biscuits, and hot coffee.

For lunch, guests can fill up on the excellent navy bean

soup or oyster stew. There are a variety of salads, fresh Apalachicola oysters, country ham, pork chops, native fish, and a good, reasonably priced steak. The waitresses are mostly local and friendly; the service is leisurely but good. Dinner adds a few fancier entrées, like frogs' legs and a seafood platter. There is also a children's menu. Desserts are rich and tempting: pecan pie, Key lime pie, strawberry short-cake. Prices are as low as you'd expect in a state park.

In the off season, Wakulla Springs is particularly popular with ornithologists and conservationists, though the conference center hosts a variety of business, church, and professional groups. There are small conference rooms in the lodge itself and a larger, separate conference area near the boat dock. Another popular room for groups is part of Edward Ball's original private quarters. With a large conference table as well as a comfortable sofa and easy chairs, it's suitable not only as a small conference room but as a parlor suite for re-unions and vacationing groups.

Adjoining the parlor/conference room are the two best guest rooms in the lodge. These rooms, which can be rented separately or together, have marble floors with Oriental rugs, huge walk-in closets, and beautiful Spanish grilles over the windows.

The other guest rooms are less spectacular but have recently been spruced up with new bedspreads and drapes. The furniture is well-worn, and some of the Oriental rugs on the marble floors are threadbare, but still good. Though the rooms are austere, they're high-ceilinged and spacious. Closets are all walk-in. The bathrooms have big, old-fashioned porcelain sinks and tubs that are long enough to stretch out in. Furnishings include antiques and serviceable wooden furniture. All rooms have heating and air conditioning. There are telephones, but no TVs or radios.

The fact that most of the rooms are spare will hardly cramp your visit. Nobody comes to Wakulla Lodge to sit in a room all day. The lobby is a favorite gathering place for visitors in cool weather. The one TV in the lodge is here, and there are magazines, games, and a checkers table.

During balmy weather in the spring and fall, everyone is outside. A charming stone path winds across the wide lawn and back garden to the spring. In winter, the big camellia bushes that line the path are in bloom. It's easy to spend an hour or two here on one of the Victorian-style white iron and wood benches, watching the birds swoop, mullets leap from the water, and hyperactive gray squirrels strew nutshells all over the path.

Miles of nature trails in the state park wind through fields and vine-entangled forests of beech, pine, hickory, live oak, maple, and wild magnolia. The soil here is not sandy like most of Florida's but a pale coppery red. Apply insect repellent liberally when walking on the nature trails or anywhere at Wakulla Springs. The birds are not the only flying creatures who thrive here.

If possible, visit Wakulla Springs in the off season or on a summer weekday. On summer weekends, the place can be mobbed with day visitors, and the boat rides lose some of their charm when there are two more boats behind you with guides broadcasting their tour spiel. Still, glass-bottom boat trips, a bargain at $4 for adults and $2 for children, are the highlight of most people's visit — but don't feed the alligators!

Wakulla Springs has a long, legend-filled history. The Indians called it the "mysteries of strange water" and often visited the springs for their healing powers. Ponce de Leon sailed up the St. Marks River to reach Wakulla in 1513, apparently certain that this was the true Fountain of Youth. On a later visit in 1521, he was attacked by Indians defending their territory and died in Cuba of his wounds, deliriously begging to return to the springs. Wakulla Springs has always had an aura of mystery and grandeur for those who came here, no matter what they were seeking. Perhaps the most striking thought for visitors skimming over the clean, crystal waters in a boat today, past vultures and long-necked herons, is that this is what the subtropical world was like before modern man changed it so drastically.

Central Florida and Disney World

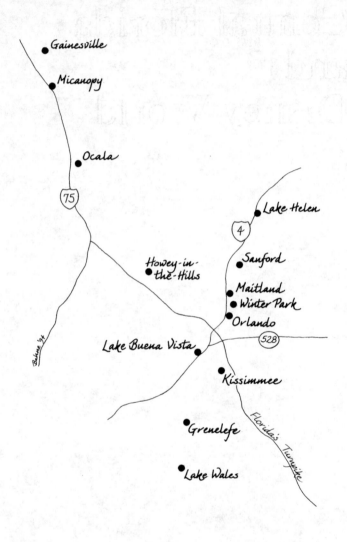

Gainesville
Magnolia Plantation, 168
Micanopy
Herlong Mansion, 196
Ocala
Seven Sisters Inn, 199
Lake Helen
Clauser's Bed and Breakfast, 188
Sanford
Higgins House, 215
Howey-in-the-Hills
Mission Inn, 174
Maitland
Thurston House, 194
Winter Park
The Fortnightly Inn, 217
Park Plaza, 219
Orlando
Courtyard at Lake Lucerne, 202
Hyatt Regency Grand Cypress, 206
Omni Orlando Hotel, 208
The Peabody Orlando, 210
Sonesta Villa Resort, 212
Wynfield Inn-Westwood, 214
Lake Buena Vista
The Dolphin and the Swan, 177
Vistana Resort, 179
The Walt Disney World Resorts, 181
Kissimmee
Wynfield Inn–Main Gate East, 176
Lake Wales
Chalet Suzanne, 190
Grenelefe
Grenelefe Resort, 171

Best B&Bs

Gainesville
  Magnolia Plantation
Lake Helen
  Clauser's B&B
Maitland
  Thurston House
Micanopy
  Herlong Mansion
Ocala
  Seven Sisters Inn
Orlando
  Courtyard at Lake Lucerne
Sanford
  Higgins House
Winter Park
  The Fortnightly Inn
  Park Plaza

Best Budget Finds

Kissimmee
  Wynfield Inn–Main Gate East
Orlando
  Wynfield Inn–Westwood

Best City Stops

Orlando
  Omni Orlando Hotel

Best Eclectic Finds

Lake Wales
  Chalet Suzanne

Best Resorts and Spas

Grenelefe
  Grenelefe
Howey-in-the-Hills
  Mission Inn
Lake Buena Vista
  The Dolphin and The Swan
  Vistana Resort
  The Walt Disney World Resort
Orlando
  Hyatt Regency Grand Cypress
  The Peabody Orlando
  Sonesta Villa Resort Orlando

Central Florida was at one time the least developed part of Florida — a fact not lost on Walt Disney when he sent his minions out to buy land. In the center of the state, the geological origins of the Florida peninsula are at their most obvious. Much of the soil is a grayish white mix of sand and limestone, excellent for growing citrus. Of course, many of the citrus groves in this agricultural region have been cut down to make way for housing developments, mobile home parks, restaurants, Disney World, and various secondary attractions. Nonetheless, it is still possible to go for a Sunday ride in the citrus-growing regions south of **Orlando** and **Lake Buena Vista** and smell the orange blossoms.

Palmettos grow in profusion in the sandy soil, with tall pine trees above. Some parts of central Florida along highways that run east and west, like Route 60, are almost desert-like, with only low plant growth. But when you add topsoil to the sand and plant flowers and trees and give them plenty of water, even these areas become lush. Orlando and all of the areas developed just south of the city have a profusion of flowering and green plants, both native and imported. The landscaping at Disney World and Sea World is particularly beautiful.

In culinary offerings, central Florida is given over to fast food, though there are gourmet restaurants north of Orlando in **Winter Park** and to the south at Chalet Suzanne in **Lake Wales,** as well as in Orlando proper. The Walt Disney World hotels, the Hyatt Grand Cypress Hotel, and other major hostelries near Disney World have good, sometimes outstanding, dining.

Northeast of Orlando is the city of **Gainesville,** the site of the University of Florida. Farther south is Florida's beautiful horse country and the historic town of **Ocala.** These two towns, as well as **Sanford** to the northeast of Orlando, have historic districts that are worth exploring. But the city most often visited in central Florida is, of course, Orlando, the site of a number of corporate headquarters, and Buena Vista, the town just south of the city that is synonymous with Disney.

Disney World is made up of the Magic Kingdom, EPCOT, and the Disney-MGM Studios. The Magic Kingdom itself has four separate "kingdoms": Fantasyland, Adventureland, Frontierland, and Tomorrowland. Fantasyland is usually the favorite of young children, while older children love the other three. However, it's not easy to predict who will like what at what age, so it's best to try to see a bit of each "land" the first day and then decide on where to go on succeeding days. Although many people who haven't visited Disney World assume that the Magic Kingdom is the place for families with small children, the Magic Kingdom is fun for all ages, including grandparents and honeymooners.

EPCOT has two entities: futuristic technology and international culture. Although EPCOT used to be thought of as the park that was most appropriate for teenagers and adults, it has become a disappointment to people of all ages. Some of the buildings at the front of the park are looking shabby and a bit absurd in their futuristic pretensions — essentially looking like tired Star Trek sets. The Land and Sea exhibits are interesting and well done, but some of the other science exhibits are lackluster. Perhaps we're all spoiled by good Nova shows on TV and hometown science museums, but EPCOT definitely needs a shot in the arm.

The Disney-MGM Studios Theme Park, on the other hand, allows itself simply to be fun and flashy. It is similar to the traditional California and Florida movie studio game parks, but with rides, performances, and shops and restaurants — many of these decorated in a glitzy, Art Deco style. Disney-MGM Studios is especially fun at night, so many tourists enter the gates in the late afternoon and stay till midnight.

There is a running debate over whether it's better to stay at a hotel on Disney property or somewhere off the grounds. This comes down to a matter of budget and taste. If you're going to Florida to relax or play tennis and plan to make Disney World a one-day side trip, it's probably better to stay in one of the excellent resorts or B&Bs nearby, far from the madding crowd. If you have small children and are traveling to Florida exclusively to see Disney World, consider staying at one of the Disney hotels or resorts on the monorail, which goes directly to the Magic Kingdom. Most of the hotels on the monorail are quite expensive, but being able to get on this futuristic conveyance with little kids every morning and back again at the end of a long day is worth the extra money for most families.

Disney accommodations need to be reserved as much as a year in advance if you're arriving during the summer or a holiday; four to six months if you're coming at a less popular time of year. This is particularly true of the three hotels on the monorail. However, cancellations do occur. When you call the Disney people at Central Reservations, even if they tell you there are no vacancies, get directions and go directly to the hotel where you want to stay at 3 P.M. on the day you want a room. You might luck out.

A few tips for enjoying Disney World: start early, bring sunscreen, and wear your most comfortable shoes. If you aren't burdened with a lot of baby bottles and paraphernalia, bring a second light pair of shoes to change into after lunch. Be certain to make dinner reservations at least 24 hours ahead, especially at EPCOT's ethnic restaurants in the World Showcase. Consider visiting the parks from mid-September to mid-December. Many locals visit during the weeks between Thanksgiving and Christmas, a good sign that this is a quiet time. If you don't have this much flexibility, try planning your vacation so that you are visiting the parks on Thursday, Friday (the lightest day of the week), or on Sunday morning. For more information, write to the Walt Disney World Central Reservations Office, P.O. Box 10100, Lake Buena Vista, FL 32830, and read and plan as much as you can before going.

Another tip: when you go through the gates at the Magic Kingdom, head left — not right, like everybody else; it makes for less crowding. At EPCOT, walk to the international exhibits in World Showcase at the back of the park first, eat lunch at one of the ethnic restaurants there, and then visit Future World at the front of the park in the afternoon when everybody else is at the international exhibits. If you're going to be visiting Disney World for an entire week, it's wise to invest in one of the paperbacks on Disney World; Birnbaum's guidebook is the most comprehensive.

GAINESVILLE

The Magnolia Plantation

309 S.E. Seventh Street
Gainesville, FL 32601
904-375-6653

A step back in time to a quieter, more gracious era

Proprietors: Cindy and Joe Montalto. **Accommodations:** 6 rooms. **Rates:** Rooms $60–$90; special rates for corporate and weekday guests; wedding packages; special rates for extended stays and reunions. **Included:** Complimentary full breakfast, beverages and home-baked snacks during the day. **Minimum stay:** 2 nights, during football weekends and some special events. **Added:** 9% tax. **Payment:** Major credit cards; traveler's checks. **Children:** Discouraged due to antique furnishings. **Smoking:** On verandahs only. **Open:** Year-round.

Innkeepers Cindy and Joe Montalto met and fell in love as students at Gainesville's University of Florida. Their Victorian B&B is the fulfillment of a long-held dream. After leaving the university and pursuing their careers, Cindy and Joe dreamed of returning to Gainesville and opening a B&B. The realization of their dream was a true labor of love — and a nearly backbreaking one — as they shoveled out debris, refinished floors, and painted the walls of the faded Victorian mansion they bought in Gainesville's historic district.

The architecture of the house, usually called French Second Empire, looks more like New Orleans than Old Florida. The mansard roof is of red and green slate tiles in the variety of shapes popular during the Victorian era: rectangular, hexagonal, square, and fish scale. Along the left side of the house is a four-story tower, and on the front and back are old-fashioned verandahs with Italianate brackets. Cindy and Joe painted the Victorian details of the clapboard structure in several different historic colors.

> **Views from the large, double-hung windows are of magnolia trees and flowers on the sides and front of the house, and in the back, of a brick-paved patio and a pond. This wonderful retreat also has two waterfalls of native limestone. A tiny arched bridge leads to a natural wood gazebo.**

The house was originally the home of Mr. and Mrs. Emmet Baird and their seven children. The Bairds had had hard times before coming to Gainesville, but Emmet opened a successful basket and crate factory there — so successful that rumors began to circulate that he had found buried treasure at Suwannee River. The tale was that an old man, just before he died, had given Mr. Baird a map to treasure buried near bluffs above the river and that Baird had found a pirate's chest of gold and jewels. The story was so compelling that after the mansion passed out of the Bairds' heirs' hands, a treasure hunter destroyed much of the front parlor fireplace looking for hidden loot.

Cindy and Joe have now replaced the fireplace in this front room, built as a gentleman's parlor. Other renovations in the parlor involved removing plywood that covered archways ornamented with Italianate plaster brackets and painstakingly refinishing the pine floors.

There is also a ladies' parlor with still another fireplace (there are nine altogether). This one was left intact, with the original faux marble design painted on the slate and a beautiful tile hearth. The parlors are furnished with an old piano and a pedal organ, wing chairs, and other period antiques. Walls are a soft ocher.

At the large oval table in the dining room, Cindy and Joe

serve imaginative breakfasts of what they call "funk food": chocolate chip pancakes, French toast stuffed with orange marmalade, honey, and cream cheese, macadamia nut French toast, piña colada muffins, waffles with whipped cream and apples, soufflés and quiches. There is always fresh fruit, juice, coffee, and tea. A complimentary glass of wine is served upon each guest's arrival.

In the back of the house is the Magnolia Plantation's only first-floor bedroom, Jasmine. It has an antique brass double bed, marbleized slate and tile fireplace, old-fashioned paddle fan, and an ensemble of family pictures on the mantel. Windows are tall and the ceiling high, as was common in Florida before the advent of air conditioning. Bath towels tied with a satin ribbon are set out for guests. In all the rooms, Cindy and Joe have worked hard "to give people an idea of what life was like" a century ago. As a result, they do not have separate modern showers, but have opted for brass shower attachments above old-fashioned tubs.

The five second-floor guest rooms are also named after flowers. Daisy and Heather are small back rooms that share a bathroom. Daisy is a soft blue and has a queen-size sleigh bed. Heather has pink walls and a white iron double bed covered with a quilt. Both these rooms have individual sinks, which makes sharing a bath easier.

Azalea has a clawfoot tub right in the room. The toilet and corner sink are in the little bathroom, a converted closet. The four-poster bed is queen-size, and the rest of the furniture is white wicker. The walls are rose and the large windows are framed by green and rose stenciling.

Gardenia is Magnolia Plantation's bridal chamber. On the pale yellow walls are wedding photographs of Montalto family members and other memorabilia. The four-poster double bed has a regular mattress topped by a thick feather bed and white lace spread. Above is a crocheted canopy. Two wing chairs stand before the lace-curtained windows. A clawfoot tub, its underside painted a deep cobalt blue, is right in the room, draped in white netting, while a porcelain sink and toilet are in a little bathroom.

Magnolia, the former master bedroom, has its original clawfoot tub, push-button toilet, and old sink. This room has an antique bedstead that accommodates a queen-size mattress. The walls are a light teal, and ruffled balloon curtains in deep rose are at the windows. The fireplace (another one!) is of heart pine, intricately carved and incised with gold.

Magnolia Plantation has been a family effort in many ways. Joe's father, a landscape architect, helped Joe build the pond and waterfalls, and his mother hunted down antique furnishings for the house. His aunt and uncle donated their German lace curtains, and Cindy's aunt gave them heirlooms that had belonged to her grandparents. Cindy's mother, who lives in a little carriage house out back, takes care of the gardens and manages the inn when the couple are away. Magnolia Plantation is truly a family home, and Cindy and Joe love sharing it with guests.

GRENELEFE

Grenelefe Resort and Conference Center

3200 State Road 546
Grenelefe, FL 33844-9732
813-422-7511
800-237-9549

A sophisticated Florida resort in citrus country

General manager: Joseph Hunter. **Accommodations:** 950 rooms. **Rates:** Rooms $85–$180, 1-bedroom villas $105–$220, 2-bedroom villas $180–$385; packages available. **Minimum stay:** 2, 3, or 5 nights with packages. **Added:** 9% tax. **Payment:** Major credit cards; personal checks. **Children:** Under 18 free in room with parents. **Smoking:** Nonsmoking rooms available. **Open:** Year-round.

Grenelefe is only 30 minutes from Disney World, but there is a country feel to this citrus-growing region, reflected in the split-rail fences and broad velvety lawns of the resort. This is a place where you can get away to play tennis or golf (and, if you're here for a convention, to work a little), but it's close enough to EPCOT and the Magic Kingdom for a day or two of Disney fun.

A large percentage of Grenelefe's business is in conventions and executive retreats. The reception center and conference center are on a rise overlooking a championship golf course. The conference center, which can accommodate up to 2,000 people, provides high-tech equipment and professional staging and lighting. Facilities include an outdoor pavilion overlooking the pool that can seat up to 600 and is often used for barbecues. The conference center is well away from the villa accommodations. This is appreciated by families and couples on vacation as well as by businesspeople who wish to have a self-contained environment without children underfoot during the day.

This is one of the best resorts in Florida for golf and tennis; it is also a great place to fish. Spring-fed Lake Marion has 6,400 square acres of fresh water, and there is a rustic tackle shop and dock. A large blue heron lives near the dock and walks the weathered pier in a deliberate way. He seems merely to tolerate resort guests and the local fishermen who take them out on the lake. Dense native forests skirt the lake, and hundreds of alligators make their home here, the babies sunning themselves on lily pads while big gators dive underneath when boats pass. Needless to say, swimming is forbidden in the lake.

For exciting landlubber activity, there is always tennis and golf. Grenelefe has 20 well-tended courts, two of grass and 11 lighted. The complex includes a 1,700-seat tennis stadium. Every year, the resort hosts adult and junior tournaments. This is a good place to watch, learn, and play the game.

Golf is just as impressive. There are three beautiful courses: the East Course, with level greens and traps to the sides; the South Course, a British design with numerous sand traps and water hazards; and the challenging West Course, which has been ranked best in Florida for several years by

Golfweek magazine. All three courses have been sculpted out of the forests, marshlands, and fields of Grenelefe.

The clustered low-rise villas overlook the fairways. Grenelefe has over 900 accommodations, with spacious kitchens, pullout couches in the living/dining rooms, double beds in all bedrooms, and decks overlooking the fairways. Kitchens come with ice makers, full refrigerators, and coffeemakers, and the living rooms have cable TVs with movie channels. All the villas are privately owned and individually decorated, and all have been recently refurbished.

The groups of villas form small communities, with shared swimming pools and recreation areas tucked into the woods. Although there is a large pool behind the conference center, most vacationers use the private ones. The property also has miniature golf, a basketball court, bicycle trails (with rental bikes available), and nature walks.

> **Even if you aren't an avid fisher, the experience of fishing here should not be missed. The locals who take guests out in their boats are an independent lot and have many colorful stories to tell.**

The abundance of herons in the resort's marshes inspired the name of the resort's premier restaurant, the Grene Heron. Apart from Chalet Suzanne in nearby Lake Wales, this is the best restaurant in the area. The menu features both Continental and traditional American dishes.

Also on the property is Camelot, a large, airy restaurant serving three meals a day, with excellent service and an imaginative menu. This casual eatery has an open feel, with lots of windows overlooking the South Golf Course and a patio. The seafood buffet is especially good. Lancelot's, a lounge, is open to the public in the evening. It serves some food during the day and has a soup and sandwich buffet from 11:30 A.M. to 2:00 P.M. for busy conventioneers and golfers in a rush to get back on the links.

Grenelefe is named after a character in *Robin Hood* and has borrowed many names from English myths and storybooks. The roads running through the woods to the villas have names like Canterbury Drive and Robyn Lane. But apart from the names, there is nothing cute about Grenelefe, and nothing glitzy either. This is a down-to-earth place for tennis, golf, and fishing, wildlife watching, fine food, and sound sleep.

HOWEY-IN-THE-HILLS

Mission Inn Golf and Tennis Resort

Highways 19 & 48
10400 County Road 48
Howey-in-the-Hills, FL 34737
904-324-3101
800-874-9053
Fax: 904-324-2636

> *A Spanish-style
> golf and tennis
> resort in
> hill country*

Manager: Bernard Vissher. **Accommodations:** 160 rooms. **Rates:** Rooms $95–$185, suites $115–$350, villas $174–$345; packages available. **Minimum stay:** 2 nights with packages. **Added:** 9% tax; $7 rollaway. **Payment:** Major credit cards; personal checks. **Children:** Under 12 free in room with parents. **Smoking:** Nonsmoking rooms available. **Open:** Year-round.

Howey-in-the-Hills is in the low, rolling hills of this citrus-growing region. To those used to the Appalachians or Rocky Mountain foothills, these "hills" will look like little rises in the landscape, but you have to remember that most of the rest of Florida is as flat as a pancake. Another stretch of the imagination is in the resort's name: there never was a mission here. The family who bought this one-time private estate with the idea of creating a resort simply wanted to design it on a Spanish mission theme.

The Mission Inn still feels like a secluded estate, though

it's only 35 minutes northwest of Walt Disney World, EPCOT, and Sea World, and about 15 minutes from the charming town of Mount Dora. But Mission Hills is very much a destination resort, with plenty to fill every day on the property itself. The 18-hole championship golf course that has been here since Mission Hill's opening is consistently rated among the top 20 in a state with over 800 of them. Recently, a second golf course was added, making a total of 36 holes. There are also tennis, shuffleboard, and volleyball courts, jogging trails, and bicycles for rent. For children there is a little playhouse with a Spanish tile roof.

> The resort is meticulously maintained, with lots of flower beds and clay pots of colorful annuals on the patios. The buildings have buff-colored stucco walls and terra cotta tile roofs. Arched walkways lead through lovely courtyards with copper and wood benches. Spanish tiles are everywhere: on the floors, in the fountains and pool, and even embedded in some of the walls.

The inn is surrounded by lakes and ponds, affording plenty of opportunity for sailing, motorboating, and fishing. Marina del Ray is the yachting center, and the inn has a 1930s yacht, *La Reina,* that you can take for a cruise down the river.

El Conquistador, the inn's elegant dining room, serves both American and Continental cuisine. Many dishes have delicious cream sauces, and the desserts are rich. El Patio is an informal alfresco eating area overlooking the golf course, with buffet tables almost spilling over with food throughout the morning and afternoon. The 19th Hole Restaurant overlooks another part of the course and is famous for its site on one of the highest points in Florida. La Hacienda, the newest restaurant at the inn, has good views as well.

Guest rooms, all of which overlook either the golf course or the tennis courts, are luxurious and beautifully appointed. Deluxe hotel rooms, one- and two-bedroom penthouse suites, and club suites are available in the center of the resort. The most secluded accommodations are the Mission Santa Cruz villas: small, luxurious homes with two or three bedrooms, a living room, kitchen, dining area, wet bar, patio, private courtyard, and garage. No two are exactly alike.

No accommodation is inexpensive at Mission Inn, but the amenities justify the price. In the villas, you can cut down on expenses by cooking some of your own meals. Holiday packages are available for all accommodations; inquire about them when calling for information.

The Mission Inn has excellent conference facilities, with some meeting rooms off the charming arched walkways. The main conference center is near the Plaza de la Fontana, a romantic spot with a tiled fountain and mission bell. The inn also has a small shopping arcade near the fountain, with a Christmas store, a clothing store, and pro shop.

KISSIMMEE

Wynfield Inn–Main Gate East

5335 U.S. Highway 192 East
Kissimmee, FL 32741-9401
407-396-2121
800-468-8374

*A budget motel
a few minutes
from Disney*

Innkeeper: Clay Theophilus. **Accommodations:** 120 rooms. **Rates:** $52–$62. **Included:** Coffee, tea, and fruit in lobby. **Minimum stay:** None. **Added:** 11% tax; $10 roll-away; cribs free. **Payment:** Major credit cards. **Children:** Under 17 free in room with parents. **Smoking:** Nonsmoking rooms available. **Open:** Year-round.

For anyone looking for reasonably priced accommodations close to Walt Disney World, this is the place to be. The Wynfield Inn is very much a family motel, with a well-designed outdoor recreational area and a friendly staff.

This is an immaculate New England–style inn of white clapboard. The lounge feels like a friend's living room, with comfortable camelback sofas. Free coffee, tea, and fruit are served in the lobby 24 hours a day.

Near the lobby lounge but sequestered from it is an electronic game room used night and day by teens and their younger brothers and sisters. Also well away from the lobby and living room are vending machines and laundry facilities.

> **The Wynfield is about 10 minutes from the main entrance to the Magic Kingdom and 15 minutes from EPCOT and Sea World. The inn provides bus transportation to these attractions for a small fee.**

The Wynfield has a large landscaped patio with a pool for adults, an adjacent wading pool for little ones, and a chickee-hut snack bar. Guests receive a 10 percent discount at the Village Inn Restaurant next door. There are plenty of restaurants at Disney World and other area attractions.

The rooms are identical, with serviceable motel furniture and carpeting. The rooms are in three-story units built around the pool, so most have views of the swimming pool and grounds. Unlike many places in the Orlando/Disney World region, the Wynfield Inn has no convention space, making for a quiet family retreat as well as substantial savings.

LAKE BUENA VISTA

The Swan

1200 EPCOT Resorts Boulevard
Lake Buena Vista, FL 32830
407-934-3000
Fax: 407-934-1399
1-800-248-SWAN
800-228-3000 (Westin)

> *A tongue-in-cheek Disney resort*

Managing director: Ron Olstad. **Accommodations:** 758 rooms and suites. **Rates:** Rooms $235–$260, suites $675–$935; packages available; $25 extra person. **Minimum stay:** 4 nights with some packages. **Added:** 10% tax. **Payment:** Major credit cards. **Children:** Under 18 free in room with parents. **Smoking:** Nonsmoking rooms available. **Open:** Year-round.

The Swan and the Dolphin (see below) are referred to as "EPCOT resorts" and are next to Disney's EPCOT resorts, the Yacht Club and the Beach Club. But the Swan and the Dolphin are owned and managed by Westin and Sheraton, respectively. Designed by eccentric architect Michael Graves, they are absurd and fantastic, quite a departure from the usual Disney hotels.

> **It's an improbable looking place, particularly to those who have come to expect everything about Disney to be picture-perfect.**

The Swan exhibits a flamboyance reminiscent of Florida's Art Deco era. Aqua waves are painted on the stucco exterior. Two massive swan statues "ride" the painted waves on top of the hotel. The swan motif is carried out everywhere inside the hotel, with swan mosaics, swan benches, swan statues, swan fountains.

Walkways lead to a recreational area and a bridge to the back of the Dolphin hotel. The hotels are linked by a canal-like waterway, which also leads to EPCOT and to the Yacht Club and Beach Club Resorts. A crescent-shaped manmade beach at the end of the waterway forms a shared playground that's landscaped with palm trees, natural grasses, and flower beds. There are three swimming pools and a jungle gym for little ones.

The Dolphin

1500 EPCOT Resorts Boulevard
Lake Buena Vista, FL 32830
407-934-4000
800/325-3535 (Sheraton)

> *Fun on a massive scale*

General manager: Bill McCreary.
Accommodations: 1,500 rooms. **Rates:** Rooms $220–$365, suites $450–$525; packages available. **Minimum stay:** 4 nights. **Added:** 10% tax. **Payment:** Major credit cards. **Chil-**

dren: Under 18 free in room with parents. **Smoking:** Non-smoking rooms available. **Open:** Year-round.

This hotel is just as much fun as the Swan, especially for small children. Everything is oversize and fantastical. The Dolphin's exterior is painted with tropical leaves on the sides and six-story dolphins at each end of the building. The fountain in back is one of the best things about the hotel: water surges over a series of aqua shells several stories high and then tumbles into a large dolphin fountain.

> **Tendrils of fake wisteria (with blossoms in several unlikely colors) climb up the green-latticed columns of the lobby.**

Public rooms at the Dolphin are designed on a massive scale. The rotunda lobby is several floors high, its canopy ceiling painted in aqua, red and ivory stripes. The rooms at both the Swan and the Dolphin have a West Indian feel. Stripes on the doors give the rooms a cabana feel. At the Dolphin, custom-made wallpaper and carpets in the hallways create a beach scene; the carpet is patterned with a boardwalk and beach towels laid out on sand.

Vistana Resort

State Road 535
P.O. Box 22051
Lake Buena Vista, FL 32830
407-239-3100
800-877-8787

> *A large resort with a feeling of community*

General managers: Raymond Gallein and Art Zimand. **Accommodations:** 800 villas **Rates:** 2-bedroom villas $225–$275. **Minimum stay:** 3 nights. **Added:** 10% tax. **Payment:** American Express, Visa. **Children:** Free in room with parents. **Smoking:** Allowed. **Open:** Year-round.

Vistana is an extremely pretty resort and a good value. Manmade streams, waterfalls, and fountains accent the rolling lawns and flower beds. Each cluster of villas has a theme based on one of the resort's landscaping features, such as the Palms, the Springs, or the Falls. Most of the villas are of stucco and stained wood. The newest, the Fountains, has Old Florida architecture: a blue and buff exterior with latticed trim and a tin roof.

The two-bedroom, two-bath villas have whirlpools in the master bathrooms, ceiling fans, TV/VCRs, screened porches, and a washer and dryer. The well-equipped kitchens have a microwave and a dishwasher — maid service includes loading and unloading it. Most villas come with a barbecue grill outside. With a pullout couch in the living room, each villa can sleep six to eight people comfortably.

> **Although Vistana caters to families, the resort is romantic enough for an anniversary celebration or a honeymoon.**

The resort has a general store for supplies (though the prices are lower at the local supermarket). If you wish, your refrigerator will be stocked before your arrival with items you request. The area has many restaurants, and Vistana competes respectably with its Flamingo Café and Zimmie's Casual Eatery and Bar.

For those who come to the resort for R&R, there are flower-bordered walkways and bridges, a massage therapist, and a sauna and steam room. Vistana's four swimming pools have bubbling-hot Jacuzzis, some secluded among grotto outcroppings. One is a lap pool; another has a water slide; and the Super Pool holds 250,000 gallons of water. For those who want electronic entertainment, there's a video game room at one of the resort's three recreation centers.

In addition to the spectacular swimming pools, there are 14 championship tennis courts, a tennis pro shop and pros to give lessons, shuffleboard, basketball, a fitness center, and a 12-station fitness course.

The staff at the recreation centers organize activities for kids, and bicycles and pool floats can be rented. For younger kids, there's a climbing structure. Kiddie pools are next to the adult pools, and children as young as four can play tennis.

Meanwhile, all of Disney World awaits just a few miles outside the security gates. Vistana has a number of packages that include admission to the Disney parks and other attractions, such as King Henry's Feast and Mardi Gras. Without a doubt, Vistana is a perfect resort for active families.

The Walt Disney World Resorts

Central Reservations
P.O. Box 10100
Lake Buena Vista, FL 32830-0100
407-WDISNEY (407-934-7639)

> *More than a dozen hotels and resorts, each with a different fantasy theme*

Accommodations: More than 10,000 rooms, suites, villas, and campsites. **Rates:** Beach Club Resort & Yacht Club Resort $205–$390, Caribbean Beach Resort $89–$119, Contemporary Resort $195–$780, Disney Vacation Club $190–$755, Disney Village Resort Villas $185–$825, Dixie Landings Resort & Port Orleans Resort $89–$121, Fort Wilderness Campsites $35–$52, Fort Wilderness Fleetwood Homes $195, Grand Floridian Beach Resort $245–$495, Polynesian Resort $195–$520; packages available. **Included:** Transportation to and from Disney attractions via monorail, bus, or boat. **Minimum stay:** With some packages. **Added:** 10% tax; $12–$15 extra person in hotels, $5 in trailers, $2 in campsites. **Payment:** Major credit cards; personal checks. **Children:** Under 18 free in room with parents. **Smoking:** Nonsmoking rooms available. **Open:** Year-round.

The Walt Disney World Resort corporation operates this mind-boggling array of accommodations. All the hotels and resorts are well planned, lavishly landscaped, very comfortable, and superlatively maintained. Smoking, nonsmoking, and handicapped-accessible rooms are available. Some hotels have concierge service, others do not. All offer free transportation to Disney attractions, some by boat or the monorail, others by bus.

The Contemporary Resort, the Polynesian Village Resort, and the Grand Floridian Beach Resort are on the monorail to the Magic Kingdom. These are good for those with small children who are in Orlando principally to see the Magic Kingdom. The ability to get on the monorail in the morning without having to drive or wait for a bus or tram can save time and anguish. These three resorts are expensive, particularly the Grand Floridian.

The Fort Wilderness Campground and the Caribbean Beach Resort, Port Orleans, and Dixie Landings are the least expensive accommodations. Maps of all the accommodation locations seem to indicate that the campground is fairly close to the Magic Kingdom and that the other three are close to EPCOT or Disney–MGM Studios. This is not the case, however, and at closing time in peak season, the wait for a bus back to these resorts can seem awfully long — another good reason to consider coming to Disney during the "value season."

Though they will not be reviewed until the next edition of *Best Places to Stay in Florida,* the Wilderness Lodge, opened in May 1994, and the less expensive Allstar Resort, opened in June 1994, are two more options.

All of the Disney resorts have an astounding list of amenities: children's playgrounds and electronic game rooms, fitness centers, jogging tracks, shopping malls, laundry rooms, swimming pools, boat and water sports rentals, marinas, manmade beaches, movies and a stage theater, restaurants, snack bars, lounges, and lots of organized activities for both the day and evening.

When planning a vacation, call or write to Walt Disney World Central Reservations several months ahead and request their "Vacation Information" booklet, which lists individual amenities, prices during high season and "value season," and special packages. It includes complete descriptions of properties and a map of Walt Disney World that allows you to see precisely where each hotel and resort is located with respect to Disney attractions. At the most popular Disney resorts, reservations should be made four months in advance, and for stays in winter and during school vacations, as much as twelve months in advance.

The Beach Club
The Yacht Club

The Beach Club Resort and the Yacht Club Resort are known as Disney's EPCOT resorts, although plenty of people staying at these accommodations go to all of the Disney attractions. A galleon-style bridge spans the lagoonlike waterway between the resorts, and a festive launch travels between them and EPCOT, as well as to the Swan and Dolphin resorts. Trolleys also run every few minutes between the Beach Club and the Yacht Club and EPCOT.

The Beach Club and the Yacht Club are similar architecturally and are sometimes thought of as one resort: the clapboards simply change width and color as you move from one to the other. They are more subdued than some of the other Disney fantasy resorts — they look like New England waterfront hotels. Both have turrets and other Victorian touches. The outdoor areas are planted extensively with hundreds of azaleas, begonias, and other annuals and perennials. The two resorts share a meandering grotto swimming pool with some shallow parts that are perfect for children under six. Here and there are waterfalls and tropical plantings. The fantasy pool includes a windmill and a large shipwreck, where kids can climb up to a water slide. Adults can retire to a little "island" for a soak in a Jacuzzi. The atmosphere is active here but not frenetic.

> **For all its polish, there's a relaxed, informal feel at the Beach Club, particularly on the beach and in the restaurants. The two resorts share restaurants and lounges, and many people walk from one resort to the other on the flower-bordered pathways that are well lit at night.**

The Beach Club's atmosphere and decor are similar to the Yacht Club's, but without the nautical theme. Generally, the Beach Club is a little more understated. Outside are pretty flower beds and a Queen Anne–style porte cochere. Inside, the lobby invites sitting, with lots of wicker and tassled Victorian sofas and polished floors. Lobby windows overlook the gardens and water, and large urns of fresh flowers accent the marble floors. The male staff are dressed in striped blazers and bow ties; female staff wear blue sailor outfits or long dresses with leg-o'-mutton sleeves. Everyone — waiters, housekeepers, lobby clerks — makes a point of saying hello and seems genuinely welcoming.

At the Yacht Club, wrought iron and brass street lamps grace the brick and wooden walkways. White wooden rockers on the porch await guests who want to rest and rock a spell. First-floor hallways open out onto interior brick courtyards with white garden benches cushioned in blue gingham. Guest rooms are decorated in fresh colors and have roomy baths. At the very least, rooms look out over the beautifully planted gardens; some have both garden and water views. A few have red and white awnings over the windows. The lobby has several sitting areas furnished with cherry or mahogony reproduction pieces and leather chairs. The staff work in period costumes, with band marches or classical music playing in the background.

The Caribbean Beach Resort

With 2,112 guest rooms, the Caribbean Beach Resort is the fifth-largest hotel complex in the United States. Located on 200 acres not far from EPCOT Center and the Disney–MGM Studios, the resort surrounds a 42-acre lake and is made up of five "villages," each named after a Caribbean island. This is indeed a fantasy resort and includes a large pool patio with Disney rocks and the "ruins" of a fort rising above the lagoon-like swimming pool. The Caribbean-style rooms are extremely comfortable, and the prices are fair.

The Contemporary Resort

The Contemporary Resort is like something out of Tomorrowland. The monorail comes right into the middle of this A-shaped hotel, making it the most accessible to the Magic Kingdom. It is an enormous place, crammed with more kids than a Y camp in August. There are 1,050 rooms in the tower, along with two garden wings, four restaurants, two snack bars, two lounges, six shops, a marina, a manmade beach, a health club, two swimming pools, and convention space.

Some people find the Contemporary overwhelmingly large, but the accessibility to the monorail, which come through the hotel every few minutes, makes this hotel very desirable for families with young children.

Disney Vacation Club

The concept behind the Disney Vacation Club is similar to a time-share, but with fewer disadvantages. A couple (or couples) or a family buys a membership, usually one week a year. But it doesn't have to be the same week each year, so there's more flexibility with the plan than there is with a time-share. At press time, not all the shares in the resort were sold, so short-term rentals are still possible.

The units are like spacious apartments with full kitchens, so families can save a little cash by cooking some meals. The Key West–style buildings have tin roofs, fish-scale shingle and clapboard siding in pastels and tropical colors, gingerbread detailing on the verandahs, and louvered shutters at the windows. The buildings are in clusters, and there seems to be an effort to create a sense of community.

Disney Village Resort

The Disney Village Resort, near Disney Village Marketplace, is a huge complex of villas that provide visitors with a number of choices. Most have kitchens, or at least refrigerators and sinks, and are good for large or extended families. Though these accommodations are more expensive than some Disney hotel rooms, they can be more economical in the long run if you plan on preparing most of your own meals.

There are five kinds of villas in the Village Resort: one- and two-bedrooms near the village clubhouse; club suites with either a bed/sitting area or a larger duplex floor plan with a living room with foldout couch downstairs and two queen-size beds upstairs; spacious two-bedroom "fairway" villas with some handicapped-accessible units and views of the Lake Buena Vista Golf Course; conical, three-bedroom "treehouse" villas on concrete supports, with decks overlooking the pines or the golf course; and "grand vista" suites, super-deluxe homes with well-stocked refrigerators. Bicycles and a golf cart are included in vista suite rates.

These accommodations may seem off the beaten path, but after a couple of days at Fantasyland with ten zillion kids, the seclusion is nice. Walt Disney World shuttle buses make frequent stops throughout the grounds, taking guests to the Disney attractions and the village clubhouse.

Fort Wilderness Campground

Fort Wilderness Campground is the least expensive of Disney lodgings. Located between the Magic Kingdom and EPCOT on 740 acres of woodlands, the campground has laundries, showers, and a full schedule of activities that are fun for children and adults. There are two options here: fully equipped campsites and Fleetwood trailers. Each of the 817 campsites has a 110-volt electric outlet, a picnic table, and a barbecue a short distance from the portable bathrooms. The trailers have fully equipped galley kitchens, spacious, attractive bathrooms, color TVs, linens, and housekeeping service — you're not exactly roughing it here.

The Grand Floridian

The Disney people have outdone themselves at the Grand Floridian. This is a fairly authentic replica of a turn-of-the-century grand hotel, with white clapboards, stained glass, latticework, lacy railings on the verandahs, and turrets, towers, and dormers rising from the red shingled roof. The grounds have brick terraces and are planted with masses of flowers. Bellhops at the front portico wear knickers and white golf sweaters. Inside are huge planters of flowers, furniture custom-made in Spain, original artwork, intricately crafted moldings, and an Oriental bird cage with peach-colored parakeets especially bred for the Grand Floridian.

The lobby is five stories high, with stained glass domes and massive chandeliers. The guest rooms are just as impressive. Despite the high rates, the Grand Floridian usually has a 100 percent occupancy rate. This is partly due, no doubt, to the articulate and courteous staff. All personnel at the reservation desks have bachelor's or master's degrees and are multilingual. The resort has two lounges and five excellent restaurants, with food well complemented by decor.

High tea is served every afternoon in the Edwardian-style Garden View Lounge.

Polynesian Village

For those who want a fantasy South Seas experience, there's the Polynesian Village. Its jungle motif is carried out spectacularly in the lobby, where an atrium planted with ferns, banana trees, orchids, gardenias, and other tropical plants rises three stories high; waterfalls splash in the midst of it all. Service is friendly and courteous, and the atmosphere is low-key.

The clean, attractive accommodations are in 11 low-rise lodges, each named for a Pacific island. There are 855 rooms, but because they're spread out, guests don't feel crowded. Many rooms have a balcony or patio and views of the Seven Seas Lagoons or the swimming pools and gardens. With two queen-size beds and a daybed, the rooms can easily accommodate five. The jungle theme extends throughout the complex, in the decor of the rooms and in the lagoons, rustic bridges, and tiki figures that accent the grounds. As at all the Disney resorts, there are lots of activities for adults and children.

Port Orleans Resort

Port Orleans and its sister resort, Dixie Landings, are located between EPCOT and Disney Village. They are both quite large but designed so well they are not overwhelming. Port Orleans has a New Orleans and Mardi Gras theme, with buildings that have French Quarter–style grillework, verandahs, and mansard roofs. A landscaped promenade leads to a fantasy lagoon pool and play area. The arched tail of a blue and pink plastic serpent forms a bridge over the pool, which has a couple of shallow areas for small children.

Accommodations are in three-story stucco "townhouses." Black iron gates and ivy-covered brick posts at the entrance to the townhouse groupings create a feeling of authenticity — it's not all plastic. The entire resort is landscaped beautifully with many willow trees, magnolias, and curly-bark birches growing along the banks of a manmade lagoon. Guests can take a launch along the waterway to neighboring Dixie Landings, or stroll along the curving path beside the water.

Dixie Landings Resort

The guest accommodations at Dixie Landings are straight out of a Southern movie set: large, white mansions with pillars, verandahs, and green louvered shutters. The imposing brick entryways that lead to the mansions include fountains, gazebos, black wrought-iron archways, lanterns, and formal flower beds. Inside are the standard features of Disney resorts: a choice of rooms with king beds or two doubles; fresh, clean bathrooms; and small touches that extend the fantasy theme.

At the reception center and play area, the theme is a combination of Tom Sawyer and King Cotton. Guests check in at a brass- and marble-appointed "bank," have a drink at the "cotton coop," dine at the "Colonel's cotton mill," and then stroll outside along a manmade riverfront to rustic-timbered Dixie Landing. Recreation is out on "Ol' Man Island" and includes the Muddy Rivers Bar, a "fishin' hole," a playground, and a swimming pool that meanders around a big oak tree and worn-looking wooden steps that lead to a water slide. It's a combination of Frontierland and Adventureland — very appealing for school-age kids who might find the pink-plastic fantasy of the Port Orleans pool a little childish. Guests can use the facilities of both resorts and can also take a free riverboat ride to Pleasure Island entertainments and the Disney Marketplace shops that are just across Buena Vista Lagoon.

LAKE HELEN

Clauser's Bed and Breakfast

201 E. Kicklighter Road
Lake Helen, FL 32744
904-228-0310

> *One of the few real country B&Bs in Florida*

Innkeepers: Tom and Marge Clauser. **Accommodations:** 2 rooms. **Rates:** $60–$80. **Included:** Full breakfast. **Minimum stay:** 2 nights during special events. **Added:** 10% tax. **Payment:** Discover, MasterCard, Visa; personal checks. **Smoking:** Prohibited. **Open:** Year-round.

Lake Helen and the surrounding towns are so small they are little more than attractive crossroads set in the midst of woods and thickets. Yet there's easy access to I-4; the Atlantic is less than a half hour away; and Disney World is only about an hour from here. This is country, with easy access to civilization — if you really want it. You might not want it, once you get to Clauser's Bed and Breakfast and put in some time rocking on the front porch.

The Clausers are interesting, well-educated people; "homebody" is written all over them. Tom is a clever workman, and

Marge is a great cook and craftswoman. Together they have created a restful country retreat. Built in the 1880s and listed in the Register of Historic Places, this farmhouse is a fine example of Old Florida architecture, with tin roof, white clapboards, slate-blue shutters, and a gingerbread-trimmed porch that wraps around three sides of the house. The Clausers have added flower beds and flowering shrubs to the rich growth of pines, live oaks, and magnolias already on the property.

> **Many people staying at Clauser's Bed and Breakfast take off for a state park or go antiquing in the area for the afternoon. But it's just as pleasurable to stick around "home." Guests can play croquet, horseshoes, badminton, or volleyball in the yard, or relax on the porch swing and rockers on the front verandah.**

The big kitchen and screened back porch overlook a screened-in Victorian gazebo with a cupola and a tin roof to match the house. Inside is a hot tub with scented water. Behind the house are new accommodations in a converted carriage house.

On the second floor in the main house are a reading room and two guest rooms with private baths. Lilac and Lace has lilac walls and many touches of lace. Just off the room is a verandah, a wonderful place to sit when the tall magnolia tree in the front yard is in bloom. Peaches and Cream, decorated in soft peach shades, has a private bath across the hall.

The upstairs sitting room for guests has stenciled walls, gauzy curtains, and a sofa. There's a television set and a lending library of Tom and Marge's books. In what was once the room's closet, Marge has her handmade gifts for sale, such as dolls and stuffed animals and heart-shaped pillows.

Downstairs are the kitchen, family room, and a front parlor that is used as a breakfast room. Breakfast is everything one would expect from a great country cook: homemade apple muffins or coffee cake, homemade jams and jellies, French toast or bacon and eggs, bananas and cream, strawberries, and fresh-ground coffee.

The front parlor, called the Tea Room, serves as a gathering spot for both guests and local people. Marge serves tea sandwiches and homemade pastries with traditional English and

American teas and soft drinks. The array of treats, such as scones and lemon tarts, shows off Marge's love of cooking and her flair for the authentic. The Tea Room is available for group functions and has become popular in the area for small wedding receptions and showers.

On the back of the house, the wraparound porch has been enclosed and is furnished with cushioned bamboo chairs. Though this is part of the downstairs family quarters, the Clausers share it with guests. Here, Marge serves fruit and beverages and homemade goodies in the afternoon and a glass of sherry in the evening. For a true country B&B experience, Clauser's is hard to beat.

LAKE WALES

Chalet Suzanne

3800 Chalet Suzanne Drive
(U.S. Highway 27 and County
 Road 17A)
Lake Wales, FL 33853
813-676-6011

*A famous
gourmet getaway
and fantasyland*

Owners: Carl and Vita Hinshaw.
Accommodations: 30 rooms. **Rates:** $125–$185; special packages available. **Included:** Full breakfast. **Minimum stay:** None. **Added:** 9% tax; $12 extra person; $10 for crib. **Payment:** Major credit cards; personal checks. **Children:** Wel-

come. **Pets:** Allowed in designated rooms; $20 extra. **Smoking:** Allowed. **Open:** Year-round.

Chalet Suzanne was Fantasyland before Walt Disney ever thought of it: Tyrolean towers and terraces and turrets, rambling in all directions and painted in ice cream and sherbet colors. You might wonder if the people who've recommended it in guidebooks have lost their minds. This crazy place? With masonry cracks on half the buildings and broken bricks in the walkways? Well, yes, especially if you love good food.

Chalet Suzanne has been owned and run as a country inn and restaurant by the same family since its creation 50 years ago. Its founder was a brilliant eccentric named Bertha Hinshaw. She and her husband were both from wealthy families and Bertha spent a good deal of her early married life collecting antiques, artwork, and fine china and silver in Europe. The Hinshaws lost almost all their money in the 1929 crash, and took to raising chickens and rabbits on the central Florida land that is now the Chalet Suzanne.

Then Mr. Hinshaw died, leaving Bertha with two children and no apparent means of support. However, Bertha had two assets she could capitalize on: the land she was living on, and an imaginative genius in the kitchen. She opened a restaurant that would soon become famous and a "Tyrolean village" to house her overnight guests. After a fire in the 1940s, she rebuilt part of the village out of chicken coops, stables, and rabbit hutches. Much of the time, she slept on a narrow bed in her tiny office.

Over the years, Bertha added more guest rooms to her storybook inn and more dining rooms to the restaurant. As she became more prosperous, she began collecting in Europe again, and Chalet Suzanne became a mix of Austrian, Italian, French, Spanish, and Oriental architecture and decor.

Bertha's son Carl and his wife, Vita, now run the inn and oversee the restaurant with their grown children. Carl is in charge of the kitchen and the cannery that cans and mails out the famous Chalet soups and sauces, while Vita runs the dining room and oversees the wait staff.

Each dining room is a different size and shape and distinctively decorated. The Swiss dining room has stained glass windows along one wall, a paneled ceiling, and a tiled mantel. The English dining room has wooden beams and intricate stenciling on the ceiling. The main dining room is octagonal, with a mix of interesting hanging lamps over the tables and a view of Lake Suzanne. All of the rooms in the restuarant have eclectic combinations of antique chairs and wood or tile-topped tables, which are set with lace tablecloths, fine silver, and unmatched china. The place settings include unusual soup bowls made by a Yugoslavian couple who have a studio on the chalet property.

> Anyone who wants to can design and make a commemorative tile. The autographed tiles are added to the border of the rose-garden wall. Some have been made by celebrities, but most were done by honeymooning couples.

The meals at Chalet Suzanne are outstanding but extremely expensive. Most visitors opt for a room-and-meal package to soften the blow. Dinner begins with a chalet specialty, a cinnamon-broiled half grapefruit with a succulent chicken liver in its center. Next there might be romaine soup, with mushrooms, spinach, chopped onions, and carrots. Entrées include lump crab with herb butter, broiled shad roe, filet mignon, shrimp curry, London chop grill, lobster Newburg, and chicken Suzanne — probably the most famous of the chalet specialties. Every part of the meal is slowly, carefully prepared.

After the meal, every guest is served a crêpe Suzanne. This and perhaps a liqueur from the Hinshaw's wine cellar finish off a meal nicely. Other desserts include cherries Romanoff, brandied fruit, and Gâteau Christina, a creation of the Hinshaws' daughter, Tina, that consists of thin layers of almond meringue and semisweet chocolate.

For breakfast, popular selections are the chalet's egg dishes and silver-dollar pancakes with a warm berry sauce. Lunch, which also begins with grapefruit and soup romaine, is lighter fare such as salads and ham, as well as a delectable lobster thermidor and chicken Suzanne. Children's menus are available at all three meals. Off-season packages include breakfast and dinner.

Each accommodation, like the dining rooms, is different. The first-floor Lakeview Room is one of the nicest, decorated in shades of blue. The Banana Room, of course, is decorated in yellow. The Balcony Suite, popular with honeymooners, has a big, round bed surrounded by a gauzy drape suspended from the ceiling. The room includes a balcony dining nook overlooking one of the dining rooms. The pistachio green Tower Room has a balcony overlooking the lake. All guest rooms have private bathrooms.

Little effort has been put into upgrading the rooms, and unfortunately, the defects are not of the charming sort that can be excused by "the patina of time." Some of the colors in the rooms are garish, and shag carpeting that was stained and worn five years ago is still on the floor. Many people come out here to eat at the spectacular restaurant, and some of them stay the night, but they don't come for the luxury accommodations.

The exterior of the accommodations and the grounds are still beautifully cared for, however. Bertha Hinshaw's creative use of the tile she collected from all over the world is one of the most impressive things about Chalet Suzanne. On the exteriors of some of the buildings, she had brightly colored Spanish and Italian tiles embedded in the stucco. In the bathrooms, she used a variety of European and domestic tiles. Those used in the deep Roman tub might be dark green, while the rest of the bathroom might be tiled in yellow and blue, with broken pieces used along with whole pieces.

This is a place for people who like to stroll. The accommodations, the gift shop, the cannery, and the ceramic studio are connected by charming brick paths, many of which were laid by Carl Hinshaw as a boy. The cracks and unevenness that have occurred over the years add to the charm. One pathway leads to the chalet's lovely rose garden, a favorite of honeymooners.

The garden is near the Chalet's 2,450-foot lighted airstrip (both Carl and his son are pilots), so, if you happen to have a private plane, just call ahead for clearance. The airstrip is about the only thing on the property that brings you back to the 20th century. There is a storybook feeling everywhere at Chalet Suzanne. To stay here is to eat like a king and sleep like a princess.

MAITLAND

Thurston House

851 Lake Avenue
Maitland, FL 32751
407-539-1911

*A carefully
restored Victorian
overlooking a lake*

Innkeeper: Carole Ballard. **Accommodations:** 4 rooms. **Rates:** $70–$80. **Included:** Continental breakfast; wine and snacks. **Minimum stay:** None. **Added:** 10% tax. **Payment:** Personal checks; Visa, MasterCard. **Children:** 12 and older welcome. **Smoking:** Outside only. **Open:** Year-round.

Innkeeper Carole Ballard moved with her husband from Massachusetts to Florida with the hope of finding a historic house in central Florida that she could make into a B&B. This is not easy here, where so many old houses were demolished decades ago. But she found a beautiful example of Queen Anne Victorian architecture in the Thurston House and did an exemplary job of bringing it back to its original beauty.

   The building had been standing empty for some time and, fortunately, no disfiguring "modernizations" had been made. There was, however, a good deal of paint on every surface in the house. It took Carole six months to strip the accumulation from the cypress and pine woodwork. She also stripped and polished the brass drawer pulls and fixtures in the house that, amazingly, were intact. The result of Carole's hard work is extremely gratifying for anyone who loves the grace and detail of fine old houses.

The risers and treads of the heart pine staircase have an unusual swirled grain. Carole points out that a plainer grain was used on the risers past the landing, out of sight of visitors in the parlor. A stained and leaded glass window casts muted shadows of green and gold on the staircase.

The four bedrooms are named after the families who lived in the house. Thurston, the smallest, is in the back of the house. It has a four-poster double bed and sponged yellow walls. The old fireplace bricks have also been sponge-painted, a tech-

> **The yard and gardens at Thurston House have tall old palms, 20-foot-high camellias, and a hundred-year-plus camphor tree that is so broad Carol has planted flowers in its flat center.**

nique that many New Englanders used and that Carole revived in all four rooms.

The other three bedrooms are named after the families who lived here in the present century. The O'Hare has a queen-size bed with pillow slips embroidered by Carole's grandmother. Furnishings are good reproductions or antiques.

The Hirsch Room has a four-poster double bed with a hand-crocheted canopy. The walls and fireplace are sponged blue. The bathroom has the original clawfoot tub with a brass shower head above. Like all of the rooms at Thurston House, the Hirsch has a desk and telephone. This room also has a sleep sofa and a highboy to make up for its little closet.

The Cubbedges were the most recent family to live in the house. Their namesake room is decorated in shades of green, with a queen-size bed and a handmade quilt. Although Carol decorates with restraint, and there are none of the fussy, "country" knick-knacks that clutter some Victorian B&Bs, she does have some special touches. One of these is her practice of leaving bath towels on the bed, tied into a little "package" with ribbon.

Downstairs are more natural wood floors and comfortable furnishings. The back parlor has a pine and tile fireplace and a sofa and chairs. Here guests can enjoy a glass of wine in the afternoon, read or chat, or watch television.

The dining room is dominated by a built-in cabinet of cypress, where a generous Continental breakfast is served each morning. A typical breakfast might be French toast, fresh fruit and juices, carrot muffins, and dry cereal. Guests who wish to may finish the meal with tea or coffee in the sitting room, on one of the screened-in porches, or outside on the old-fashioned bench sheltered by a trellis of bougainvillea.

The grounds overlook a peaceful lake, with wild grasses and reeds growing along its edges. There is fishing but no swimming here, and there is boating nearby. Guests can also play horseshoes or croquet on the lawn. Carol and Joe have an herb and vegetable garden out back, and they have lovingly brought back mature plants and trees that were languishing before their arrival. Although Thurston House is only 20 minutes north of Orlando and about 40 minutes from Disney World, there is a country feeling to the place. Joe and Carol have a little more than one acre of land and the property backs onto a wooded area, creating still more privacy.

MICANOPY

The Herlong Mansion

Cholokka Boulevard
Micanopy, FL 32667
904-466-3322

A white-columned mansion in a quiet antebellum town

Owner: Sonny Howard. **Accommodations:** 7 rooms; 3 suites, 1 cottage. **Rates:** Rooms $75–$120, suites $110–$160; rates reduced on weeknights; special group discounts on request. **Included:** Full breakfast on weekends; Continental during week. **Minimum stay:** None. **Added:** 9% tax; $5 roll-away; $10 extra person in room. **Payment:** Master-Card, Visa; personal checks. **Children:** Welcome. **Smoking:** Only on verandah. **Open:** Year-round.

Anyone visiting Gainesville or Ocala should make a point of driving to nearby Micanopy. It's the clichéd "little town that time forgot." Micanopy is reputed in these parts to be the oldest town in Florida after St. Augustine. It feels even older, perhaps because it's never been a large center of commerce.

> **The Herlong Mansion hosts many weddings and receptions. The wide verandah lends itself to bands playing and garlands draped over the white balustrades. The brides must feel like Scarlett O'Hara at Tara.**

There is a peace and an unchanging feel about this town that's extraordinary. Spanish moss drapes the big old oak and pecan trees that form a canopy above the main street, Cholokka Boulevard, on which there are an ancient cemetery and a park with a gazebo. Picturesque brick and wood frame stores line the street. No doubt these were once groceries and feed and grain stores; they are now mostly antique and craft shops. Dominating the boulevard — and the town — is the Herlong Mansion.

It is truly a southern mansion. The house that was originally on the site was a simple two-story farmhouse with a detached kitchen, built in 1845. Between 1909 and 1913, the Herlongs, who made their fortune in timber and citrus, built a brick Greek Revival structure around the farmhouse with Corinthian columns and first- and second-story verandahs. The house has ten fireplaces and leaded glass windows that reach nearly to the ceilings. The finest lumber went into paneled wainscoting and hardwood floors.

But like so many homes of this era, the mansion was neglected. In the mid-1980s, Kim and Simone Evans, a couple from the Orlando area who had worked at a Disney hotel, bought the Herlong. With hundreds of hours of labor and more than 150 gallons of paint stripper, they gave the house newfound glory.

The front parlor was perhaps their greatest achievement,

its Mission-style wainscoting and mahogany-inlaid oak floor now revealed in all their beauty. The Evanses added fine appointments to create a Victorian parlor that befits the Herlong's stature: brocade swags above lacy sheers at the long windows, leather-topped end tables, a brocade sofa and wing chairs, and a Chinese rug. They ran the Herlong Mansion successfully for several years and then handed it over to the present owner, Sonny Howard, a former insurance executive.

Sonny Howard is making the Herlong his own. He has spruced up the yard and added some beautiful new rooms on the third floor of the mansion with the help of his daughter, who is an architect. Though he says he's no great chef, he remodeled the Herlong's kitchen and presents quite a good breakfast — full on weekends, Continental during the week.

Each guest room is individually decorated. The Pink Room has white wicker furniture and a pastel dhurrie. The bathroom has an old sink and clawfoot tub but a new tile floor. The Pine Room has cypress woodwork and a maple floor. Its modern bath has a deep red Oriental rug. The pleasant Blue Room still has the wavy old glass window panes. It's furnished with old rockers and a small Chinese rug.

The Herlong Suite has a canopied mahogony bed; a big brick and oak fireplace lends the room an imposing air. The sitting room has diamond-paned leaded windows and a sofa. In this suite, its original tile floor intact, is the first indoor bathroom in Micanopy.

At the end of the wide upstairs hallway is a door leading to the second-floor verandah, which Mrs. Herlong used as a sleeping porch. Now it is a lovely spot to sit and sip a glass of wine or iced tea while surveying the quiet street below.

On the third floor are six large rooms built in 1993. All are beautifully decorated and furnished, but the Governor's Suite and Inez's Suite are especially nice. The Governor's Suite has its original leaded glass windows, and the queen bed is ensconced in an antique faux-grained bedstead. Inez's Suite is even more impressive, with a brass queen bed and a Jacuzzi in addition to a separate tiled bathroom. Appointments include elaborate sconces flanking the leaded glass windows that can be dimmed during a soak in the big Jacuzzi.

Amber's Suite, on the first floor, is no larger than the other original bedrooms but is impressive largely because of the adjoining bathroom. Originally Mr. Herlong's office, it has a big whirlpool tub and a gas-log fireplace with an old wood mantel. A dark wood Victorian dressing table, heavy drapes, a chair upholstered in needlepoint, and an old-fashioned porcelain sink complete the picture. The bedroom has a wood bedstead carved with tropical leaves and flowers.

One of the Herlong Mansion's newest accommodations is the Cottage, an original building that was essentially a utility shed until Sonny renovated it. The room has a queen-size bed, parquet floor, new tile bath, and a kitchenette. Gnarled old trees shelter the little cottage.

OCALA

Seven Sisters Inn

820 S. E. Fort King Street
Ocala, FL 32671
904-867-1170

> *The B&B standard for graciousness and beauty*

Owners: Bonnie Morehardt Oden and Ken Oden. **Accommodations:** 7 rooms and suites. **Rates:** $85–$125; packages available; special discounts. **Included:** Full breakfast. **Minimum stay:** With some packages. **Added:** 6% tax. **Payment:** American Express, MasterCard, Visa; personal checks. **Children:** Under 14 not allowed. **Smoking:** Only on the porch. **Open:** Year-round.

Built in 1888 and opened as a B&B in 1985 after an extensive renovation, this Queen Anne Victorian is considered by many critics to be Florida's finest historic B&B. Much of the credit goes to Ken and Bonnie Oden, the young couple who own and operate the Seven Sisters Inn. Bonnie and Ken have expanded the space devoted to guests by opening up a beautiful new dining room and slowly redecorating bedrooms.

The Odens cater to businesspeople as well as B&B enthusiasts and tourists. Their first-floor guest room is especially good for corporate travelers, with a laptop computer hook-up as well as a sturdy desk. The Seven Sisters Inn also hosts those who canoe in the nearby Ocala National Forest and sets up murder mystery weekends for groups, office Christmas parties, business retreats, special candlelit dinners, and weddings. Despite the range of activities, the Odens are also considerate of their B&B guests, limiting most special events to weeknights only.

Among the wonders that overnight guests enjoy is a gourmet breakfast. A choice of fruit juices is followed by strawberries and cream, muffins or sweet bread. The entrée might be blueberry or peach and cheese French toast. The several-course meal is served elegantly, on fine china, crystal, and silver. Usually, it is also leisurely, but business travelers who need to eat early and quickly are always accommodated.

The breakfast room/dining room, decorated by Bonnie, has a French country feel. Walls are painted a soft yellow, with designer fabric draping the nearly floor-to-ceiling windows. The view from the table is of the Victorian house next door and a large oak tree. After breakfast, guests can retire to the upstairs club room or see the sights in Ocala or nearby Silver Springs. Some guests simply go back to their rooms, which are almost too pretty to leave.

The first owner of this B&B did indeed have seven sisters. Each guest room was named after a sister and decorated according to that sister's taste. The result has been impressive, with awards from magazines and organizations across the country, including a Best Restoration Project in Florida award given by the state Historic Preservation Society.

Perhaps the most frequently photographed of the seven rooms is Sylvia's, also the largest. Four big windows form a lacy backdrop for the elaborately dressed king-size bed. The pale pink walls contrast with the dark wood of the fireplace and the fluted woodwork around the windows. Another special room is called Lottie's Loft, a large attic room with sloped ceilings and dormer windows that bring in a surprising amount of sunshine. The big space almost seems like three rooms, with a bed and cozy sitting area arranged under the eaves. The color scheme is green and sparkling white with wicker and pine furniture and white linens and lace. The other rooms are just as delicately fashioned into perfect pictures of good taste and comfort.

The furnishings in all the rooms are period antiques, wicker, or reproduction French country pieces that have been painted to match the room. The armoires are particularly beautiful, some hand-painted and some with inlaid and burled woods and oval mirrors. There are plenty of special touches: Dresden plates, lacy pillows, grapevine wreaths, a wood goose atop an armoire, rose-papered hatboxes, or a quilt thrown over a banister.

Guests share a second-floor club room, which also has been decorated with exquisite detail. A brass and wood ceiling fan swirls above a sofa upholstered in black watch plaid and green leather club chairs. In winter, a fire crackles in the tile and wood fireplace. As everywhere, beautiful appointments enhance the theme: leatherbound volumes of the classics, an intricately carved chess set on a polished side table, brass reading lamps, a leaded crystal vase holding red flowers, a richly patterned Oriental rug before the fireplace.

> **Ocala is known as an unspoiled Florida town; it is out of the way yet bustling with a life of its own. The town is in the center of Florida horse country, and there are plenty of horse farms to visit. This is beautiful, peaceful country, with sweeping, grassy hillsides and acres of thick woods.**

The exterior of the house is just as perfect, with a manicured lawn and a broad walkway to the front steps and wraparound porch. In the center of the walkway is a circle of bright flowers. Surrounding the house are beds of impatiens and other colorful flowers, and baskets and pots of more flowers adorn the balustraded porch. The wood clapboards are painted a soft ivory, accented with blue-gray trim. On one side of the house is a Queen Anne–style turret; in the center on the second floor is a small railed porch tucked between two windows.

The Seven Sisters Inn is in Ocala's Historic District. There are many other examples of turn-of-the-century architecture in the neighborhood, which makes it fun to stroll through for history and architecture buffs. The only jarring note is the modern apartment building directly across the street.

In 1990, Seven Sisters was judged one of the 12 best inns in North America. Under the care of Bonnie and Ken Oden, the place should continue to garner awards. It has become famous not simply because it is beautifully decorated and furnished, but also because of the way things are done. The fine cotton sheets are freshly ironed, and talc is scattered between them. Breakfast and special dinners are served on china and silver. These are details that truly take one back to another era.

ORLANDO

Courtyard at Lake Lucerne

211 N. Lucerne Circle East
Orlando, FL 32801
407-648-5188
800-444-5289

> *An oasis in downtown Orlando*

Owners: Charles and Sam Meiner and Paula Bowers. **Accommodations:** 6 rooms, 4 suites, 12 1-bedroom apartments. **Rates:** Rooms $65–$85, suites $100–$150, apartments $85–$150. **Included:** Continental breakfast and complimentary wine. **Minimum stay:** None. **Added:** 10%

tax. **Payment:** Major credit cards; personal checks. **Children:** Allowed, with supervision. **Smoking:** Nonsmoking rooms in the Norment-Parry. **Open:** Year-round.

Orlando was once a sleepy southern town of turn-of-the-century mansions, wood-frame family homes, and low-slung bungalows. Ladies and gentlemen sat in wicker rockers on their grand porticoes or modest porches, fanning themselves and gazing out at the lakes and ponds that fringed their quiet neighborhoods. Today, the casual visitor to this overdeveloped metropolis might see this as a "once upon a time" story, but that's not quite the case. At the Courtyard at Lake Lucerne, the southern grace and hospitality of old Orlando survive. The Courtyard comprises three inns: the Norment-Parry Inn, the I. W. Phillips House, and the Wellborn.

The front verandah of the Norment-Parry, the first B&B of the three to open, sets the mood. With gingerbread detailing on the pillars and white wicker furniture, it overlooks Lake Lucerne and the Orlando skyline. Unfortunately, an exit ramp from the expressway obstructs some of the lake view. Still, the lake is beautiful, and so are the rooms at the inn.

The Norment-Parry Inn is the oldest house in the city and looks the part, with an exterior of buff-colored clapboard siding, white trim, and slate-blue shutters. In its history, which stretches over a hundred years, this inn has been the home of a judge (Norment) and a tax collector (Parry), a rooming house, a Salvation Army dormitory, and a halfway house. Several years ago it was bought by a local attorney, Charles Meiner, who gathered antiques for it on trips to England.

Meiner asked several area interior designers to take a room or suite and decorate it in a distinctive style, using the Victorian furnishings of his collection. Most rooms, in fact, are named after their designers. The first-floor Crawford has a blue and white bedroom and a large sitting room with two daybeds. Because of the antiques, families with young children are not encouraged at the Norment-Parry, though older children are welcome.

The Honeymoon Suite has a bathroom big enough to accommodate a couple of curved-back antique chairs, as well as an old clawfoot tub and a modern shower. The small Gena Ellis Suite is perhaps the cleverest in the house. Since it had no bathroom and no space nearby to build one, the decorator simply created one right in the bedroom, separating it with a change from bedroom carpeting to white ceramic tile.

All of the rooms are furnished with Meiner's antiques and have deep-pile carpeting, vases of fresh flowers, and no TVs (except for the Crawford and Clippinger suites). The colors, furnishings, and fabrics in the rooms are baroque and sensual — guests revel in the Victorian plushness.

> **By purchasing the Norment-Parry's neighbor, the Wellborn, and then moving the Phillips House behind the Norment-Parry, Meiner created a space of several hundred square feet that he could transform into a peaceful garden.**

The I. W. Phillips was an old beach house that Meiner had moved a few hundred feet behind the Norment-Parry several years ago. He set about transforming it into an elegant hostelry, adding French doors leading out to verandahs on both the first and second floors and sparing no expense in materials, fixtures, or craftsmanship. He installed stained glass windows that he had saved for years and had the oak floors, staircases, and woodwork refinished. As with the Norment-Parry Inn, Meiner furnished the house with his own English and American antiques. The result is wonderful.

The Honeymoon Suite at the I. W. Phillips House is spacious and elegant, with pink and ivory curtains at the large windows, a settee upholstered in rose satin, a large Victorian wardrobe, and a queen bed. Two sets of French doors open onto a porch overlooking the brick courtyard. All of the bathrooms in the Phillips House are posh, and the Honeymoon Suite's is perhaps *la prima* of the posh: it has a deep Roman tub with a stained glass window above, a shower, a modern toilet and bidet, a sink and vanity in the dressing room, and another sink in the bathroom proper.

The other rooms are decorated lushly with rich satins and brocades on the sofas and easy chairs, marble-topped tables, wardrobes of burled wood, and solid bedsteads. Suites have generous sitting areas and private verandahs. The mood is turn-of-the-century ease and elegance.

At the Wellborn, on the other hand, Meiner and his decorators let their imaginations go wild, giving it a real sense of fun. Originally a small, genteel apartment building, the Wellborn is one of Orlando's best examples of Art Deco architecture — it has both sharp and curved lines, a metal balustrade, and corner windows. Inside, there are 13 one-bedroom apartments, each with a small bedroom and bathroom, a living and dining area, and a small but well-equipped kitchen. The decor is classic 1950s, with a zebra-striped couch in one suite, black polka-dot chairs in another, and whimsical treasures from Thailand in yet another. The room colors are red and black, black and white, banana, or off-white. Some of the wall sconces and a few pieces of furniture are originals.

The best room at the Wellborn is the Honeymoon Suite. It has a bathroom big enough to live in, with a wall of glass bricks above the double whirlpool bath and mirrors on all four walls. The suite is elegant and eclectic, with a gorgeous rose and green Chinese rug and a 1930s Japanese safe inlaid with mother-of-pearl that serves as a night table.

The bathrooms and kitchens in all the Wellborn apartments are freshly tiled and painted. Artwork is generally along the lines of posters of Fred Astaire and Ginger Rogers. The rooms are airy and sunny, most with corner windows in the living rooms that have narrow venetian blinds. There is a variety of bed sizes to choose from: doubles, twins, queens, and some kings. Many of the apartments have pullout sofas in the living rooms; the largest suites can fit a family comfortably. Front rooms overlook the Orlando skyline, Lake Lucerne, and, unfortunately, the highway. Back rooms face the courtyard fountain and gardens, and first-floor suites have paths to the courtyard.

The courtyard itself is one of the best reasons for staying here. There are curving brick pathways, flower beds of azaleas and impatiens, magnolias, palm and banana trees, plaster urns of subtropical flowers, and English park benches. Water splashes soothingly in the fountain. It is no wonder that dozens of weddings and receptions are held here.

The Courtyard at Lake Lucerne was recently named one of the top ten inns in Florida, and Meiner and his staff do all they can to maintain their enviable reputation. Upon arrival, all guests are offered a glass of sherry or a cup of tea and are given a complimentary bottle of French wine. Also complimentary is the generous Continental breakfast, served in the large drawing room of the Phillips House. Breakfast includes bagels or English muffins with whipped strawberry cream, a fresh fruit compote, orange juice, and coffee or tea. Guests may eat breakfast leisurely in the drawing room, out on the porch, or on one of the garden benches by the fountain.

The Norment-Parry does not have a swimming pool or

recreational activities for guests, but all of Orlando — including Church Street Station and the Historic District — is right at the doorstep. There are also some lovely residential brick streets near Lucerne Circle that are ideal for a stroll. A number of side streets off Delaney end at quiet Lake Avenue, which curves around a small lake — home to ducks and other wildlife. These streets, with their gracious homes and huge oak trees dripping with Spanish moss, offer lovely reminders of old Orlando.

Hyatt Regency Grand Cypress

One Grand Cypress Boulevard
Orlando, FL 32836
407-239-1234
800-233-1234

> *A grand destination resort close to Disney*

General manager: Jack Hardy. **Accommodations:** 750 rooms, 72 suites, 48 villas. **Rates:** Rooms $185–$380, suites $600–$850; ask for current villa rate; packages available. **Minimum stay:** Depending on season. **Added:** 10% tax; cribs free. **Payment:** Major credit cards. **Children:** Under 18 free in room with parents. **Smoking:** Nonsmoking. **Open:** Year-round.

The Grand Cypress is not only close to Disney World, it's also one of the most exciting resorts in Florida. Outdoors, the recreation area is the centerpiece. Huge swimming pools with grottoes, waterfalls, and lush greenery are all the rage now in Florida, and the Grand Cypress's vies with the best of them. Guests walk out the back door to landscaped grounds and a rope and wood slatted bridge across part of the pool. The area is a little overdone with statuary, but kids and adults love this aquatic playground. The pool twists around outcroppings of volcanic rock and palms, several waterfalls, and an 80-foot water slide.

At one end of the lobby is an exquisitely carved Chinese jade ship in a museum case — a great draw for wide-eyed children. Elsewhere are other works of Oriental art and mammoth vases of birds-of-paradise and orchids.

Just beyond the pool is 21-acre Lake Windsong. On the walkway that runs along the lake are bicycles for rent, some with infant carriers, which reflects the family atmosphere here. The lake has a pretty beach and a small marina with sailboats, canoes, and paddleboats for guests. Adjacent are the tennis courts and racquetball and shuffleboard courts. There's also a fitness center and several miles of jogging trails. Golf is at the Grand Cypress Golf Club, with a 45-hole course designed by Jack Nicklaus. There's a pitch-and-putt course to practice on as well. The Grand Cypress Equestrian Center offers expert instruction in both western and English riding. There's also a day-care center and a children's program.

Each of the resort's four restaurants appeals to a different palate and pocketbook. Hemingway's, at the end of a covered walkway on the grotto of the huge pool, has a Key West decor and specializes in seafood. Children love the location, and the menu appeals to the whole family. Cascades is the Grand Cypress's main dining room. It is quite dramatic, with a floor-to-ceiling mermaid wall fountain and views of the lush grounds outside. Cascades serves Italian, American, and Oriental food and has outdoor and indoor service. The Palm Café is casual, serving pizza, salads, and sandwiches for lunch and a traditional menu for breakfast and dinner.

More formal is the elegant La Coquina, with nouvelle cuisine in a small dining room overlooking a lagoon. The Sunday champagne brunch may be the best in Florida: a huge buffet is spread out in the spotless kitchen. The first time through, guests choose from dozens of different salads, breads, cheeses, and whipped butter spreads; the second time they choose from a variety of delicious brunch entrées; finally, they create their own grand finale with a tart, Key lime pie, fresh fruit, cheesecake, or chocolate torte. Ladies receive a lavender rose upon leaving.

Accommodations are comfortable, with pretty decor and Hyatt's standard amenities. The best rooms, particularly for conventioneers, are the executive-style Regency Club suites and deluxe rooms. Services include a concierge, a club lounge stocked with magazines, Continental breakfast and evening cocktails in the club, daily newspaper delivery, secretarial services, and an extra dollop of luxury in the room itself.

The Grand Cypress is a great place to stroll and sit and people-watch. The lobby is one of the most impressive in any hotel in the region, if perhaps a little overdone. Guests walk into a tropical garden, with large palm trees growing in beds set in the tile floor and a profusion of philodendrons cascading from atrium planters several floors above. Here and there are large pieces of driftwood planted with exotic tropical greenery and small pieces of statuary. Orchids sprout from the trunks of the palm trees, colorful parrots jabber from their cages, and an improbable little brook runs through it all.

Omni Orlando Hotel at Centroplex

400 W. Livingston Street
Orlando, FL 32801
407-THE-OMNI
Fax: 407-648-5414
Reservations:
Omni Reservations
800-THE-OMNI

A high-style hotel with high-tech business services

General manager: John Meunier. **Accommodations:** 309 rooms and suites. **Rates:** Rooms $89–$154, Omni Club rooms $144–$184; packages available. **Minimum stay:** With some packages. **Added:** 10% tax. **Payment:** Major credit cards. **Children:** Under 18 free in room with parents. **Smoking:** Nonsmoking rooms available. **Open:** Year-round.

The Omni Orlando Hotel is a modern city hotel in every way. Just off I-4, it has over 5,000 square feet of meeting space, including a large ballroom on the mezzanine floor and seven individual meeting rooms. Business services include access to a professional audiovisual service and the assistance of a well-trained convention staff. The Omni adjoins Orlando's Expo Centre, which has additional meeting and exhibit space totaling 86,000 square feet.

If you're planning a convention or meeting in Orlando and want to be right in the city, this is the place.

In addition to banquet facilities, the hotel has a good Italian restaurant, Petrones, as well as the Livingston Street Café, serving three meals a day, and the Ozone Lounge, just off the lobby. In downtown Orlando, there are a number of restaurants and casual cafés in the Church Street Exchange, a shopping, dining, and entertainment complex near the old Church Street depot.

Although the Omni is primarily considered a hotel for businesspeople, many conventioneers bring their families, who enjoy day trips to Walt Disney World, Epcot, and Sea World — all only about 30 minutes away. Across the street from the hotel is the Bob Carr Performing Arts Center, and next door is Orlando's Centroplex, a sports complex that offers a range of activities including lighted tennis courts. Centroplex facilities are available to all Omni guests. The hotel also has a deck with a swimming pool and large whirlpool.

Guest rooms at the Omni are both businesslike and luxurious, with desks and chairs of dark polished wood and modern tile baths. Unfortunately, the views are not always beautiful. This is, after all, a city hotel, and one of the adjoining neighborhoods is a bit dilapidated. But if you request a room on a top floor, you can see cityscapes and perhaps one of Orlando's lakes. The top two floors have the added advantage of being Club floors, offering concierge services and various perks.

After work or sightseeing, the nicest place to unwind in the hotel is the Lobby Lounge, where tea, cocktails, and snacks are served. Above, an atrium lets the sun shine in brilliantly. Decor is Art Nouveau, with lots of dark wood furnishings that are influenced in style by Japanese restraint and fluidity. The sunken lounge has a number of small groups of chairs and sofas, and plants and flowers spill out of built-in planters. Soft music from the highly polished grand piano accompanies evening cocktails.

Peabody Orlando

9801 International Drive
Orlando, FL 32819
407-352-4000
800-732-2639 or 800-PEABODY

A luxury hotel with easy access to the convention center

General manager: Allan C. Villa-verde. **Accommodations:** 891 rooms and suites. **Rates:** Rooms $190–$230, suites $395–$925; packages available. **Minimum stay:** With some packages. **Added:** 11% tax. **Payment:** Major credit cards. **Children:** Under 18 free in room with parents. **Smoking:** Nonsmoking rooms available. **Open:** Year-round.

In an area full of hotels and motels, the Peabody, with its stucco and glass exterior, looks like nothing special at first glance. But the spectacular entrance, with tropical plantings and the sound of rushing water from a pair of massive stone and tile fountains, will change your mind.

Inside is more rushing water from fountains in the lobby and lounge areas. In the Mallard Lounge, several ducks spend their days paddling in the fountain. At 11:00 every morning, yards of red carpet are laid out for the mallards to walk across to their lounge domain for a day of quacking, preening, and swimming. At 5:00 in the evening, they waddle back across the lobby to be returned to their nighttime home. This may sound bizarre, but at the Peabody it's just part of the fun.

In addition to being fun, the hotel is also quite elegant. There is a feeling of tropical richness throughout the public rooms. Everywhere there are lovely arrangements of orchids and other exotic flowers, interesting art and pottery, marble floors and deep-pile carpeting, beautifully furnished sitting areas, and enormous stucco baskets of flowers and palms.

There are 54,000 square feet of meeting and banquet space here. If that's not enough, across the street is the 350,000-square-foot Orlando/Orange County Convention Center, the largest meeting facility in central Florida. The Peabody offers good deals for conventions and other functions, particularly during the off-season.

The food at Peabody's several restaurants is uniformly good. Capriccio serves northern Italian cuisine in an elegant atmosphere, while Dux provides nouvelle American

> **Next door to the athletic club is a "children's hotel" where kids can stay while parents work out, dine, or go sightseeing. The colorful room is set up like a nursery school and staffed by professionals. Children seem happy to stay here for hours.**

in an intimate one. The B-Line Diner, a 1950s-style diner and deli, is open 24 hours. The atrium Lobby Bar and the Mallard Lounge serve drinks, coffee, and pastries.

There's plenty of recreation available to work off culinary indulgence. The Peabody has four tennis courts lit for night play, an outdoor whirlpool, a heated double Olympic-size pool, and a large children's pool. All of these are found on a rooftop recreational floor, with the street noise four stories below — lush plantings all around add to the sense of isolation. The athletic club inside has 15 Nautilus stations, as well as a sauna, a steam room, a whirlpool, and rooms for facials and massages.

Sooner or later, even conventioneers spend time at EPCOT, MGM-Disney, or Disney World, and the Peabody has transportation to and from all of them. After several hours of walking through the theme parks, it's pleasant to come back to the guest rooms here. The duplex presidential suites are the best accommodations, but the standard accommodations are far from shabby: designer spreads and drapes, thick carpeting, comfortable easy chairs, remote control TV, turndown service, and the morning paper delivered to your door. The modern baths have a hair dryer and mini-TVs, which kids love.

Sonesta Villa Resort Orlando

10000 Turkey Lake Road
Orlando, FL 32819
407-352-8051
407-345-0000
800-424-0708
800-766-3782 (Sonesta
   Reservations)

> *A lakeside villa
> resort with plenty
> of water sports*

General manager: Hugh Barrett. **Accommodations:** 369 villas. **Rates:** 1-bedroom single-level villas $95–$140, 1-bedroom bi-level villas $110–$165, 2-bedroom villas $180–$260; packages available. **Minimum stay:** With some packages. **Added:** 10% tax. **Payment:** Major credit cards; personal checks. **Children:** Free in room with parents. **Smoking:** Nonsmoking rooms available upon request. **Open:** Year-round.

The Sonesta is one of the nicest places to stay in the Orlando area for families tired of the crowded hotels closer to Walt Disney World. It's also an excellent convention and conference hotel. The complex has 369 one- and two-bedroom villas with fully equipped kitchenettes, living/dining rooms, separate bedrooms, and daily maid service. There are patios on the first floors and balconies on the upper floors. The villas are clustered so guests don't feel overwhelmed, with each cluster grouped around a whirlpool spa. There's almost a clubby feel to the villa groupings.

The older villas have recently been redecorated with cushiony carpets and pretty drapes and spreads. The two-bedroom villas are spacious and are ideal for those who will be in the area for a week and want some room to spread out. One bedroom is on the first floor along with a kitchen and dining and living room area. At the summit of a curved stairway is a loft bedroom. The first-floor bedrooms have outside entrances, so older kids can run outside when parents upstairs are still sleeping, or parents can stay up late downstairs without waking the kids in the loft.

The one-bedroom two-level villas also have a loft bedroom and are just as beautifully decorated. With a pullout couch in the sitting area, these accommodations are spacious enough for a family

> **There's a high level of service here, with a personal service manager on duty to help you rent tennis equipment or a car, hire a babysitter, or give you information on how to get to the many nearby attractions. Sea World is just five minutes away, and Disney World is about 15 minutes down the road.**

of four. This is where you can save money and still feel you are living a life of luxury. When you telephone for reservations, ask the clerk where to buy groceries on your way in so you can save by making breakfast, sandwiches, and snacks. The kitchens also make life easier for families traveling with babies whose bottles need refrigeration.

The best value at the Sonesta is the single-level one-bedroom villa. These villas have all the amenities of the higher-priced accommodations, but no stairs to deal with.

When you're ready to treat yourself to dinner out, the Sonesta has the pretty Greenhouse restaurant, which also serves breakfast and lunch. The informal Terrace Café, overlooking the pool and grounds, serves great sandwiches and fresh fruits. For a special dessert or afternoon ice cream cone, kids love the Scoops ice cream shop next to the pool. Both children and parents enjoy the Cabana Pool Bar and Grill, where barbecued hamburgers and hot dogs and cool drinks are available all day. In the evening, there's the Terrace Lounge for exotic cocktails, snacks, and live entertainment.

A tremendous range of activities is available on the Sonesta's 300 acres overlooking Sand Lake. There's a small beach at the lake and a pier running out to a dock where you can rent

Jet Skis and various boats. Water skiing and Jet Skiing lessons are also available — the staff will help you with whatever water sport you're interested in. Many types of waterfowl can be seen fishing and preening here; it's fun to watch.

You'll also find a free-form swimming pool, a jogging path, health club, sauna, game room, and shuffleboard, as well as lighted tennis courts, a volleyball court, and bicycle rentals. For young children, there's a wooden jungle gym and a play area in an attractively planted setting. Throughout the property, the landscaping is beautiful and well maintained.

For those mixing business with pleasure, the Sonesta is ideal. The crush of conventioneers that is common at some Orlando hotels is not a worry here: there are plenty of corporate conferences held at the Sonesta, but they are carried out quietly. The hotel uses the impressive Oleander Ballroom for large groups and has seven smaller function rooms overlooking Sand Lake. Businesspeople can get plenty of work done while their families enjoy the pool and the lake.

Wynfield Inn–Westwood

6263 Westwood Boulevard
Orlando, FL 32821
407-345-8000

A well-managed family motel with easy access to Disney

Innkeeper: Beth Arnold. **Accommodations:** 300 rooms. **Rates:** $52–$62. **Minimum stay:** None. **Added:** 11% tax; $10 roll-away; cribs free. **Payment:** Major credit cards. **Children:** Under 17 free in room with parents. **Smoking:** Nonsmoking rooms available. **Open:** Year-round.

The Wynfield Inn–Westwood is near Wet 'n' Wild on International Drive, Walt Disney World, and several other attractions in the region, so there's lots to see within easy driving distance. It is much like the Wynfield Inn–Main Gate East (see listing under Kissimmee) — the same pleasant lobby with 24-hour snacks, the same decor and furnishings, and the same friendly service. The only difference is that the Wynfield Inn–Westwood has more rooms and a bigger pool. This Wynfield is farther from Disney's Magic Kingdom but closer to Sea World.

SANFORD

The Higgins House

420 South Oak Avenue
Sanford, FL 32771
407-324-9238

A Victorian B&B in a historic town 20 minutes from Orlando

Innkeepers: Walter and Roberta Padgett. **Accommodations:** 3 rooms and 1 cottage. **Rates:** Rooms $75–$85, cottage $100–$125. **Included:** Continental breakfast; afternoon wine and cheese. **Minimum stay:** None. **Added:** 10% tax. **Payment:** Major credit cards; personal checks. **Children:** Welcome in cottage; under 12 not allowed in main house. **Smoking:** Outside only. **Open:** Year-round.

The Higgins House was built in 1894 by James Cochrane Higgins, a superintendent for the railroad in Sanford who raised 13 children here. At the time, Sanford was probably more important than sleepy little Orlando. Incorporated in 1877, the town was named after a pioneer citrus farmer who grew 140 kinds of citrus and various other tropical fruits from Africa and South America. Sanford is still the county seat of Seminole County and, in recent years, there has been an effort to promote it as a historic place. Old brick and embossed concrete buildings line lakeside streets and walkways, some of which are paved in brick. Lake Monroe feeds the St. Johns River, which wends its way east to the city of Jacksonville.

Oak Avenue runs from downtown up to the Cultural Arts Center and Centennial Park, a large square of lawn and trees with a gazebo where several weddings have taken place. Across from the park is the Higgins House, a beautifully preserved example of Queen Anne architecture — a rarity in central Florida. The house is painted a rich blue. White planters of ferns and flowers hang from the spindle-railed porch. On the second floor above the porch is a tiny gabled verandah, with more hanging planters and a window box of bright flowers.

> **The Padgetts make their own beer, called Cochran after James Cochran Higgins, and enjoy sharing it with guests in the bar.**

Inside are heart pine floors, paddle fans, natural woodwork, spacious common rooms, and Victorian-era bedrooms. All the rooms have queen-size beds. The Queen Anne is on the first floor and is decorated in rose and blue. The private bath has a clawfoot tub with an underside of deep rose.

Upstairs are the pink and white Wicker Room and the Victorian Room, with lace curtains and Victoriana touches. These share a bathroom and are ideal for a family. Also upstairs is a small gift shop and the little verandah that is perched above the front door. Innkeepers Walter and Bertie lived in each of the rooms as they finished them so that they could see for themselves what the noise level was and what little things needed fixing.

The three guest rooms are not really appropriate for small children, so Bertie and Walter bought a cottage next door to provide for families and for those who wish to rent by the week or month. This two-bedroom, two-bath accommodation is one of a small group of privately owned clapboard cottages. The Padgetts' is painted a pale yellow and has a master bedroom with private bath and a smaller bedroom with a bathroom off the living room. The house has a small porch and a well-equipped galley kitchen. A roll-away bed lets the cottage accommodate a family of five.

The health-conscious breakfast includes seasonal fruit, granola, yogurt, juice, fresh-baked muffins, homemade jams and jellies, tea, and coffee. The formal dining room is rather unusual, the walls covered with gathered rose fabric. In the back of the house is an informal sitting room and bar with a comfortable sofa and big TV.

Throughout Higgins House, large windows provide views of the lawn and flower beds and mature trees outside. Behind the house is the Padgetts' prize garden. Steps lead from the back porch to a bi-level deck and hot tub. Beyond is a landscaped area and raised beds of beautifully tended herbs, vegetables, and flowers. Mandavia vines, with trumpet-shaped, deep pink flowers, climb along the wooden fence and latticework trellises. On the side of the house is another smaller, crescent-shaped deck and a curving brick path that leads to more flower beds.

The front porch, with its swings and hanging planters, is another favorite spot for guests. Historic Sanford, the lake, and the marina are a short walk away. Nearby are fishing, sailing, and canoeing. Sanford is known as a cultural and recreatonal area and the Padgetts are planning future events that will contribute, such as a wine-tasting party in November, Christmas festivities, and cultural activities in conjunction with the Arts Center.

WINTER PARK

The Fortnightly Inn

377 E. Fairbanks Avenue
Winter Park, FL 32789-4422
407-645-4440

> *A well-restored house handy to Rollins College*

Innkeepers: Frank and Judi Daley. **Accommodations:** 3 rooms and 2 suites. **Rates:** Rooms $75–$85, suites $85–$95. **Included:** Full breakfast; sherry; bicycles. **Minimum stay:** During some special events. **Added:** 10% tax. **Payment:** Major credit cards; personal checks. **Children:** Not encouraged; no infants or small children. **Smoking:** Only on exterior porches. **Open:** Year-round.

With Rollins College and a mixed population of older people and young professionals, Winter Park has long needed a good B&B where people can stay while visiting friends or relatives. Now it finally has one. The Fortnightly Inn is on the residential end of Fairbanks Avenue, which leads to Winter Park's gracious downtown area, Rollins College, and the park. The Fortnightly Inn is an easy walk into town, past large, well-kept homes and small businesses.

Set back a bit from the street, the Fortnightly Inn is painted a soft, rosy beige. Nicely landscaped with some big old trees, pretty flower beds, and pots of flowers on the porch, the house looks like the kind of comfortable place F. Scott and Zelda Fitzgerald might have lived in. Built in 1922, the house has some lovely features,

> Downstairs are the common rooms, a large sitting room and adjoining dining room. Here folks may sit and talk all evening, play the piano, or have a good read.

which the Daleys have accentuated. There are a great many windows in the house, some with the original wavy glass, kept sparkling clean. The Daleys have made the most of the sunshine that filters into the downstairs windows by having pretty lace curtains on their bottom half while keeping the paned windows above free of any treatment.

The Daleys have five bedrooms, straightforwardly numbered. They're of different sizes and shapes, and each is decorated distinctively. Except for a few good reproductions, all the furnishings are antiques. The upstairs rooms feature a carved walnut bed, a mahogany sleigh bed, two antique iron beds, and a rice bed. One is a queen bed, the others are full-size. Soft paint and provincial wallpaper complement the antiques. Handmade quilts and lacy white pillows add homey touches.

Many of the private baths adjoining the rooms, though remodeled, have clawfoot bathtubs. All rooms come equipped with alarm clocks and flashlights, and guests can request a television. Most of the rooms are spacious and have sitting areas with settees or wicker chairs. The two suites have sunny enclosed porches.

An honor fridge on the back porch is stocked with soft drinks, juices, and plenty of ice. There's complimentary sherry in all the guest rooms. The Daleys do not live in the house, but a staff member is on hand from 8:00 A.M. until 9:00 P.M., and guests are asked to turn out the lights in the common rooms before they go to bed. Though guests can sit in the common rooms as late as they wish, quiet is appreciated after 10 P.M.

Guests staying in suites may have breakfast on their sun porch, but most guests eat in the formal dining room. Breakfast varies from day to day and is always a gourmet feast, with dishes like quiche tarts, shirred or coddled eggs, French toast, country-style ham biscuits, muffins, hot apple oatmeal, fresh fruit, juices, and hot coffee and tea. The morning repast is served on antique china and silver, with fresh flowers in the center of the polished dining room table. A cordial, professional staff prepares and serves the meal and will answer any questions guests may have about how to spend their day.

Park Plaza

307 Park Avenue
Winter Park, FL 32789
305-647-1072
800-228-7220
Fax: 407-647-4081

*An Old Florida
oasis overlooking
the town park*

Manager: Sandra Spang. **Accommodations:** 16 rooms, 11 suites. **Rates:** Rooms $80–$125, suites $150–$175; weekly and monthly rates available; special discounts. **Included:** Continental breakfast. **Minimum stay:** None. **Added:** 10% tax. **Payment:** Major credit cards. **Children:** Ages 5 to 10 free in room with parents; under 5 not permitted. **Smoking:** Nonsmoking rooms available. **Open:** Year-round.

The sophisticated enclave of Winter Park, northeast of Orlando, is a haven from the crowds and traffic of Orlando and Disney World, overlooking the wonderful park from which the town derives its name. The Park Plaza is a small place, with old-fashioned polished mahogany paneling. It feels like the Florida of the 1920s.

The guest rooms can be reached by elevator or up one flight of stairs. Rooms all have natural or painted wicker furniture, brass beds, Oriental rugs, plants, and ceiling fans. Some are fairly small; others have a sitting area and a large alcove for the bed. The clean and refurbished private baths are as homey and individual as the rooms. Travelers used to pastels and lots of windows may find the rooms a bit dark, but it's authentic Old Florida. One of the best of the suites is 212, which has a king bed and a sitting room furnished in white wicker. Suite 214, with a queen and a twin bed, is good for those traveling with a child.

Most of the guest rooms have French doors onto a balcony reminiscent of New Orleans's French Quarter, with a wrought-iron railing and an awning above. Dozens of flowers and ferns are in pots on the wood floor of the balcony; tendrils of flowers and vines spill through the railings to the streets below.

> Orlando has expanded so much that Winter Park almost seems like a section of it, making the Park Plaza an even better location for people who are doing business in the city.
> But both Winter Park and the Park Plaza are really worlds apart from the hectic pace of Orlando.

The best balcony views are from rooms on New England Avenue, overlooking the park. Rooms on the other side of the hallway make up for a slightly less desirable location by being a bit larger. The balcony is not deep, but there is plenty of room for white wicker chairs and small round tables, each of which holds a flower pot. Continental breakfast is part of the room rate and can be served in your room or on your little wedge of balcony. Breakfast alfresco is always a high point of a stay at the Plaza Hotel. Only leafy plants screen each individual section of the balcony outside guest rooms, allowing guests to get to know their neighbors if they wish.

The Park Plaza is a good choice for travelers who don't want to drive. The Amtrak station is a walk away, and the Orlando airport is only a 20-minute cab ride. Winter Park is a real town, a rarity in Florida. Park Avenue itself is an upscale shopping area. There are many restaurants here, among the best of which is the Park Plaza Gardens, next to the hotel. While it is no longer run by the owners of the hotel, hotel guests still have many meals here. The restaurant has a garden feeling, with a brick floor, green pillars, lots of potted plants and trees, and a glass roof. Tables are set with pink and white linens and white china. The ice cream parlor chairs fit right in. There is a European sophistication to this well-managed restaurant, and the Continental cuisine has won many awards. The Sunday brunch is particularly good.

The
Southeast Coast

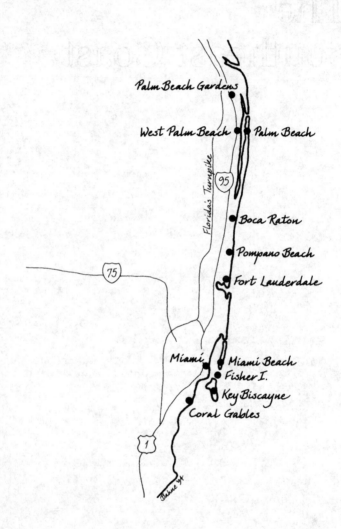

Aventura (North Miami)
The Spa at Turnberry Isle Yacht and Country Club, 229
Boca Raton
Boca Raton Resort & Country Club, 232
Coral Gables
The Biltmore Hotel, 235
Hotel Place St. Michel, 237
Omni Colonnade Hotel, 239
Ft. Lauderdale
Bonaventure Resort & Spa, 244
Ft Lauderdale Marriott Hotel & Marina, 246
Lago Mar, 248
Marriott's Harbor Beach Resort, 250
Riverside Hotel, 252
Key Biscayne
Sonesta Beach Hotel, 254
Miami
Doral Saturnia International Spa Resort, 256
Hyatt Regency Miami, 264
Hotel Inter-Continental Miami, 262
Fisher Island, 241
Mayfair House, 266
Grand Bay Hotel, 260
Miami Beach
The Alexander Hotel, 268
Art Deco Hotels (The Cavalier), 270
The Betsy Ross Hotel, 272
Colony Hotel, 274
Essex House Hotel, 275
Palm Beach
Brazilian Court, 277
The Breakers, 278
The Chesterfield, 281
Four Seasons Ocean Grand, 282
Palm Beach Historic Inn, 284
Ritz-Carlton, 284
Palm Beach Gardens
PGA National Resort, 288
Pompano Beach
Palm-Aire Spa Resort and Country Club, 289
West Palm Beach
Palm Beach Polo and Country Club, 291

Best B&Bs

Palm Beach
Palm Beach Historic Inn

Best Beachside Accommodations

Miami Beach
The Alexander
Palm Beach
The Breakers
Fort Lauderdale
Lago Mar Resort
Marriott's Harbor Beach Hotel
Palm Beach
Four Seasons Ocean Grand
Ritz-Carlton, Palm Beach

Best City Stops

Coral Gables
Omni Colonnade Hotel
Miami
Grand Bay Hotel
Hotel Inter-continental Miami
Hyatt Regency Miami
Mayfair House

Best Eclectic Finds

Miami Beach
Art Deco Hotels (Cavalier)
Colony Hotel
Essex House Hotel

Best Island Getaways

Fisher Island (Miami)
Fisher Island

Key Biscayne
   Sonesta Beach Hotel

Best Resorts and Spas

Aventura (North Miami)
   The Spa at Turnberry Isle Yacht and Country Club
Boca Raton
   Boca Raton Resort and Country Club
Coral Gables
   The Biltmore Hotel
Fort Lauderdale
   Bonaventure Resort and Spa
   Fort Lauderdale Marriott Marina
Miami
   Doral Saturnia International Spa Resort
Pompano Beach
   Palm-Aire Spa Resort and Country Club
West Palm Beach
   Palm Beach Polo and Country Club
Palm Beach Gardens
   PGA National Resort and Spa

Best Small Hotels, Inns, and Motels

Miami Beach
   The Betsy Ross Hotel
Palm Beach
   Brazilian Court
   The Chesterfield
Coral Gables
   Hotel Place St. Michel
Fort Lauderdale
   Riverside Hotel

The Atlantic coast of Florida is so thickly settled that it's sometimes difficult to see the geographical features of the land. At first the only thing obvious about the coast is a string of famous beach towns and fabled cities stretching from north to south: Palm Beach, Boca Raton, Fort Lauderdale, Miami Beach, Miami, and the thin green ribbon of the Keys stretching south and west into the Gulf of Mexico. But to look at a map with no cities printed on it is to see that many of these beautiful beaches are on barrier islands and peninsulas. The narrow rivers, inlets, and elongated lakes between these barrier islands and peninsulas form channels for Florida's Intracoastal Waterway. Some of the most famous vacation spots on the east coast are on islands that are little more than sandbars, with the Atlantic on one side and the Intracoastal on the other, making for breezes and a perfect environment for water sports.

The Southeast Coast is often called "the Gold Coast." Though there is some discussion about where, exactly, the Gold Coast begins, **Palm Beach** is as good a guess as any. The name refers to a town, an island, and a county. The county, striving to overcome its pampered image, includes **Palm Beach Gardens** and **West Palm Beach,** which are actually on the mainland. Originally built by Flagler for his railroad workers and the servants at Palm Beach mansions, West Palm Beach is now a vibrant center that has a much larger population than the town of Palm Beach. Palm Beach Gardens was developed by John MacArthur and is home to the PGA National Resort as well as a smashing bilevel shopping mall, the Gardens.

To the west of West Palm Beach and Palm Beach Gardens is Lake Okeechobee, the huge body of water that appears as a big blue spot on aerial photographs of the United States. The lake is a mecca for people who love to fish. A good side trip from Palm Beach is a drive along the southern end of Okeechobee to Clewiston, a small agricultural city in the middle of cane country. When Florida was first settled, the area south of Lake Okeechobee was part of the Everglades. Much of the marsh was drained, starting in 1881, to create land for sugar cane production.

The town of Palm Beach is beautifully situated, overlooking Lake Worth on the west and the Atlantic on the east. The municipality of Palm Beach is an enclave of the rich, with plenty of antiques shops, galleries, and boutiques.

Half an hour south of Palm Beach is **Boca Raton,** a wealthy coastal city with a colorful history of pirates and Spanish explorers. The name in Spanish means "mouth of the rat," referring to the sharp rocks lining the mouth of the harbor that brought many a Spanish bark aground. Like Palm Beach, Boca Raton has many Addison Mizner mansions built in an elegant Spanish Renaissance style.

The best-known towns south of Boca Raton are **Pompano Beach,** Lauderdale-by-the-Sea, and **Fort Lauderdale.** All share the beautiful Atlantic beach, but Fort Lauderdale has a distinct reputation as a wild beach town, particularly when college students descend in hordes during spring break. However, Fort Lauderdale is also a city of canals and beautiful residential areas, and it offers excellent shopping. The town has some European-style restaurants on Las Olas, a museum of art, and a few Mizner buildings. Those who wish to avoid the spring-break crowds can simply pick a lodging in a quiet part of town or come at another time of year.

South of Fort Lauderdale are beach towns and then the northern outskirts of **Miami.** An international city of commerce, finance, and culture, Miami is sophisticated and cosmopolitan. It is also, in certain areas, one of the most beautiful cities in the United States. The downtown area along Brickell Avenue and Biscayne Bay rivals modern sections of San Francisco. At the same time, certain areas of Miami are among the most troubled and economically depressed of any city in the world. Visit the Miami Center and the Coconut Grove section, as well as nearby Coral Gables and Key Biscayne, just south of the city.

Although Miami has certainly been overdeveloped, there is a new sensitivity to preserving what is extant. The Fairchild Tropical Garden on Old Cutter Road has 83 acres of flowering trees, orchids, and ferns and one of the world's largest collections of palms and cycads. Some of the most interesting diversions acknowledge Miami's Spanish and Cuban heritage, like the Vizcaya Museum and Gardens and Little Havana.

Dining in the Miami area is an adventure in itself, with the restaurants often reflecting the international flavor of the city. Little Havana, on the Tamiami Trail (Highway 41), has many Cuban restaurants. There is also good Vietnamese food in the city. Across the bay, several Miami Beach hotels have gourmet offerings, and there is also a run-down but delightful New York-style deli, Wolfie's, on lower Collins Avenue in South Beach.

Miami Beach is sometimes mistakenly thought of as part of the city of Miami. In fact, Miami Beach is an island running north and south along Biscayne Bay and the eastern edge of Miami — a little like Manhattan, but thinner. The areas first developed in Miami Beach — mostly for the elderly and the wealthy of New York — were South Collins Avenue, Ocean Drive, and neighborhoods west to the bay. Some of the most exciting and innovative development occurred during the 1930s and 1940s, resulting in the Art Deco neighborhoods that have recently had a resurgence in popularity.

The Art Deco style was so popular and the South Beach neighborhood of Ocean Drive and South Collins Avenue so fashionable that the building boom here lasted for years. But to many, the style began to look silly and dated after its heyday. The neighborhood declined in the 1960s as development moved north along Collins Avenue, and eventually the area became economically depressed and socially fragmented.

An interest in Art Deco led to the restoration of individual buildings and some revitalization of the neighborhood in the 1970s and 1980s. But even today, the Art Deco district of South Beach is not consistently thriving. Although the hotels are popular again, particularly among Europeans and budget-minded Americans, rooms may be small, service minimal, and a good night's rest difficult because of the Ocean Drive noise and loud bands.

South of Miami and Miami Beach is a series of keys in Biscayne Bay. The most famous is **Key Biscayne,** with the town and a number of accommodations in the center of the island and a good deal of open land and public beach. Crandon Park, with ample parking and a long stretch of beach, is at the northern end of the island, and Cape Florida State Park, with a fine old lighthouse, is at the southern end. There are also many inlets and coves along the shores of Key Biscayne, and there's also a marina. Though some residents of Key Biscayne grumble that the place is becoming too commercial, it is peaceful compared to most of the Miami area.

The Everglades, the largest subtropical wilderness in the United States, are so vast they stretch nearly to the outskirts of Miami. It is still possible to get a taste of this wilderness by driving on Highway 41, the Tamiami Trail, from Miami to Tampa. The populations of waterfowl, alligators, and other animals here have been greatly reduced in recent years, and there are no longer any wild flamingos. But kingfishers still sit on telephone wires and dive for fish, and herons and egrets stalk the swampy gulleys beside the road. The wild vines and native trees of Florida, as well as plants imported decades ago, grow luxuriantly.

An alternate route through the Everglades is Highway 84 (also known as Alligator Alley), which runs through the Big Cypress Seminole Indian Reservation. If you have an interest in the Everglades and its "River of Grass," consider exploring Everglades National Park, where you can get a closer look at the wildlife on boardwalks built over the swamps and inlets. Except for houseboats and lodge rooms at Flamingo, there are no accommodations in this vast park, but there are many well-maintained campgrounds. (See camping guides under Recommended Guidebooks. For reservations and information, write or call Flamingo Lodge, Marina and Outpost, Flamingo, FL 33030, 813-695-3101 or Superintendent, Campsites, Everglades National Park, P.O. Box 279, Homestead, FL 33030, 305-247-6211.)

AVENTURA

The Spa at Turnberry Isle Yacht & Country Club

19999 West Country Club Drive
(Spa: 19735 Turnberry Way)
North Miami, Aventura, FL 33180
305-932-6200
800-223-1588 or 800-327-7028
Fax: 305-937-0528

> *Also a marina, hotel, and spectacular spa*

Accommodations: 340 rooms and suites. **Rates:** Yacht club rooms $140–$285, marina rooms $160–$335, country club rooms $175–$395, suites $275–$1,800, 2-night mini-spa package $249–$449/person double occupancy, 4-night spa package $909–$1,299/person double occupancy, other spa packages available. **Included:** Exercise classes, tennis; spa and beauty treatments; club privileges; tax, service charges for spa packages. Higher priced packages also include airport transfer and spa wardrobe. **Minimum stay:** With spa packages. **Added:** 12½% tax; $30 extra person in room for rooms and suites; $50 charge for non-spa occupant in spa room. **Payment:** Diners, Discover, MasterCard, Visa preferred; American Express accepted. **Children:** 12 and under free in room with parents; no children under 16 for spa packages. **Smoking:** Allowed in most of resort; restricted at spa. **Open:** Year-round.

Turnberry Isle truly is an isle — a lush, subtropical sliver of land in Biscayne Bay between Miami Beach and the North Miami mainland. Turnberry's spa, one of the best in the country, is on the island, while its country club and resort are on the mainland.

The Turnberry Isle complex is devoted to enabling club members and guests to indulge themselves and live the good life. Some come here in order to see and be seen, and the resort and country club are reputed to be rather cliquey. But this need not impinge on a guest's experience at the spa itself. Spa guests are mostly interested in getting healthy, losing weight if they need to, and indulging in a well-earned rest.

The spa allows only 10 guests at a time, and those 10 are given a great deal of attention. If you are one of the lucky few, even before your arrival you will get a minimum of two phone calls from spa personnel to discuss your individual needs. On the day of your arrival, you give your name at the security gate, the guard calls ahead, and someone will make a special trip to the gate to escort you to the spa. A nutritionist and medical personnel discuss your tailor-made program with you before the regimen begins.

> **Turnberry Isle is beautiful, with curving flower beds and greenery everywhere all meticulously cared for. One of the highlights of the day is taking a morning walk through the grounds and along the bay. After the morning walk, guests enjoy breakfast in a luxurious dining room overlooking the marina.**

The spa itself is outfitted with the best equipment: 15-station Nautilus equipment, Treadmaster, Stairmaster, free weights, stationary bicycles, and rowing machines. Spa guests have the use of three championship racquetball courts, an outdoor swimming pool, a Vitacourse jogging track with exercise stations, a Swedish sauna, massage rooms, and a Turkish bath. With some spa packages, all the clothing needed for a stay is provided: leotards, warm-up suits, terrycloth bath-robes, and slippers.

Skin and body treatments include herbal wraps, aromatherapy baths, facials, saltglo-loofah treatments, Swiss shower treatments, massages, pedicures, and manicures. Some of these are carried out in the spa's spectacular, multilevel beauty salon overlooking the marina and Biscayne Bay. The entire Turnberry Spa experience is one of being quietly cared for and guided into better physical health and self-confidence.

When it comes to food, don't think a stay at the spa will

mean dry toast and mineral water. Meals are delicious, with enormous variety. A typical breakfast is a Jarlsberg omelet, melon-flavored yogurt, and ripe fresh fruits. Diets for participants here to lose weight are generally designed to provide what Turnberry calls "calcium counters" and "muscle retainers," providing plenty of energy for daily exercise. With that in mind, lunch might be a mushroom and spinach salad, grilled swordfish, and a broiled half-grapefruit or vanilla custard for dessert. Dinners have delicious vegetables and entrées like eggplant Parmesan or lobster with dill sauce, followed by fresh fruit or a special apricot crème.

Most spa guests stay at the resort's Marina Hotel or Yacht Club, which are closest to the spa building. Rooms are understatedly opulent. At the same time, there is plenty of Florida white wicker. The most extravagant of these accommodations are the Marina Hotel's two tower suites. Bathrooms include a long marble vanity and a large Jacuzzi. The pièce de résistance is the tri-level sun deck, reached by a spiral staircase. Here you can stretch out in the huge Jacuzzi and look out over the Miami skyline and Biscayne Bay.

When guests have spare time from the rigors of their program, the hotel's lounges are fun to spend time in. On hot days, the lobby of the hotel is a cool, pleasant area to sit. It's paneled with expanses of beautifully grained wood, and its terra cotta tile floors are covered with sumptuous Orientals. The staff, like the personnel at the spa, are soft-spoken and attentive.

Those traveling with their families or with a golfing or tennis-playing spouse can also stay at the Turnberry Isle Resort and Country Club. The club is a spectacular place, with polished marble floors and Oriental appointments in the lounges and public rooms. Guest rooms are in three hotel buildings named after exotic flowers that face a large pool and patio. Orchid accommodations, the oldest here, are near the tennis courts. Guests reach their rooms by way of a trellised garden of orchids and bromeliads. Rooms are larger than those in the other two buildings.

Newer and more smashing in decor are the Hibiscus and Magnolia accommodations, with Mediterranean architecture and decor. Turnberry will accommodate as far as possible guests' choice of rooms and how serious a spa regime they carry out. When making reservatons, be sure to ask about all the spa packages and what treatments they include, as well as the various accommodations available.

BOCA RATON

Boca Raton Resort and Country Club

501 E. Camino Real
Boca Raton, FL 33431-0825
407-395-3000
800-327-0101

> *One of the grand old resorts of Florida*

Accommodations: 963 rooms, 39 suites, 60 1-bedroom villas. **Rates:** Rooms $110–$220, suites $225–$450, golf villas $150–$380; packages available. **Minimum stay:** 3 nights with all packages. **Added:** 10% tax. **Payment:** Major credit cards. **Children:** Under 16 free in room with parents. **Smoking:** Nonsmoking rooms available. **Open:** Year-round.

Addison Mizner, self-taught architect and Florida promoter, built the Boca Raton in 1926 as the Cloister Inn. Mizner spared no expense in building, furnishing, and landscaping his grand "inn." The picturesque building is a mix of Mediterranean styles, with arched colonnades, Venetian detailing around windows, and rooftop decorative spires reminiscent of a fancy wedding cake. Renamed the Boca Raton Hotel and Club after Mizner went bankrupt and left town, it eventually became a premier resort of the wealthy.

Although the Boca Raton now comprises the Boca Raton Beach Club, the Tower, golf villas, and the Boca Country Club, the old Cloisters lobby and the original accommodations are still the heart of the resort.

From the arched courtyard, guests enter the spectacular lobby through a row of mahogany and beveled glass French doors. Furnished with dark, intricately carved antiques upholstered in fine leather and vibrant fabrics, the lobby has the feel of a Mediterranean colonnade. Beams of heavy cypress arch over the Venetian-style room, and hand-tied Oriental rugs cover the polished terra cotta floors. Oil paintings hang on the pale stucco walls, many of them found by Mizner in old churches and universities in Spain and Central America.

The Country Club gives guests a great choice of recreation, including 36 tennis courts. A well-organized children's program is tailored to four age groups, from toddlers to teenagers. Activities are both educational and recreational and include kids' art shows, scavenger hunts, kite flying, sports, banana boat rides, dance parties, and teens-only cruises.

> **Although there are people dressed to the nines, attire is mostly casual, except at dinner. This is, after all, a resort, and many guests come primarily to play tennis, swim in the pool overlooking the water, or golf on the excellent courses.**

The resort's Beach Club is just across the Intracoastal Waterway from the Cloisters, accessible by ferry and shuttle bus. The Club rents sailboats and motor boats, Windsurfers, and scuba and snorkeling equipment. Staff members offer windsurfing lessons and will arrange for scuba diving, fishing, and snorkeling charters through the marina. The excellent fitness center has a weight room and an aerobics studio, as well as steam, massage, and sauna rooms. Rounding out the choices are two pools and a heated whirlpool.

The Beach Club's guest rooms have views of either the Intracoastal or the Atlantic from private balconies. The restaurant, Shells, serves beautifully presented nouvelle French cuisine, and the service is excellent. The dining room itself is lovely, with banquettes of white leather and views of the Atlantic. More casual is the Cabana, which serves three meals a day and a generous seafood buffet on Friday nights.

History buffs and aficionados of grand hotels may feel that the Beach Club is too modern in architecture and lacks the Cloisters' character. But the beach alone makes a trip across the Intracoastal Waterway worthwhile. The covered open-air launch, *Mizner's Dream*, while not as fast as the resort's shuttle bus, offers twice the fun and romance.

Guests board the launch at a landing next to the Tower, a Boca addition of many years ago that, like the Club, has its detractors and its adherents. Perhaps someday, this 27-story, free-standing high-rise will be thought of as funky and interesting, like the Art Deco hotels in Miami Beach. Right now, painted to match the Cloisters, it looks too big, too pink, and too towering. The Tower does provide great views of the Intracoastal from guest rooms, a good deal of conference space, and an excellent rooftop restaurant.

The resort also offers pleasant golf villas, perfect for golfing foursomes because of their proximity to the course and their views of the greens.

Wherever resort guests are staying or dining, sooner or later they come back to the Cloisters. Here there are Spanish-tiled fountains in little hideaway gardens, small shops and an art gallery off the lobby, charming guest rooms, and some wonderful restaurants and lounges.

The Cathedral Dining Room, with its adjoining Patio Royale, mixes Mediterranean and Moorish decor. On the terra cotta floors of its anteroom are ornate wrought-iron Moorish candlesticks that stand about six feet tall. These set the mood for the dining room with its soaring pillars, rich carpets, and elegant napery and china. This is a place where you can feast with your eyes as well as your mouth.

The breakfast buffet offers a cornucopia overflowing with fresh fruits and berries, silver serving dishes of eggs and breakfast meats, a variety of fresh pastries, and omelets made to order. Occasionally, the sheer numbers of guests in the dining room can cause hitches — special-order pancakes at breakfast may be rubbery, or a spot of jam may be on the tablecloth at lunch. And making oneself understood with a non-English-speaking waiter can be frustrating. Still, this is the most romantic place to eat at the Boca Raton.

Standard rooms at the Cloisters are smaller than those at the Beach Club, but their charm cannot be denied. Large windows have a heavy, room-darkening drape to draw when guests wish to sleep late or take an afternoon siesta. The traditional furnishings are reproductions in beautiful walnut and mahogany. Even the standard rooms come with a mirrored desk, an "in-room butler" stocked with gourmet snacks and beverages, and closet safes.

The bathrooms are marble, with polished brass 1920s-style fixtures. Guest rooms also have separate dressing rooms with vanities that hold china jars stocked with niceties like cotton balls and emery boards, and a porcelain basket holds more thoughtful amenities, including a sewing kit, a shoeshine kit, and potpourri sachets.

Each guest at the Boca Raton receives a complimentary bottle of iced champagne. This and other special touches make visitors feel like royalty.

CORAL GABLES

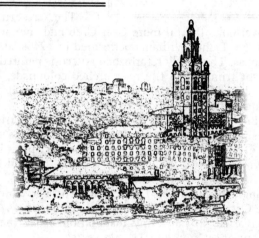

The Biltmore Hotel

1200 Anastasia Avenue
Coral Gables, FL 33134
305-445-1926
800-228-3000
Fax: 305-448-9976

> *The world's largest hotel pool, where Esther Williams swam*

General Manager: Peter Shepherd.
Accommodations: 275 rooms and suites. **Rates:** Rooms $129–$249, suites $289–$1,100; special packages. **Added:** 12.5% tax. **Payment:** Major credit cards. **Children:** Welcome; free in room with parent. **Smoking:** Nonsmoking rooms available. **Open:** Year-round.

The Biltmore has a long and colorful history, which the present owners and managers are proud to share with visitors who know little of this Florida legend. The hotel looks like a Spanish palace rising above Miami and the small city of Coral Gables — itself a 1920s version of a Spanish town. After years of neglect, this fine old hotel has been restored with the help of $55 million from its owners, Seaway Hotels Corp., the expert management of Westin, and the devotion of its staff.

> **Most guests eventually end up in the courtyard, with its colonnade and vividly tiled fountain. This is a restful place for reading or sitting in the sunshine.**

The crescent-shaped hotel overlooks the Biltmore Golf Club and the swimming pool where Esther Williams performed in 1940s aquatic extravaganzas. The newly refurbished stucco is painted salmon with light trim. A red tile roof, arched colonnade, 315-foot bell tower, and eclectic mix of Moorish and Mediterranean styles make the hotel a local treasure.

The Biltmore was built in 1926 by George Merrick, who also designed the limestone archways and streets of Coral Gables in this country's first venture into city planning. Less than two years after the Biltmore opened, the land boom in Florida collapsed (along with Merrick's finances), and the hotel languished. Like the Don CeSar on St. Petersburg Beach and the Casa Marina in Key West, the Biltmore was eventually converted into an army installation. After the service moved out, it sat empty for several years.

Now the hotel attracts people from Europe, Asia, and Latin America as well as Floridians and other Americans. The beautiful lobby has massive Corinthian columns soaring from a pink and gray marble floor to a vaulted gothic ceiling painted blue with gold stars. The plaster walls are buff, faintly mottled for a slight patina. Furniture is dark, carved, and ornate. The grand ballroom and the formal dining room have painted and coffered ceilings. Drapes and upholstery fabrics are heavy brocades, damasks, velvets, and tapestries. Rugs on the marble floors are intricately patterned Orientals.

The Biltmore has 42,000 square feet of function space, with two ballrooms and a number of smaller meeting rooms including the clubby Biltmore Lounge. Tennis is played on 10 lighted courts, and golf is on a Donald Ross-designed course that begins its lush green meanderings just beyond the huge swimming pool. The hotel's health club has more than 70 pieces of fitness equipment, sauna and steams rooms, and services that include some excellent spa treatments.

The courtyard is very pleasant for lunch or for dinner on balmy nights. The casual Courtyard Cafe also provides service indoors in a Spanish-style restaurant decorated with beautiful Mediterranean tiles. The Cafe serves three meals a day, including a delicious lunchtime buffet and a popular Sunday brunch. Formal dining is in Il Ristorante, with artful presentations of authentic Italian cuisine.

Coral Gables is a lushly beautiful city, and there are some spectacular views of it from the Biltmore's elegant rooms. A typical room has ornately painted Mediterranean bedsteads, new firm beds, armoires, and new tile baths. The deluxe king rooms, with a king-size bed and a velvet sleep sofa, are good for a family.

If you want to splurge, you might try the Everglades suite. Al Capone once hid out here, stationing his bodyguards at the floor-to-ceiling windows where they could see out over Coral Gables in four directions. The oak doors and timbers of this Spanish-style suite look as if they've been salvaged from the Armada. The floors of terra cotta tile are covered with Oriental rugs. In addition to bedrooms with balconies, there is a large central living/dining room area with a carved coral fireplace, and an oversize marble bath with a Jacuzzi and a shower with three massaging showerheads.

There are rumors of ghosts at the Biltmore — men in 1920s style dinner jackets and women in nurses' uniforms from the 1940s. Surprisingly, there are no reports of Spanish courtiers.

Hotel Place St. Michel

162 Alcazar Avenue
Coral Gables, FL 33134
305-444-1666
800-848-4683

A European-style hotel in fashionable Coral Gables

Owners: Stuart Bornstein and Alan Potamkin. **Accommodations:** 24 rooms and 3 suites. **Rates:** Rooms $109–$125, suites $165. **Included:** Continental breakfast, fruit and cheese basket, morning newspaper. **Minimum stay:** During some major events. **Added:** 12.5% tax; $10 extra person. **Payment:** Major credit cards except Discover. **Children:** Under 12 free in room with parents. **Smoking:** Allowed. **Open:** Year-round.

The name recalls Paris, and well it should, for the Hotel Place St. Michel is reminiscent of a good Parisian hotel. And the name Alcazar, the elegant Coral Gables boulevard on which the hotel is located, brings to mind a Spanish palace with Moorish archways and Spanish tiles. The hotel has that kind of palatial beauty — just on a smaller scale.

> **The Hotel St. Michel was built in 1926 as the Hotel Sevilla and, from the outside, looks somewhat like a small European palazzo — the sort of place where a lesser relative of the Medicis might reside.**

The entrance sets the mood: a red canvas awning above an arched doorway with a coat of arms above. Inside, cool terrazzo tile floors, buff-colored stucco walls, archways of rich ceramic tiles, and French windows open into a bistro-style restaurant on one side of the hallway and the hotel lobby on the other. A concierge presides at the ornately carved registry desk, with an Eastlake mirror and pigeonhole postal cases mounted on the wall behind. French doors lead into a sitting/breakfast room of velvet settees.

A brass elevator takes guests up to rooms on the second and third floors. Hallways are furnished with breakfronts and other period pieces. Above each room are stained glass transoms in Art Nouveau designs of green, mustard yellow, and cream. Guests can choose a room with two double beds, a queen-size bed, or a king.

Each room is different in shape, size, and decor. The parquet floors are covered with fine old rugs, and the furnishings are Victorian antiques. Rather than building closets, the owners furnished the rooms with large antique armoires. Televisions sit on old Singer sewing machine tables. Some rooms are smaller than others, so be certain to inquire about space when making reservations.

The modern tile bathrooms have pedestal sinks and stenciling on the walls. Beautifully veined marble and new brass fixtures were installed in the bathrooms during a recent major renovation.

Two especially nice rooms are 306, with two corner windows, and 302, with its own Victorian-style sitting room. There are special touches in all the guest rooms: vases of flowers, gold and white French telephones, carved antique bedsteads, bentwood armchairs upholstered in fine fabrics, and good paintings.

Guests enjoy a Continental breakfast in their rooms with the morning newspaper, or they may take their morning meal downstairs in the sitting room. Breakfast features fresh croissants with jam and marmalade, fruit juice, and tea or coffee. Other complimentary offerings are a fruit basket and cheese on arrival and chocolates on the pillow with nightly turndown.

For lunch and dinner, there are a number of charming cafés and restaurants on Ponce de Leon Boulevard and elsewhere in Coral Gables, one of the most beautiful cities in Florida. The Cuban section of Miami, on the Tamiami Trail, offers many dining options. Closer to home is the Restaurant St. Michel, just across the tiled lobby entryway. This is a favorite dining spot for Miamians as well as hotel guests. The mood is European, and the menu is even more so, with escargots, grilled swordfish with Mediterranean pepper relish, lobster sautéed in mushrooms and scallions, and crêpes for dessert.

Like many old Florida hotels, the Hotel St. Michel has had its ups and downs, and it's heartening that the management is preserving the beauty and dignity of such a worthy place.

Omni Colonnade Hotel

180 Aragon Avenue
Coral Gables, FL 33134
305-441-2600
800-533-1337
305-445-3929
Telex: 305-445-3929

An elegant hotel built around Greek revival–style offices

Accommodations: 140 rooms, 14 suites, 2 presidential suites. **Rates:** Rooms $195–$255, suites $425; discount weekend rates available. **Minimum stay:** 2 nights during special events and holidays. **Added:** 12½% tax. **Payment:** Major credit cards. **Children:** Under 16 free in room with parents. **Smoking:** Nonsmoking floor. **Open:** Year-round.

Coral Gables was developed by a longtime Florida resident, George Merrick, during the Miami land boom of the early 1920s. Unlike many other developers, George Merrick did not simply pave over cleared jungle and build houses. Next to the Coconut Grove section of Miami, he designed a Mediterranean-style town that had broad boulevards, fountained rotaries, and well-built houses tucked behind thick vegetation.

> On the first floor of the hotel are two good restaurants, Doc Dammers Bar and Grill and the more formal Aragon Café; both have established excellent reputations in a short time. There are also some boutiques and the rotunda, where bar mitzvahs, luncheons, and receptions are held. The ballroom is on the second floor.

When the 1926 hurricane hit the city of Miami and the surrounding area twice within 24 hours, the only houses that remained in one piece were those built by Merrick. Among them was the Colonnade, Merrick's office building, from which Merrick sold $150 million in Coral Gables real estate. Merrick lost all his money in the Florida real estate crash of 1926, but luckily, both the Colonnade and Coral Gables survived.

The original Colonnade building is a Greek Revival rotunda in pale pink stucco. Inside are fine coral and deep green marble floors, elaborate moldings, and white columns that reach up to a Greek Revival atrium. The hotel was built behind the original Colonnade in 1988. The shift from one to the other is nearly seamless from the inside, largely because the designers used the same marble columns and archways that Merrick favored. They were even able to closely match the marble.

The public rooms and individual accommodations display attention to detail and excellence. Even the hallways are attractive, with plaster friezes and brass and etched crystal light fixtures that hark back to the 1920s. The marble and tile bathrooms have polished brass and ceramic fixtures and a vase of fresh flowers. The hotel has 17 suites, including several bilevel suites with spiral staircases, that are tempting if a guest wants to really live in opulence. But this is an expensive hotel even for Coral Gables, and most guests find the superior and deluxe rooms more than adequate. The superior rooms, with double beds, have plenty of space for a family and include a small sitting area with a sofa. Mahogany furnishings include hand-tooled armoires that hide a remote control color TV. There are two telephones and a mini-bar in every room.

Since early 1994, the hotel has been managed by Omni Hotels, which has invested quite a bit in upgrading rooms. Services include champagne on arrival, nightly turndown, and tea or coffee with a wake-up call. The staff is friendly and professional. For recreation on the property, there's a rooftop sundeck with a pool and Jacuzzi and a fitness club with sauna. Nearby are boating and fishing, tennis and golf, museums, theater, and shopping in the boutiques of Coral Gables.

FISHER ISLAND

Fisher Island

One Fisher Island Drive
Fisher Island, FL 33109
305-535-6000
800-537-3708

*A private, plush
community
a few minutes
from Miami*

General manager: Pamela Forsberg.
Accommodations: Number of accommodations in rental pool varies. **Rates:** Suites $350–$475, villas $425–$750, 2-bedroom condos $575–$1,000, cottages $700–$1,075; $25 membership

fee per day per couple for nonmembers; separate rates for spa packages. **Included:** Complimentary golf cart with some units. **Minimum stay:** 3–7 nights over some holidays. **Added:** 12½% tax. **Payment:** Major credit cards. **Children:** Under 12 free in room with parents. **Smoking:** Allowed. **Open:** Year-round.

This secluded 216-acre island in Biscayne Bay is named after Carl Fisher, who developed Miami Beach in the 1920s. Covetous of the 254-foot yacht of his friend William Vanderbilt, great-grandson of the famous Commodore, Fisher exchanged his island paradise for it. Fisher was quite pleased and Vanderbilt was too, creating a hideaway vacation estate for himself and his family.

Recently, the estate has been converted into an exclusive country club and condominium community. Exclusive is an understatement: the security on the island is so tight, Secret Service men have complained that it's harder to get onto Fisher Island than into the White House. Though most of those who stay here belong to the Fisher Island Club or own a condominium, a limited number of cottages, condos, and club villas can be rented by the public.

Although the island feels away from it all, it's 15 minutes or less from Miami, depending on whether you arrive by ferry, motor launch, seaplane, helicopter, or your own boat. As quickly as you can get on the island, you can also get off, to enjoy the cultural offerings and night life of Miami. But it's unlikely that you'll get bored on Fisher Island. There are 17 tennis courts, three of them grass, four courts for paddle tennis, a jogging trail, and a 9-hole golf course. There is one marina for club members and residents and another for guests. Swimming is at the island's beautifully tiled pools, including the one originally installed by Vanderbilt. Landscaping is lush, and everywhere there are lovely places to walk.

New to Fisher Island is the European-style spa. It has private treatment rooms, a lap pool, sauna, aerobics rooms, and a bougainvillea-draped Roman whirlpool and waterfall. Treatments include hydromassage, herbal wraps, and facials. The spa has its own salon and a good café with outdoor seating.

The accommodations are as splendid as everything else at Fisher Island. The most costly is Rosemary's Cottage, beside William Vanderbilt's mansion and named for his daughter. Built on the same Mediterranean lines as Vanderbilt's house, the cottage is white stucco with a tile roof and decorative wrought-iron grilles over the windows. The floors are gray marble, and the full kitchen has counters of decorative Italian tile. The enclosed back porch has terra cotta tile and a hot tub. Rosemary's Cottage is furnished with fine antiques and has old-fashioned cushioned window seats under most of the windows. The cottage has two bedrooms, a sitting room, and a dining room that can be made into a third bedroom. The high-season $900 per night rate is easier to manage if three couples rent the place; off-season rates are considerably less.

Across the broad lawn are the original servants' quarters. These are rented by the night or longer for a rate about half that of Rosemary's Cottage. They are charming, with country pine furniture, dhurrie rugs on the marble floors, king-size beds, distinctively decorated bathrooms with whirlpool tubs, and spacious patios.

> **If you want a sybaritic, secluded island getaway in Florida, this is it: tennis, golf, swimming, and an outstanding new spa that is among the best in Florida. Gardens and lawns are luxuriant, and the club even maintains a plant nursery where the island's tropical and subtropical plants and flowers are grown. The beach is glorious.**

Some part-time residents rent their seaside villas for a few weeks or months of the year. Like all the accommodations here, these are decorated with beautiful furnishings and a generous display of marble and ceramic tile. All have an outdoor hot tub and patios or balconies. Views of the water and pristine beach are nothing short of spectacular.

Fisher Island has a bank, dry cleaner, grocery store, and a pizza parlor that delivers to your door. Restaurants include the friendly Beach Club; Café Porto Cervo, serving gourmet pasta dishes under Mediterranean-style archways and exposed juniper beams; the Mesquite Grill, with its spacious patio overlooking the marina; the Racquet Club snack bar; and the formal dining rooms of the Club. The Club is in the original Vanderbilt mansion, and if you dine nowhere else on the island, you should dine here. It is worth it just to see the lovely rooms of the mansion, which have been beautifully restored by expert craftspeople, some from Europe and Cuba.

The main dining room, the Vanderbilt Room, blends beautifully with the rest of the old home. It has paneled walls painted a delicate green, with hand-painted flowers and fine moldings. A pianist plays sonatas on a grand piano. Both the gourmet cuisine and the service are excellent.

Just outside the Vanderbilt Room is a coral-paved patio and the swimming pool that Vanderbilt had installed in the '20s, complete with an ornate fountain, Mediterranean-style stone railings, and statues of lions standing guard. Brown Jordan lawn furniture and tables with umbrellas encircle the pool. The view is of the ocean and palm trees.

Next to the main dining room and also overlooking the pool and the sea is the Vanderbilt library. Now used as a lounge or dining room for small groups, it has a clubby ambience, with mahogany paneling, floor-to-ceiling arched windows, and a large marble fireplace. Upstairs are three bedrooms that have been converted into small dining rooms. All rooms in the original mansion have fireplaces and are beautifully appointed with antique furniture, silver candelabra, and fine art collections.

Many corporate meetings take place on the second floor of the mansion, as well as in the separate conference center. Fisher Island is popular for corporate retreats because it is so quiet and free of distractions.

The Club rooms — both the original mansion living quarters and recent construction — were built with the finest materials and the truest craftsmanship. Window frames are bronze; wall and ceiling paneling is of teak, oak, or mahogany; Spanish-style grilles are of heavy black wrought iron; marble and ceramic tiles are imported from Europe; and carving on the moldings and pillars is expert. Nothing is out of plumb, nothing mismatched.

The Club is the focal point of the island community, and the condominium villas and other new construction on the property are influenced by its Mediterranean architecture. But there is also a strong feeling of Old Florida here. The stucco of the mansion's exterior is embellished around doors and windows with bleached coral stone from southern Florida. The circular courtyard is paved with large blocks of the same beautiful coral. Dominating the courtyard is a huge old banyan tree whose limbs spread over the old stones. The gardens are lush with oleander, bougainvillea, palms, and ferns. Aviaries house colorful cockatoos and macaws, and peacocks strut before their hens.

FORT LAUDERDALE

Bonaventure Resort and Spa

250 Racquet Club Road
Fort Lauderdale, FL 33326
305-389-3300
800-327-8090

> *A resort and spa dedicated to refreshing body, mind, and spirit*

Accommodations: 496 rooms and suites. **Rates:** Rooms $95–$195, suites $150–$275. **Minimum stay:** None. **Added:** 9% tax; spa treatments. **Payment:** Major credit cards. **Children:** Under 17 free in room with parents. **Smoking:** Nonsmoking rooms available. **Open:** Year-round.

Although the address of the Bonaventure is Fort Lauderdale, the spa and resort is quite far out of town, so far that cows and horses graze in the green fields near the highway. And the name Bonaventure does not refer to just a resort and spa; it's an entire complex that includes a residential section. Guests can feel quite removed from the world, yet the resort is full of active, interesting people, here for any number of reasons.

Many people coming to Bonaventure combine spa treatments with games of golf or tennis. The golf course meanders around and behind the spa and hotel buildings. The tennis courts are a few blocks from the spa — a nice walk in the morning, or you can take the free van.

The Bonaventure is a friendly place with an element of tropical elegance. The lobby is dominated by a huge aquarium of exotic fish. The conference center at the other end of the main building has its own lobby and reception area with a sunken living room and a waterfall of coral stone. Between the two reception areas is the spa dining room, with excellent cuisine.

Behind the main building is a patio and lagoon pool, complete with manmade rocks and a waterfall. Nearby is the spa, which, along with the dining room, was recently renovated and redecorated. The Bonaventure offers guests a good variety in rooms and suites with different combinations of bed sizes. Rooms with king-size beds have bathrooms with bidets and double sinks. All the accommodations have pretty views of the pool, golf course, or garden.

Spa guests can feel part of the action at the resort but also enjoy the peace and privacy of the spa and special dining room. The spa has a full complement of treatments and a supportive staff. Prices for spa packages include treatments such as facials, herbal wraps, massages, pedicures and manicures as well as hair salon sevices. There are few extra costs. The two-night package is particularly good for working people who are stressed out and want a short R&R. A short stay at Bonaventure can be surprisingly recuperative.

Ft. Lauderdale Marina Marriott

1881 S.E. 17th Street
Ft. Lauderdale, FL 33316
305-463-4000
800-433-2254
800-228-9290

A relaxing marina resort with beach privileges

Accommodations: 583 rooms and 7 suites. **Rates:** Rooms $118–$214, suites $350–$625; packages available; discounts for weekends, advance purchase, etc. **Minimum stay:** None. **Added:** 9% tax. **Payment:** Major credit cards; personal checks. **Children:** Free in room with parents. **Smoking:** Nonsmoking. **Open:** Year-round.

This Marriott has a fresh nautical feel; even when there isn't a breeze off the marina, you feel as if there is. The marina location is accentuated with generous windows in each guest room, 20-foot windows in the lobby, and more windows overlooking the marina on guest room floors near elevators and at the end of hallways. If the mere sight of water helps you unwind, you'll be in a state of profound relaxation in no time.

The pool and marina have laid-back atmospheres and a Tahitian and Old Florida motif. The snack bar and marina buildings have thatched or wooden shake roofs. You can spend the whole day in your swimsuit. Start the day with a swim, then relax by the pool; you don't have to move very far to get a drink or a snack. If you get too warm, take a stroll along the boardwalk at the breezy marina under shady tropical trees.

The Marriott has four tennis courts and can arrange for scuba diving, fishing, and sailing from the marina. There's a game room for the nimble-fingered and a health club. Nearby are golf, Jet Skiing, parasailing, and some good restaurants. But you don't have to go far to eat well. You'll find plenty of variety at the Marriott's two indoor restaurants and outdoor mesquite grill.

Best of all, guests really get two resorts for the

> **You don't have to have a yacht to enjoy yourself here. There are sailboat rentals (and lessons), windsurfing, paddle boards, boogie boards, and floats for rent by the hour or day. There's also tennis, a fitness room, a sauna, and a pool.**

price of one, for they can take a shuttle to the Marriott's other Fort Lauderdale resort, Harbor Beach. Here there's an enormous grotto pool and health club as well as a wide beach.

Other services at the hotel and marina include valet or self-parking, safety deposit boxes, auto rentals, a tour desk for area attractions, a gift shop, room service, and — especially nice for mariners — a guest laundry facility. The marina has 55 slips and, as at any busy marina, it's important to call ahead for space. Visitors should be forewarned that this is a *working* marina. Across the waterway from the hotel is a rusting corrugated steel marina building. It's all part of the scene for a seasoned mariner but might be a surprise for someone expecting only pretty yachts.

Accommodations in this high-rise overlooking the water are varied. Altogether, there are 583 guest rooms and seven large suites, each with color TV with free HBO, radio, minibar and refrigerator, iron and ironing board, large closet, and attractive tile bath. (Bathrooms in the standard rooms might be a little snug for some people.) The West Villa rooms are the least desirable, with views of the parking lot, so it's wise to discuss view when making reservations. Weekend and Marriott Getaway rates are the best throughout the year. All the rooms have balconies, and the higher up you go, the more fantastic the views of the marina, Port Everglades, and the Intracoastal Waterway.

Lago Mar Resort

1700 S. Ocean Lane
Fort Lauderdale, FL 33316
305-523-6511
800-255-5246

*A beachside resort
where people come
back for generations*

General manager: Dan Sladden.
Accommodations: 45 rooms and
135 suites. **Rates:** Rooms $85–$155, suites $120–$285, 2-bed-
room suites $175–$350; packages available. **Minimum stay:**
None. **Added:** 9% tax. **Payment:** Major credit cards. **Children:**
17 and under free in room with parents. **Smoking:** Allowed.
Open: Year-round.

Lago Mar is friendly and quiet (but not too quiet), an ideal
family resort that is, in fact, family-run. The resort has undergone a number of changes recently, including a new three-
story main building, expanded ground-floor lobby and conference center, new suites, refurbished bathrooms, a huge swimming lagoon, and a new garden dining area — all of which
make for greater service and elegance.

Guests enter through a new stucco and brick-paved portico
with a large tiled fountain. The elegant lobby and reception
area are perhaps three times their previous size so that large
groups can be accommodated with ease. On the walls are
rather haunting paintings of the tropics — the kind of thing
Magritte might have done if he'd sojourned in Florida.

The accommodations give guests a good deal of choice,
with one- and two-bedroom suites, efficiencies, and a few
smaller guest rooms. Views are of the ocean or the landscaped

garden and pool. Rooms in the hotel's newest building are the most elegant. Even the hallways have coffered ceilings and graceful moldings. The new guest rooms have a kitchen that includes a microwave and coffeemaker. The dining area in the oceanfront suites is a little small for a family of four or five, with an iron table and chairs that might be more appropriate on the balcony. Other than that, the appointments are handsome.

> **Over the years, sedimentation has broadened the Fort Lauderdale coastline; the beach is now wider than ever.**

Bathrooms in the suites include an oval tub large enough to wash the salt and sand off several little kids or provide a romantic soak for two when the kids have gone to bed. Everywhere in the rooms and suites, it is obvious there has been a desire to provide lasting beauty and comfort.

Although it is oriented toward families, Lago Mar is also popular for corporate meetings and retreats. The Executive Conference Center is self-contained and has a private elevator to the luxurious one- and two-bedroom suites on the upper floors. The living/dining areas double as hospitality or small meeting rooms. The center has its own lobby, a private reception patio, and four meeting rooms, which can handle up to 200 people. High-tech support is available, of course, but this is the sort of place where corporate decisions can be thoughtfully made while gazing out at the dappled greenery of the garden. Seventy-five percent of Lago Mar's conference clients are returnees.

The resort is wonderful during holidays. Thanksgiving is a week-long feast, with brunches and parties in the dining room overlooking the pool or in the new Lakeview Room overlooking pretty Lake Mayan and the dock. Many families book for the week of Christmas and enjoy a holiday barbecue, caroling around the tree on Christmas Eve, and the arrival of Santa Claus — by helicopter. At Easter, there's a massive egg hunt on the lawn.

Activities include miniature golf, a putting green, shuffleboard, tennis, volleyball, fishing off the dock, a new lagoon swimming pool, lap pool, and kiddie pool, Jacuzzis, an electronic game room, and a playground. Shop Row has a health club, clothing stores, liquor store, gift shop, and tennis shop.

A step away from Shop Row is Lago Mar's private beach,

with the blue Atlantic surging beyond. Property to the north and south of Lago Mar is owned by Marriott and residential condo communities, so the beach is secluded and private. Amenities include chaise longues and hooded cabanas.

The dining room and lounge have been redecorated, with a New Orleans-style overhang extending from the dining room for alfresco dining overlooking the lagoon pool and sea grape trees. There's also the Soda Shop for snacks (with a mini-grocery in the back) and a poolside snack bar. The weekend brunch at Lago Mar includes omelets made to order and fresh tropical fruits. Food is not four-star but is more than adequate. Many families cook their own meals. The always-cordial staff at the front desk also advise guests on the many excellent restaurants in the Fort Lauderdale area.

Lago Mar Resort is only a 10-minute drive from the airport and a few city blocks from the overdeveloped Fort Lauderdale "strip" on Route A1A. Whether you drive from the airport in a rented car or the resort's white limo, you'll pass Lake Mayan before veering west away from the beach. The area between the lake and the ocean is residential and secluded; there are private homes and small condominium developments, as well as Marriott's Harbor Beach Resort and Lago Mar. Picturesque canals join the lake to the back gardens of homes and the Lago Mar's docks.

Marriott's Harbor Beach Hotel

3030 Holiday Drive
Fort Lauderdale, FL 33316
305-525-4000
800-222-6543
Reservations:
800-228-9290 or 800-233-1234

An informal, sophisticated resort with 1,100 feet of beachfront

Accommodations: 625 rooms; 25 suites. **Rates:** Rooms $140–$275, suites $500–$1,400; packages available. **Minimum stay:** None. **Added:** 9% tax. **Payment:** Major credit cards. **Children:** Free in room with parents. **Smoking:** Nonsmoking rooms available. **Open:** Year-round.

On 17 acres of land of prime beachfront land, the 15-story Harbor Beach Marriott is in the quiet Harbor Beach section of

Fort Lauderdale — not far from the Fort Lauderdale "strip," but worlds away in spirit. Service is friendly, and the atmosphere is informal.

A weathered boardwalk leads to the beach, a wide swath of pale sand with warm Atlantic waters that have just enough wave action. The beach is dotted with striped hooded cabanas for rent, along with water sports equipment. Also on property are tennis courts and, nearby, championship golf. The fitness center has a sauna and exercise and massage rooms.

The beach is nice for lazy strolling as well as sunbathing. Walk south past the residential condos and Lago Mar Resort to Port Everglades, where hundreds of ships dock every year. Or go past the front of the resort through the pretty residential neighborhood of Harbor Beach to Lake Mayan and the canals.

Windsurfing lessons are offered by the hour.
For those who want a less rigorous water activity, floats are rented by the day.

For those who prefer freshwater swimming and a chaise longue by the patio, the Harbor Beach Hotel has an enormous free-form pool with a waterfall surrounded by palm trees. You can easily spend all day sunning and relaxing here. When you get hungry, you need move only a few feet to get a grilled sandwich or salad at Cascades.

For a change of pace in the evening, try the Kinoko, a Japanese restaurant and steakhouse, or Sheffield's, an English-style restaurant. Both require jackets for men. The Sea Breeze Grille is less formal, with offerings such as duck breast salad, smoked chicken, and salmon and tuna sashimi. OceanView, with the atmosphere of an island plantation house, has more standard fare. The Lobby Bar, the Oyster Bar, and the poolside Cascades Bar all serve drinks. Service in the various restaurants and bars is friendly but not as swift as it could be.

The decor of the resort's Japanese restaurant is carried into the lobby, which has Asian appointments and a great deal of brass and mahogany. The lobby gives the Marriott a sophisticated feel that is unusual in a beach resort.

Most of the resort's rooms could be called "standard luxury." There is nothing special about them, but all are attractively furnished, with bamboo-style furniture and tile baths. All accommodations at Harbor Beach Hotel have balconies from which you can see the port, the ocean, and the canals of the city. If you can afford it, ask for an oceanview room. The oceanfront rooms have an even more impressive view, but they are more expensive, and the sliding glass doors to the balcony sometimes whistle unnervingly when the wind off the ocean is strong. When making reservations, ask about the views and try to get up as high as possible. If you cannot afford an oceanview room, you might be able to get something with a view of Fort Lauderdale canals.

Riverside Hotel

620 E. Las Olas Boulevard
Fort Lauderdale, FL 33301
305-467-0671
800-325-3280

> *A small hotel with Continental and Floridian charm*

General manager: Eric Mushovic. **Accommodations:** 112 rooms. **Rates:** Rooms $70–$175, suites $125–$175; special packages; weekend rates; corporate rates. **Minimum stay:** With some packages. **Added:** 9% tax. **Payment:** Major credit cards. **Children:** Under 16 free in room with parents. **Smoking:** Nonsmoking rooms available. **Open:** Year-round.

Facing fashionable Las Olas Boulevard and with its back on the New River, the Riverside is one of the finest small hotels on the Gold Coast. Built in 1936, it is owned by one of Ft. Lauderdale's first families, with the second generation now running the hotel.

The best rooms are tower rooms, which overlook the alfresco eating area and pool and the resort's private docks on the river (write ahead to reserve mooring space if you want to bring your boat). Each room is a bit different, but all have whitewashed stucco walls and comfortable beds. The bureaus and bedsteads in the guest rooms are carved Jacobean oak. The owners even had TV stands made by a local woodworker to match the Jacobean pieces.

The canopy king riverview rooms are especially nice for a honeymoon or anniversary couple. Even the standard rooms have a small fridge and cable TV. Rooms have ceiling fans and are also air conditioned, though the hallways are not. The immaculate bathrooms are a bit

> Having "real wood" furniture in a hotel room may seem insignificant to a New Englander or Midwesterner accustomed to old country inns, but in Fort Lauderdale, any hotel room not furnished with plastic is worth noting.

small in some rooms but are very attractive, with generous use of Italian tile. Several rooms were recently combined to form spacious suites, and two wheelchair-accessible rooms have been added.

The lobby looks both Continental and Old Florida, with terra cotta tile floors, cushioned wicker chairs in several sitting groups, and two wonderful old fireplaces of carved coral tabby. For fine dining or brunch, Le Café International, just off the lobby, serves award-winning cuisine. The larger Six Twenty Dining Room, serving breakfast and lunch, is next door. Accessible from the street, a vibrantly colored mural is painted on its facade. The outstanding food is popular with both guests at the hotel and residents and visitors to the city. The hotel has room for business functions and a lounge off the lobby that is dimly lit and restful at night.

KEY BISCAYNE

Sonesta Beach Hotel Key Biscayne

350 Ocean Drive
Key Biscayne, FL 33149
305-361-2021
Reservations: 800-766-3782
(European toll-free numbers also
available at this number)
Fax: 305-365-2082

> *A favorite of
> both Americans
> and Europeans*

Accommodations: 290 rooms, 2 villas. **Rates:** Villas $800–
$900; packages available; MAP $55 per adult, $40 per child,
plus 8.5% food tax, 15% gratuity; FAP $70 per adult, $51 per
child, plus 8.5% food tax, 15% gratuity. **Minimum stay:** With
some packages. **Added:** 12.5% tax; $35 extra adult; refrigera-
tor $15/day. **Payment:** Major credit cards except Discover.
Children: Free in room with parents. **Smoking:** Nonsmoking
rooms available. **Open:** Year-round.

In a quiet residential section of Key Biscayne, with Biscayne
Bay to the west and the Atlantic to the east, the Sonesta
Beach Hotel looks like an expansive ziggurat. It's big, but
because the architects spurned the original skyscraper design,
it doesn't look it at first. Although like most of Key Biscayne,
the Sonesta was beaten badly by Hurricane Andrew in 1992,
the hotel has bounced back beautifully. Service is friendly for
a chain hotel, and the location and amenities cannot be beat.
Guests are only 20 minutes from the excitement and nightlife
of Miami.

Guests walk out the Sonesta's back door to an impressive
view of the Atlantic. This isn't just a plain strip of beach;
tropical plants and palms dot the sand, here and there small
huts give shelter from the sun, and right on the sand is an interesting Tahitian-style bar with a banyan tree growing
through its thatched roof. Chaise longues and hooded cabanas
are available for rent, along with kayaks, Windsurfers, catamarans, Sunfish, and aquacycles. Scuba diving and snorkeling
can be arranged through the hotel.

The Sonesta's free children's program, for ages 5 to 13,
transports kids to area attractions like the Monkey Jungle,
the Science Museum, the local bowling alley and skating

rink, and sometimes a nearby Burger King. At the Sonesta itself, there's swimming and castle building on the beach, arts and crafts, including jewelry making on the oceanside patio, shuffleboard, miniature golf, tennis clinics, and movies.

The Sonesta's fitness center has the finest in workout equipment and offers a lecture series as well as exercise classes, saltglo-loofah treatments, steam room, sauna, and whirlpool. There's also an Olympic-size heated pool with a Jacuzzi. Bicycles can be rented for $8 a day, and the residential neigh-borhood surrounding the

> **The resort's 10 Laykold tennis courts (three of them lighted for night play) are in a parklike setting opposite the Sonesta entrance.**
> **The tennis program, operated by two full-time pros, includes lessons, tournaments, and clinics with video playback.**

Sonesta Beach Hotel is ideal for cycling. There is no golf on the property, but the Key Biscayne Golf Course, considered the best public course in the state, is just a few minutes away.

In the evening, there is all of Miami and Miami Beach to enjoy. But the hotel can keep those who want to stay closer to home entertained and well fed. You can dance to the oldies spun by the disc jockey in Desires, a lounge and bar off the lobby with a pool table. Desires has a big-screen TV and is a popular gathering spot for local Miami Dolphins fans during big games.

The Purple Dolphin serves breakfast, lunch, and dinner, with a menu influenced by Caribbean, American, Floridian, and South American flavors. The Friday night buffet should not be missed. The Jasmine Cafe serves American cuisine at breakfast, lunch, and dinner. The Two Dragons Restaurant is like eating in a miniature "teahouse of the August Moon." In addition to regular tables, some spaces have been divided into small eating areas sheltered by peaked, natural wicker Chinese canopies. This is a good place to take children for dinner; the eating areas are relaxed and fun, and a variety of foods can be sampled. On the beach, the Seagrape Bar and the Snackerie serve beverages as well as sandwiches and light meals.

Every accommodation at the Sonesta has views of the Atlantic or Key Biscayne. All rooms and suites have balconies or patios. Which of the two water views is the more beautiful is difficult to say, but the best views are from the corner rooms, which overlook both the bay and the ocean as well as the impressive Miami skyline. These have walk-in closets, tile bathrooms, and large bedrooms.

Those who can spend a bit more or who wish to eat in will like the Sonesta's villas. These have fully equipped kitchens, daily maid service, a private heated swimming pool, spacious bedrooms, and at least two baths. The two-bedroom suites have just enough extra space to make them convenient for a family. All accommodations have carpeting, wicker and wood furniture, and sliding glass doors to the furnished balcony or patio. Services for all guests include one-day dry cleaning and laundry, safe-deposit boxes, a beauty salon, and a newsstand.

The Sonesta has a healthy convention business. Facilities include a 7,000-square-foot ballroom overlooking the ocean and 12 meeting rooms. Banquets are held inside or, even better, by the pool overlooking the beach. A convention manager and banquet staff oversee meetings and meals.

MIAMI

Doral Saturnia International Spa Resort

8755 N.W. 36th Street
Miami, FL 33178-2401
305-593-6030
800-247-8901 in Florida
800-331-7768 in U.S.
Telex: 990471
Fax: 305-591-9266

> *One of the best spas in Florida — and in the world*

Spa director: Carol Upper. **Accommodations:** 48 rooms. **Rates:** Rates vary; 4 night/3 day spa package begins at $1,280 per person double occupancy; other packages available at various seasonal rates. **Included:** All meals, facilities, classes, several treatments and services depending on package. **Minimum stay:** Varies, depending on spa program. **Added:** 6% tax; 17% service charge. **Payment:** Major credit cards; personal checks. **Children:** Under 16 not permitted. **Smoking:** Discouraged; allowed outside only. **Open:** Year-round.

The Doral Saturnia is fashioned after the Terme di Saturnia, a famous Italian spa that uses volcanic mineral water and fango, a volcanic mud, for spa treatments. The Doral Saturnia in Miami imports the purple-tinted fango for mud treatments said to tone the skin and soothe the body. This may sound like a lot of hocus-pocus to the uninitiated, but this is a well-run and beautifully designed spa that pampers and shapes up its clients. Skeptics leave as enthusiasts.

The cool reception area leads to fitness and aerobics rooms. Off the hallways are rooms for massages, mud treatments, and herbal wraps. These are small and softly lit.

The spa was founded only a few years ago by Howard Doral (of the Doral Hotel and Country Club family), who teamed up with Leandro Gaultieri, the owner of the Saturnia spa in Italy. What they have achieved is superlative in terms of program, design, and the overall spa experience.

All personnel are quiet and respectful of clients' privacy when passing by, so guests can totally unwind during treatments.

Doral Saturnia specializes in an amazing array of treatments: full body massages, facials, hydrotherapy, aromatherapy, and fango mud treatments — which sound crazy, but they feel great. All guests have a nutritional consultation and dietary computer analysis after arriving. The Doral Saturnia has long been sensitive to the benefits of herbs, especially the therapeutic value of inhaling their strong aromas or having them applied to the body. Two of the most relaxing herbal treatments are the herbal wrap and aromatherapy massage.

The herbal wrap is a treatment that dates back thousands of years to the Egyptians. At Doral, it begins with several sips of hot herbal tea and a few minutes spent in the steam room, which is perfumed with eucalyptus. Next, the client lies flat on a padded bed in a dimly lit room. Muslin sheets have been soaking for hours in a large tub of hot water in which float bags packed with sage, rosemary, juniper, comfrey, calendula, chamomile, rosebuds, and ginger. These are chosen for various properties that stimulate, cleanse, or soothe the body. A technician wrings out a few sheets, places them on and around the guest's body, and then puts a thick rubberized sheet on top. A large blanket goes over it all, and cold compresses are placed on the client's forehead to avoid dehydration and a too-high body temperature. The lights are dimmed in the treatment room and classical music is played softly while the guest rests for 25 minutes. The various herbs are supposed to rid the body of toxins. One thing is certain: this is *extremely* relaxing and wonderful for smoothing skin.

The aromatherapy massage is even more relaxing, if that's possible. Spicy aromatic oils are smoothed onto the face and body and then gently, deeply rubbed in by an expert masseuse. The combination of deep, smoothing massage and the aroma of the fragrant oils results in an experience that is almost ethereal. If all world leaders had one of these each morning, there would be no war.

A wide range of activities balance all this relaxation: power walks, boxaerobics, yoga, aqua-aerobics, tap dancing, and high energy workouts. The Spa has steam baths, sauna, Swiss showers, whirlpools, indoor and outdoor swimming pools, a large aerobics room, and a dance studio. Guests have access to the Doral Hotel and Country Club, with its tennis courts and championship golf courses. Two extras that many spas lack are a library and a theater.

The Doral Saturnia gives lectures and talks on subjects like nutrition and home exercise, but it isn't all serious. The dance studio offers tap dancing just for the fun of it. The theater shows movies in the evenings, with popcorn for everybody (no salt or butter). The indoor pool is quite beautiful, with floor-to-ceiling etched-glass panels. The influence of Italian design is evident here and throughout the interior.

The outdoor spaces behind the spa are just as elegant. Oblong blocks of coral stone pave the colonnade just outside the back doors. A long balustrade stretches along the terrace. Several steps below is an arching fountain and a reflecting pool with more fountains and candleflame cypress trees. Surrounding this symmetrical perfection are formal Italian gardens — it's like stepping into a Roman palazzo. In the pool in the garden, hundreds of gallons of hot mineral water gush out of spouts and cascade into the pool, pummeling the tired back muscles of guests.

In the Villa Montepaldi, a summer house–style dining room, guests can be serious about dieting and still enjoy the food. In this airy, sun-washed room, spa participants are given small, medium, or large portions, depending on their needs as determined during an earlier consultation with a nutritionist.

Menu selections are made with an eye toward "fat points" as well as calories and nutritional benefits. All food items are listed with a calorie count, and menus come with a calculator so that guests can keep track when ordering. The chef makes eating right painless by preparing food that is appetizing and beautifully presented. A meal might include a leafy salad, roast chicken with lemon, and a baked potato with yogurt and chives, followed by fresh fruit.

No one lives a spartan life at bedtime, either. The 48 rooms and suites, some designed by Piero Pinto, are nothing short of palatial. Some of the suites were designed to be shared by two friends, or by a mother and daughter or father and son. They have two double beds on raised platforms at opposite ends of the room. Bed

> **The Ristorante di Saturnia, the focal point of the four-story atrium, has the same calorie-conscious nouvelle cuisine as the Villa Monte-paldi. Trays of sculpted raw vegetables and fresh fruits and berries are available all day in the lounges. There are also pulp-rich fruit juices in big pitchers and plenty of hot herbal tea. No one starves here.**

hangings of striped raw silk can be pulled around the bed to give privacy. Each side of the room has its own television and opulently appointed bathroom with Jacuzzi. The sitting area has a stereo and a television set with a VCR (movies can be borrowed from the library).

Suites designed for couples are just as luxurious, with a formal foyer, a king-size bed, and an attractive sitting area. The furniture in the accommodations is mostly bleached oak in an Art Nouveau style. Floors are of white ceramic tile or marble or contemporary carpets.

All accommodations include safes and padded satin hangers in the spacious closets. Each room door has a doorbell, rather than a knocker, so that a guest need not be disturbed by loud rapping from a friend or the maid. Rooms also come with Do Not Disturb lights in the hallway that guests can turn on by pushing a button inside the room. At Doral Saturnia, everything has been thought of to insure invigorating exercise, rest, and sybaritic luxury. If guests lose a few pounds as well, that's great.

Grand Bay Hotel

2669 South Bayshore Drive
Coconut Grove
Miami, FL 33133
305-858-9600
800-327-2788

> *The premier
> business hotel
> in Miami*

Managing director: David Kurland.
Accommodations: 181 rooms and suites. **Rates:** Rooms $195–$325, suites $325–$750, penthouse $1,100; corporate rates and packages available. **Minimum stay:** With packages. **Added:** 12.5% tax. **Payment:** Major credit cards. **Children:** 18 and under free in room with parents. **Smoking:** Nonsmoking rooms available. **Open:** Year-round.

The Grand Bay, much sought after for corporate retreats and small conventions, is also a popular sophisticated vacation-weekend destination, with good reason. The prices are high, but so are the standards.

The hotel is on Bayshore Drive in Coconut Grove, just opposite the grove's marina. The Grand Bay looms like a Mayan temple, with brilliant purple bougainvillea spilling from concrete planters along the sloping side of the building. European influence is evident everywhere. Guests register as they would at a fine Continental hotel: at inlaid Louis XIV desks in a quiet anteroom off the entrance. While guests sign in, they are served a glass of champagne or orange juice.

Guests can finish their champagne in the elegant lounge, which has floor-to-ceiling windows and Moroccan leather sofas. Philodendron plants cascade halfway to the floor from planters on the mezzanine. Tea is served here each afternoon, with apéritifs, canapés, and scones.

The Grand Bay has the feel of a small European hotel, but it offers 181 rooms, 49 of them suites. The standard rooms come with a king-size bed, two doubles, or a Murphy bed. The junior suites are a bit larger, with a desk and plenty of work space. The pent-house and deluxe suites are spectacular. Two are bilevel, with spiral stair-cases to the second-floor bedroom and bath. Stan-dard rooms and small ju-nior suites have bal-conies, while the more costly suites and penthouses have large private terraces.

> **The pool is U-shaped, with a whirlpool at each end and a gentle waterfall in a recessed grotto just a few steps away. Above loom the other 11 floors of this Mayan palace, with their balconies and massive planters of cascading bougainvillea.**

All of the rooms and suites are a cut above an average hotel's best and have recently been redecorated. Bathrooms are luxurious, with amenities from a hair dryer and telephone to heat lamps and a bidet. Some suites have Jacuzzis in the baths, large living rooms, and fine wood floors. Even rooms in the lowest price range have a spacious sitting area. Other amenities include mini-bars, remote control television, clock radios, padded hangers, terrycloth robes, and maid service twice a day, including evening turndown with mineral water.

Business services available include excellent telecommunications and secretarial services. The large Continental Ballroom can be divided into three smaller rooms, and there are three other 450-square-foot meeting rooms. All the space is beautifully appointed.

The hotel is owned by Compagnia Italiana Grandi Alberghi (CIGA), one of the finest hotel companies in Europe. The CIGA Bar is a popular meeting place for Miami executives and overnight business guests. This softly lit lounge is reminiscent of a men's club. The Grand Café, overlooking an austere Italian garden, is an airy bilevel dining room decorated in Art Nouveau style. Food is nouvelle cuisine, with crisp vegetables and beautiful presentations.

Service everywhere at the Grand Bay is reminiscent of the best small hotels in New York and London. The staff is cordial, intelligent, and dignified. In a city where hoteliers have great difficulty hiring courteous workers, the Grand Bay maintains high standards.

Outside, on the mezzanine, is a swimming pool and patio screened by a tropical garden, as well as a small but well-equipped health club. Poolside services include a beverage and snack bar and a masseur. After a long day, this is a wonderful place to unwind.

Hotel Inter-Continental Miami

100 Chopin Plaza
Miami, FL 33131
305-577-1000
800-327-0200

A big-city hotel with a cosmopolitan clientele and Continental ambience

General manager: Alvaro Diago. **Accommodations:** 644 rooms. **Rates:** Rooms $199–$259, suites $389. **Minimum stay:** None. **Added:** 12½% tax. **Payment:** Major credit cards. **Children:** Under 13 free in room with parents. **Smoking:** Nonsmoking rooms available. **Open:** Year-round.

The Hotel Inter-Continental Miami, a tower of Italian marble, stands majestically on the shores of Biscayne Bay and the

Miami River. Accessible by elevator to its architectural twin, the Miami Center office building, the Inter-Continental is one of the best business hotels in Florida. Nearby is the financial and business district and, just a few miles beyond, the upscale shops and residences of Coconut Grove.

The 30 deluxe suites have an interesting mix of Oriental and Art Deco decor, including mahogany armoires, red lacquered chairs, and chrome and black granite tables. Every suite has two luxury bathrooms, one with a Roman shower bath.

Altogether, there are 644 rooms and suites in the 31 stories of this marble and glass tower. A standard room has a king-size bed or two doubles, a refrigerator with mini-bar, a clock radio, and a large marble bath. Terrycloth robes hang in the mirrored closets.

Convention space and services at the Inter-Continental are outstanding.

> The view from the rooftop pool is nothing short of astounding — the city spreads below, and Biscayne Bay and the Miami River stretch out to bay islands and the Atlantic beyond. Cruise ships are docked nearby at the Port of Miami. Many guests stay here the night before embarking on one of them.

A total of 55,000 square feet of meeting space includes the hotel's Grand Ballroom, which can accommodate up to 2,700 people for receptions and 1,350 for banquets. There are more than 20 smaller rooms for informal meetings, private dinner parties and receptions, and conferences. Facilities include a well-equipped business center with photocopying, fax, and telex machines.

A favorite lounge for guests attending conventions or conferences is the Oak Room, which has the air of a private club and is frequented by Miami executives as well as hotel guests. This is a popular place at happy hour and during sports events. The room is paneled with dark-stained oak, and the low bar has armchairs of rich leather.

The four-star restaurant at the Inter-Continental is the elegant Pavilion Grill. The restaurant has won a number of awards for its American and regional gourmet cuisine.

The Royal Palm Court, just off the lobby, serves breakfast, lunch, and dinner and resembles a large gazebo. Its green latticework panels are trimmed with pink molding, and overhead is a charming ceiling mural of tropical birds and foliage. Food is good, and while the service can be a bit slow, waiters are friendly and polite.

The hotel is sited on several acres of land, and there is room for a rooftop recreational wing with a swimming pool and a jogging trail landscaped with subtropical foliage.

The high-ceilinged lobby on the first floor is a meeting place for a cosmopolitan clientele. Thirty-foot-tall palm trees reach to an atrium ceiling paneled with tiger maple. Dominating the center of the big room is a 70-ton marble sculpture by Henry Moore surrounded by a fountain with dozens of water jets. The sculpture is representative of the hotel itself: modern and distinctive, but sometimes lacking warmth.

Hyatt Regency Miami

City Center at Riverwalk
400 S.E. Second Avenue
Miami, FL 33131-2197
305-358-1234
800-228-9000 in U.S.
Telex: 514316
Fax: 305-358-0529

A first-rate hotel in a busy, active part of town

Accommodations: 615 rooms and suites. **Rates:** Rooms $105–$195, suites $195–$700; rates lowest on weekends, some unannounced specials. **Minimum stay:** None. **Added:** 12½% tax. **Payment:** Major credit cards. **Children:** Under 18 free in room with parents. **Smoking:** Nonsmoking rooms available. **Open:** Year-round.

Although the Regency is surrounded by a number of hotels, it stands out as a result of its excellence as a convention hotel, its service, and its restful ambience. Approximately 60 percent of this Hyatt's business is from meetings and conventions. The hotel is adjacent to the Miami Convention Center and has three floors of meeting space, including an impressive ballroom, a concert hall, a 28,000-square-foot exhibit center, an auditorium that seats 444 and has facilities to simultaneously translate up to six languages, and more than two dozen smaller function rooms. Much of the meeting space has been recently redecorated.

Miami is the "cruise ship capital of the world": the nearby Port of Miami welcomes millions of cruise ship passengers every year. Many of these passengers stay at the Hyatt before embarking on their trips, including some teenage school groups who can be a little boisterous. But the international staff takes it in stride; the staff members are friendly and professional. In a city where service is sometimes a problem, the Hyatt Regency's staff seems genuinely happy to be working here, and the hotel has one of the lowest turnover rates among service personnel in the city.

> **The lobby's centerpiece is an atrium sitting area dominated by a contemporary sculpture rising three floors high. Throughout the day, guests gather here on sofas and easy chairs to read or talk with the soothing sound of the coral fountains in the background.**

Against the far walls of the lobby are small shops, the informal Riverwalk Café, and Currents lounge. Beyond them is the Esplanade Restaurant, open for lunch and dinner. Although this restaurant looks formal, with its black lacquered Oriental chairs and dramatic gray and black place settings, the mood is informal. Many Miamians come here to relax and enjoy the American menu, which features grilled food. In the winter, the stone crabs are particularly popular. An additional draw for the Esplanade Restuarant is its view of the Miami River, which more accurately could be called a canal.

For a closer look at this interesting, busy waterway, sit outside on the cut coral patio or stroll along the palm-lined Riverwalk. Sightseeing boats pull up at the Hyatt's dock.

The Hyatt's recreational area includes a heated swimming pool accented by white planters of bougainvillea, white chaise longues, and tables with umbrellas. Large planters of tropical plants rimming this recreational area create a buffer between the noise of the city and the pool. A poolside bar is open on weekends and holidays.

Even the standard rooms at the Hyatt are huge and have many extras, including a comfortable sitting area and a small furnished balcony. All the rooms have a clock radio and TV with pay movies. The bathrooms are large and have a separate dressing area.

Gold Passport and Regency rooms and suites are even better, with larger sitting areas and complimentary food offered in special guest lounges that overlook the water. A variety of bed sizes are available in all three room types, and there's flexibility to make a standard room into a parlor suite. If you can afford it, request a room with a view. The higher you go in this skyscraper, the better the view of the Miami River, Biscayne Bay, and the busy city.

Mayfair House

3000 Florida Avenue
Coconut Grove
Miami, FL 33133
305-441-0000
800-433-4555
800-341-0809 in Florida
Telex: 506728

*An unusual
Art Nouveau
hotel in trendy
Coconut Grove*

Accommodations: 181 suites. **Rates:** 1-room suite $195–$250, 1-bedroom suite $260–$395, 2-bedroom suite $450–$500. **Minimum stay:** With some packages. **Added:** 12.5% tax; $35 extra person. **Payment:** Major credit cards; personal checks with major credit card. **Children:** Under 12 free in room with parents. **Smoking:** Nonsmoking rooms available. **Open:** Year-round.

The Mayfair House is part of the World of Mayfair, an imaginative shopping complex in Coconut Grove, on the southern edge of Miami. Though it's fallen on hard times, with more vacancies than the owners would like, this shopping complex is one of the most beautiful on the east coast of Florida. There's greenery everywhere, waterfalls and fountains, and imported tile cleverly worked into the design of fountains, benches, walkways, and murals.

Yet the Mayfair House is self-contained; guests don't feel as if they're in the middle of a shopping mall. There is a hushed gentility to the place that seems stuffy to some visitors, upscale to others.

The plaster walls of the public rooms and hallways are sculpted curves, with unexpected angles in the corners of the ceiling. Appointments in the lobby include Art Nouveau brass floor lamps in the shape of a snarling serpent and modern oil paintings. Many of the mahogany doors are hand-carved in intricate Oriental or Art Nouveau patterns.

> **Guests need never fear boredom at Mayfair House. Besides the diversions of World of Mayfair, where there are restaurants, sidewalk cafés, bakeries, and a number of shops and boutiques, visitors also enjoy the Coconut Grove nightlife at CocoWalk, which accommodates everyone from latter-day hippies to yuppies.**

Each of the 181 suites is different in shape, decor, and size. Some have room dividers of Art Nouveau etched glass or wooden slates that have an Oriental look. Most of the artwork and appointments are new, but the designers preserved some original panels of Tiffany stained glass. Furniture includes hand-carved bedsteads and, in 39 of the suites, antique English pianos.

The suites share some wonderful characteristics. Each has a Jacuzzi, in the bedroom, the living room, or on a trellised balcony. The furniture in each is custom-designed — all bedrooms have a sofa, table, and chairs, and there are TVs and telephones in the bathrooms as well as in the bedrooms. The custom-made closets have heavy mahogany doors with built-in drawers and cabinets. The baths are of marble; all have extras such as a clothes hamper, hair dryer, and makeup mirror. The ceramic tile floors have mahogany detailing. Kimonos are left on the bed at turndown.

Other services include limousine transportation within a

limited area and 24-hour room service, which includes in-suite catering for private dining. The hotel also has a rooftop pool and spacious sun deck.

The hotel's restaurant, the Mayfair Grill, is under new management, and it is very good. Twenty-seven suites have separate dining rooms for formal board meetings and business entertaining; a separate executive conference center has various meeting rooms and a wide range of audiovisual equipment. The Mayfair Ballroom, with striking use of copper and marble, can accommodate up to 700 people theater-style or be divided into three separate rooms.

MIAMI BEACH

The Alexander

5225 Collins Avenue
Miami Beach, FL 33140
800-327-6121
305-865-6500

*An all-suite hotel
on Miami Beach's
glittery hotel strip*

Accommodations: 170 suites. **Rates:** 1-bedroom suites $225–$660, 2-bedroom suites $325–$900; packages available; $25 extra person. **Minimum stay:** With some packages. **Added:** 11½% tax. **Payment:** Major credit cards. **Children:** 17 and under free in room with parent. **Smoking:** Allowed. **Open:** Year-round.

The Alexander is painted a bright tropical pink and has an Art Deco panel running along its facade, reminding one that South Beach, Miami's 1930s Art Deco district, is just down the street. Balconies stretch along the back and sides of the hotel, so everyone views at least a slice of the ocean or Biscayne Bay, often both.

Many suites for rent at the Alexander are as large as apartments or small houses. All have fully equipped kitchens with refrigerators, stoves, and microwaves. The hotel's pantry service will deliver groceries. All suites have a well-stocked mini-bar. There is a remote-control color TV in the living room and another one hidden in an armoire in the bedroom.

There are two full bathrooms, one off the living/dining area and another off the bedroom, and plenty of closet space. Best of all are the terraces overlooking the water. These are roomier than most hotel balconies, with a chaise longue, a small table, and lawn chairs — they're a wonderful place to sit with a drink and watch the sun set over Biscayne Bay.

Even the least expensive suites are luxurious, with wall-to-wall carpeting and lovely artwork. The standard one-bedroom suites have either a king bed or two doubles, with a pullout couch in the den area. The two-bedroom suites have a king-size bed in one bedroom and two doubles in the second.

> **Out back is a two-acre tropical garden with lush plants and lagoonlike swimming pools and Jacuzzis. Beyond that is the Atlantic and an elevated boardwalk to famous Miami Beach.**

The Alexander has extensive convention space. The Orchid Ballroom covers nearly 5,000 square feet and can be divided into three separate rooms. The mezzanine is ideal for small receptions and informal tête-à-têtes. A former restaurant was converted to 2,000 square feet of additional meeting space. The suites themselves are ideal for small meetings, with bedrooms that can be closed off and a bath off the living room.

You can dine at the poolside Top of the Falls or Dominique's, the Alexander's premier gourmet restaurant. It is easy to understand why Dominique's, founded by a French resistance fighter who moved to the states to work in a nightclub, has won numerous culinary awards over the years. For all the elegant decor and fastidious presentation of the food, there is little pretension here, and the atmosphere is relaxed. Fine Oriental rugs cover the ivory marble floors. Chairs upholstered in velvet face comfortable banquettes along the walls, and fringed lamps hang over some of the tables. Other antiques include a railing from a Vanderbilt mansion and an ornate mirror that hung in the Blumenthal house. The bright foyer has bubbled stained-glass windows.

The garden terrace is a pleasant place to stroll after dinner. The lush garden is on two levels, with a fountain and a little stream tumbling into a pool on the lower level. The fountain is quite romantic when lit at night.

The Art Deco Hotels (The Cavalier)

1320 Ocean Drive
Miami Beach, FL 33139
305-531-8800
800-338-9076 or
   1-800-OUTPOST
Fax: 305-531-5543

> *An Art Deco standby
> with better-than-
> average service*

Accommodations: 46 in the Cavalier; 116 rooms and suites total in the four Art Deco Hotels. **Rates:** Rooms $135–$160, suites $180. **Included:** Continental breakfast. **Minimum stay:** 3 nights during special events; 2 nights on weekends for all but the Leslie. **Added:** 11½% tax; 10% service charge; free cribs. **Payment:** Major credit cards. **Children:** 12 and under free in room with parents. **Smoking:** Some nonsmoking rooms available. **Open:** Year-round.

The Art Deco Hotels is a management group that operates four hotels on Ocean Drive and South Collins Avenue in the Art Deco district of Maimi Beach. South Collins Avenue still has a way to go in restoration, although there are some intriguing hotels here; one of them is the Marlin, which has an intricate facade painted in blues, purple, aqua, and ocher. It's also managed by the Art Deco group, and if the Cavalier is full, guests sometimes stay here instead. Ocean Drive has become a neon "hot spot," with sidewalk cafés, restaurants, clubs, and refurbished hotels that are hopping night and day.

Much has been written about the Art Deco district, and it is sometimes difficult to separate the actual experience of staying at a hotel here from all the hoopla about the hotels' architecture. The Art Deco district was the first 20th-century neighborhood to be put on the National Register of Historic Places, and South Miami Beach has more examples of Art Deco design than any other area in the United States.

In Miami Beach, buildings in the Art Deco style generally are made of stucco and painted bright ice cream colors like raspberry or pistachio, with smooth, streamlined corners and entryways. The architects played with many decorative elements: plaster friezes, panels, shields, borders, bands. The interior design is usually modern, with banded terrazzo floors, chrome embellishments, etched glass, and beveled mirrors. The hotels reflect the neighborhood's role as a playground for the rich and famous in the '30s and '40s.

In the 1950s and '60s, the area deteriorated, and there is still a crime problem on some blocks of South Collins Avenue. On both Ocean Drive and Collins, hotels have closed after a great deal of fanfare surrounded their restoration and opening. Therefore, travelers to this fascinating neighborhood must pick a hotel carefully. Some Art Deco hotels written up in the guidebooks of the 1980s were part of the first restoration efforts and are already looking dilapidated. Others look all right on the surface but have indifferent service, small guest rooms, and harried management. Some get the noise of late-night revelers outside or jazz from nearby clubs through the thin walls.

On the beach and along the sidewalks, one passes elderly ladies speaking Yiddish, young Hispanic families, elderly couples still holding hands after all these years, fashionable yuppies, sun worshipers, bikers, Rollerblade fanatics, and earnest-looking architecture students scribbling in notebooks.

A good bet for an enjoyable stay is the Cavalier Hotel, right in the middle of the ever-changing scene on South Beach. The suites and rooms in front are the most desirable, overlooking Ocean Drive, Lumus Park (a somewhat shabby oceanfront park), and the Atlantic. Though small by today's standards, rooms have some nice features: comfortable, firm double beds with batik bedspreads, interesting artwork, and wood furniture. Additional amenities are radio and cable TV, CD and casette player, VCR, direct-dial phones, vases of fresh flowers, and bottles of Evian water.

In a typical room, walls might be sponged a warm mustard color and the floorboards and doors painted purple and orange or bright turquoise. The furnishings are eclectic, with African, European, and American influences. The service can sometimes be nonchalant and the outside noise level high on weekend nights. In some rooms, the lights may blink when you turn on the bathroom fan. But if you have a taste for the bohemian and a free and easy attitude about your stay in the Art Deco district, you can have a great time here.

Complimentary breakfast is no longer served at the Cavalier or at the other hotels managed by Art Deco Hotels, though plans call for a restaurant to be built in the Leslie Hotel that would serve guests at all the hotels. People now go out for breakfast at one of the cafés on Ocean Drive, often returning to sit in the rather exotic lobby, reading or chatting.

The Art Deco Hotels also operate Casa Grande on Ocean Drive as well as the Leslie and the Marlin. Sometimes these take spillover from the Cavalier during high-season weekends, so when making reservations you may wish to ask what the odds are for this happening — not such a bad thing, especially if you wind up in the newly refurbished Casa Grande.

At all these hotels, guests love to people-watch. Fashion photographers and their pouty young models from Los Angeles, New York, and Europe use the district as a backdrop for fashion layouts. Strolling along the sidewalk, you may come upon a photographer with a group of bored-looking models dressed in neon pink. Sometimes producers rent fin-tailed cars from the 1950s and park them along Ocean Drive to complete the look for a layout.

Though it's unwise to walk on the beach or in the park late at night, some young people take evening strolls and visit South Beach clubs till the early morning hours. It should be noted that Ocean Drive hotel owners pay for extra security on their street, but Collins Avenue is not patroled as consistently and is not a good place for tourists late at night.

The Betsy Ross Hotel

1440 Ocean Drive
Miami Beach, FL 33139
305-531-3934
800-755-4601
Fax: 305-531-5282

Pleasant rooms and two good restaurants in the Art Deco district

Owner: Novel Penabad. **Accommodations:** 76 rooms and suites. **Rates:** Rooms $95–$140, suites $190; group and packages rates available. **Minimum stay:** 2 or 3 nights for some special events and holidays. **Added:** 11½% tax; $10 for extra person. **Payment:** Major credit cards. **Children:** Free in room with parents. **Smoking:** Allowed. **Open:** Year-round.

The Betsy Ross is unusual in Miami Beach's South Beach Art Deco district (SoBe) in that it is traditional in design, inside and out. The outside of the hotel is white brick and stucco, trimmed with slate blue plaster moldings. Some of the windows have wooden shutters, giving the hotel a New England look. Compared to many hotels on South Beach, the Betsy Ross is fairly spread out and has the imposing look of a mansion. Inside are camelback sofas and a brass chandelier in the lobby, French doors, and floor-to-ceiling paned windows. Yet there are also hallmarks of the Art Deco era such as terrazzo floors.

> **The Betsy Ross is one place in South Beach where a visitor can actually get a good night's sleep. This may sound like an odd thing to say about a hotel, but the Art Deco district is known for its lively nightlife, and a few blocks down the street this can be too much of a good thing.**

Beyond the lobby and small reception area is a pool that is enclosed by walls and by the hotel itself. The light walls reflect the sun, making the narrow pool patio a warm spot in the cool months.

The rooms of some Art Deco hotels that were renovated in the 1970s are now shabby and dirty. The Betsy Ross was refurbished only a few years ago, and the rooms have been well cared for. They are well lighted, decorated in traditional colors. Bathrooms are tiled in marble and, in some cases, the original ceramic. All rooms have direct dial telephones and remote-control cable TV with free movie channels.

The hotel is on the north end of Ocean Drive, directly across from the beach, which is bordered by a low coral stone wall. This end of Ocean Drive is definitely quieter than the area farther south, where there may be more "action" but there is also less sleep, especially on a Saturday night.

There is a restaurant at each end of the lobby. E Mano and Mediterraneo are attractive spots with European ambience and good food. Novel Penabad, who operates the restaurants and hotel as a family business, is a warm, gregarious man.

Some guests complain that the attractive lobby is largely taken up with the two restaurants, but in the hotel survival game on South Beach, any hotel that makes it should be given some slack. The Betsy Ross seems to have the right combination for success.

Colony Hotel

736 Ocean Drive
Miami Beach, FL 33139
305-673-0088
1-800-2-COLONY
Fax: 305-532-0762

> *A well-run hotel and restaurant in the heart of South Beach*

General manager: Julie Davis. **Accommodations:** 36 rooms. **Rates:** Rooms at flat rate $89–$200, rooms at American plan rate $129–$240; group and package rates. **Included:** Continental breakfast at flat rate, breakfast, lunch, and dinner at American plan rate. **Minimum stay:** None. **Added:** 11½% tax; $10 additional person flat rate, $50 American plan rate. **Payment:** Major credit cards except Discover. **Children:** Age 16 and under free in room with parent. **Smoking:** Smoking allowed. **Open:** Year-round.

In the few years it's been open, the Colony Hotel has established a very good reputation. Its gourmet French restaurant, the Colony Bistro, is one of the most successful on Ocean Drive. While the facade of the hotel boasts few sculpted embellishments, its restoration has been faithful to its Art Deco heritage: a smooth stucco exterior with 1930s-style "streamline" detailing, recessed windows outlined in chrome, narrow overhangs bordered with a horizontal aqua stripe, white cloth awnings on the first-floor windows, and its name in neon on a wraparound marquee.

The small lobby is furnished in a mid-20th-century style, with zebra and leather chairs, a zebra rug, and brass pots of palms and banana trees. The wraparound registration desk has pigeonhole key boxes behind. All that's missing is a Humphrey Bogart character to ask mysteriously for his key.

The oceanfront rooms are the best in the house. All rooms are furnished in keeping with the mood of the era: venetian blinds hang at the windows, ceiling fans twirl slowly overhead, and Art Deco appointments complete the look. Rooms have double or queen-size beds, modern baths, and cable TV. Compared with new hotel rooms, the Colony's seem small, but they are typical of the era. Decor is attractive and appropriate for the period, rather than outlandish or arty. Amenities include concierge service, in-room safes, beach towels, cable TV and in-room movies, and valet parking.

The flat room rate includes only breakfast, while the American Plan provides three meals a day. The Continental breakfast is the same for all guests: muffins, croissants, orange juice, coffee and tea. The lunch and dinner menu is similar to the menu for regular bistro customers, though with fewer selections. The Colony is centrally located, so you are never far from "home" at mealtime, whether you're at the beach or the local art museum.

> **A good housekeeping staff keeps the sheets clean and the furniture dusted — something that cannot be said for every hotel in the Art Deco district. Colony management runs a tight ship.**

South Beach is one of the best places in the world to people-watch, and an oceanside room is a good vantage point. Guests also enjoy sitting at the sidewalk tables of the Colony Bistro, which is open to the public and busy day and night. If you want to get closer to the action, there's the beach across the street and the street itself. The eclectic group here includes teenagers on Rollerblades and skateboards, young women in bikinis, retired couples, would-be models, actors, and singers, art students, and photographers. A sidewalk table at the Bistro is a good place to take it all in, day or night. While there, try the salade Niçoise or pasta for lunch and the grilled tuna steak with Cajun spices or steak au poivre for dinner.

Essex House Hotel

1001 Collins Avenue
Miami Beach, FL 33139
305-534-2700
Fax: 305-532-3827
Reservations: Travelodge
   1-800-255-3050

> *An Art Deco hotel, run by a chain updating its staid image*

Rates: Rooms $75–$125, suites $115–$140; discounts available. **Minimum stay:** During some holidays. **Added:** 11.5% tax. **Payment:** Visa and MasterCard. **Children:** Free in room with parents. **Smoking:** Allowed. **Open:** Year-round.

Fuchsia flamingos, bands of ice cream colors above geometric moldings, etched glass windows and portholes, terrazzo floors, a moody tropical mural — it's all here, the best of Art Deco. The thorough and faithful restoration of this hotel took many months of hard work. The mural, which runs nearly the length of the lobby's front wall, was painted in 1938 by Earl LaPan and restored by the same artist in 1989. The Essex House is listed on the National Register and has won awards for its restoration. This, coupled with the professional hotel staff, bodes well for the hotel, which is now owned by Travelodge. The hotel is particularly fun to visit during the Art Deco Festival in January.

> The lobby of the Essex could serve as a movie set. The bright colors are fun rather than jarring, and the furniture is overstuffed, comfortable 1930s-style. The original registration desk is still here, with its wooden pigeonholes for mail. A grand piano completes the look.

Located at the corner of Collins Avenue and 10th Street, the Essex House is close to the action of the beach and the clubs of the Art Deco district. There may be a good deal of noise from the loud bands on nearby Ocean Drive, especially on weekends. The "streamline moderne" exterior is white stucco with curves and columns and recessed windows. Guests may have their complimentary Continental breakfast in the small sunny courtyard.

Upstairs are three floors of guest rooms. Through the venetian blinds, views are of the street scene, a slice of ocean, the building next door, or the garden and street — not a full ocean view, but then Miami Beach has an urban as well as a beach atmosphere. All the rooms and suites have wall-to-wall carpeting, private baths, color TV with cable, and telephone. The air conditioning works well, and there are also Casablanca-style ceiling fans. Suite 206 is particularly nice and worth the higher rate, which is still considerably less than that for a similar suite farther north on Collins Avenue.

Attention to detail is apparent everywhere at the Essex House. It's clean and well cared for, unlike so many other Art Deco hotels that were refurbished in the 1980s and then neglected because of the owners' financial problems.

PALM BEACH

Brazilian Court

301 Australian Avenue
Palm Beach, FL 33480
407-655-7740
800-552-0335 in U.S.
800-228-6852 in Canada
Fax: 407-655-0801

> *A hotel with a
> quality that sets
> it apart from the
> ordinary*

General manager: James Metzger.
Accommodations: 128 rooms and 6 suites. **Rates:** Rooms $95–$290, suites $525–$850. **Minimum stay:** With some packages. **Added:** 10% tax; $25 extra person. **Payment:** Major credit cards; personal checks. **Children:** Under 12 free in room with parents. **Smoking:** Nonsmoking rooms available. **Open:** Year-round.

In a town that considers itself the epitome of style, the Brazilian Court is *très chic*. It is also restful, charming, and colorful. A stucco and tile-roofed low-rise building that meanders around lovely courtyards, the Brazilian Court is "Old Florida." A color scheme of tropical pastels and white accentuates the sunny, airy feel of the sitting area and lobby.

Frequent refurbishings have made the Brazilian Court one of the brightest, most beautiful hotels in the area. Most of the floors are pickled oak or pine, with new rugs. The rooms are beautifully appointed, with wood furniture and TVs in armoires. Number 106, an espe-

> **The courtyards are delightful. Everywhere there are beautiful plantings and the restful sound of splashing fountains.**
> **In the corner of one is a large cage of finches.**
> **The private pool area has the sense of enclosure and quiet that characterizes the entire hotel.**

cially nice room, has a vibrant yellow and green color scheme and two deep chairs in front of a large bow window overlooking the courtyard.

Dining is in the fountain courtyard, the casual bistro, or the main dining room, which has a wonderful Venetian flavor. For large groups there is a ballroom, surprisingly spacious for a hotel this size. Parties and receptions are also accommodated in the courtyard. The Rio bar, with its soft piano music, is popular with both guests and locals. The Brazilian Court is in a lovely residential section of Palm Beach, nice for a morning or balmy evening walk. There is also the beach nearby and the galleries and shops of elegant Worth Avenue.

The Breakers

1 S. County Road
Palm Beach, FL 33480
407-655-6611
800-833-3141
Reservations: 407-659-8440
Fax reservations: 407-655-3577

A traditional gathering place for the wealthy and influential

General manager: Phyllis Lipger.
Accommodations: 562 rooms and 57 suites. **Rates:** Rooms $125–$445, suites $310–$810; Presidential suites available; packages available; MAP meal plan $55 plus $20 service charge. **Added:** 10% tax; $25 extra person. **Payment:** Major credit cards. **Children:** Under 17 free in room with parents. **Smoking:** Nonsmoking rooms available. **Open:** Year-round.

The Breakers is a Flagler hotel, the second built by the railroad baron and the first oceanfront hotel in South Florida. Unlike so many other grand hotels in Florida, it has never suffered financial disaster or neglect.

But its early history was not without its difficulties. The first hostelry on this spectacular site was the Palm Beach Inn, built in 1895. The inn was so successful it was enlarged three times, but was destroyed by fire in 1903. When it was rebuilt as the Breakers it entered one of its most illustrious periods, when finely dressed ladies and gentlemen, children and nannies would come down to Palm Beach for the season by way of Flagler's famous railroad. At the depot at the end of Royal Poinciana Way, they would be met by donkey-drawn surreys that carried them along the Old Pine Walk to the grand hotel.

When this mostly wood structure also succumbed to fire in 1925, Flagler's heirs decided to build an invulnerable hotel to rival Florida's best. They chose Leonard Schultze, architect of New York's Waldorf-Astoria, to design it. The hotel was built in 1926 on a round-the-clock schedule that included over a thousand workers, among them artists and artisans from Europe, most notably Italy. What they created is amazing, particularly considering that the hotel reopened in less than 12 months. The Breakers is one of the few grand hotels whose beautiful exterior has survived intact through the Depression and two world wars.

> **The Breakers offers a variety of activities for many interests and ages, with outstanding guidance from an energetic professional staff: golf clinics for adults, teens, and children; bicycling, croquet clinics, aerobics classes, scuba diving, and snorkeling; historic and garden tours; card and game nights; and ice cream parties.**

Schultze's design was inspired by the Villa Medici in Florence. Of ivory stucco, it has a red tile roof with belvedere towers at each side, arched, recessed windows on the top two floors, and long colonnades. In 1969 two oceanfront wings were added, in keeping with the architecture of the original. Throughout, the Breakers follows the Italian palatial tradition — elegant, but without undue ornamentation.

First-time guests are prone to gasps of awe. The ceilings of the lobby are vaulted and frescoed; the stucco walls and solid columns have a soft patina. On the walls are oil paintings and 15th-century Flemish tapestries. From the lobby, with its arched loggias, French doors lead out to colonnades and arched courtyards. Fountains are set with richly colored European tiles. Everywhere are palm trees and luxuriant gardens.

The grand ballroom and the dining rooms are equally breathtaking. Circling the palatial Gold Room, just below a ceiling of gold leaf, is a series of portraits of Renaissance rulers and Old World explorers. The ceilings of other dining rooms have intricate carved moldings in teal and gold and are painted with scenes of Italian cities. The frescoes and paintings are lit by chandeliers of Austrian crystal and bronze.

Behind the hotel is the inspiration for the hotel's name: the warm waves of the Atlantic breaking on the narrow strip of sand on the private beach. The beach club has an attractive patio and a large swimming pool and Jacuzzi.

There are 20 tennis courts and two golf courses: the original Ocean course at the hotel and a newer one at nearby Breakers West. It's easy to imagine tennis greats of the 1930s playing here in their whites, or men in plus fours and women in white skirts and middies golfing on the Ocean course.

Befitting the upscale legacy of Palm Beach, children's programs include a money management camp for kids and an etiquette camp as well as the Mini Day Camp. Worth Avenue, with its elegant boutiques, galleries, antique shops, and restaurants, is just a few miles away.

Accommodations at the Breakers are beautifully decorated and maintained. A typical room has light stucco walls (sometimes accented with delicate stenciling) and deep-pile carpeting. Some of the bathrooms have original tile floors and walls and old-fashioned fixtures; others have a more contemporary ambience, with wooden shutters over the windows.

A long-range refurbishment plan begun in 1993 has freshened up the hallways and the guest rooms. Wood furniture is lighter, wall colors softer, and marble has been installed in many of the bathrooms. When making reservations, ask for the most recently renovated rooms.

The Breakers has long been thought of as a winter resort, but it has been open year-round since 1969, and many of its most interesting children's programs take place in the summer. In recent years, the Breakers has attracted more and more families, and more rooms are furnished with two beds. Rates during spring and fall are relatively reasonable, and the staff urge wintertime visitors to try the Breakers in the summer, too, when the temperature is not much higher than it is farther north and ocean breezes keep things cool.

The Chesterfield

363 Coconut Row
Palm Beach, FL 33480
407-659-5800
800-CHESTR-1
Fax: 407-659-6707

> *A small hotel with
> the refinements
> of both Europe
> and Palm Beach*

General manager: Michael Platt.
Accommodations: 57 rooms and
suites. **Rates:** Rooms $75–$265, suites: $175–$700. **Minimum stay:** None. **Added:** 10% tax. **Payment:** Major credit cards. **Children:** Under 12 free in room with parents. **Smoking:** Non-smoking rooms available. **Open:** Year-round.

The Chesterfield, just down the street from the Brazilian Court, is part of the Chesterfield Hotel Deluxe Collection, an English firm that has a small hotel in London as well as Palm Beach. The new ownership has enhanced the stylish, European feel the hotel has always had.

Built in the Mediterranean style favored by renowned Palm Beach architect Addison Mizner, the Chesterfield is painted pink and has French-style awnings over the front windows. Guests walk through an ornate white iron gate into a pretty courtyard, which also serves as the outdoor dining area for the excellent restaurant. French doors lead into a small but elegant lobby.

All of the public rooms on the first floor, including the restaurant's dining room and lounge, are richly appointed and decorated. The Leopard Lounge is both whimsical and elegant, with bright red upholstered chairs, a leopard-spotted carpet, and a leopard and floral wallpaper border accenting the walls. The restaurant, Butler's, has seating both inside and out in the courtyard.

A favorite public room for many overnight guests is the Card Room. Again the colors are brillant: red felt-topped game tables and red lacquered chairs. There's a TV here as well as games. Just down the hall is the paneled library, which carries national and international newspapers. It's furnished with a green leather sofa and wing chairs that are upholstered in a rich designer fabric. In the winter, a fire crackles in the fireplace.

Fresh flowers are everywhere. The floors are of marble, hardwood, or plush carpeting, and furnishings are antiques or good reproductions. The Chesterfield's pool and Jacuzzi are encircled in a pretty aqua tile, and the patio has pink cement paving — very Palm Beach.

The room amenities are above the ordinary: fine English toiletries and a hair dryer in the bathroom, thick bathrobes, bottled mineral water, and a remote control TV with free cable movies.

> **A traditional English tea is served in the afternoon, with delicate sandwiches and fresh scones. On Monday night, there's a barbeque in the courtyard.**

The baths are clean and fresh, some with the original ceramic tile and others with new marble. A variety of bed sizes and room sizes are available, including suites with queen-size sofa beds and two baths. All beds are either queen or king. If you're traveling with children, the best bet is probably a one-bedroom suite with a sleep sofa.

Views from the rooms are usually "cityscape": the building next door, the street, perhaps the pretty courtyard and the pool. Outside, the scene is quiet in the evening as well as during the day, since the restaurant crowd is a gentle group. Ideally located on the corner of Australian Avenue and Coconut Row, the Chesterfield is only a few minutes from Worth Avenue shops. The airport is an unharried 10-minute drive.

Four Seasons Ocean Grand

2800 S. Ocean Boulevard
Palm Beach, FL 33480
407-582-2800
800-432-2335 in U.S.
800-648-2335 in Canada
Fax: 407-547-1557

> *A hotel in the tradition of the grand Old Florida resort*

Managing Director: Pierre Zreik. **Accommodations:** 210 rooms, suites, and penthouses. **Rates:** Rooms $135–$420 2 doubles or king, club rooms $240–$485, suites $550–$750, penthouse suites available; packages available. **Included:** Continental breakfast and snacks with club rate. **Minimum stay:** 2–3 nights with some packages. **Added:** 10% tax, daily parking charge. **Payment:** Major credit cards. **Children:** 17 and under free in room with parents. **Smoking:** Nonsmoking rooms available. **Open:** Year-round.

From the high ceilings and cut coral columns at the entrance to the great vistas of the Atlantic from its French windows in the back, the Ocean Grand is indeed grand. The ground floor hallways and public rooms are of marble, and fine art adorns the walls.

The hotel has a number of charming sitting areas. Its Living Room lounge is like a French drawing room, with empire furniture. A nearby card room has intricate, inlaid-wood game tables and beautiful wainscoting. The only jarring element is a carpet with a pattern that looks like leopard spots encircling yellow flowers.

> **The accommodations at the Ocean Grand are so luxurious that most people will be more than satisfied with the least expensive rooms. A standard room with two double beds is large enough for a family of four. Prices tend to go up with height and view.**

The restaurants are elegant; each has high ceilings and expansive windows. Even the Bistro café, which is advertised as the least formal, has an upscale air in the evening. The service and the food are quite good at all the restaurants.

Standard rooms have a choice of bed sizes, a large armoire that holds a TV, a bureau, a small desk with a telephone, lots of closet space, a mini-bar, and a furnished terrace. The marble bathrooms, with a telephone and a mini-TV, are quite beautiful. All rooms have a safe in the bedside cabinet. The one-bedroom suites have much more space for a family, a pullout king sofa, a powder room, balconies off both the sitting area and the bedroom, and a VCR and stereo. A variety of suites, Grand Club rooms, and penthouses are also available.

For exercise, there's swimming in the hotel's freshwater pool or the warm Atlantic, tennis on three Har-Tru courts, and golf nearby, which can be arranged at the concierge desk. The Ocean Grand has ample facilities for group meetings and banquets to accommodate conferences and executive retreats.

When making reservations, be sure to ask about packages. The hotel's Grand Getaway is wonderful for a honeymoon or an anniversary weekend, with two breakfasts and one dinner, complimentary valet parking, and reserved time for a tennis court. For those who want to splurge, there's a spa package that includes a facial and massage, manicure, aerobics, a power walk on the beach, and access to all the exercise equipment in the hotel's immaculate spa.

Service throughout the Ocean Grand is excellent, comparable to that at esteemed resorts such as the Breakers or the Boca Raton Club. But don't worry that this hotel is *too* grand: the relaxing atmosphere and amiable staff will make you feel at home.

Palm Beach Historic Inn

365 South County Road
Palm Beach, FL 33480
407-832-4009
Fax:407-832-6255

> *A Victorian-style B&B with surprisingly sensible rates*

Innkeepers: Barbara and Harry Kehr. **Accommodations:** 9 rooms and 4 suites. **Rates:** Rooms $75–$110, suites $125–$210. **Included:** Continental breakfast. **Minimum stay:** None. **Added:** 10% tax; $10 extra person. **Payment:** Major credit cards; personal checks with credit card. **Children:** Under 14 not recommended, 14 to 18 free in room with parent. **Smoking:** Nonsmoking rooms available. **Open:** Year-round.

A reasonably priced B&B in downtown Palm Beach! Impossible! This is what anyone would have said about this exclusive enclave before the Palm Beach Historic Inn opened in 1993. But the impossible has finally happened. For under $100, guests can stay in a historic building just a few minutes' walk from chic Worth Avenue and the Atlantic.

Mind you, corners have been cut here. The brass beds are not heavy-gauge antique, and the prints on the walls look like the kind of art one might buy in Woolworth's by the yard. But the attempt to create a Victorian retreat at affordable prices is sincere, and the location at such prices makes the heart stop.

The inn is in the loveliest part of town, across the street from the Spanish-style town hall. Within walking distance are Mizner mansions, the boutiques, art galleries, and flower-draped archways of Worth Avenue, and a beautiful beach. At a small reception desk in the Victorian parlor, veteran hoteliers Barbara and and Harry Kehr welcome guests.

Upstairs are rooms and suites decorated with antiques, firm beds, and frothy Victorian touches. All rooms and suites have cable TV and telephones and modern bathrooms with old-fashioned fixtures. The curtains at the windows or festoon above a bed may not be the finest fabric, as one would find in

> **In the afternoon, the parlor tea service is warmed up, and tea is served in the small downstairs library and parlor.**

the Breakers or the Brazilian Court. But an effort has been made to create a mood. Each room is individually decorated and of a unique shape and size, so there is the feeling of being in a home rather than a motel.

The suites have sitting areas that recall the grace and ease of the upper classes during the Victorian era. Especially nice is Suite 121, done up in pink and ruffles, with a daybed and queen in the bedroom and another daybed in the sitting room. A family of four could be quite comfortable here.

Harry and Barbara are professional yet friendly. They seem to like their role as innkeepers after years of working for large hotel corporations. Every morning, they deliver to each guest room a Continental breakfast that includes a hot muffin or a bagel and cream cheese, melon or other fresh fruit, yogurt, juice, coffee and tea. Guests also receive a complimentary morning newspaper. There is no pool or other recreation here, but pretty Palm Beach is just outside the door.

Ritz-Carlton, Palm Beach

100 S. Ocean Boulevard
Manalapan, FL 33462
407-533-6000
800-241-3333

> *An elegant beach-side hotel with all the traditions of the Ritz*

General manager: Wolfgang Baere.
Accommodations: 270 rooms and suites. **Rates:** Rooms $130–$500, 1-bedroom suites $525–$1,450; packages available. **Minimum stay:** With some packages. **Added:** 10% tax; $15 for fourth

person in double coccupancy room. **Payment:** Major credit cards; personal checks. **Children:** 18 and under free in room with parents. **Smoking:** Nonsmoking rooms available. **Open:** Year-round.

The town of Palm Beach receives so much publicity that visitors to Florida often aren't aware that the island of Palm Beach has many other small communities. Manalapan, just eight miles from the mansions and exclusive boutiques of Worth Avenue, is one of the nicest. The new Ritz-Carlton here is on a slight incline above Ocean Boulevard on the southern end of the island. Stately royal palms line the curved drive up to the entrance, where the Ritz lion-and-crown emblem is emblazoned on an elegant porte cochere. Everything about the Ritz feels substantial, rooted in the traditions of this world-renowned hostelry and the finer things of Palm Beach life.

The hotel forms an E-shape with the prongs of the E facing the ocean, a clever design that makes the most of the Ritz's seven acres. The architecture is influenced by the eclectic Spanish style of Palm Beach's seaside villas. Its smooth, buff-colored stucco exterior is embellished with mission bell towers and fine Italianate detailing beneath the terra cotta tile roof. On the back of the hotel, iron railings outline the balconies of the rooms, which overlook the Atlantic and the bi-level courtyard and pool patio.

Many rooms have sweeping views of the ocean. Lower-priced rooms look out at landscaped gardens or, on the first floor, have tiled patios next to the pool. All the rooms have a little more space and a few more extras than a standard hotel room. All have three telephones, including one in the bathroom, cable TV hidden in an armoire, a safe, and a mini-fridge stocked with beverages and other treats (there is, of course, a charge for these). Terrycloth robes hang in the closets. French doors lead to the furnished private terraces.

The oversize bathrooms have floor-to-ceiling marble and both a tub shower and a stall shower. All bathrooms have double sinks, a makeup mirror, hair dryer, and bath scale. Suites have a separate dressing room; many suites also have a second bathroom.

It's not just the elegance of the baths that makes the Ritz special. Another is the service. Manager Wolfgang Baere, a native of Germany, has years of hotel management experience. Staff members nearly bend over backwards to give attentive, courteous service. Occasionally they may seem a bit self-conscious, as if they're serving tea sandwiches to Mother's guests for the first time and are nervous about spilling something on the tablecloth. But this is a welcome change from the languid service that visitors to Florida often find in hotels.

> **All employees of the hotel are trained in the Ritz-Carlton creed: they are "ladies and gentlemen serving ladies and gentlemen."**

The hotel has three restaurants, a lounge, and a poolside bar and café. The food is outstanding. Dinner menus offer appetizers such as wild mushrooms in scallion cream sauce, barbecued shrimp, tomato-leek soup, and oysters on the half shell. Entrées include grilled chops and steaks, North Atlantic salmon, and Colorado lamb chops, and some exotic dishes like Gulf shrimp basted in hazelnuts and almonds and a veal paillard in a pine nut Parmesan crust. Desserts are both traditional American (warm apple pie or bread pudding) and Floridian (Key lime pie and passion fruit sorbet).

The conference facilities include a banquet service that provides the same superlative cuisine. The Ritz has a skilled concierge team that arranges the details for large and small meetings. Conference space includes two ballrooms that can be divided into smaller meeting rooms and two boardrooms.

For diversion, there are the Worth Avenue boutiques and galleries and the nearby golf courses. But it is difficult to top the Atlantic Ocean. The breeze from the water can make this expanse of the coast cooler in summer than cities hundreds of miles north. The water is pleasantly warm in the winter without being "bathtub warm" in the hotter off-season months. Swimmers should beware of the rocky shelf in the water. For freshwater swimmers, there's a pool with a large Jacuzzi overlooking the ocean. Everywhere, there are beautiful plantings of traditional annuals and luscious subtropical plants, creating a feeling of gentility and exotica.

PALM BEACH GARDENS

PGA National Resort and Spa

400 Avenue of the Champions
Palm Beach Gardens, FL 33418
407-627-2000
800-633-9150
Fax: 407-622-0261

A resort where golf is played with intensity, commitment, and humor

General manager: Dave Bagwell. **Accommodations:** 336 rooms and suites, 79 cottages. **Rates:** Rooms $99–$300; junior suites $175–$375; 2-bedroom, 2-bath club cottages $230–$365; packages available. **Minimum stay:** 2 nights with packages. **Added:** 10% tax; $15 roll-away. **Payment:** Major credit cards; personal checks. **Children:** 17 and under free in room with parents. **Smoking:** Allowed. **Open:** Year-round.

In addition to the formidable PGA Champion Course at this resort, there are three other excellent courses, named after golfing greats: the General, for Arnold Palmer, reminding fans of his great "charges"; the Haig, after Walter Hagen; and the Squire, after Gene Sarazen, the first professional to win a Grand Slam. All these courses challenge pro and amateur alike and are meticulously cared for year-round.

Apart from the outstanding golf, this resort offers an abundance of activities for all ages and interests. The PGA National has an excellent health club, with an aerobic dance studio, racquetball courts, exercise rooms with Nautilus machines, and sauna and massage rooms. The spa and New Image Center offer hydrotherapy and other treatments, massages, and tanning areas. Outdoors, there are whirlpools for soaking well-exercised muscles, as well as swimming pools surrounded by chaises. A jogging path winds under palms and pines past velvety greens.

The U.S. Croquet Association has its home here, so this is the place to go for croquet. The croquet complex has five tournament-size courts, including one for instruction. The association's national school is held here each spring, with instructors from the Solomon Trophy Team of Great Britain and the USCA National Team.

The resort does not slack off when it come to tennis, either. There are 19 clay courts, 10 of them lighted for night play. Chris Evert and Martina Navratilova have played here on the Virginia Slims circuit.

For those who still have the energy after the rigors of the day, Palm Beach is a shopper's paradise. Worth Avenue has excellent boutiques, galleries and antique shops.

> **The breezy manmade beach, overlooking a 26-acre lake, is a favorite spot, especially for families. Aquacycles, kayaks, sailboats, canoes, and aquatic equipment are for rent at dockside.**

The resort offers an excellent recreational program for children ages six to thirteen. Activities include sand castle building, cookie decorating, arts and crafts, picnics, and movies.

The standard guest rooms are quite spacious, and the PGA National also has a selection of one- and two-bedroom suites. All rooms come with safes and well-stocked mini-bars. Upstairs rooms and suites have balconies overlooking the fairways or grounds; first-floor rooms have Mexican terra cotta tile in the rooms and patios outside. These ground-floor rooms are perfect for the golfing addict who can't even wait for breakfast before getting out on the course.

POMPANO BEACH

Palm-Aire Spa Resort and Country Club

2601 Palm-Aire Drive North
Pompano Beach, FL 33069
305-972-3300
800-336-2108

> *A spa with over 20 years of success helping guests feel healthy*

Managing director: Marc Mastrangelo. **Accommodations:** 191 rooms. **Rates:** Room $357 per person double occupancy, $337 for returning guest. **Included:** Golf and tennis fees, 4 spa services or treatments, tax and gratuities; three meals a day and airport transportation with some packages. **Minimum stay:** With some packages. **Payment:** Major credit cards; personal checks. **Children:** Under 16 not permitted in spa. **Smoking:** Discouraged; outside only. **Open:** Year-round.

The Palm-Aire Spa Resort has two separate but identical spa facilities, one for men and one for women, plus some coed areas and an airy dining room. The spa program includes informal lectures by a registered dietitian in an informal living room setting. Each spa facility has exercise rooms with aerobics machines and weight-training equipment, exercise pools, saunas, steam rooms, whirlpool tubs, hot and cold plunge pools, a lap pool, and a Parcourse jogging track with exercise stations. Outdoors, spa guests have access to golf courses and all-weather tennis courts. The recreational facilities are so spectacular because the spa is part of the 1,500-acre Palm-Aire Resort and Country Club. Spa guests take a van to tennis courts and other recreational facilities.

> **The landscaping around the buildings and the outdoor recreational facilities is exotic and beautifully maintained. Although there is so much to do here that there is no need (and little time) to go anywhere else, Palm-Aire is located near some beautiful beaches. There's also harness and greyhound racing nearby.**

Staff people are apt role models for guests — but there is no tongue-clucking when clients are not as trim and self-disciplined as the personnel who minister to them. The professionally trained staff are caring without being patronizing. They aim to help clients achieve their weight loss or fitness goals and motivate them to maintain their health after they leave Palm-Aire. Many of the guests are local residents who belong to the country club and come here for exercise and fitness classes and relaxing spa treatments.

When dining, guests can choose between a regular menu and a spa menu. A typical spa menu might offer a seafood salad or salmon salad, twice-baked potato with Jarlsberg cheese, teriyaki swordfish with ginger relish, or a burger on bagel thins. Food is surprisingly filling and satisfying and includes some clever low-calorie desserts.

Accommodations at the spa are extremely comfortable and attractive. Standard rooms have two double beds (10 have kings), color TV, telephone, a private terrace, and spacious bathrooms with separate dressing areas. One- and two-bedroom suites are available, some with an attractive kitchenette. Rooms have two bathrooms, which is especially nice for friends sharing double occupancy.

The spa offers a number of different programs and packages. One of the most respected is the University Health Center (UHC) program, restricted to 12 people. This two-week weight loss plan, developed by medical experts from several universities, includes individual and group counseling, personalized exercise and diet programs, instruction in weight control and stress management, unlimited use of all spa facilities, and an exercise videotape and follow-up manual to take home.

WEST PALM BEACH

Palm Beach Polo and Country Club

13198 Forest Hill Boulevard
West Palm Beach, FL 33414
407-798-7000
Telex: 803489
Fax: 407-798-7230

A first-rate facility for golf, tennis, and riding

Manager: Mark Norman. **Accommodations:** Number in rental pool varies. **Rates:** Studios $90–$195, 1-bedroom villas $115–$290, 2-bedroom villas $205–$460, 3-bedroom villas $290–$515; packages available. **Minimum stay:** With some packages. **Added:** 10% tax. **Payment:** Major credit cards. **Children:** Free in room with parents. **Smoking:** Allowed. **Open:** Year-round.

The Palm Beach Polo Club is not as intimidating as one might expect, with all that polo and Palm Beach conjure for the average person. Yes, this is a playground for millionaires, but it is also a very sporty place with rather down-to-earth people who are usually more concerned about their horses than about how to impress each other. They have passions that are easy to admire: physical fitness, sportsmanship and good manners, loving care for animals, and environmental beauty.

In 1993, the club was bought by an energetic businessman, Glenn Straub, a move that relieved residents and sportspeople who had been concerned about the financial health of the place. Straub's long-range plans include the construction of more residences and restaurants, some shops, a hotel, a new polo field and covered arena, and a spa. His business acumen and financial resources should result in a revitalized club and community.

The club is sited on two and a half square miles in West Palm Beach, with acreage devoted to tennis, golf, polo, and equestrian competitions. The equestrian programs and polo have the most impressive facilities, though golf and tennis are hardly shabby. The equestrian center is certainly the best in Florida and, no doubt, one of the best in the world. Equestrians and polo players come here from Europe and Latin America, India, Canada — everywhere — to play and work, and, in some cases, to live. Scattered among the facilities and lush golf courses are condominiums and large residences where people make their homes, usually just for the winter months.

Some privately owned condominiums are available for guests for short-term stays. These are in well-designed low-rise natural wood and stucco buildings, about four units to a building, with landscaping and a walkway in front. Studios and one-, two-, and three-bedroom accommodations are available. Some have small swimming pools on a fenced back patio. All have spacious bathrooms, a washer and dryer, and distinctive features such as cathedral ceilings or fireplaces in both the bedroom and living room.

There are some luxurious features in the accommodations; for example, sliding glass doors may open to a tiny walled garden opposite the tub. But surprisingly, some of the accommodations are imperfectly maintained: the whirlpool might not work, or wallpaper may be peeling a bit. In one bathroom, carpeting was not affixed properly to the nailed strip underneath, and the tacks were sticking up through the thin carpet. It seems ironic that a place synonymous with luxury and privilege should have rental units that are not quite up to snuff in a competitive resort market — the Polo Club's emphasis may be on residents and members rather than overnight guests.

In a town where every resort is trying to outdo the others with dramatic entryways and exotic Florida flora, the Polo Club's reception center is rather pedestrian: a functional railed walkway above a cement waterfall softened by a few flowers. But perhaps that's the point: visitors are here for various sports, and nobody is too interested in having a grand entryway. It's one of the small ironies about Palm Beach Polo Club — it is both rarified and down-to-earth.

> **Polo is a spectacular sport that requires timing, coordination, and speed. At the Polo Club, it is played by people who have a genuine passion for it. It's exhilarating simply to watch horses and riders thunder down the playing field.**

The resort is organized around different sporting areas. Wimbledon Circle, with its Tennis Lodges and Wimbledon Patio Lodges, is near the Tennis Club House, courts, and clubhouse pool and patio. The resort offers three playing surfaces: clay, grass, and hard. Tennis pro Carey Powell gives upbeat instruction to both adults and youngsters and operates tennis camps during the summer. The clubhouse facilities include reception and eating areas and a pro shop.

Golf is up the road from the Tennis Club House, just past the manicured croquet lawns. Large arched windows in the dining room overlook one of the resort's two 18-hole courses; there is also a 9-hole course designed by Tom and George Fazio. The clubhouse dining room serves three meals a day and is the only restaurant open all year. Although there has been criticism in the past about the food at Palm Beach Polo Club, there is a new chef, and the restaurants on the property now offer old standards and imaginative new entrées.

Scattered among the golf links and fairways are condominiums and large residences where an international sports crowd lives, mostly during the Palm Beach winter season. Polo Club Drive winds a serpentine path from the Golf Club House up to the Polo Club House, with many more elegant houses and clusters of condos along the way. The Polo Club House is a Spanish-style building with a dining room that carries out the Spanish theme in leather and tack-studded Mediterranean chairs and a dark-beamed cathedral ceiling. The ceiling is of rare pecky cypress, which unfortunately was painted white.

Beyond the dining room is an enclosed porch where one can eat overlooking plush, sweeping fields. Downstairs is the Players' Club, a brass and mahogany bar room with a wonderfully sporty feel to it. Photos of Prince Charles and other celebrity polo players are on the walls.

Outside are the playing fields, stadium, and horse barns, which are quite beautiful. The split rail fences and atmosphere of the grounds remind one of the Kentucky bluegrass country or Ocala, the horse country of Florida. Polo is popular with many locals as well as the international sporting set, and weekend games are well attended. Although celebrities do frequent games, and wealthy Palm Beach residents dress to the nines for some events, there are plenty of people in the stadium wearing shorts and camp shirts.

A short distance from the Polo Club House and stadium is the new $12 million Equestrian Club, one of the finest in the world. It includes four show rings, schooling areas, a grand prix ring with viewing mounds, and immaculate stables. The Club hosts Palm Beach's Winter Equestrian Festival, attracting people from all over the world as well as local residents. As with the polo games, there is something for everyone at this event.

There are also a number of swimming pools on the property and pleasant patios for sunning and relaxing. All the clubhouses have well-equipped locker rooms and lounges with saunas. The grounds are very pretty, with lots of winding roads and banks of bright flowers at the entryways to the various clubhouses and residential enclaves. A 92-acre cypress preserve is ideal for long walks and gives a glimpse of what this playground for sport and horse lovers was like when it was simply a Florida jungle.

The Keys

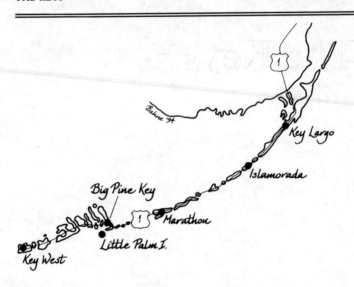

Big Pine Key
Bahia Honda Bayside Cabins, 305
Bed and Breakfast on the Ocean: Casa Grande, 303
Islamorada
Cheeca Lodge, 308
Chesapeake Resort, 311
Pelican Cove Resort, 313
Key Largo
Largo Lodge, 314
Sheraton Key Largo Resort, 317
Marina Del Mar, 315
Key West
The Artist House, 320
The Banyan Resort, 322
Duval House, 324
Eden House, 326
Heron House, 328
Hyatt Key West, 330

Island City House, 333
La Mer Hotel, 336
La Pensione, 334
The Marquesa Hotel, 338
Marriott's Casa Marina, 341
Ocean Key House Resort and Marina, 344
Pier House Resort and Caribbean Spa, 346
Marriott Reach Resort, 348
Simonton Court, 349
South Beach Oceanfront Motel, 351
Southernmost Motel in the USA, 352
Little Palm Island
Little Palm Island, 354
Marathon
Faro Blanco Marine Resort, 358
Hawk's Cay Resort, 360

Best B&Bs

Big Pine
   Bed and Breakfast on the Ocean: Casa Grande
Key West
   The Artist House
   Duval House
   Heron House
   Island City House
   La Mer Hotel
   La Pensione
   Simonton Court

Best Beachside Accommodations

Islamorada
   Cheeca Lodge
   Chesapeake Resort
Key West
   The Reach

Best Budget Finds

Big Pine
   Bahia Honda Bayside Cabins
Key Largo
   Largo Lodge

Best Island Getaways

Little Palm Island
   Little Palm Island

Best Resorts and Spas

Duck Key
   Hawk's Cay Resort & Marina
Islamorada
   Pelican Cove Resort

Key Largo
Marina Del Mar
Sheraton Key Largo
Key West
Hyatt at Key West
Marriott's Casa Marina
Ocean Key House Resort & Marina
Pier House Resort and Caribbean Spa
Marathon
Faro Blanco Marine Resort

Best Small Hotels, Inns, and Motels

Key West
The Banyan Resort
Eden House
The Marquesa Hotel
South Beach Oceanfront Motel
Southernmost Motel in the U.S.A.

South of Miami and Key Biscayne are what could be called the "Keys proper" — the chain of tiny islands that have a reputation for being laid-back and unpretentious, with some of the best fishing in the world. The Keys can be disappointing at first, until you learn where to go to fulfill your particular fantasy or expectation. Many people who go to **Key Largo** — the first and largest of the Keys — expect the wild, remote beauty they remember from Bogart and Bacall's film *Key Largo*. They are disappointed to find two-lane Route 1 lined with ramshackle food stands, bars, bait shops, souvenir stores, and uninspired accommodations. You have to leave Route 1 to find the "real" Key Largo. There are interesting, attractive places to stay on narrow roads that end at the water — the Atlantic and Straits of Florida on the east, Florida Bay on the west. Like Fort Lauderdale, Key Largo has many inlets, marinas, and canals.

A nature walk at John Pennekamp Coral Reef State Park provides insight into the physical characteristics of all the Keys, with its unusual vegetation and sandy soil. An excellent staff of rangers and diving experts can take you by boat to the enormous living coral reef several miles offshore. The reef is long, stretching from Key Largo to the Dry Tortugas south of Key West. Divers will see not only the beautiful lacy coral but also many varieties of colorful fish.

The reef is responsible for the lack of natural beaches everywhere but on Bahia Honda and Key West. All the Keys on Route 1 are made of dead coral rock. Originally, Key Largo was a series of rock-and-sand keys that were filled in when Flagler's railroad came in. The railroad was completed with much fanfare in 1912, just a few months before Flagler's death. Though the railroad no longer exists, Route 1, which links all the Keys, was constructed on the old railroad bed, much of it washed out during a hurricane. The railroad was supposed to create prosperity for the Keys by transporting the fruits and vegetables grown on plantations and struggling farms to major markets. Ironically, Key West became a distribution center for cheaper South American and Caribbean produce. Eventually, many farms and plantations failed because of this competition and because there wasn't enough topsoil to support their crops. Always beset by economic woes, the Keys survived on fishing. Until recently, the leading industry in Key West was shrimping. Today, of course, it is tourism.

The lack of fresh water and the desolation of the Keys kept them off most tourists' itineraries in the earlier part of this century. There were mosquitoes and deadly hurricanes. The worst of these occurred in 1935, when a train was blown off the tracks in Islamorada, south of Key Largo, and much of the track elsewhere in the Keys was swept away. The Great Depression hit the Keys hard. Although work was begun to convert the railroad into a highway after 1935, the hurricane took the heart out of development for many years. Today, some would say there has been too much development, but tourism has saved the region economically. The Keys have become popular for their informality and funky charm, as well as for the excellent fishing. A swimsuit, a pair of shorts, several T-shirts, and a pair of sandals are all you need to pack unless you plan to go out to dinner, in which case you might want to bring a pair of slacks or a sundress.

Getting around is pretty easy too. You can fly into Ft. Lauderdale, Naples, or Key West and rent a car or, if your only destination is **Key West,** fly there, take a taxi to your guesthouse, and rent a moped, bicycle, or car in town. If you're staying in Old Town, you can simply walk everywhere and forgo the rentals. If you're driving from a mainland airport, you'll eventually get on Route 1, the only highway that runs the length of the Keys. Along Route 1, you will notice mile marker signs with an MM followed by a number. These orient people to what's where on the Keys and are used in place of street numbers. Accommodations and restaurants on side streets off

Route 1 often use mile markers to indicate their addresses.

Fishing is still important in the Keys, for both food and sport. Tavernier and Plantation keys and Upper and Lower Matecumbe keys are popular for saltwater fishing. **Islamorada** is the largest town on the Upper Keys, with big marinas and a nightspot, Holiday Isle, that draws tourists and natives. There are some good restaurants here, a post office, souvenir shops, resorts, and the Theater of the Sea, a dolphin show and marine education center. Occasionally, the Upper Keys and various other Keys in the chain have a problem with water pressure. This usually means only that you might shorten your morning shower by a few minutes, but you should be sensitive to the fact that the natives don't like to see water or other resources wasted in the Keys.

Southwest of Islamorada are several tiny uninhabited islands inaccessible by car throughout this stretch of waterway, many made of mangroves. One Key that has built up over the centuries is Lignumvitae, an unspoiled island of wild vegetation accessible only by boat. The Key is named after lignumvitae, a tree with unusually dense wood that is extremely rare and is reputed to be nonflammable.

The next big community is **Marathon,** at the center of the Middle Keys. Founded as a base camp for railroad workers in 1906, this is a good place to buy supplies and fishing bait and equipment. Marathon is at its prettiest on back roads and beside its long canals.

South of Marathon, the Keys shed their tourist quality and become more rural up to the outskirts of Key West. Pigeon Key is the start of the old Seven-Mile Bridge, Flagler's great engineering achievement and the longest of the Keys' bridges. After 1935, it was widened and became a highway bridge. It was replaced in 1982. Altogether, there are 42 bridges linking the various Keys.

Bahia Honda State Park, adjacent to the Bahia Honda Bridge, is the tail end of the Middle Keys, with the best beach on the Keys and good diving in the deep waters near the bridge pilings. You can see corals and sponges as well as fish. But the current is swift in some areas, and there are stinging fire coral and sea urchins, as well as occasional hammerhead sharks when the tarpon are running. It's best to get advice from state park personnel on where not to go off Bahia Honda, or simply stay at the state park for safer swimming.

Many of the islands in the Upper and Middle Keys are elongated, but south of Bahia Honda they broaden out a bit. Beyond the Keys proper, there are dozens of smaller islands. Big Pine Key is the most settled area before Key West, with a big shopping center and a good deal of development. Otherwise there is little commercialism. Tiny Key deer live here, with fawns that weigh less than five pounds at birth, and it's important to drive carefully at night and in the early morning hours when they may be out. The National Key Deer Refuge (MM 31) is worth visiting, though it is tough to spot the deer themselves except in the early morning and late evening when they feed. There are plentiful waterfowl, hawks, and smaller birds in this area. The vegetation is dense on the Keys, and includes hammocks of hardwoods.

When Ernest Hemingway first moved to Key West, he said it was "the best place I've ever been any time anywhere." Throughout this century, Key West has had an aura that many visitors find difficult to explain. At the southernmost tip of the continental United States, Key West is closer to Havana than Miami and, both geographically and atmospherically, is a world unto itself. It is a zany, laid-back, tolerant place with an international citizenry that at times delights in the bizarre. Key West is sometimes called the "Conch Republic," and natives are called "conchs." Key West actually declared itself a republic briefly in 1982 in response to roadblocks set up to search cars for smuggled drugs. Key West seceded from the union on April 23, 1982 at high noon, raised a quickly designed Conch Republic flag, declared war against the United States, formally surrendered in order to be "eligible for foreign aid," and then held a party that lasted several days. Only in Key West could this happen.

Despite its designation as the southernmost region of the United States, more northerners than southerners live in Key West, as well as Cubans and natives of various Caribbean islands. Except for conchs who own small shops and fishermen, most people are from someplace else. Many of them, particularly gays, moved here specifically because of the island's openness and fair-mindedness. A small segment of the population is really down-and-out and probably living here because of the mild climate as well as the tolerance for any lifestyle. There are bag ladies and bag men and a few people who took one too many acid trips and never fully returned. Several famous artists live here and any number of bon vivants and bohemians. At its best, Key West gives a glimpse of what the rest of American society could be in its diversity, tolerance, and sense of fair play. When little kids play in their sandy front yards at dusk, it is not unusual to see children of three or four different racial or ethnic groups together. Many biracial couples from northern cities choose Key West for their honeymoon. Residents are outside a lot, walking or bicycling to their destinations rather than driving their cars. No one is in a big hurry or makes a big fuss about anything.

At night, some of the tourists and local fishermen get drunk at places like Sloppy Joe's, a favorite hangout of Ernest Hemingway's. Though wild and woolly, the town is really pretty safe. The Key West community is very close, and there is an unwritten rule that tourists are to be protected — largely because they are cruicial to the economic health of a place that has seen many precarious times, but also because of the sense of fair play in Key West. There is virtually no violent crime here, and although there are occasional robberies, they tend to be local against locals. It is still wise to watch your wallet or purse, especially if you are drinking, since out-of-towners sometimes prey on inebriated tourists.

A favorite haunt of visitors is the Old Town, particularly Mallory Square and Duval Street. To orient yourself and decide what attractions to see, take one of the "Conch Train" tours during the day. The loquacious guides of these toylike trams point out old Victorian "conch houses" and "shotgun houses" while providing information about the town's checkered past and its famous residents.

Also worth some time and money is a tour of the Currier Mansion, a marvelous example of Victorian architecture with a bird's-eye view of Old Town from its widow's walk. Lately, maintenance has slipped and the place is not as immaculate as it was when first opened. But it is worth seeing for those who are fascinated by Victorian island architecture and are willing to ignore the dust and air of neglect.

In recent years, Mallory Square and the Duval near Front Street have become extremely commercial, a blatant tourist trap. There are some lovely shops here, but there are also stores selling profane T-shirts and souvenirs at ridiculously high prices. The owners of one of these stores once sold some German tourists four T-shirts for $600 until a local resident overhearing the sale intervened and called the police. Avoid these places; there are better shirts and nicer people further up the street. Some of the most interesting shops featuring local craftspeople are several blocks from Mallory Square at the far end of Duval Street and along quiet side streets.

Key West's guesthouses and hotels reflect the many qualities of the island and appeal to a wide range of visitors. Some are enclaves for gays and the free-spirited, others for the chic and wealthy, still others for history buffs who love Victoriana and gingerbread. A few, like the Marquesa, have restaurants that have become renowned in their own right. Generally, restaurants in Key West, like so many other things on the island, go up and down. A place that is outstanding one year may be overpriced and mediocre the next, so ask the proprietors of your hotel or guesthouse for suggestions. Louie's Backyard is dependably good, though expensive. For authentic, cheap Cuban food, try El Seboney on Catherine Street. At the high end of Duval Street is Camille's, also inexpensive and a favorite of locals for breakfast.

For a look at some wildlife and native plant life on Key West that has survived development, visit the Riggs Wildlife Refuge through the Audubon House in town. Although Key West prides itself on its natural beaches, most are privately owned by resorts. One good public beach is Higgs Memorial, at the end of White Street. Slightly rockier is Fort Taylor, at the end of Southard Street at the Truman Annex.

BIG PINE KEY

Bed & Breakfast on the Ocean: Casa Grande

P.O. Box 378
Big Pine Key, FL 33043
305-872-2878

> *A standard for Keys guesthouses*

Owners: Jon and Kathleen Threlkeld. **Accommodations:** 3 rooms. **Rates:** $75–$85; $20 extra person in room. **Included:** Full breakfast; water sports equipment. **Minimum stay:** 2 or 3 nights on some holidays. **Added:** 11% tax. **Payment:** Personal check; cash. **Children:** Not allowed. **Smoking:** Only in restricted area. **Open:** Year-round.

Bed & Breakfast on the Ocean is so perfect as a B&B, any guest would swear that Jon and Kathleen Threlkeld designed their

oceanside home with future guests in mind. All the bedrooms, decorated in green, ivory, melon, and other rich colors,
have private baths —unusual in a family home. But according
to Kathy and Jon, who moved to Big Pine Key in 1967, the
individual baths were a
response to having five
teenagers living at home.
They built their Spanish-
style house with a hand-
some bathroom for each
bedroom. Several years
later, when the teenagers
had grown up and gone,
the Threlkelds started Bed
& Breakfast on the Ocean.
The design of the house
follows that of a traditional hacienda, with a cres-
cent of bedrooms opening
onto a garden patio. The
screened-in patio is a focal
point, with a hot tub overlooking the water, lawn
furniture, and a breakfast
table with umbrella.

> **Guests have free access to
> what the Threlkelds call
> their "beach junk": Wind-
> surfers, rafts, snorkeling
> equipment, and paddle-
> boats. Bicycles are avail-
> able for those who want to
> bike around the neighbor-
> hood or trek into town.
> The town of Big Pine Key,
> one of the larger settle-
> ments on the Keys, has
> some small, inexpensive
> restaurants for lunch.**

Bed &Breakfast on the Ocean was one of the first B&Bs to
open in the Keys, and it has maintained a consistently high
standard throughout the years. As with everything, breakfast
is superb. It begins with hot tea or coffee and proceeds to
juice, fresh tropical and native fruits, cold cereal, and a hot
entrée: lobster Benedict, waffles, stone crab quiche, or a special omelette. The Threlkelds sometimes will serve a true
English breakfast: eggs and fish, with local seafood such as
tuna, dolphin, or yellowtail. "We like to serve as much native
food as possible. We also like educating people about seafood
or dishes that they might not have had at home."

The patio, where the morning meal is served, is surrounded
by subtropical and tropical flowers and profuse greenery. The
table is always set with pretty china and flatware, and there is
an arrangement of tropical flowers and ferns at the center.
From the table, guests can see the ocean.

The Threlkelds' secluded beach, directly behind the house,
is a good place to spend a morning. The beach is shaded with
trees near the house and has open stretches closer to the

water. It's a pretty, restful spot with a boat ramp and dock for fishing, a chikee hut, and a barbecue grill.

Many people come to the Keys to snorkle. The Threlkelds have three pedal boats available — one for each guest room at the Casa. These are fun to pedal around in, and they can also be used as a jumping-off spot for snorkeling by throwing out the anchor. The water is clear and warm and offers a variety of underwater sights. Big Pine Key is only about 33 miles from Key West, so there is a balmy feel to the air and a breeze from the water most of the year.

After a morning of swimming and lounging on the beach, a nap under the ceiling fan in the bedroom is always nice. Each room has a small refrigerator for soft drinks and snacks, and there's an attractive sitting room with a fireplace and television. Take some time to look around at Casa Grande: the house makes dramatic use of many natural materials, such as coral, pine, terra cotta tile, and ceramic tile. The spectacular fireplace in the sitting room is of rough coral.

Some days, it's nice to take a drive into Key West, stay for dinner, and then come back for a soak in the hot tub. At night, stars blink above the steaming tub, and the tropical plants around the patio give off a moist, earthy fragrance.

Bahia Honda Bayside Cabins

Bahia Honda State Recreation Area
Route 1, Box 782
Big Pine Key, FL 33043
305-872-2353

A bargain for families and nature lovers

Park director: Carl Nielsen. **Accommodations:** 6 cabins. **Rates:** $96.85–$124.60. **Included:** All applicable taxes and charges. **Minimum stay:** 2 nights; 7-night maximum stay. **Added:** $5.55 extra adult. **Payment:** MasterCard, Visa. **Children:** Free in room with parents (up to 8 family members allowed per cabin). **Smoking:** Allowed. **Open:** Year-round.

Bahia Honda State Recreation Area is on Bahia Honda Key, near Big Pine Key, with the Bay of Florida on one side and the Atlantic Ocean on the other. Pronounced *bay-ya hahn-da*, the name means "deep bay." Many people come here for the day because Bahia Honda is reputed to have the most beautiful beach in the Keys. There are plenty of overnighters here, too, camping out or staying in the state park's reasonably priced cabins. From one end of the beach, visitors can see part of the picturesque old railroad bridge that juts into the water at the farthest point of land, running roughly parallel to a new bridge. A small marina on the bay side of the island has two boat ramps. The marina also has a gift shop and snack bar, barbecue grills, picnic tables, and a parking lot. This is a good place for boaters and families who want to vacation in clean, moderately priced accommodations.

> As one would expect, this environment attracts many birds: roseate spoonbills, reddish egrets, white-crowned pigeons, ospreys, terns, herons, and brown pelicans are among them.

There are many treasures here. This small state park has some of the most diverse terrain in the United States, with coral outcroppings, beach dunes, berms, mangrove forests, and, of course, a real sand beach. The beach near the marina has a state park feel to it, with picnic tables and palm trees. Walk up a bank of old cement steps past the old bridge, and you are on the Atlantic side of the island. This beach, which runs for several thousand feet, has flat areas near the water, dunes and berms dotted with sea oats, other grasses, and, in some areas, a bank of exposed coral. The ocean is warm and has many shallow stretches that are ideal for young children to wade in.

This is also the perfect place to go beachcombing: the gentle waters of Bahia Honda encourage deposits of treasures like pieces of coral, seaweed, and sponges to wash ashore. The color of the water is remarkable — it's pale blue near the shore and then darker farther out, particularly above seaweed beds, where the water looks almost purple.

The park's camping ground and cabins are on the bay side of Bahia Honda, overlooking a small inlet; to get to this area, you have to drive under the highway bridge. The three cabins are only a few hundred yards from the highway, so there can be some highway noise when the air conditioning is not on. Each cabin is set up like a small two-bedroom apartment and has a full bath with combination shower and tub, so there is no stumbling through the dark to a campground shower. One bedroom has a double bed and the other a double bed and two twins, so the cabin can sleep four to six people quite comfortably. Two roll-aways can also be used in the living room, though this makes the space a little tight.

The cabins are rustic, with polyurethaned plywood walls, linoleum floors, and simple blinds at the windows. Furniture is serviceable but attractive; there are nightstands and dressers in the bedrooms and bamboo furniture in the sitting and dining area. The kitchen has a small refrigerator-freezer and a full set of pots and pans and tableware. The cabins have no telephone, TV, or radio. Clean linens and towels are provided, but you should bring large beach towels and soap and shampoo — the little store adjacent to the marina has sundries for sale. On the way to Bahia Honda, it may be wise to stop at the supermarket in the town of Big Pine. Big Pine, one of the larger commercial settlements in the Keys, also has a number of good little shops.

Each of the three cabins has a deck overlooking the bay inlet with a barbecue grill and picnic table. The living quarters, all on the second floors of the cabins, are constructed on pilings with a wooden staircase along the side that leads to a railed verandah and the entrance. The verandah runs along the length of the cabin and is a wonderful vantage point from which to view the inlet and the peaceful bay beyond. The inlet is not good for swimming because the edge is rather rocky; most people who want to swim drive to the beaches in the main part of the park. Although there are a few places to explore in the bay side of the campground, the ocean side of the park is quite appealing for the nature lover.

A number of wildflowers grow at Bahia Honda that cannot be found anywhere else in the United States, their seeds carried by hurricanes, the ocean, and birds from the Caribbean islands hundreds of years ago. An unusual species of morning glory thrives here as well as small-flowered lily thorn, yellow satinwood, silver palm, and a variety of other flowers and trees. Some of the flora are rare or endangered, and visitors are cautioned to step with care when taking nature walks.

Bahia Honda is an ideal place for anyone who loves bird watching, nature walks, beaching, boating, or camping out. One could come back here year after year for a lifetime and never begin to see all that there is in this small, peaceful place.

ISLAMORADA

Cheeca Lodge

U.S. Highway 1, Mile Marker 82
P.O. Box 527
Islamorada, FL 33036
305-664-4651
800-327-2888

> *A longtime
> favorite of those
> who can afford
> excellence*

General manager: Tomas B. Zeisel.
Accommodations: 139 rooms, 64 suites. **Rates:** Rooms $125–$425, suites $200–$550; packages available. **Minimum stay:** 2 or 3 nights on some weekends and holidays. **Added:** 11% tax; $25 extra adult; $25 roll-away. **Payment:** Major credit cards; personal check with credit card. **Children:** Under 16 free in room with parents. **Smoking:** Nonsmoking available. **Open:** Year-round.

After his 1989 inauguration, President Bush went for a vacation at Cheeca Lodge on Islamorada. The Presidential Suite he stayed in is the most beautiful accommodation on the property, with expansive rooms, a Jacuzzi in the master bathroom, and luxurious appointments. But it is also warm and informal, with French country furniture, bright rugs accenting the marble floors, and a simple terrace overlooking the water. The Presidential Suite reflects the ambience of the entire lodge — luxurious yet informal, with the focus on both comfort and natural beauty.

Every accommodation at Cheeca Lodge either has been recently decorated or is completely new. There are 49 guest rooms and penthouse suites in the main lodge, as well as 155 villa rooms and suites in villas scattered around the property. All the buildings are of ivory stucco, with deep blue tile roofs and blue shutters. The individual villas are on thick concrete stilts — insurance against hurricane damage — with carports below.

All guest rooms have thick wall-to-wall carpeting or area rugs on marble or tile floors, teak and oak furniture, queen-size and king-size beds, mini-bars, remote control color TV, VCR, and bathrobes. The new baths have large double sinks, glass and tile showers or shower baths, and hair dryers. Many of the porches are screened in and are a pleasure to sit on in any kind of weather, with their views of the water or the landscaped grounds — both, if you're lucky. With the sliding glass doors drawn open, you can bring the outdoors into your room any time of day.

> Cheeca Lodge has plenty of options for those who want to do more than just unwind. There are lighted, all-weather tennis courts; a charming children's playground; a modest nine-hole golf course designed by Jack Nicklaus; sailing and water sports; and great fishing off the 525-foot lighted fishing pier. Deep-sea fishing and various excursions can also be arranged.

The most reasonably priced rooms are in the original lodge building overlooking rooftops or, better, the courtyard. These are spacious, and their bathrooms have a tub/shower, whereas bathrooms in the new cottages have only a large shower stall. The bathrooms also have a second sink and vanity top outside the bathroom proper, opposite a mini-bar and countertop. Natural wooden shutters slide over the big windows. Furnishings are similar to that of the cottages: wood bureaus, double beds, and a glass and bamboo table with wicker chairs. The same type of room in the main lodge is also available overlooking the water, although the rate is a good deal higher.

Cheeca Lodge has always been one of the most beautiful properties on the Keys, with a rich variety of old mahogany, ficus, orchid, gum, palm, and other trees. During the renovation, these were carefully preserved, and areas between the lodge building and the ocean were landscaped with flower beds and small oases of green plants and trees. The lodge grounds are now a greater delight to walk through than ever, night or day.

The recreation area between the main lodge and the ocean is the sort of place where you can linger. There is a lagoon-style swimming pool adjacent to a real lagoon with two springs feeding directly into it from the ocean. Just beyond is the Atlantic, which can always be depended on to provide a cooling breeze. The poolside terrace has a new surface of white concrete and shellstone, which gives the whole area a fresh, clean look. Chaises longues are scattered here and there, and Seminole-built chickee huts give shelter from the sun. You can order a cool drink or a light meal at the snack bar, or call for a waiter from the Ocean Terrace Grill. This patio — with poolside restaurant service, comfortable lawn furniture, a whirlpool spa, and fresh- and saltwater lagoons — provides both fun and rest in the midst of beauty.

For businesspeople, Cheeca Lodge has added the Pavilion, a versatile 4,000-square-foot conference center that accommodates up to 200 people. The Cheeca Lodge is only 75 miles from the Miami Airport, close enough to be accessible but far enough from civilization to give business executives and professionals a sense of getting away from it all.

It's also one of the best places in the Keys to eat. The two restaurants at Cheeca Lodge are the Atlantic Edge, an elegant, semicircular room overlooking the ocean, and the Ocean Terrace Grille, an airy new dining room with oak casement windows that open onto the poolside terrace and the beach. The Light Tackle Lounge, for those who enjoy a drink before or after dinner, is popular with fishermen and other local residents. There are huge mounted fish on the walls, windows overlooking the ocean, a solid teak horseshoe bar, and teak tables. There's live entertainment here till late at night.

The Light Tackle Lounge, the restaurants, and the lodge's boutiques are all in the main building, just off the lobby. The floors of shellstone and concrete are accented with cobalt blue tiles; above are the original cedar beams. French doors lead out to the courtyard and the archway of the front entrance. The shellstone walkway of the courtyard loggia is lined with big clay pots of bougainvillea and several varieties of hibiscus. At night, the loggia and the paths through the grounds of the lodge are lighted for romantic walks. When it's finally time to walk down the lovely loggia for the last time, it's hard to leave this beautiful, restful place.

Chesapeake Resort

Mile Marker 83.5
P.O. Box 909
Islamorada, FL 33036
305-664-4662
800-338-3395

The kind of place families come back to year after year

General manager: Christian Fleisher. **Accommodations:** 65 rooms and suites. **Rates:** Motel rooms $96–$140, efficiencies $110–$160, oceanfront rooms $130–$190, oceanfront suites $200–$425, villas $190–$375; packages available; 15% discount for 7 nights or more. **Minimum stay:** 3 nights on holiday weekends and with some packages. **Added:** 11% tax. **Payment:** Major credit cards; cash. **Children:** 12 and under free in room with parents. **Smoking:** Allowed. **Open:** Year-round.

This is not only a winter vacation spot; Floridians and other Southerners stay at the Chesapeake in the summer, mostly for the island breezes and the relaxed atmosphere. The feeling here is informal and unpretentious. People are here simply to enjoy the salty air and the work and fun of boating or fishing. The Chesapeake is not for the sophisticated — room numbers are painted on baby whales, and the restaurant is plastered with shells that look a bit corny. The informality, the friendly staff, and the availability of both bargain accommodations and more expensive waterfront suites are the attraction.

Islamorada calls itself the "sport fishing capital of the world," and you'll find out why. Boat dockage and the resort's launch ramp are available to guests who arrive by water or have their boat hitched to their car. Amenities do not include hook-ups, and space is limited to boats that are less than 28 feet long. Chesapeake of Whale Harbor charters fishing boats and rents water-sports equipment.

> **For those who love to relax in the sun, the resort's salt-water lagoon is wonderful. The lagoon is suitable for swimming, and its far end is accessible to the Atlantic.**

The villas are the resort's oldest accommodations. Really more like beach cottages, these are 1950s-style, one-story units. There are small lawns in front, and palm and orchid trees dot the area. All of the cottages have full kitchens, a color TV, and a telephone. The furnishings are functional; their ordinariness is relieved by prints on the walls and nice bedspreads. The cottages are well cared for, freshly painted and extremely clean. For a family planning to cook most meals, these are a real bargain.

Next to the office (and closer to the highway) is a two-story motel. Like the other Chesapeake accommodations, these rooms are extremely clean, and the owners have made an effort to compensate for the motel atmosphere. The units are pleasantly decorated and have small balconies and pretty stenciling in the tile baths. Available to all guests are shuffle-board, two swimming pools, a gym, a whirlpool, tennis, and a child's playground. At night, guests and locals gather at the Whale Harbor Restaurant for drinks, hearty food, and live entertainment.

Overlooking the lagoon and the Atlantic are the Chesapeake's newest accommodations, the oceanfront suites. These are in three-story pink stucco buildings that have tin roofs in the tradition of old Florida hostelries. The suites are luxury accommodations that have a Jacuzzi right in the bedroom, and railed balconies have unhindered views of the Atlantic. These are the most sought-after accommodations at the Chesapeake for those who are not on a budget — except for families who've been coming for years and have a favorite cottage.

Pelican Cove Resort

84457 Overseas Highway
Mile Marker 84.5
P.O. Box 633
Islamorada, FL 33036
305-664-4435
800-445-4690

> *A small,*
> *well-cared-for*
> *waterfront resort*

General manager: Cathy Salvatori. **Accommodations:** 39 rooms, suites, and efficiencies. **Rates:** Rooms $105–$155, oceanfront efficiencies $125–175, oceanfront 1-bedroom suites $175–$265. **Minimum stay:** 2 nights on holidays and some weekends. **Added:** 11% tax; $15 extra person. **Children:** Under 16 free in room with parents. **Payment:** Major credit cards. **Smoking:** Allowed. **Open:** Year-round.

The Pelican Cove is on two-lane Route 1, next door to the Theater of the Sea, a dolphin show and educational center. Because the crowds are at the shows during the day, the resort is surprisingly quiet except for occasional highway noise. Activity centers around the swimming pool and a Jacuzzi that overlook the Atlantic. Both are decorated with striking Mediterranean tile. The surrounding patio has light paving stones broken up by little islands of palm trees and other vegetation. The shake-roofed cabana by the pool sells drinks to quench your midday thirst.

Guests arriving by sea can tie up their boats at the Pelican Cove dock. The beach is manmade, like so many in the Keys, where the Atlantic waves have been too gentle over the centuries to turn rock into sand. The white sand of this little beach is dotted with palm trees, and the rock sea wall along the water is picturesque.

The resort arranges deep-sea fishing, and guests may also fish off the dock. Islamorada has the largest charter fleet in the Keys for deep-sea and backcountry fishing. Expert scuba and snorkeling instruction is available at the John Penne-kamp Coral Reef State Park, just down the road. The live coral reef is worth diving to see, even if you have never dived before. There are also new tennis courts for guests only.

> **Guests can rent sailboats at the resort and explore the warm Key Largo waters.**

The resort's accommodations can house a family comfortably. All have either two queen-size beds or a queen and a pullout couch. Deluxe efficiencies have a bed, a sofa bed, and a kitchenette. For couples on a honeymoon, there are luxury one-bedroom suites with Jacuzzi. All of the rooms are decorated in soft pastels with deep blue-gray carpeting, oak furniture, light walls, and prints of waterfowl on the walls. The kitchens in the efficiencies include a counter that wraps around to form a breakfast bar with two chairs.

Railed balconies sweep around the three-story complex. The architecture is Old Florida, with crimped tin roofs and sliding shutters. The palm trees shading the balconies and the pelicans who come to roost on the pilings let you know you're in the subtropics.

KEY LARGO

Largo Lodge Motel

101740 Overseas Highway,
  Mile Marker 101.5
Key Largo, FL 33037
800-IN-THE-SUN; 305/451-0424

> *The real Key Largo, on a budget*

Owner/manager: Harriet Stokes.
Accommodations: 6 duplex apartments. **Rates:** $75–$95. **Minimum stay:** 2 nights. **Added:** 11% tax. **Payment:** MasterCard, Visa. **Children:** 16 and over. **Smoking:** Allowed. **Open:** Year-round.

The Largo Lodge is hidden away several hundred feet off busy Route 1, at the end of a long, narrow driveway canopied with tropical trees and plants. The big wooden sign looks a bit worn, but the honky-tonk of the highway is just a funky memory once guests arrive at this unpretentious motel. This is another world — with exotic ibis, ducks, lizards, and squirrels sharing the grounds. It feels almost as if guests are the intruders here.

> **Snorkeling and scuba diving are available at nearby John Pennekamp Coral Reef Park, one of the best places for diving in the United States.**

Largo Lodge has a dock with dockage space for guests' boats and a typical Florida Keys beach: small and manmade. A wide lawn runs directly to the beach, and this is where many of the animals wander, unconcerned with human onlookers. Under small shade trees near the dock are cushioned PVC lawn chairs and chaise longues.

The lodge's accommodations are tucked away in its canopied "jungle." All are white brick, one-story 1950s duplexes. They have a living/dining room furnished with attractive bamboo furniture, kitchen, bedroom, bathroom with shower, and a screened-in porch. The appointments are "motel modern," and everything is clean and well cared for. The landscaping around the duplexes has been allowed to grow profusely but not out of control. Pots of colorful hibiscus and poinsettia on the doorsteps accent all the green.

The Largo Lodge offers fishing off the dock (bring your own equipment), swimming, and beaching. The beach is a boon in the Keys, where there are few sandy beaches with open-water swimming.

Marina Del Mar

527 Caribbean Drive,
   Mile Marker 100
P.O. Box 1050
Key Largo, FL 33037
305-451-4107
800-451-3483

> *A great place to tie up your boat or just hang your hat*

Assistant general manager: Fay Bailey. **Accommodations:** 76 rooms and suites. **Rates:** Rooms $89–$130, studios $120–

$160, suites $955–$310; packages available; weekday rates reduced. **Included:** Continental breakfast. **Minimum stay:** On some holidays. **Added:** 11% tax; surcharge for some holidays. **Payment:** Major credit cards. **Children:** Free in room with parent. **Smoking:** Nonsmoking available. **Open:** Year-round.

At least 40 percent of the Marina Del Mar's guests come for the scuba diving at nearby John Pennekamp Coral Reef State Park. But they also come for the fantastic fishing and the resort's excellent deep-water marina. For those who don't own a boat, Marina Del Mar is a low-key, relaxing place with a lively restaurant and lounge.

The hotel is built on coral on the Atlantic side of Key Largo. Because of the reefs offshore, there is no heavy water action, and therefore no sandy beach. The lack of a beach and small waves disappoint some people, but the gentle waves make for great diving. If you're not interested in diving, it is enough to relax on a bench overlooking the marina and watch the boats and the people.

Marina Del Mar succeeds in looking unmanicured and pretty at the same time. Square, wooden planters hold a profuse array of bougainvillea in coral, dusty pink, and cream. The swimming pool and expanded sun deck have similar plantings. In the evening, the patio and the railings of the wooden ramps to the resort's restaurant are lit with tiny lights The one drawback to this area is that pool maintenance has slipped recently, and the tiling and cement paving is not as clean as it should be.

A few steps from the patio is Coconuts Restaurant and Lounge, a lively, though never wild, meeting place for fishermen, divers, boaters, and other locals. There's a handsome bar overlooking the boat slips, and clusters of small tables and chairs here and there. The sounds of nightly live entertainment in the lounge float into the adjoining restaurant, which serves lunch and dinner. Food is hearty, and the chef uses his imagination.

The restaurant, pool, and lounge are located well away from the accommodations, to allow guests a good night's rest. Rooms and apartments are reasonably priced for the area, and a great deal of effort is made to make them attractive. All are housed in three main buildings of light green stucco, with pink railed verandahs that overlook the water. There are five types of lodging: standard rooms, marina-view rooms, marina-view studios, one-bedroom suites, two-bedroom marina-view suites, and three-bedroom marina-view suites. All have color TV with movies, radios, refrigerators, and exceptional tiled bathrooms with whirlpool tubs.

The studios and suites have completely equipped kitchens with full-size refrigerators, coffeemakers, toasters, dishes, and plenty of pots and pans. They also have built-in entertainment centers in the living room and a dining room set for four. Studio apartments have a couch in the living room and a Murphy bed. The two- and three-bedroom suites are more luxurious, with pretty sofas and love seats, and two tiled bathrooms.

> **The one-bedroom suites are so well designed and roomy that a family of four can live quite comfortably for many days without feeling cramped.**

In all of the accommodations, an effort has been made to give a feeling of space and luxury. Rates in all the accommodations include daily maid service.

The marina and the main buildings of Marina Del Mar are on the Atlantic side of Key Largo, but the resort now also has Bayside, a suite hotel just off Route 1. Standard rooms have two double beds, and nice bathrooms. The king standard room is the same but with a king-size bed. Suites overlooking the water above the patio have tile floors, a kitchenette with a full stove and refrigerator, small bedroom with a king bed, and a Murphy bed in the dining and living room. Bayside includes first-floor wheelchair-accessible rooms, with parking space right next to the room's entrance and a sidewalk and ramps up to the door.

Sheraton Key Largo Resort

97000 S. Overseas Highway,
  Mile Marker 97
Key Largo, FL 33037
305-852-5553
800-325-3535

> *A choice getaway spot on Florida Bay*

Accommodations: 200 rooms and suites. **Rates:** Rooms $145–$255, suites $189–$410. **Minimum stay:** With some packages. **Added:** 11% tax; $15 extra person. **Children:** Under 17 free in room with parents. **Payment:** Major credit cards. **Smoking:** Nonsmoking rooms available. **Open:** Year-round.

Just a little over an hour from the Miami airport, the Sheraton Key Largo is an ideal hotel for executives who want to work in a businesslike atmosphere removed from the city. The location feels remote, even though guests are just a few minutes' walk from busy Route 1. With its romantic bayfront location and some convivial nearby watering holes, it is a great place for honeymooners, and the outdoor swimming pool and native hammock make the Sheraton nice for families, too. This is a place where you can leave your troubles behind and play hard or work hard without the hassles of civilization.

The resort has two lagoon-shaped pools on two levels connected by a grotto and waterfalls, one pool for children (and their parents) and another for adults. Bright bougainvillea and other tropical plants spilling over the rocks make the grotto and patio festive. At the upper-level pool, Splashes serves kids and adults light meals and cool drinks.

Across the hotel grounds is the dock, with 21 slips and a manmade beach overlooking Florida Bay. It's too rocky for comfortable swimming until you get out pretty far, but the crescent-shaped beach is a nice place to stretch out in one of the hotel's chaises. Between the beach and the hotel is a boardwalk with wooden stairs to the hotel. These traverse a dense hammock (an Indian word for a tropical hardwood forest), with many rare and endangered trees. This is a favorite place for nature walks for children and parents, though it is important to protect the trees by staying on the boardwalk. Just above the nature boardwalk is Tree Tops, a bar that commands romantic views of the bay and the leafy treetops in the forest, particularly at dusk and at night.

Accommodations include standard, superior, and deluxe rooms, and spacious suites. Prices reflect square footage and views; some rooms overlook the bay, others the parking lot and pool. All accommodations are decorated in light colors and light pine furniture. All have balconies. The bathrooms are surprisingly large, with double sinks, a tile shower bath, and a makeup mirror above the sinks.

Tennis and swimming are popular here. Fishing and boating are great fun on Key Largo, and the Sheraton staff will make arrangements for both. Nearby is snorkeling and scuba diving at the John Pennekamp State Park, which has a storied coral reef that should not be missed. A 14-mile bike and jogging path traverses the Key. The Sheraton property itself, landscaped with brilliant flowers and lush greenery, is an enjoyable place to explore.

A sense of tropical tranquility and beauty descends as you step onto the cool terra cotta tiles of the lobby. Behind the check-in counter is an unusual coral rock mural. The shells and coral that formed naturally within the rock itself are accentuated with bright enameled tropical fish painted by the artist.

Just off the lobby and lounge are the conference facilities, which include a

> **Fishtales, on the top floor of the hotel, is the place for dancing and music. The gourmet restaurant at the Sheraton is Christina's, where the specialty is seafood. Café Key Largo is more casual. Its Sunday brunch, popular with Key Largo residents as well as hotel guests, is a must for anyone staying the weekend.**

ballroom and a spacious boardroom. French doors lead from the lounge to a patio that can be transformed into a reception area. The larger suites can double as hospitality suites and small meeting rooms for executive work sessions.

This is not just another Sheraton. Care has been taken by those who operate the resort to provide a pleasant environment. All guest rooms were refurbished in 1993. The one drawback is a recent lowering of standards in upkeep in the lounge and lobby. Sadly, throughout Florida, this has been one result of the recession and the downturn in tourism.

KEY WEST

The Artist House

534 Eaton Street
Key West, FL 33040
305-296-3977
800-582-7882

> *A lavender and*
> *white confection*

Innkeeper: Darryl Meyer. **Accommodations:** 2 rooms, 3 suites, 1 master suite. **Rates:** $79–$225. **Included:** Continental breakfast off season, full breakfast in season. **Minimum stay:** 3 nights during holidays. **Added:** 11% tax. **Payment:** Major credit cards. **Children:** Under 10 not permitted. **Smoking:** Only on balconies and back patio. **Open:** Year-round.

The Artist House is a dream for anyone who loves Victoriana: intricate scrolling on the brackets of the verandahs, louvered shutters, etched-glass transoms above doors, a tin-roofed turret, and a black wrought-iron fence enclosing the azaleas in the little front garden. If an art historian — or a movie producer — were looking for the perfect Key West Victorian, this would be it. A recent slip in the standards of cleanliness is sad to see in such a jewel, even considering this *is* laid-back Key West.

The Artist House is just one block from busy, touristy Duval Street — close enough to be near all the excitement but far enough to provide respite from it. Built in 1890 and once owned by Key West painter Gene Otto, the house has been beautifully restored. Guest rooms have four-poster and brass beds, hand-painted wallpapers, wood floors, wing chairs, and lace curtains at the large double-hung windows. The furnishings are antique or good reproductions. Appointments include oil paintings and Oriental vases and lamps.

> A large Jacuzzi in the garden is surrounded by terra cotta pots of flowering and green plants. A dwarf palm tree shades an ornate iron garden bench on the brick patio. Later in the day, this is the perfect place to unwind after taking in the sights of Key West's Old Town.

One of the most popular rooms (which must be reserved well in advance) is the Turret Suite on the second floor. Its sitting room bay has wing chairs and a sofa complemented by faux marble tables. Floors are polished pine, with a blue and cream Oriental rug on the floor. Through narrow double doors opposite the brass and porcelain spindled bedstead is an enclosed porch. Adjacent to the doors is a winding staircase that leads up to the third-floor turret. From this vantage point, one can look out over Key West.

Anne's Suite is one of the quietest rooms, with a private entrance and stairway as well as a hallway door that shuts it off from the house. The mahogany four-poster is queen-size, covered with a white eyelet spread and set against a backdrop of four paisley-curtained windows. Walls are a deep rose. The Chinese rug on the pine floors is pretty, but on our last visit was quite soiled. The bathroom is original, with a clawfoot tub, horizontal white-painted paneling, and blue and white tile border of festooned ribbons and flowers — very Victorian.

The other rooms have interesting features and furniture: a desk with a hand-tooled leather top, an Oriental chest, a fireplace, or a carved bedstead. Though each guest room has individual character, they are in keeping with the Queen Anne Victorian architecture of the house, which includes carved mahogany banisters and crown moldings. But comfort is not sacrificed for authenticity. A telephone and television are found in every room. The private bathrooms have been recently replumbed, and in most cases, newly tiled.

In season, a full breakfast is served to guests in the back garden. A typical winter breakfast includes an egg dish with a breakfast meat or pancakes. The Continental breakfast, served off-season, usually consists of fresh fruit, homemade muffins, cereal, and coffee.

The Banyan Resort

323 Whitehead Street
Key West, FL 33040
800-225-0639
305-296-7786
Fax: 305-294-1107

A Key West institution

General manager: Gilbert Russell. **Accommodations:** 38 suites. **Rates:** Studios $115–$185, suites $130–$265; weekly rates available. **Minimum stay:** During some holidays, weekends, and special events. **Added:** 11% tax; $20 for extra person. **Payment:** Major credit cards. **Children:** Older children preferred. **Smoking:** Allowed. **Open:** Year round.

You spend the first few minutes after arriving at the Banyan Resort gaping and gasping. Spectacular banyan trees dominate the gardens around the white Victorian mansions of the Banyan Resort. Guests drive into the brick-paved drive of the white mansion whose front parlor serves as a reception area and first look up at the huge banyan tree that is in the middle of the front garden. Next door is another white Victorian house with a lacy banistered verandah that is also part of the complex. These two houses back onto a garden where there are six more Victorian houses and a banyan tree (trees) many centuries old. During those hundreds of years, more and more tendrils kept descending to the ground and forming more baby trees, so that the banyans here are more like a family of trees, forming a huge canopy of branches above and a vertical web of tree trunks below. They are fascinating.

The eight Victorian houses that compose the resort, most of which are on the National Register of Historic Places, have their own fascinating features: tin roofs, ornate porch brackets, lacy balustrades, fish-scale shingles, leaded glass doors, large bay windows. They're all very pretty, very gracious. Inside are surprisingly fresh, contemporary furnishings and designer fabrics.

There's a great deal to choose from here: studios, one-bedroom suites, and two-bedroom suites with one or two baths. Some of the suites have loft bedrooms, and the spacious studios have Murphy beds. All rooms have furnished kitchens, modern private bathrooms, color TV, and telephones. The one-bedroom suites have a sleep sofa and they can sleep a total of four people, while the two-bedroom suites (which also have a dining area) have a sleep sofa and can accommodate six.

> **There are a total of 200 varieties of tropical and subtropical flora at the Banyan, in flower beds connected by curving pathways to the swimming pools and the eight houses.**

Guests who are light sleepers will probably want to be in one of the studios or suites toward the back of the resort, since Whitehead Street can be a little noisy with mopeds and cars roaring along. Many people like the upstairs rooms that have a romantic balcony and a bird's-eye view of the gardens. Other long-time guests think that the best rooms are those that are on the ground floor with their own little patio area shielded by a high wood fence. Ask what's available when you make reservations.

One very nice feature of staying here is the Banyan's custom of allowing guests to use the pool and facilities after they have checked out. You can keep your bags in the little luggage sheds near the pools until you're ready to leave.

All accommodations have a private patio or a verandah overlooking the garden flourishing beneath the big banyan tree. It is this backyard area that makes the Banyan feel like a world apart. There are two pools and a Jacuzzi to soak in here, but it is really the shaded tropical garden that creates the mood of a hidden Caribbean retreat.

Although all accommodations have a kitchen, many guests do little cooking. A Continental breakfast is served every morning except Sunday from the rustic-looking Tiki bar under the banyan tree. Coffee is complimentary, and croissants, bagels, yogurt, cereal, fruit, juice, and specialty coffees and teas are available at a reasonable charge. Lunch is served "noonish to sometime around 5" and includes Caesar salad, grilled chicken, and hamburgers and hot dogs. Most guests eat meals at quite a leisurely pace, lounging around the pool or on their private verandah or deck while they eat and drink. The Tiki bar also offers beer, wine, and iced tea.

Bicycles are for rent at $8 for a full day, although the major Key West attractions and shopping are within walking distance — that is, if you can bear to leave this place.

Duval House

815 Duval Street
Key West, FL 33040
305-294-1666

> *One of Key West's most beautiful and restful guesthouses*

Owner: Richard Kamradt. **Accommodations:** 28 rooms and suites. **Rates:** Rooms $95–$165 ($75–$110 with shared bath), suites $110–$220; slightly higher during some holidays, lower for weekly stays. **Included:** Continental breakfast buffet. **Minimum stay:** None. **Added:** 11% tax; $15 for extra adult. **Payment:** Major credit cards. **Children:** Under 14 preferred. **Smoking:** Allowed. **Open:** Year-round.

Duval Street is essentially the main street of historic Old Town and sees a lot of action; late at night, it can get downright wild. But at Duval House, most guests are oblivious to the Key West rowdies, with whom Hemingway might have hung out at Sloppy Joe's. The three Victorian houses that make up the inn are just far enough from Mallory Square and the center of the action that there is little to interfere with a guest's relaxation, night or day. At the same time, the charming historic district and the boutiques and galleries at the high end of Duval Street are at the doorstep, to say nothing of the gulf and the Atlantic at opposite ends of the street.

Guests are an adults-only mixture of gays and straights who want to enjoy Key West in an oasislike setting. The feeling of seclusion is largely due to the lovely back garden the three houses share, with a huge banyan tree dripping rust-colored roots from its limbs, a variety of palms and other large subtropical and tropical trees, and many flowering plants.

Connecting the houses and garden is a pathway and an attractive wooden sun deck. The airy pool lounge overlooking the Spanish-tile swimming pool has a deep jungle green awning that shades the French doors of its entrance. Inside are a comfortable couch and rockers, a communal kitchen, color television, a small library, and a number of puzzles and games. A Continental breakfast buffet is laid out here every morning.

The first two houses that were first made into guest quarters were originally tenements for cigar makers in the 1800s. They were vacant and neglected when the previous owners bought them in the early 1980s. Atten-

> **Restoration was done expertly, always with an eye to comfort and making the most of the Key West breezes.**

tion to detail shows in the renovation of these two houses — and the third that was added later. With pale salmon-colored clapboard siding, white trim, and dark green wooden shutters, the houses are charming examples of Key West Victoriana. The rooms have lots of windows, and most open onto verandahs with white railings and gingerbread detailing. Although all the rooms are air conditioned, they don't need to be if the windows are open and the paddle fan is whirring overhead.

Duval House now has a number of suites that have private patios and kitchens. Furnishings in all the guest rooms are an interesting mix of West Indies and turn-of-the-century style. The armoires are great fun, with inlaid burled woods and odd curves and moldings. Beds are firm and comfortable, and the vibrant tropical bedspreads contrast well with the delicate wall colors. Some rooms have high ceilings with intricate crown moldings or stenciling, and all have immaculate baths. Special touches, like decorative antiques and small stone carvings placed on a shelf or table, show how much thought has gone into creating the ambience of each room.

For anyone who wants to sample the glories — and the excesses — of Key West, Duval Street is the place to be. But the Duval House has more to offer than that. The historic authenticity of these three homes, their charming verandahs, and the spectacular jungle garden they overlook are the features best loved by people who come back year after year.

Eden House

1015 Fleming Street
Key West, FL 33040
800-533-KEYS
305-296-6868
Fax 305-294-1221

> *Varied accom-*
> *modations with*
> *an artistic owner*

Owner: Mark Eden. **Accommodations:** 40 rooms and suites. **Rates:** Rooms with shared baths $55–$75, rooms with semi-private baths $60–$90, rooms with private baths $70–$125, suites $90–$275; reduced weekly rates available off season. **Included:** Afternoon refreshments during high season. **Minimum stay:** With packages. **Added:** 11% tax. **Payment:** Major credit cards. **Children:** Welcome at additional charge. **Smoking:** Outside. **Open:** Year-round.

The Eden House is another one of those Florida institutions where the out-of-town visitor, with reservations and the glowing reports of friends, drives up and thinks, "Oh, no, this *can't* be right." The place almost looks like a converted gas station from the 1920s. It sits squarely facing Fleming Street with just a perfunctory sidewalk in front. Its architectural style could maybe be called 1920s Art Deco–bungalow–Mediterannean, with traces of Aztec. The stucco exterior is painted white, with squarish pillars on the front porch, and a timbered, Spanish-style verandah above. At the top of the hotel is a ziggurat cut-out design that looks both Art Deco and Aztecian.

On the front porch are painted metal rockers that have been there since the 1930s, along with some potted and hanging plants and, often, somebody's bicycle resting against a porch pillar. Everything looks fresh and clean, so there's reason to be encouraged. Inside are more reasons: a pleasant, cool-looking lobby furnished in white wicker with touches of white lattice and Victorian spindles and brackets at the registration desk. On the left side of the lobby is a door to the pool patio and garden. This is where even the most jaded traveler can get really excited. The garden patio is a wonderful space. Three Victorian houses that owner Mark Eden bought to convert into luxury accommodations form an enclave with the original Art Deco hotel.

The location of the Eden House is perfect for those who want to be within walking or bicycling distance of Old Town but don't want to be right in the middle of it all. Bikes are availble for a reasonable fee. The Eden House staff pride themselves on service and enjoy pointing guests to island restuarants and Key West events.

Many guesthouses in Key West are composed of several individual houses that back up onto each other, forming a patio and pool area. But the one at the Eden House is especially impressive. Odd little stairs and bridges crisscross between the houses and go up and down between floors. A small wooden bridge curves over a goldfish pond surrounded by greenery and a slender tree festooned with Spanish moss. There are lots of unnecessary and sometimes even slightly loopy but purely wonderful details like this. Mark Eden's sense of play and artistry is evident everywhere.

At the same time, the Eden House is a well-run hotel. For example, two large wicker baskets sit on the wooden deck by the pool, one for wet towels and one for freshly laundered and carefully rolled ones. The patio and boardwalks between the various buildings are well-swept and always in good repair.

The houses that back onto the pool patio were expertly restored and are largely responsible for the hotel's historic preservation awards. The turn-of-the-century Victorian facing Fleming Street is particularly pretty, with teal clapboards and gingerbread details. All four houses have porches or verandahs, most of them overlooking the garden patio and pool.

Meals and snacks are available at Rich's Cafe, which has outdoor seating near the pool and Jacuzzi.

In some ways, the Eden House is a luxury guesthouse. The three Victorian houses have deluxe rooms and suites with features like queen-size beds, lofts, and private terraces. The honeymoon suite has an oak spiral staircase that leads to a sleeping loft and balcony above the pool and garden. But the original hotel was once a budget hostelry that attracted bohemian residents and visitors to Key West. When Mark Eden bought the place in 1975, he slowly repaired and repainted the place, offering bargain rates to artists and low-budget travelers who would put up with the sawdust and wet paint.

As the place became more popular, Mark Eden could have gutted the interior of the original Art Deco building and converted the old rooms into luxury accommodations. Fortunately for longtime guests and for anyone who is appalled by present Key West room rates, he chose not to do this. As a result, it is still possible to get a basic but attractive room here, with a sink in the corner and the bathroom down the hall. These 10 guest rooms are referred to as "European" and do, in fact, attract a good many Continental travelers who can't understand our prissy insistence on private baths. They're also popular with American students. Other budget accommodations available are guest rooms that share baths between two rooms. These are particularly good for families and friends who want connecting rooms.

Heron House

512 Simonton
Key West, FL 33040
305-294-9227
Fax: 305-294-5692

*A labor of love
and a haven of
rest and beauty*

Owner: Fred Geibelt. **Accommodations:** 21 rooms. **Rates:** Rooms $75–$185; seventh night of weekly stay free except in February and March. **Included:** Continental breakfast buffet. **Minimum stay:** Some holidays. **Added:** 11% tax; $20 for extra person in winter, $10 in summer. **Payment:** Major credit cards. **Children:** Under 15 not permitted. **Smoking:** Not permitted. **Open:** Year-round.

In a town where guesthouse owners pride themselves on their gardens, innkeeper Fred Geibelt has one of the loveliest. The entrance to the Heron House is through a pair of large cedar gates set in a coral stone wall. Inside are brick patios and a garden shaded with mango and avocado trees and palms.

Fred Giebelt has also created special accommodations. Three old homes make up Heron House, their backs or sides opening onto the garden and pool deck. The newest rooms are the best, with walls of beveled wood, granite vanities, and old-fashioned verandahs.

Terra cotta pots of fig trees are placed around the swimming pool near well-tended beds of bougainvillea, jasmine, and bird-of-paradise. Orchids and ferns drape down from little wire planters attached to palm trunks.

New rooms upstairs have handcrafted stained glass transoms above each door. Some older accommodations have walls of the original pine. Recent changes include wet bars in some of the rooms and the replacement of queen beds with kings. Though some rooms are larger and more spectacular than others, all are furnished with West Indian–style wicker and have pretty bedspreads in tropical colors. Irma Quigley's watercolors decorate the walls, and thin venetian blinds at the windows filter the subtropical light. Bathrooms are interesting and modern, constantly being upgraded by Fred, who loves to work around the place.

In the morning, Fred serves an informal, do-it-yourself Continental breakfast under a breezeway. A table near the pool is set with a pitcher of fruit juice, a toaster, a basket of homemade muffins, English muffins, and bread, butter and jam, and coffee. Guests usually eat on chairs and chaises around the pool or in the cool breezeway. Heron House's guests tend to be well-traveled, congenial, and dedicated to the B&B experience.

The swimming pool at Heron House is small, but the deck is so attractive it hardly matters. Beside the pool are oversize coral planters that Fred put in along with brick paving. At the bottom of the pool is a mosaic of a blue heron done by a friend of Fred's. Unusual features like this reflect the mood of this exceptional guesthouse.

Hyatt Key West

601 Front Street
Key West, FL 33040
305-296-9900
800-233-1234
Telex: 529667
Fax: 305-292-1038

> *A breezy,*
> *tropical respite*

Managing director: Ernst Bacher. **Accommodations:** 128 rooms, 8 suites, 8 king salons. **Rates:** Rooms $190–$345, suites $325–$600. **Minimum stay:** With packages. **Added:** 11% tax. **Payment:** Major credit cards. **Children:** Under 18 free in room with parents. **Smoking:** Nonsmoking rooms available. **Open:** Year-round.

The turquoise waters of the Gulf of Mexico provide the setting for one of Key West's most refreshing hotels, the Hyatt Key West. The Hyatt is built in Old Florida style with tin roofs, smooth peach stucco exteriors, French doors opening onto verandahs, and white-railed balustrades.

Guests enter a small lobby, checking in at a cherrywood registration counter. A full-time concierge is ready to arrange for any Key West activity that a guest can conjure up. Many guests simply want to rest between excursions and enjoy the tropical breeze that blows across this pretty corner of Old Town. Just off the lobby, a fish pond and gentle waterfall set the mood for relaxation, while a mosaic wall mural of Key West echoes the vibrancy of the town. The mural and fish pond lead to the Hyatt's airy patio and pool. Here, a kiosk has a posting of the day's events in the town of Key West and at the hotel. Also posted is the national weather, which compares the balmy Key West temperature to that of Chicago and other frigid cities.

Wooden decks and walkways lead guests to the Hyatt's restaurants and bars and the pier and marina on the gulf. Large clay pots of tropical plants and flowers and groupings of palms and fig trees accent the patio and decks. All the lawn furniture is sparkling white, kept so by a vigilant maintenance staff. The Hyatt's swimming pool is the centerpiece of the patio, with the Hyatt's popular restaurant, Nick's, and the pier and beach beyond. A gazebo overlooks the Jacuzzi and the pool, where bands sometimes play in the evening.

The beach is small and manmade but well maintained,

rimmed by large chunks of rough coral called key stone. The Hyatt's marina offers dockage to guests staying at the hotel. A 65-foot yacht, *Floridays,* is docked here and can be rented by guests for daytime fishing, snorkeling, or romantic evening cruises.

One of the nicest things about the pier and dock is the deck that leads to them, where there's plenty of room for sunning on chaises. It's pleasant to hear the marina traffic but to be lazily removed from it. Deck service from Scuttles, the poolside bar and grill, makes it unnecessary to get up even for lunch or drinks.

When you do summon the energy to get up, there are a couple of choices for light lunches, drinks, and dinner. Scuttles, which closes at sunset, has an

> **Women for Sail, a sailing school, operates from the Hyatt's marina. The hotel also has Yamaha wave-runners for rent and can arrange for snorkeling, scuba diving, and fishing trips.**

unusual tiled bar and overlooks the water. Nicole's is the resort's seafood restuarant, located downstairs from Nick's Grill. Both restuarants are in a clapboard building with an Old Florida–style tin roof that is reminiscent of turn-of-the-century Key West. Both have indoor and outdoor dining overlooking a slice of the gulf — ideal for leisurely meals. In the evenings, many guests start out with drinks on the deck above the gulf and the sunset.

Accommodations at the Hyatt are in five-floor buildings that include a range of prices, sizes, beds, and views. The Hyatt has six handicapped-accessible rooms and two floors in each building with nonsmoking rooms. As more families visiting Key West have chosen to stay at the Hyatt, the hotel has increased the number of rooms with two double beds. Some rooms have better views than others, and the Hyatt usually compensates for a mediocre view with more space. If you are traveling with children and know you'll be spending most of your time outdoors, ask about these larger standard rooms. The Hyatt will make an effort to upgrade your room during low season whenever possible.

The rooms and suites have very pretty decor: tropical pastels in bedspreads and sofas and a generous use of a deep green in upholstery fabrics. Furniture is of oak or wicker with white stain, and some of the floor lamps and entryway tables are of bleached coral stone. The tiled bathrooms have oversize tubs with a grab bar. There are shining porcelain and chrome fixtures, hair dryers, and a conch shell with a natural sponge and complimentary toiletries. Suites have double sinks and a little more room in the bathroom. Cotton waffle-weave robes hang in the spacious closets.

All the rooms have large balconies with a small table and two chairs; the suites have double balconies furnished with chaises and a table and chairs. The higher-priced suites on the top floors have a large sitting room with tile floors and area rugs, a desk and two phones, and sliding glass doors out to the large balcony. Views of the gulf and the small islands beyond the marina will take your breath away, especially at sunset.

The Hyatt offers a lot more for visitors of all ages. Bicycles and mopeds are available for rent, and various water sports and excursions can be arranged through the Hyatt's helpful concierge. Babysitting service, strollers, wheelchairs, and crutches are available to all guests. A children's program, Camp Hyatt, is open during summer vacations and holidays. It includes special activities such as an underwater Easter egg hunt. At Christmastime there is a visit from Santa, and all guests enjoy watching a fireworks display and the boats in the marina that are decorated for the holidays.

Throughout the year, the Hyatt staff organize a number of conferences and executive retreats. The resort has meeting and banquet facilities, with a 448-square-foot executive boardroom overlooking the gulf and a larger meeting facility that can accommodate up to 120 people. The clientele at the Hyatt Key West is varied, with many businesspeople, vacationing couples and families. The clientele is also international, with many visitors from the United Kingdom, Canada, and South America.

At the manager's cocktail reception on Wednesday evenings, guests can meet Ernst Bacher, the general manager. A gracious Austrian with years of experience in the hotel business, Bacher is enthusiastic about the relaxing Key West lifestyle and the Hyatt's contribution to it. The Hyatt has greater privacy than most hotels in Key West. Most hotels here have all or part of the place open to outsiders. Except for power lunches at Nick's, which Key West businesspeople come to, the Hyatt is here for its guests only. "Then too," he smiles, "a lot of our success is just Key West itself. We all love it here."

Island City House

411 William Street
Key West, FL 33040
305-294-5702
800-634-8230
Fax: 305-294-1289

> *Three historic houses clustered around a tropical garden*

Manager: Stanley and Janet Corneal. **Accommodations:** 24 suites. **Rates:** Studios $95–$165, 1-bedroom suites $115–$210, 2-bedroom suites $145–$275; packages available. **Included:** Continental breakfast. **Minimum stay:** 2 nights during holidays. **Added:** 11% tax; $20 for extra person in room; charges for crib, futon. **Payment:** MasterCard, Visa. **Children:** Under 12 free in room with parents. **Smoking:** Allowed. **Open:** Year-round.

The main house of Island City House is a tall, narrow Victorian trimmed with gingerbread and graced with breezy verandahs on all three floors. Its top floor, capped with a pediment and four improbable-looking wedding cake spires, was added in 1912. The original owner, Samuel Lowe, heard that Flagler's railroad was coming and added the third floor to turn his family home into a hotel. The Lowes also owned an interesting oddity called the Arch House on Eaton Street. Eaton is perpendicular to Williams, so the rear of the Arch House backs up onto the back yard of the Williams Street House. The Arch House is like a double house, with an ornate gingerbread archway between the two buildings through which a horse and carriage could drive to reach the cigar factory behind. It is the only extant carriage house on the island. The third house that makes up Island City House B&B is a replica of a cigar house that stood on the same spot.

Those who call early get their choice of one- and two-bedroom suites. The rooms in the Arch House and the Island City House are very Victorian, with wonderful dark antiques, lace and rose bedspreads, old-fashioned curtains, and memorabilia. The spindle-railed verandahs onto which the rooms open are charming.

But there is much to be said for the Cigar House, built in the 1980s by the previous owners, who were preservationists with a keen interest in Key West history. This reproduction of the Alfonso Cigar Factory was built of natural cypress, with louvered doors and hardwood floors. All the suites have a spacious sitting area with a pullout sofa, separate bedroom, full kitchen, and roomy bath. The decor is contemporary, with bright tropical colors. The first-floor suites open onto the pool and sun deck, while those on the second floor have a balcony overlooking the pool and Jacuzzi. These parlor suites are good for families and couples traveling together.

> The tropical garden is shaded by big trees, while the deck that surrounds the Jacuzzi and pool is sunny. Brick pathways connect the three houses and the little office cottage. Under one tree is a brick patio with a covered breakfast bar, where fruit and danish is spread out every morning.

The Island City House is the sort of place where you can feel at home right away. Unlike some guesthouses in Key West that cater only to adults and have a large gay clientele, here there are guests of all ages and lifestyles, including many families.

La Pensione

809 Truman Avenue
Key West, FL 33040
305-292-9923
Fax: 305-296-6509

> *A skillfully restored historic house*

Innkeeper: Vincent Cerrito and Joseph Rimkus. **Accommodations:** 7 rooms. **Rates:** $98–$148; holiday rates slightly higher. **Included:** Expanded Continental breakfast. **Minimum stay:** 2 nights on weekends, 4 nights on holidays. **Added:** 11% tax. **Payment:** Visa, MasterCard, Discover; personal check with 10-day advance. **Children:** Discouraged. **Smoking:** Allowed; preferred outside. **Open:** Year round.

Innkeepers Vince Cerrito and Joe Rimkus owned another B&B in Key West before buying the 19th-century clapboard structure that was to become La Pensione. They therefore knew how to preserve the physical beauty of an old house and at the same time provide the modern amenities that vacationers want. A strict preservationist, knowing that the house dates back to the late 1800s, might express surprise that the old pine floors aren't exposed in the bedrooms or that there aren't clawfoot tubs in all the baths. However, in their last B&B venture, Vince and Joe learned that wooden floors are noisy floors and that old tubs strung up with gerrymandered shower heads can lose their charm quickly. Consequently they endeavored to and succeeded in preserving important interior and exterior features of the house while creating fresh, modern bathrooms and a pretty pool patio off the parking lot.

> **Apart from swimming and relaxing by the pool, guests at La Pensione have an easy walk or ride to the heart of Old Town Key West, where there are any number of places to hang out and soak up the island atmosphere.**

The Italian word *pensione* means a room in a private home, and there is certainly that feeling of hominess in this B&B. But the guest rooms are also a little more spacious than many rooms in historic guesthouses in Key West, and they are immaculate. Each room is furnished in Ethan Allen furniture (no sticky antique bureau drawers here) and has a firm king bed. The designer fabric spreads match upholstered loveseats that are set in a corner or before a bank of lace-curtained windows. The tile bathrooms have new sinks and fixtures in traditional styles that nicely blend appropriate Victorian design with modern dependability. Room number 7 has a dressing area, which makes it a bit larger than the average room, and also has access to the upstairs verandah, as do 8 and 9. On the first floor is La Pensione's wheelchair-accessible guest room.

Also downstairs is a front parlor that now serves as a reception area and, behind that, a dining room that has been beautifully restored. This is a fairly small room, but it has the original tile fireplace intact. Breakfast is served here or can be taken out on one of the verandahs. It's difficult to know whether to call this a Continental or full breakfast since the only items missing from what would usually be termed "full" are sausage and eggs. The innkeepers usually serve a main dish like Belgian waffles and fresh fruit, homemade muffins and breads, orange juice, coffee, tea, and decaf. For honeymooners, they will create a special breakfast that might include a cranberry morning cake or their renowned lemon banana walnut creation. The fragrances waft up the hallway from the kitchen — no need for a wake-up call.

In the dining room there are books for guests to borrow and photo albums of old Key West to look through. La Pensione, built in 1891, is certainly a part of the history of Old Town. The house is on Truman Avenue, a fairly busy street since it's the main route of arrival for tourists but also a great location for getting to know Key West on foot.

1991 marked the 100th anniversary of the house and was also the year that innkeepers Joe and Vince completed its restoration. They preserved the fluted moldings around the windows and repaired the newel post at the foot of the front stairway, which was composed of more than 200 pieces of wood. They painted the clapboards of the exterior a deep yellow. The trim and the verandah banisters are white and the louvered shutters green, a typical Victorian color scheme. Vince and Joe put in a swimming pool on the east side of the house, building a wooden fence around the patio for privacy.

La Mer Hotel

506 South Street
Key West, FL 33040
305-296-5611
Reservations:
Old Town Resorts
1319 Duval Street
Key West, FL 33040
305-296-5611
800-354-4455

> *The Victorian charm of Key West with the amenities of a resort motel*

Group sales and information: 305-294-5539
Fax: 305-294-8272

Accommodations: 11 rooms. **Rates:** $105–$245. **Included:** Continental breakfast. **Minimum stay:** 2 nights during holidays and winter. **Added:** 11% tax. **Payment:** Major credit cards. **Children:** Under 12 not permitted. **Smoking:** Allowed. **Open:** Year-round.

La Mer, a Queen Anne–style B&B, is one of Key West's three Old Town Resorts. The other two are the Southernmost

Motel in the USA and South Beach Oceanfront Motel. La Mer and the South Beach Motel both front South Street, with the Atlantic and tiny South Beach in back. The Southernmost Motel is across the street, straddling South and United streets, which run perpendicular to busy, bizarre Duval Street. Actually, Duval Street becomes relatively sedate here, making this location ideal: close enough to the Key West action for younger guests and quiet enough for older guests. All the Old Town Resorts have color cable TV and modern private baths and share swimming pools and other recreational facilities.

> **The front and side gardens are extremely pretty, boasting a variety of flowering and green plants as well as mature trees. The back porch of La Mer looks out at the palm trees of South Beach — a long stretch of sand with wave-smoothed rocks, the calm ocean beyond.**

La Mer was built at the turn of the century and is a wonderful example of Key West conch house architecture, with a gabled tin roof, white clapboards with gray trim, double-hung windows, and spindle balusters on the gingerbread verandah. Rooms open out onto balconies upstairs and verandahs and wooden decks downstairs. There is a low white wall at the front of the house and lattice fences. A brick walkway leads to the front porch.

Rooms at La Mer vary in size and shape, as one would expect in an old Victorian, but they share the same decor and modern amenities. Entrance to some of the rooms is from the pretty verandahs, which have views of the side garden or water, usually both. The rooms are immaculate, with traditional touches like paneled doors, bay windows, paddle fans on the high ceilings, and wood venetian blinds.

Among the rooms, spacious number 407 is particularly good for small families, with a king-size bed and pull-out sofa. Windows look out over treetops to the street and the pretty front garden. At one end of the room is a kitchenette with a refrigerator and small stove, hardwood cabinets, and a tiled breakfast bar that doubles as extra counter space. The efficient room has a small sitting area so that a family need not feel too cramped. The one drawback is the small closet.

Continental breakfast is served on a long table in the reception office. Guests can eat here, take their pastries and coffee up to their room, or — the preference for most — have breakfast on their private deck, looking out at the palm trees and the water.

The reception office at La Mer is all business, with a 24-hour concierge. The office space is just off the front porch and, in an earlier day, was probably a spacious entryway or small front parlor. It's attractive, but it is not the sort of place where guests would linger or feel homey. One complaint of guests who visit B&Bs in Key West and elsewhere is that there is often no sitting room or other common room where guests can sit and read or talk. However, most people visiting Key West don't spend a lot of time indoors.

For recreation, guests have their pick of the beach and swimming in the Atlantic, just outside the back door, one of the swimming pools at the Southernmost Motel, or the South Beach Motel pool just across the parking lot. The Southernmost Motel offers water sports rentals and mopeds, and the South Beach Motel has its own dive shop. For lunch and dinner, there's an all-you-can-eat buffet at the restaurant just behind La Mer, accessible by a little path across South Beach. Even better are Louie's Backyard on Waddell Avenue and Antonia's at 615 Duvall Street.

The Marquesa Hotel

600 Fleming Street
Key West, FL 33040
800-UNWIND-1
305-292-1919
Fax: 305-294-2121

A Key West reprobate, now polished into a beautiful gem

General manager: Carol Wightman. **Accommodations:** 15 rooms and suites. **Rates:** Rooms $115–$215, junior suites $150–$245, 1-bedroom suites $165–$260. **Minimum stay:** During holidays. **Added:** 11% tax; $15 for extra person. **Payment:** Major credit cards. **Children:** Under 16 discouraged. **Smoking:** Allowed. **Open:** Year-round.

On the wall near the front parlor of the Marquesa Hotel is a framed collage of before and after pictures. Anyone visiting the Marquesa is impressed by its restful charm, and seeing these photos, one can appreciate how far the old rooming house has come. More than a million dollars was spent on the restoration by the owners, Richard Manley and Erik DeBoer. For their work on the Marquesa, Manley and DeBoer were presented with the Master Craftsmanship Award of the Historic Florida Keys Preservation Board.

When this elegant yet laid-back hotel was a rooming house, called the Q-Rooms, it was frequented by rowdy drunks. Now it attracts a quiet crowd who come here to relax in luxury and to enjoy the creative atmosphere of Key West. The Marquesa is beautifully run, offering 24-hour service, as one would expect at a fine city hotel. A concierge is always on hand to make suggestions for daytime excursions in Key West and give excellent, honest advice about restaurants and entertainment.

The staff are polite and professional, knowledgeable about the Key West scene without succumbing — or allowing unwary guests to succumb — to

> **Each room has something special: a dhurrie rug in soft pastels, original pine walls, a pillowed window seat, an antique secretary, a private verandah on the street, or an extra-large deck overlooking the pool. Flowers are in every room, and turndown service includes Godiva chocolates. A newspaper is at the door of each room in the morning.**

its flashier trendy side. They will do everything possible to save guests from a wasted morning or a bad meal. The staff is one of the many assets that puts the Marquesa in a class by itself in the growing guesthouse market of Key West's Old Town.

The Marquesa is at the corner of Simonton and Fleming streets (just one street over from famous Duval), four blocks from the gulf, and eleven blocks from the Atlantic. The hotel comprises two fine old clapboard homes, one facing Simonton and the other Fleming, and two additions. Now listed on the National Register of Historic Places, the 19th-century buildings were meticulously restored after a shoddy history as boarding houses and an auto dealership. Most of the accommodations are in the main house and the two additions that face Fleming Street. On the first floor of the house on Simonton is the Café Marquesa, with more rooms on the second and third floors.

The hotel is painted turquoise with slate blue shutters and white trim, an unusual combination that works. Handsome double mahogany front doors and long windows face the white verandah. There's also a gingerbread verandah on the second floor of the house.

Standard rooms overlook the pool, while junior suites overlook the front yard and historic Key West streets. Most rooms and suites are a generous size, but smaller rooms have some compensation, such as a large deck. Rooms are reached by white-railed stairs or, in the main house, a polished mahogany balustrade. All the poolside rooms have French doors that open onto a private deck. Suites have TVs and a sitting room with a pull-out sofa as well as the queen-size bed that is standard in all Marquesa accommodations.

The hotel's decor makes the most of the interesting configurations of each room. Baths have floors of green-veined marble or white tile and pedestal sinks. Terrycloth robes hang in the closets. Even the brass and enamel European-style telephones are special. Framed Key West prints and ceiling fans add a tropical feel to the Victorian elegance. Furnishings in the rooms are eclectic, with a mix of mahogany reproductions, bamboo and wicker, country pine armoires, restored furniture, and authentic antiques.

The lobby of the hotel was probably the front parlor of the original house. It has lovely proportions, floor-to-ceiling windows, and fine moldings. The juxtaposition of different styles or textures can be exciting but not entirely successful: a dolphin-footed glass table with walnut club chairs rests next to a mahogany reproduction table and chairs; opposite is an easy chair of woven grass next to a traditional sofa with a large, abstract painting above.

The swimming pool, heated by solar panels on a side roof of the addition, is just beyond French doors. Old-fashioned striped awnings hang above some of the windows and French doors overlooking the pool. A fence of lattice and vertical siding is a backdrop for clay pots of flowers and the blue and aqua tiled pool. The steady trickle of a small Italianate fountain gives a peaceful sound to the patio. White chaises and chairs and two glass-topped tables allow guests to lounge. Most people enjoy their breakfast here, although guests can also eat in the lobby, in their room, or on their room's private deck or verandah.

A Continental breakfast is prepared for all hotel guests by the chef at Café Marquesa, and it is delicious: grapefruit with wildflower honey, homemade granola, muffins and croissants, tea and freshly brewed coffee, espresso, or cappuccino. The breakfast is beautifully presented and includes fresh tropical fruits as well as traditional Florida orange juice and grapefruits. Breakfast costs $6, a bit more with deck or room service. In the afternoon by the pool, guests can order from the bar at the Café or sip a complimentary glass of iced tea.

The Café Marquesa is a whimsical, unpretentious place with Cuban tile on the front stoop, rough plaster walls inside painted a deep marigold, and a variety of seating that includes an old sofa behind one set of tables. The food appeals to a sophisticated palate: snails and shrimp and corn for appetizers, fried tomato salad and duck breast salad, homemade pasta, and delicious entrées like salmon, pork loin, Delmonico steak, fresh shrimp, and dolphin fish. Guests staying at the hotel can make arrangements to use the restaurant for meetings: 20 to 50 people can be seated here.

Marriott's Casa Marina

1500 Reynolds Street
Key West, FL 33040
305-296-3535
800-228-9290 in U.S.
800-235-4837 in Florida

> *Henry Flagler's*
> *last grand hotel*

General manager: Michael Tierney. **Accommodations:** 314 rooms and suites. **Rates:** Rooms $170–$335, suites $345–$695; seasonal packages. **Minimum stay:** For special packages. **Added:** 11% tax. **Payment:** Major credit cards. **Children:** Under 18 free in room with parents. **Smoking:** Nonsmoking rooms available. **Open:** Year-round.

Built at the terminus of Henry Flagler's Florida railroad line and completed in 1921, several years after his death, the Casa Marina shone throughout the 1920s, 1930s, and early 1940s as Key West's premier hotel. The Casa was a gathering place for writers, statesmen, and movie stars, and its style was indeed grand. The rich and famous posed with their friends and rivals on the terrace behind the Mediterranean-style hotel, with its elegant arched loggia and cool Spanish tile roofs. They sunned themselves on chaises overlooking the picture-perfect grounds and the ocean beyond, and delighted in the pampering of a solicitous staff.

World War II changed all that, when the government leased the Casa Marina to the U.S. Navy for housing. The Casa became a hotel again in 1945 but was taken over by the Army in 1962 during the Cuban missile crisis. After this service, it could not survive as a hotel.

In the late '70s, new owners bought the hotel and spent $13 million renovating it. They enlarged and refurbished accommodations in the original 1920s building, giving odd but interesting angles to the rooms and making for bigger, more comfortable rooms and suites. The new owners also modernized the bathrooms and added new fixtures throughout the hotel. They restored the Mediterranean exterior and the lobby, always two of the hotel's strongest points. In 1984, Interstate Hotels bought the Casa, giving Marriott an operating franchise.

Today, the old pine floors in the lobby are polished and beautiful. Overhead, the black cypress beams of the vaulted ceiling stretch across the big room to French doors with fanlights above. The doors open out onto the loggia and terrace, and to the swimming pool and beautiful grounds beyond. The mood of the era has been captured best here in the lobby.

However, there have been some mistakes. When the first renovation was done, the intricately molded fireplace and the original brass and wood registration area were restored. But during a later renovation in the 1980s, Marriott replaced the registration desk with a large, paneled front desk without the old brass detailing. Painters didn't even match the stain they were using on the desk to that of the wooden posts and beams in the rest of the lobby. Also, this new front desk was constructed right up to the side of the handsome fireplace, which used to dominate the lobby from a central position on the front wall.

Some people are also bothered by the west wing that was added to the original building in 1978. The four-story west wing is a flat-fronted, charmless, modern building. The owners made no attempt to blend new with old, except to make the exterior the same buff-colored stucco. In the mid-1980s, after the state of Florida passed more stringent laws protecting the architectural integrity of old buildings, Marriott added an east wing that successfully duplicated many fine old features of the original Casa Marina architecture. Walls in both new wings are a bit thin, but the rooms are well proportioned, and many have wonderful views of the Casa loggia and court-yard as well as the water.

The guest rooms in both the original building and the two wings are attractively decorated, with light stucco walls and bleached oak furniture. There is a good variety of accommodations, including standard and oceanfront balcony rooms, junior suites, corner suites, and two-bedroom loft suites. As in all Marriott hotels, the baths are well designed and have many extras.

Service is efficient and friendly throughout the hotel. The service at Henry's, the main restaurant, is quicker than average for laid-back Key West, and the food is good. This restaurant, with the original coffered mahogany ceiling and French windows, has recently been lightened and brightened with lots of polished brass and wood. Henry's serves all three meals. The Sun pavilion, right on the water, with weathered decking and a West Indies look, serves lunch outdoors. Service is sometimes slow here, but the view is great, making this a wonderful spot for a leisurely lunch.

> **Swimming was once rather dangerous here because of a shelf of rocks by the beach, but Marriott has added a dock and a long pier that goes beyond the rocks, making swimming a real pleasure. The dock is also an excellent spot to push off for snorkeling, a favorite pastime of Casa guests. The Keys' waters are home to plenty of colorful fish and other marine life.**

Besides swimming off the pier, Marriott offers many other diversions, including water skiing, boating, sail boarding, tennis, and fishing. Most guests fish off the Casa's own dock, but deep-sea excursions can also be arranged. The Marriott has a great many rentals available, including mopeds and bicycles. The pool terrace, which is beautifully planted and maintained, has a Jacuzzi to soak in. It is this outdoor area, with its relaxed Riviera ambience and backdrop of Mediterranean archways, that is still the Casa Marina's greatest draw.

Ocean Key House Resort and Marina

Zero Duval Street
Key West, FL 33040
305-296-7701
800-328-9815
Fax: 305-292-7685

> *A friendly resort in the middle of Key West's waterfront scene*

Manager: Richard Grossmann. **Accommodations:** 100 rooms and suites. **Rates:** Rooms $135–$155, 1-bedroom suites $215–$525, 2-bedroom suites $295–$700. **Minimum stay:** 3, 5, and 6 nights during some holidays. **Added:** 11% tax. **Payment:** MasterCard, Visa. **Children:** 17 and under free in room with parent. **Smoking:** Nonsmoking rooms available. **Open:** Year-round.

Zero Duval Street is where Front Street, Mallory Square, and Duval (Key West's Main Street) come happily, chaotically together. Boats for fishing charters, snorkeling, cruising, and diving are docked here, with colorful signs advertising their excursions. On Mallory Square, people gather every evening to watch the sunset and the goings-on of jugglers and musicians. Close — but not too close — to this scene is the quiet and luxury of the Ocean Key House.

Although there are a few double and single rooms available with a choice of a queen or twin beds, most of the accommodations are one- and two-bedroom suites. The two-bedroom suites are quite spectacular; the master bedroom has both a king-size bed and a Jacuzzi, which is on a raised tiled platform and mirrored on two sides, with a dramatic flower arrangement on a tiled counter. Guests can soak in the Jacuzzi and look out past the big bed and through the glass balcony doors to the Gulf of Mexico.

The other rooms of the suite are a master bathroom next to the Jacuzzi, a spacious living and dining area decorated in designer fabrics, a bedroom with twin beds and a tiled bathroom, and a separate kitchen. The attractive kitchen has everything, from pots and pans to a microwave. Guests can buy their food in a supermarket in Marathon or Key West on their way in or purchase treats at the Ocean Key's Cafe Duval, just off the lobby. A mini-bar in the living room is stocked with drinks and snacks for sundowners. The balcony could be considered another room — one where guests spend a good deal of time. It extends across three rooms: the master bedroom, living/dining room, and part of the second bedroom.

> **Guests at the hotel can take advantage of the offerings of the marina for an active vacation or simply spend their time lounging by the hotel's gulfside swimming pool or people-watching on a bench at the marina.**

With the Ocean Key's corner location on two bodies of water, some suites afford a view of the sun setting over the gulf and rising over the Atlantic. Daytime views of the yachts docked below, the fishing boats setting forth, and a variety of people coming and going are fun, too.

The two-bedroom suite has a sofa that pulls down into a double bed so that this suite can accommodate six. The Ocean Key House also has what they call a "convertible two-bedroom, two-bath suite" that can accommodate up to six people. In this slightly different floor plan, the second bedroom shares the master bath instead of having a separate bath. This is a good choice for a family with two or three children but is not as good as the larger two-bedroom suite if you are traveling with another couple or with grandparents.

The Ocean Key's one-bedroom suite accommodates four and has a well-equipped kitchen, a living/dining area with a double pull-out sofa, and a king bedroom with a spacious bath and Jacuzzi. The balcony is accessible from both the bedroom and the living room. When making reservations, be sure to ask about views. The "Island-view" suites are less expensive than the "Gulf-front" suites, but ask for one with a balcony that overlooks a lot of "gulf" and a little "island," which can translate into "street."

Guests staying at the Ocean Key House in the summer need not feel that they'll stay in their air-conditioned room most of the time. Temperatures here are pleasant in the warmer months because of the breezes that sweep over the marina during the day.

The one problem at the Ocean Key House is that since there are no elevators from the lobby to the rooms, guests must traverse the ground-floor garage area to get to the elevator taking them to their rooms. To put it bluntly, the garage is ugly — coming and going, inside and out.

Pier House Resort and Caribbean Spa

1 Duval Street
Key West, FL 33040
305-296-4600
800-327-8340

A warm, uninhibited atmosphere in the middle of Old Key West

General manager: Joy Smatt. **Accommodations:** 129 rooms and 13 suites. **Rates:** Rooms $195–$400, suites $385–$950, spa rooms $300–$435 (spa services/treatments separate charge); packages available. **Minimum stay:** None. **Added:** 11% tax. **Payment:** Major credit cards. **Children:** Under 12 free in room with parents. **Smoking:** Nonsmoking rooms available. **Open:** Year-round.

Duval Street is Key West's spirited main street, and the Pier House is where a lot of the action begins. It has what most consider Key West's premier restaurant, and four of its liveliest bars. It also has one of the few beaches on the island — small, but still a beach. The atmosphere is sophisticated and uninhibited. Some old Key Westers feel that too many units have been crammed onto the resort's five acres, but the overall design has been well executed. Land is at a premium, and the Pier House has done all that it can with its first-rate location.

> **Though the Pier House does a good business in conferences and corporate retreats, it's definitely a place that encourages play.**

The Pier House is made up of Old Florida–style buildings with peaked tin roofs and railed porches, and more contemporary buildings with dramatically angled roofs. All cluster around the center of activity — the beach and the palm-studded deck and pool.

The beach is one of the few places in Key West where you can actually swim; there are no jagged or slippery rocks, just fine sand. One small section is designated for nude sunbathing. Facilities by the beach include a dock several yards offshore with wide benches, a good place to take a breather. There's freshwater swimming in the Pier House's swimming pool, partly shaded with palms, partly open to the brilliant sunshine. The water sports staff are happy to arrange for off-property fishing and diving excursions.

Accommodations are expensive, but they're also luxurious. All rooms and suites have a mini-bar and refrigerator, cable TV, and a private balcony or patio. A variety of views are available, and rooms are priced accordingly. Best are deluxe rooms overlooking the courtyard garden or pool, the "harbor front" rooms, and the suites. No two are exactly alike, but all are decorated in fresh, tropical colors with wicker furniture and Key West artwork.

Some of the most appealing rooms are in the Pier House's new Caribbean Spa building. These have hardwood floors, Bermuda shutters on the windows, and oversize bathrooms with a whirlpool or a Euro-habitat — a bathtub that can be enclosed to create a sauna. The spa program provides a full schedule of classes and treatments such as aroma therapy facials, body facials, loofah salt-glo, herbal peels, and massages.

Facilities include a workout room with the latest Kaiser equipment, sauna, steam room, and Jacuzzi, and a full-service salon. A spa menu is available for all three meals.

The famous Pier House Restaurant has an imaginative menu of American and Caribbean cuisine and an extensive wine list. The restaurant has won a number of culinary awards including a top ten designation in a rating of all Florida restaurants. You can eat inside or on the deck overlooking the harbor. The restaurant serves both lunch and dinner and has a good champagne brunch on Sunday. The resort's Harbour View Café is a good choice for day or evening, with a real Key West menu of fresh shrimp, conch chowder, and conch fritters.

Everybody who comes to the Pier House soon has a favorite bar, but the best for a sundowner is Havana Docks Lounge, where ships for Cuba once departed. The lounge's Sunset Deck has a great view over Key West's old harbor. If it's an especially impressive sunset, everybody has another drink.

Marriott Reach Resort

1435 Simonton Street
Key West, FL 33040
305-296-5000
800-874-4118
Fax: 305-296-2830

A beachside resort with an airy, fresh feeling

General Manager: Michael Tierney. **Accommodations:** 150 rooms and suites. **Rates:** Rooms $175–$270, suites $220–$465; packages available; rates lowest on weeknights. **Minimum stay:** On holidays and some weekends. **Added:** 11% tax; $40 for extra person. **Payment:** Major credit cards. **Children:** Under 18 free in room with parents. **Smoking:** Allowed. **Open:** Year-round.

The Reach faces one of the few real beaches on Key West and has taken full advantage of its prize location. Guests can sail, windsurf, parasail, snorkel, and scuba dive. There are sailing lessons for beginners and old hands. Swimming is in the freshwater pool or in the ocean. Nearby is fishing and charter boating, which the energetic staff can help you arrange. The well-equipped health club on the property offers aerobics.

The Reach's restaurant takes advantage of the beachside location with windows overlooking the water and a dining terrace where people like to sit and gaze out to sea, even when they're not eating. The resort also has banquet facilities, a deli, and a pool bar.

The resort is pale peach stucco accented with lots of white — white trim around the small-paned windows and the French doors, white Victorian-style railings and pillars on the verandahs, and lacy white gazebos on the dining terrace. The architecture mixes Old Florida

> **With its fantastic location on the beach, the Reach could have coasted by with second-rate decor and design; the original owners chose not to, much to the pleasure of their guests.**

style with a few touches of Key West Victorian gingerbread. There are a surprising number of rooms in the five-story buildings, but because of the open-air walkways leading to rooms, guests never feel crowded.

Amenities at the Reach include a library where you can stop in for a complimentary glass of sherry and a good book. There is also a conference center, unusual for Key West. The space includes two boardrooms and a larger room with French doors leading onto a balcony overlooking the ocean.

Accommodations are in a variety of room types, from Tropical Guest Room (read standard room) to rooms and suites overlooking the water. All are attractive, with tile floors covered with dhurrie rugs, ceiling fans, private balconies, coffeemakers stocked with fresh beans, mini-bars, refrigerators, and immaculate bathrooms. The suites have sleeper sofas, kitchenettes, a dining table and chairs, and whirlpools.

Simonton Court

320 Simonton Street
Key West, FL 33040
305-294-6386
800-944-2687
Fax: 305-293-8446

> *An enclave of historic Key West buildings*

Hosts: Bill Wascher and Mike Sparks. **Accommodations:** 22 rooms and cottages. **Rates:** Rooms $80–$175, cottages $180–$320, $10 extra person. **In-**

cluded: Continental breakfast. **Minimum stay:** 3 nights during off-season holidays, 5 nights during high season. **Added:** 11% tax. **Payment:** MasterCard, Visa preferred; American Express accepted. **Children:** Under 18 not allowed. **Smoking:** Allowed. **Open:** Year-round.

One of the first guesthouses to open in Key West, Simonton Court is an adults-only inn that prides itself on a free and easy atmosphere. Down a path by the main house facing Simonton is the guesthouse office; beyond that, on Hurricane Alley, is a row of modest-looking, peak-roofed cottages. A landscaped gravel path connects all the buildings of Simonton Court.

> There are two pools here, one of them heated, and a 10-person hot tub. The most interesting pool has a border of ebony tile at the top and a black coating on the sides and bottom, giving it the look of a dark pool in the depths of the tropics. Guests spend a great deal of time around the pools, and the atmosphere is relaxed and happily indolent.

The main house facing Simonton was a Cuban cigar factory in the 1880s, and the cottages on Hurricane Alley were the workers' quarters. The owners of Simonton Court respect the integrity of the buildings and have not tried to alter their 19th-century exteriors.

Inside are rooms of rustic beauty. Some rooms have the original pine on the walls and floors. Interesting spaces have been created in all the accommodations. Many of the suites have an open floor plan, with lofts reached by ladders. Beds are low to the ground and sitting areas are built-in. The decor is contemporary, tropical, and "old cigar factory."

The main house and cottages share a secluded back garden, a major drawing point for Simonton Court. The whole area is lush with flowering shrubs and green vegetation. A wood deck covers several hundred square feet. In one corner is a canvas-draped cabana. Chaises longues and small tables are placed in groups on the deck, and there are big wooden planters of tropical trees.

Because all the cottages have cooking facilities, it would be easy to settle in here and stay a long, long time.

The Keys • 351

South Beach Oceanfront Motel

508 South Street
Key West, FL 33040
305-296-5611
Fax: 305-294-8272
Reservations:
Old Town Resorts
1319 Duval Street
Key West, FL 33040
305-296-5611
800-354-4455
Group sales and information: 305-294-5539

> *A small place with a fountained pool and access to the Atlantic*

Accommodations: 47 rooms. **Rates:** $92–$195. **Minimum stay:** 2 nights during holidays and winter. **Added:** 11% tax; $10–$15 for extra person. **Payment:** Major credit cards. **Children:** Under 12 not permitted. **Smoking:** Allowed. **Open:** Year-round.

In the high season, rooms at the South Beach Oceanfront Motel are slightly more than those at its sister hostelry, the Southernmost. But the rooms and the motel itself are usually quieter, and this is *the* spot to be for ocean-lovers. One side of the motel faces South Street, diagonally across from the parking lot of the Southernmost. The motel stretches southeast toward the Atlantic, with rooms overlooking the La Mer Hotel, South Beach, an Olympic-size pool and deck, and the ocean itself.

Guests reach first-floor rooms by way of a covered wooden walkway that has sunken flower beds and clay pots of palms on each side of the louvered guest room doors — though the doors leading to the rooms look worn and have chipped paint. Upstairs rooms at the motel are generally the best, for they are quiet and have wonderful views through the sliding glass doors that lead to the verandahs. But there is one first-floor room that is very desirable: at the ocean end of the motel, it has its own little beach and looks directly out at the pier and the Atlantic. The room above it is also quite good, with a spacious verandah that hangs over the beach.

All rooms have a tropical decor with bamboo and rattan furnishings, similar to that at La Mer and the Southernmost Motel. The tiled baths are modern and immaculate. The rooms at the Atlantic end of the motel have easy access to ocean swimming, a sunning pier and deck, and a manmade beach. The rooms at the South Street end of the motel may be slightly less quiet in the evening.

The motel has a dive shop that will provide information on diving and snorkeling. Just across South Street, the Southern-most Motel has water sports and moped rentals, two swimming pools, and a poolside bar. Guests at South Beach Motel are free to use the facilities at the Southernmost; they are part of the Old Town Resorts complex and are included in the room rate.

> **All rooms in the two-story lattice-trimmed building have an ocean or pool view.**

Closer to home there is more activity, particularly for those who like ocean or lap swimming. Next to South Beach Motel is its namesake: South Beach. This small, palm-studded municipal beach is a little rocky along the water's edge, but it's the closest choice for guests who love the beach. Monroe County Beach and Smathers Beach — longer, bigger beaches — are a bike ride away. For anyone who prefers fresh-water swimming, South Beach Motel has one of the nicest pools in Key West — it's Olympic size, rimmed by wood decking and red pavers, with pretty landscaping. Mounted just below the second-floor verandah balusters are two duck heads that spout water into the pool. It is a whimsical touch that adds fun to the relaxing, beachside scene.

Southernmost Motel in the USA

1319 Duval Street
Key West, FL 33040
305-296-6577
Fax: 305-294-8272
Reservations:
Old Town Resorts
1319 Duval Street
Key West, FL 33040
305-296-5611
800-354-4455
Group sales and information: 305-294-5539

> *Unusual accommodations at the very tip of the U.S.*

Accommodations: 127 rooms. **Rates:** Rooms $72–$165, penthouse $90–$165. **Minimum stay:** 2 nights during holidays and winter. **Added:** 11% tax. **Payment:** Major credit cards. **Children:** No children under 12. **Smoking:** Allowed. **Open:** Year-round.

Calling the Southernmost a motel doesn't do it justice; it looks more like an expanded Florida-style inn. The Southernmost is on the corner of Duval and United streets, stretching down a small Key West city block to South Street, which borders the Atlantic. This glorified motel is the largest and most diverse of the three Old Town Resorts.

> Some think the first-floor rooms in the three-story building on United Street are the nicest: these have small enclosed gardens with private walkways to the pool. But much is to be said for the second-floor rooms opening onto verandahs on South Street.

The Southernmost is a collection of two- and three-story buildings finished in buff stucco or in clapboards with white or gray trim. The buildings are tied together with a lush garden and a central poolside recreation area. Most buildings have tin roofs and pretty upstairs verandahs with latticework balustrades and touches of gingerbread; the general feeling is very Key West.

All rooms have views of one of the swimming pools, the garden, or both. Most rooms are doubles; there is some variation in size and configuration simply because the motel is made up of four different buildings. There is also one spacious penthouse.

The poolside patio seems to be the center of activity — or nonactivity. Various types of flowering plants and vines spill over the wooden fences, and the white verandahs overlook the main pool. The tropical profusion and the laid-back atmosphere also make the pool popular for La Mer and South Beach motel guests who share facilities. Guests can swim, lounge by the pool, soak in the Jacuzzi, or have a drink at the Tiki Bar. There's also a smaller pool in the center of the South Street parking lot. The location is certainly odd, but this pool also has a sense of privacy because it is surrounded by a wooden fence and thick tropical vegetation. Some people prefer it to the central pool, because fewer people use it.

There are snacks but not much for the gourmand at the Southernmost. However, one of Key West's most venerable restaurants, Louie's Backyard, is a walk away. A new restaurant opened by the owner of Louie's, the Café Marquesa, is a 10-minute walk.

The only other drawback to the Southernmost is the registration office by the main pool: in the middle of the morning it becomes a noisy center of activity. Outsiders come here to rent mopeds or inquire about various excursions. There may also be teenagers using the vending machines by the pool or walking through the breezeway to get back to their rooms. But the Southernmost is more than just a motel — it is an active, fun place. It is not a resort for the reclusive.

LITTLE PALM ISLAND

Little Palm Island

Route 4, P.O. Box 1036
Little Torch Key, FL 33042
305-872-2524
800-343-8567

A favorite honeymoon and anniversary destination

Managing partner: Ben Woodson.
Accommodations: 28 suites. **Rates:**
Cottages $330–$465 per couple plus $10 service charge. MAP (two meals per day): $75 per

person per day plus 7% tax and 15% service charge. FAP (three meals a day): $95 per person per day plus tax and service. **Included:** Water sports equipment. **Minimum stay:** Two nights on weekends; 3 nights on holidays; 7 nights at Christmas and New Year's. **Added:** 11% tax. **Payment:** Major credit cards, personal checks. **Children:** Under 12 not permitted. **Smoking:** Allowed. **Open:** Year-round.

Couples come to Little Palm Island to mend their souls and get reacquainted. A recent guest described Little Palm Island succinctly: "When you come here for vacation, you better like the person you're with, because there's nothing here but palm trees and water." Escaping to beautiful surroundings to do almost nothing has been reason enough for hundreds of people to come to this island since it opened in 1988. It should be added that the cuisine and accommodations are superlative, transporting guests to the indolence of the South Seas.

The restaurant, which already has won a number of culinary awards, is in the Great House, a building of pecky cypress that was constructed in 1938 as a fishing lodge. Guests may dine on its deck, looking out at the ocean and the setting sun. Tables are set with white napery, stoneware, and hand-blown glassware from Mexico. Food served by executive chef Guy Michel Reymond and his staff is meticulously prepared and exotically presented. The delicate sauces and soups are flavored with herbs from the island's own garden.

Guests with small appetites who don't wish to have two or three gourmet meals a day can pay for their meals a la carte rather than taking the full or modified American plans. All the meals are full-course events, so many couples request only breakfast and dinner, or lunch and dinner if they sleep in. Those who stay for several days sometimes take the launch to Little Torch Key and then drive to restaurants during a day's excursion on other Keys. For the most part, though, this is the kind of place where people stay put.

Ben Woodson, a restaurateur who operated T.G.I. Friday restaurants in Memphis, jokes that he wanted to create a wind-down resort in the 1990s for all the upscale young professionals he served at his fast-paced eateries in the '80s. Woodson built the resort with five other businessmen after a long search for the "right island." He and his partners planted more coconut palms on the little island and planned thatch-style buildings to create the South Seas atmosphere. Woodson seems to be everywhere: greeting guests, picking up cigarette butts from the patio, moving a fallen palm frond from a sandy path, checking on progess in the kitchen.

A jogging track rims the island's five acres, and there are complimentary sailboats, canoes, and Windsurfers. Other activities are backwater excursions to other Keys, off-island fishing, and snorkeling and scuba diving at the coral reef at Looe Key National Marine Sanctuary. The resort has scuba instructors, fishing guides, and backcountry guides for excursions to nearby Keys.

At the Quarterdeck, a dockside administrative building, a 24-hour switchboard responds to guests' room buzzers. The staff's quick response to guests' needs has given the resort an excellent reputation for service.

Woodson and his partners like to call Little Palm Island a passive resort. They enjoy giving people "a chance to think about what life is all about. So, no tennis and no telephones or TVs." In fact, guests can rent a TV or VCR if they are so moved. But the emphasis is on rest and relaxation. Hammocks are strung between palm trees; chaises and lawn chairs form a small cluster on the sand. Many people spend the day simply lying on a chaise on the small, pretty beach, one of the few natural beaches in the Keys.

Children under nine are not allowed on Little Palm, although there are some families with older children. Except on the weekends, when people from the mainland frequently come here for dinner, there is very little noise.

A few steps up from the beach is a meandering path to the pool and bar. This is not to say, however, that you ever have to fetch your own drinks. Just put up a pink flag on the pole by your beach chair and an attendant will come running. The bar and poolside patio are convivial places, with the swimming pool itself one of the loveliest in Florida: palm trees draped with brilliant bougainvillea arch over it; a tiny waterfall sparkles and spills into a coral pond. Behind the pool is a thatched cabana where a masseuse gives soothing massages.

The pool bar prepares a number of tropical rum drinks served in coconuts grown on the island. The staff at Little Palm Island make use of many island resources. Tropical flowers are used as garnishes for food and drinks, and palm fronds are ground up and used for mulch around plants. Also, every effort is made to encourage the wildlife that make their home among the Newfound Harbor Keys, the string of islands of which Little Palm Island, often called LPI, is a part. Everyone is particularly fond of the waterfowl that congregate on the pier by the beach and the tiny Key deer who swim over at night to nibble on the hibiscus.

While the thatched cottages look basic from the outside, they are quite luxurious inside. Each cottage contains two suites, named after Little Palm birds. The suites have a sitting room and bedroom at each end and a spacious bath between. The sitting room is furnished with natural wicker and a pull-out couch that provides

> **Little Palm Island has a 40-foot yawl and a 28-foot Sharpie sailboat that can be rented for full- and half-day sails, and, of course, sunset cruises.**

additional bed space. The furniture is mostly bamboo and wicker. Each suite has a mini-safe and a mini-bar stocked with patés and other good things.

In the bedroom, the plaster walls are painted white or soft peach. Louvered windows look out over the water, and one can relax in a chaise in the corner. Tabletops are deep green marble. Bedrooms have either a king-size bed or two doubles, draped with nylon mosquito netting — purely for effect, as guests worried about mosquitoes are assured.

Overhead is a high, thatched ceiling supported by thick pine beams. It takes many different types of palm fronds to make the thatching of these roofs. Those who have stayed here during a tropical rainstorm say the sound of the rain-drops on thatch is wonderful, and there's no chance of any water seeping in.

The bathrooms in the suites deserve a paragraph of their own. Perhaps they are sybaritic because of the rustic plumbing of the past. (The outhouse Harry Truman used on his visits has been preserved and is now the guest telephone booth.) Every suite has a large whirlpool in the bathroom, vanity and sink just outside the tub, and a dressing room with louvered closet. The big bathtub has decorative tiles of palm trees and turtles custom-made in Mexico. Floors are tiled in large terra cotta squares. And on the deck of each suite is an outdoor shower with a bamboo enclosure.

The decks that wrap around each thatched cottage have an authentic South Seas look. They are a nice spot to watch birds swoop over the island. They are also a favorite place to rest and talk for the many couples who come here to get away from work and family responsibilities and renew the friendship in a marriage. One frequent guest remembers the first time his wife surprised him with a long weekend here. "It was time to finish packing and get to the launch and I started searching for the passports. I couldn't find them and started to panic. Then I remembered we didn't even have to leave the country for this!"

MARATHON

Faro Blanco Marine Resort

1996 Overseas Highway
Marathon, FL 33050
305-743-9018
800-759-3276
Fax: 305-743-2918

> *A Marathon main-stay for fishing and boating*

General manager: Melanie Tank.
Accommodations: 125 cottages, lighthouse apartments, condos, state rooms. **Rates:** Cottages $55–$119, lighthouse apartments $135–$175, 3-bedroom condos $198–$225, state rooms $75–$95; lower weekly rates available. **Minimum stay:** 3 nights during holidays and special events. **Added:** 11% tax; $10 extra person. **Payment:** Major credit cards. **Children:** Free in room with parents. **Smoking:** Allowed. **Open:** Year-round. **Pets:** Allowed except in condos; $18 deposit required.

Faro Blanco is most famous for its two full-service marinas and a wonderful lighthouse, its most interesting accommodation. If you come by boat, its whitewashed stucco pinnacle and many-paned windows are the first thing you see. Boat slips are spread out on either side of the lighthouse. Behind these, a long pier stretches out to the Gulf of Mexico.

Guests climb up a narrow flight of stairs to each apartment, with a length of sailboat line serving as the staircase "railing." The entrance door is cut at an odd angle and leads to a small sitting area with a built-in sofa and a fully equipped kitchen that, appropriately, reminds one of a ship's galley. The walls are of whitewashed paneling with knotty pine accents. A tiny bathroom with whale-handled brass faucets in the miniature sink, a small shower, and a toilet just fits into a corner off the kitchen. A stairway leads off the sitting room to a bedroom with a king-size bed, a window seat, and a claw-foot bathtub near the bed. Under the stairs leading to the bedroom above is a separate vanity, toilet, and chrome sink, with towel racks and shelves screwed into the back treads of those stairs. One is constantly reminded that this is, af-terall, a lighthouse, and modern conveniences are tucked in wherever they fit. Thankfully, there has been no effort to stan-dardize the rooms; there isn't a true square angle in either apartment.

> **Everyone in the resort's office is very friendly. The Spanish-style building houses Hall's dive center, and there is information here and at the dock office on fishing.**

The room on the next floor is the kids' room (they're young, they can climb more stairs). It has twin beds and a built-in sofa between two windows. The views of the water get more spectacular with each flight, and they make the odd little rooms seem bigger and brighter than they really are. The last set of narrow stairs leads to an open-air observa-tion deck and the beacon of the lighthouse. This is walled for about four feet and then has a black wrought-iron railing for another two feet above that; it's quite safe. From this perch, guests can see boats coming and going, the waters of the At-lantic, the Gulf of Mexico, and Florida Bay, the pretty grounds of the Faro Blanco resort, and waterfowl sunning themselves on the coral jetty. It would be easy to stay here all day, and, with the little twinkling Christmas lights that en-circle the beacon in the evening, maybe all night, too.

The lighthouse apartments are ideal for a honeymoon or anniversary couple or a family, though very young children might find the steep stairs a problem. The only other draw-back to this fascinating accommodation is that the apart-ments are not maintained as well as they could be. For exam-ple, the rug on the floor in the bathroom may be badly soiled, and some of the curtains could do with replacements.

The other offerings at the marina are condominiums and cottages. The Island Condominiums have three bedrooms, two full baths, modern kitchens, and terraces that look out over the grounds and the water. These luxury condos are set back from the water and are within a short walking distance of the resort's Olympic-size swimming pool and tennis court.

The Garden Cottages are the resort's budget and kidproof accommodations. These little stucco houses, painted in ice cream colors, have a 1950s look to them — some of the three-generation families staying in the cottages have been coming since about then. Inside, furnishings are simple but functional, with a mix of reproduction wood furniture and Formica-topped tables. The modest but comfortable lodgings are clean and well maintained, and are surrounded by trees and lawns. Just across the narrow "street" (this does have the feeling of a neighborhood) that runs between the groups of cottages is a picnic and recreation area, and beyond that, toward the marina, is the pool. On the other side of the resort by the condos is the tennis court. A family could stay in the cottages and not leave the property for days. And for those who can't bear to leave the family pet, Faro Blanco allows animals in the cottages for a small fee.

Although many people familiar with this resort think of Faro Blanco as occupying only a stretch of land from Highway 1 to the marina, there is more dock space, a dock office, and a laundry facility and shower on the Atlantic side of the highway. Also, there is another interesting group of accommodations here: Faro Blanco's "floating stateroom suites." These houseboats cost more than the cottages but have many of the same advantages. Relatively new, they have tile and porcelain baths and comfortable sitting and dining areas. Queen beds are new and firm. The floors are either varnished pine or wall-to-wall carpeting. Most of the units have an attractive kitchenette and a breakfast bar with stools, a coffeemaker, toaster, cooking utensils, and plates and flatware. Units that don't have a kitchenette have an expanded sitting room with a fold-out queen sofa. Guests go across decking or up a flight of stairs and then enter the staterooms through curtained French doors that give a feeling of modest elegance to the accommodations. The houseboats don't bob because they are fixed to a concrete slab. All have two units, one above the other. A deck in back looks out over the water. The units all have vertical siding with a weathered gray finish. The high-numbered houseboats are closer to the open water and have the best views. But they are also closer to one of the resort's four restaurants and the marina and so might be slightly noisy on weekend evenings. The low-numbered units look out at houseboats on the other side of the dock; the water views are not as nice, but it's a quieter spot for those with small ones who go to bed early.

Those who stay at this end of the resort can, of course, take advantage of all the recreation available on the gulf side of Faro Blanco. If you are coming by boat, call ahead to get dockage rates and other information about the marina. This marina is one of the few in the Keys that offers marine engine repair service. There is also a dockmaster's office, ship's store, tackle shop, and charter service.

Hawk's Cay Resort and Marina

U.S. Highway 1, Mile Marker 61
Duck Key, FL 33050
305-743-7000
800-432-2242 in Florida
800-327-7775 in U.S.

*A cool, breezy
private island*

General manager: Tom Cherniavsky. **Accommodations:** 160 rooms and 16 suites. **Rates:** Rooms $140–$335, suites $240–$615; packages available. **Minimum stay:** 2 or 3 nights with packages and on holidays. **Added:** 11% tax. **Payment:** Major credit cards. **Children:** Under 12 free in room with parents. **Smoking:** Allowed. **Open:** Year-round.

About two hours south of Miami on Route 1, just across a long bridge, is an enclave of low-rise and conical buildings spread out along a crescent-shaped sandbar and turquoise lagoon, with a channel beyond of deeper turquoise. It looks like a great place to unwind, surrounded by natural and man-made beauty. And so it is: it's Hawk's Cay, on its own private island on the five-island formation of Duck Key.

The covered, porchlike entrance to the resort, landscaped with banana trees and other tropical plants, continues the mood. The bellboys wear polo shirts and safari hats. Beveled, small-paned glass doors lead into the lobby and lounge area. The lobby is cool, with lazy ceiling fans and terra cotta floors. French doors lead to an enclosed terrace, where there are club chairs and small tables. Outside are the poolside restaurant, the Cantina, and the recreational area.

This is the focal point of the resort. There's a large swimming pool here with a couple of Jacuzzis, clay pots of brilliant bougainvillea, cushioned chaises longues and lawn chairs for lazing around. Near the pool is a wide expanse of lawn popular for volleyball games, and there is a basketball court and shuffleboard. Softball games start up whenever a few people feel like playing.

The average temperature in the winter at Hawk's Cay is 72 degrees; in the summer, 82, with a strong breeze. The water off Duck Key covers a wide range of blues and blue-greens, depending on the weather. At Hawk's Cay Resort, it is a lovely shade of turquoise, largely because of the underlying white sand of the resort's manmade beaches. Except for a few areas of Key West, there are no natural beaches on the Keys. The "sand" at the lagoon is beautiful but scratchy, so watch out for little ones' tender feet when they are playing and wading here. Various small sailboats and Windsurfers can be rented for sailing on the lagoon. Guests who want to sail larger boats in the wide channel outside the lagoon can rent them at the marina.

Built into a hammock of tropical trees between the palm-studded lagoon and the marina is the "tennis garden," with eight courts, including two clay courts lighted for night play. On the lawn that surrounds the tennis garden is a jogging trail with exercise stations accommodating three levels of fitness. Although there is no golf at Hawk's Cay, there is free shuttle service from the resort to an 18-hole course at the nearby Sombrero Country Club.

At the marina, guests can charter boats for deep-sea, bottom, or backcountry fishing. This is a 60-slip, full-service facility with a marina store that stocks fishing tackle, equipment, maps, books, compasses, and clothing. Adjacent to the marina store is a dive shop that includes the services of a PADI-certified diving instructor. The two dive boats include a 40-foot glass-bottom boat. The Keys offer some of the best scuba diving and snorkeling in the world, with the largest living coral reef in the continental United States just four miles offshore.

The recreational offerings at Hawk's Cay include an excellent children's program. The kids swim and fish, play on the playground, go on nature hikes, and participate in outdoor games. For older children, there is a game room off the lobby with Ping-Pong tables and video games.

Mindful of the beauty that surrounds Hawk's Cay, the resort also offers ecological raft tours of the waterways of Duck's Key. Experienced guides describe the beautiful vegetation, waterfowl, and history of this unique region.

The free dolphin show is enjoyable and educational. Guests who wish to pay a hefty fee can have their pictures taken with a dolphin by a professional photographer, swim in the dolphin training pool, and take a few rides between two dolphins, holding on to the gentle creatures' dorsal fins. If you are interested in riding the dolphins, be certain to reserve time at least a week in advance.

Hawk's Cay Resort includes convention facilities removed from the rest of the hotel in a center overlooking the water and the dolphin training pool. Meeting rooms include four large boardrooms and four adjoining caucus rooms for smaller meetings. All of the conference rooms are soundproofed and have very good audiovisual equipment and lighting. Large windows in the conference rooms overlook the water, with French doors that open onto wooden decks. These decks are ideal for receptions and parties.

> **Best of all for those who love marine life are the dolphins. The resort is a year-round training center for many sea animals, and one of the pleasures of a stay here is the dolphin show presented every afternoon. This is a private show, open only to resort guests, who sit up on the porch overlooking the water or at a curve of white sand by the lagoon.**

Guest accommodations are in the main building and in low-rise wings, all recently redecorated and repainted. Rooms have bleached oak furniture and walk-in closets. There is a separate vanity and sink by the closet as well as one in the bath. All rooms have terraces with lawn furniture and have views of the water or garden greenery. A drawback is that the maintenance isn't as good as it should be. Broken fixtures and crumbling concrete steps may remain that way for some time before they are repaired. Staff turnover is sometimes high, with many college-age employees going back to school or moving on to new adventures. This results in inconsistent service — if you luck out, it's fine, and if you don't, service is inadequate or indifferent.

Though Hawk's Cay is expensive and there are service glitches, you'll probably get your money's worth. The conical, pavilion-style restaurant offers a complimentary buffet breakfast near the dolphin pool, which most guests love. The atmosphere is a little like summer camp, with cheery waitresses filling your coffee cup, soft rock playing, and, in certain seasons, lots and lots of kids. The buffet has 60 hot and cold choices, including cereals, yogurt, a large selection of fresh fruits, brisket of beef, scalloped potatoes, sausage, bacon, and a variety of egg dishes, including eggs Benedict. There is a large selection of pastries, muffins, sweet breads, and éclairs. Unfortunately, some of these taste as if they've been recycled for days. It might be better to offer fewer varieties and to have them consistently fresh.

During the day, most guests have lunch at the Cantina near the pool or the Ship's Galley, a seafood restaurant at the marina. In the evening, the Courtyard Room, off the terrace, offers a variety of American and continental offerings. The salads are interesting here, and there are some good entrées, but service is inconsistent. During the winter season, Porto Cayo, the resort's formal Italian restaurant, is open. For part of their stay, many guests have dinner off the property at one of the fine restaurants elsewhere in the Keys. Key West is only an hour and a half from Hawk's Cay, and it's romantic and fun at night.

The West Coast

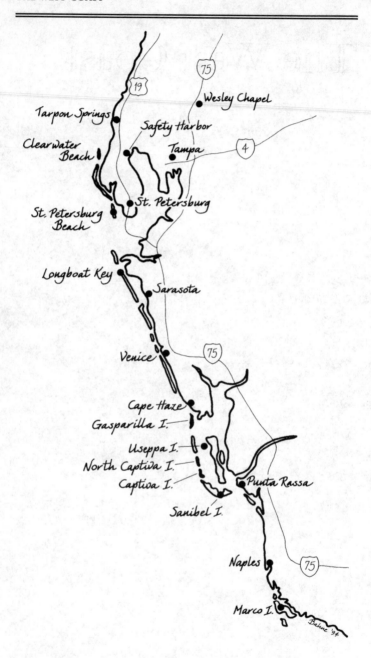

Cape Haze
Palm Island Resort, 373
Captive Island
South Seas Plantation, 375
'Tween Waters Inn, 379
Clearwater Beach
Clearwater Beach Hotel, 381
Gasparilla Island
Gasparilla Inn, 383
Keewaydin Island
Keewaydin Island, 385
Longboat Key
Colony Beach and Tennis
    Resort, 388
The Resort at Longboat Key,
    390
Marco Island
Marriott's Marco Island
    Resort, 393
Naples
Edgewater Beach Suite Hotel,
    395
Inn by the Sea, 397
Naples Bath and Tennis Club,
    399
Naples Beach Hotel and Golf
    Club, 401
The Registry Resort, 403
Ritz-Carlton, 405
World Tennis Center Resort
    and Club, 408
Punta Rassa
Sanibel Harbour Resort and
    Spa, 410
Safety Harbor
Safety Harbor Spa and Fitness
    Center, 412

St. Petersburg
Mansion House Bed and
    Breakfast, 415
Stouffer Vinoy Resort, 416
St. Petersburg Beach
Don CeSar Beach Resort, 419
Island's End Cottages, 422
Trade Winds on St. Petersburg
    Beach, 424
Sanibel Island
Casa Ybel Resort, 425
Song of the Sea, 427
Sundial Beach and Tennis
    Resort, 430
Sarasota
Half Moon Beach Club, 432
Tampa
Hyatt Regency Westshore, 434
Sheraton Grand Hotel, 436
Wyndham Harbour Island
    Hotel, 436
Tarpon Springs
Innisbrook Resort & Golf
    Club, 439
Upper Captiva Island
Safety Harbour Club, 441
Useppa Island
Useppa Island Club, 444
Venice
Banyan House, 447
Wesley Chapel
Saddlebrook Golf and Tennis
    Resort, 450

Best B&Bs

Naples
   Inn by the Sea
St. Petersburg
   Mansion House
Venice
   Banyan House

Best Beachside Accommodations

Clearwater Beach
   Clearwater Beach Resort
Lido Beach, Sarasota
   Half Moon Beach Club
Longboat Key
   Colony Beach & Tennis Resort
   Longboat Key Club
Marco Island
   Marriott's Marco Island Resort
Naples
   Edgewater Beach Suite Hotel
   Naples Beach Hotel & Golf Club
   Ritz-Carlton
St. Petersburg Beach
   Don Cesar
   Tradewinds on St. Petersburg Beach
Sanibel Island
   Casa Ybel
   Song of the Sea
   Sundial Resort

Best City Stops

Tampa
   Hyatt Regency Westshore
   Sheraton Grand Hotel
   Wyndham Harbour Island Hotel

Best Island Getaways

Cape Haze
  Palm Island Resort
Gasparilla Island
  Gasparilla Inn
Keewaydin Island
  Keewaydin Island
Upper Captiva Island
  Safety Harbour Club
Useppa Island
  Useppa Island Club

Best Small Hotels, Inns, and Motels

St. Petersburg Beach
  Island's End Cottages

Best Resorts and Spas

Captiva Island
  South Seas Plantation
  'Tween Waters Inn
Naples
  Naples Bath & Tennis Club
  The Registry Resort
  World Tennis Center
Punta Rassa
  Sanibel Harbour Resort & Spa
Safety Harbor
  Safety Harbor Spa & Fitness Center
St. Petersburg
  Stouffer Vinoy
Tarpon Springs
  Innisbrook Resort & Golf Club
Wesley Chapel
  Saddlebrook Golf & Tennis Resort

The tourism industry on the west coast reports that about a third of the visitors to Disney World travel to another part of Florida during their stay. Many of these wind up just 90 minutes west in Tampa or St. Petersburg. The two cities are on

Tampa Bay, a large natural harbor. They share some similarities to Minneapolis and St. Paul, with **Tampa** reputed to be the livelier city and **St. Petersburg** considered a staid city of old people — not exactly accurate, according to official demographics.

The west coast, with its unhurried pace and long string of islands, has become increasingly popular in the last few years. **Tampa** is a financial and commercial center, while **St. Petersburg** is less urban, with a wide range of neighborhoods, from the deteriorating to the elegant. **St. Petersburg Beach** is a residential and recreational town, with a "strip" similar to Ft. Lauderdale's. Of the attractions near Tampa and St. Petersburg, one of the most worthwhile is Busch Gardens, with more than 2,500 birds and 3,000 animals wandering the well-kept grounds. The Museum of Science and Industry in Tampa is the largest museum in Florida, and there is interesting shopping at Franklin Street Mall and Harbourside. Ybor Square, in East Tampa, is a Latin neighborhood where you can visit antique and crafts shops, dine at Cuban restaurants, and see cigars being hand-rolled.

St. Petersburg, or St. Pete, has an interesting waterfront area and two excellent museums, the Museum of Fine Arts and the Dali Museum. North of Tampa Bay are a great many beach towns and fishing villages along the Gulf of Mexico that reach up almost to the mouth of the Suwannee River in northern Florida. Tarpon Springs, a Greek enclave that was once a sponge diving center, is the most famous and the most popular with tourists. Some of the towns along the coast are charming, others are run-down. But the beach they front is generally the same: soft, powdery sand with gentle dunes, sea oats and other grasses growing on the shore, countless seashells, and warm, emerald green water.

Just south of Tampa is the city of **Sarasota,** with a rich offering of theater, music, and art. Interesting historic buildings include the Ringling Museum and Ca'D'Zan, the fantastic 1920s mansion of Ringling himself. Sarasota also offers excellent shopping and dining at St. Armands Circle.

One of the most impressive features of the southwestern coast is the number of lush islands just offshore. Some are little known outside Florida, because once people find a chunk of authenticity here, they are rarely willing to share it. Sarasota Bay has a string of small islands or keys, most notably **Lido Key,** Siesta Key, and **Longboat Key.**

Farther south, the islands adjacent or just south of Charlotte Harbor have a legend-laden history of pirates, treasure, and treachery.

Some of these islands, including **Captiva, Sanibel, Gasparilla,** and Pine Island, are accessible by causeway or bridge, off I–75 near Ft. Myers. Others, such as Cabbage Key, **Palm Island, Keewaydin, Upper Captiva,** and **Useppa,** are accessible only by boat. There are also many smaller keys, some of them formed by mangroves, whose roots extend into the water, catching sand and sediment to create islands.

Captiva Island and its larger sister island, Sanibel, were once accessible only by boat. Now a causeway links Fort Myers to Sanibel, and from Sanibel a two-lane highway reaches the tip of Captiva Island and South Seas Plantation. Many longtime residents on both islands grumble about the traffic on this little road, and it is slow going during holiday and vacation times. Of the two islands, Captiva is the least crowded with day visitors, largely because it takes longer to drive up to Captiva from the Sanibel–Fort Myers causeway.

If you can rent a boat on the mainland and travel through the Intracoastal Waterway to see some of these islands, do so. If not, book a room at one of the resorts on Sanibel, Captiva, or Gasparilla. South Seas Plantation, a resort on Captiva, has a boat excursion to Cabbage Key, a favorite haunt of past and present sailors, and to Useppa.

Farther south, near **Naples,** is **Marco Island,** accessible by means of curved, Venetian-style bridges. Both Naples and Marco Island are wealthy communities with few inexpensive accommodations. Old Naples has a wonderful shopping district on Third Street South. Though prices are high, the area is charming, with excellent restaurants and bistros.

Less well known is the Rookery Bay National Estuarine Research Reserve, a sanctuary and research facility for the study and protection of pelicans, ibis, herons, egrets, and other birds. On an estuary at a turn-off just before the State Road 951 bridge to the island, it has beautiful marshes and mangrove forests. About two thousand birds roost here every night. Like Wakulla Springs, south of Tallahassee, the reserve gives visitors a taste of the richness of Florida's wildlife as it was before man tamed it.

Marco Island is less than an hour's drive west of Everglades City, the "gateway to the Everglades." A drive from the Naples–Marco Island area to the Everglades on Highway 41 (also known as the Tamiami Trail from Tampa to Miami) is worthwhile. Much of the Everglades is inaccessible except by boat — and some areas have grasses that would clog any outboard motor. But on the Tamiami Trail you can see many types of waterfowl in the wet gullies along the road and, in the lagoons, the occasional gnarled hump of an alligator. Along the road is the Indian Village and Culture Center, a commercialized but interesting Indian enclave where you can learn about the Miccosukee Seminole Indians' way of life.

Though Floridians and longtime visitors decry the destruction of wildlife and native plants unique to Florida, there is a greater interest in preserving the environment today than ever before. Recent legislature supports rigorous protection of the environment. Because of such legislation, many new hotels, like Naples's Ritz-Carlton, also have hammocks — forests of native trees that serve as buffers between the hotel grounds and the shoreline. These harbor a variety of waterfowl and, sometimes, alligators.

Outside West Coast cities, the unique waterfowl and other wildlife of the state can easily be seen by a casual observer. Though their numbers have been greatly depleted and sightings of once-common fauna, like flamingos, are rare today, some animals are making a comeback. Various species of heron and egret may make their homes near the water hazards of golf courses or on the banks of a shopping center's manmade lagoon.

Alligators are both tolerated and protected in Florida. It is illegal to shoot them, and most residents, understandably, stay out of their way. The most important thing to remember about gators — adult or infant — is never to feed them.

The best way to see wildlife unique to Florida is to make an excursion to one of the state's wildlife sanctuaries, such as the Ding Darling Wildlife Refuge on Captiva Island. (For information about these and other sanctuaries, write to the Florida Department of Natural Resources, Office of Communication, 3900 Commonwealth Blvd., Tallahassee, FL 32399.)

CAPE HAZE

Palm Island Resort

7092 Placida Road
Cape Haze, FL 33946
813-697-4800
800-824-5412 in U.S.
Fax: 813-697-0696

> *A true getaway, where residents and visitors get along without cars quite well, thank you*

President: Dean L. Beckstead.
Accommodations: 160 suites and villas. **Rates:** Marina, 1- and 2- bedroom suites $100–$125, 1-bedroom villas $170–$210, 2-bedroom villas $190–$275, 3-bedroom villas $240–$360; packages and weekly rates available. **Minimum stay:** 2 nights; 3 nights during holidays and high season. **Added:** 8% tax. **Payment:** EnRoute, Master-Card, Visa. **Children:** Free in room with parents; charge for third child. **Smoking:** Nonsmoking available. **Open:** Year-round.

Northern escapees from ice and cold could, on waking up at Palm Island their first morning, look out at the beach and think for a minute that they're seeing snow, not beach — that's how pale the sand is. The water is a blue-green so clear you can see several feet down. And this pristine beauty is just a few miles out from the coast and the city of Fort Myers.

Palm Island was developed by some of the same people who did such a superlative job restoring nearby Useppa Island. It is accessible only by boat. There are no cars here, even for homeowners: people walk, ride bikes or golf carts, or take trams to get from place to place. Utility lines are underground, and trash is conscientiously disposed of by residents and visitors. Few day visitors make it to the island, so there are no crowds.

Guests can rent bicycles, fishing tackle, Windsurfers, tennis racquets, swim fins and masks, glass-bottom paddle boats, canoes, and small sailboats.

Palm Island is actually two resorts in one: the island itself and the marina on the mainland, where there is a ship's store, marina complex, and the white stucco buildings that house the resort's marina suites. The marina accommodations are ideal for anyone arriving by boat who wants to enjoy a night's sleep on land, or for those vacationing on the island who arrive late at night and wish to stay over before taking the launch to the island. The marina suites have a full-size kitchen, a separate bedroom, a pull-out sofa in the living and dining room, and a screened-in porch overlooking the water. Their decor and floor plan are similar to the accommodations on the island.

Most vacationers staying on Palm Island arrange for pick-up at the Fort Myers airport or rent a car and park it in the marina's lot for their entire stay. One fee takes care of parking plus the launch to the island, luggage handling, and tram service on the island.

At the end of a long ramp leading from the island's dock are a casual restaurant and a general store. Here guests can stock up on food instead of lugging groceries from a mainland supermarket (though prices are higher on the island). Guests can also call ahead and order from the "Island Shopper," a list of food staples, produce, household cleaners, and wines and liquor. For a small fee, the Palm Island staff will stock rental cottages with items guests order from the list before their arrival.

Accommodations are in square-rigger-shaped buildings that have an Old Florida look: tin roofs, gray vinyl siding with white trim, double-hung, small-paned windows, French doors, some with fan lights above, white-railed porches, and latticework. The homes are built high on concrete pilings, with storage underneath and pretty latticework concealing the concrete. All are attractively decorated, with wall-to-wall carpet and wicker furniture.

Space is well designed with open living and dining areas, loft bedrooms in the one-bedroom units, breakfast bars, kitchens with full-size refrigerators and stoves, spacious baths, washer/dryers, telephones, satellite cable TV, large closets with mirrored doors, and screened-in porches with views of the gulf. The two- and three-bedroom units have a bathroom for each bedroom. Some of the spacious beach villas also have dens with pull-out couches.

Accommodations are built in clusters, with barbecue grills and foot-washing spigots on the landings of each villa. There are tennis courts and a swimming pool with a whirlpool spa at each cluster, so guests and residents don't have to walk or ride to a central location. There are eleven courts on the property, and a full-time tennis pro provides free clinics. A scheduled children's program and a safe, wooden climbing and sliding playground keep kids busy. Deep-sea fishing is available by charter at the marina. On the mainland, there is golf at various courses near Fort Myers.

The 2½-mile beach has been carefully preserved. In the beautiful pale sand, there are more than 400 varieties of shell, as well as petrified sharks' teeth that are four or five million years old. Graceful sea oaks sway on the dunes, and the waters of the gulf lap quietly. After a few nights without city noise and glaring lights, you rest easy, and the sand doesn't look like snow in the morning.

CAPTIVA ISLAND

South Seas Plantation

P.O. Box 194
Captiva Island, FL 33924
813-472-5111
800-237-3102

A full-service resort with an informal, South Seas atmosphere

General manager: Fred Hawkins. **Accommodations:** 600 rooms, suites, and villas. **Rates:** Rooms $145–$265 rooms, junior suites $165–$285, 1-bedroom villas $150–$315, 2-bedroom villas $210–$560, 3-bedroom villas $285–$625; packages available. **Minimum stay:** 7 nights in beach homes. **Added:** 9% tax; $15–$20 extra person; $5 for crib; $3 service charge per day. **Payment:** MasterCard, Visa. **Children:** Free in room with parents. **Smoking:** Nonsmoking available. **Open:** Year-round.

In the early part of the century, this island was a plantation that produced key limes and coconuts. Today, it's a resort, producing hours of enjoyment. There is so much to do, for any age and interest, that you just can't get bored. But if you want simply to relax, there's no place better than the white, sandy beach on Captiva Island.

South Seas Plantation is a large resort with a busy marina, but it is so well designed that guests are not immediately aware of its vastness. At certain times of the year, there may be as many as 2,000 guests staying here, but the resort never feels crowded. Accommodations are clustered near the golf course, along the beach, and at the marina among beautiful native trees. Parts of the plantation are junglelike, giving a sense of seclusion to the various accommodations and activity centers.

This is a wonderful place for children, not merely for the range of children's activities, but also because of the resort's setup, right down to the speed bumps in the road and "slow" signs everywhere. Many guests don't drive at all once they get here. Dependable trolleys take guests from one part of the Plantation to another. This allows older children to go from place to place without having parents chauffeur them.

There are various recreational programs for children aged 3 to 17. All programs have age-appropriate activities like arts and crafts, kite making, games, shelling, and sand sculpture for the little ones, and canoeing, sailing, hiking, and water skiing for the older kids. The programs are provided three to five times a week, depending on the season, for half or three-quarters of a day. An enthusiastic naturalist, who works full-time at South Seas, gives intriguing talks on shells for school-age kids and leads them on shelling expeditions.

Organized family activities include crab races, nature walks, and scavenger hunts for adults. Companies that hold conventions at the resort and want spouses and children to come along get special attention, with adventure trips, theme parties, and competitions that can involve anything from pie eating to an obstacle course.

Corporations can reserve space at the northern end of the island for their family activities and for small meetings at the

Harbourside Meeting Center, or gather at the Plantation conference center, a spectacular facility at the southern end of the resort for groups of up to 500. The conference center is state of the art, with a concealed projection booth running the length and breadth of the grand ballroom, theatrical lighting, and room for vehicle drive-ons.

South Seas Plantation is sometimes referred to as a resort within a resort. Guests enter the plantation through the security gates at the South End of the property. The South End is composed of Bayside Marina, with a boat launch and scuba diving, the Tennis Center, the Conference Center, some small boutiques at Chadwick's Square, Mama Rosa's Pizzeria, and Chadwick's, a restaurant and lounge open to the public. The North End of the plantation has a larger marina, Cap'n Al's Dockside Grill, bike, boat, Windsurfer, and jet ski rentals, a sailing school and skiing school, and a game room and fitness center.

> **Captiva Island is famous for its shells, with over 400 varieties, including black sharks' teeth and paper fig shells. It was on Captiva and Sanibel that Anne Morrow Lindbergh started the shell collection that became the inspiration for her book *Gift from the Sea.***

At the North End of the property are some of the original clapboard buildings that made up the plantation. King's Crown, named after a crown-shaped shell, is the resort's gourmet restaurant. Housed in the original commissary building with a wall of small windows overlooking the water, it has a distinctly Old Florida feel. Both the wine list and the menu, which emphasizes fresh seafood, are excellent.

Cap'n Al's is still more informal and one of the best places to take children on the property. It is a cool, pavilionlike building, with outside dining at umbrella tables overlooking the marina. Food is not as outstanding here as at the King's Crown but more than adequate for family meals. Another restuarant, Chadwick's, is at the South End, just outside the plantation grounds, and is also quite informal. Mama Rosa's Pizzeria, near Chadwick's, features unusual combinations that can be eaten in, taken out, or delivered to your room.

Accommodations are in one- and two-bedroom villas. These are no more than four stories high and feature well-equipped kitchens, a living/dining area, and a private porch. Amenities include a private swimming pool and views of the tennis courts or the water. The North End has deluxe hotel rooms and two-bedroom villas within walking distance of the 9-hole golf course and Yacht Harbour. In the Harbourside hotel rooms, overlooking Pine Island Sound and the Yacht Harbour marina, there's a choice of two queen beds, a king bed, or a junior suite arrangement with a sitting area. Marina villas have two bedrooms with two baths, a kitchen, a screened-in porch overlooking the harbor, and a private pool. The two- and three-bedroom suites at Land's End Village look the most like Old Florida, with gray wooden siding, white trim, and tin roofs. These accommodations are the most luxurious and the most expensive (about $50 more than the regular villa prices). They feature separate living and dining rooms, a well-equipped kitchen, two bathrooms, a screened porch with water views, and a pool for Land's End guests with a "hydro-spa" and a poolside lanai.

The interiors of all accommodations are festively decorated, with bright spreads and drapes, pretty carpets, and light oak furniture. The bathrooms are particularly large and well designed. Even the hotel rooms have big bathrooms with a closet area, dressing room, and separate vanity at one end, and a toilet and oval tub at the other. Above the tub is a cord for hanging wet clothes. Hotel rooms, when outfitted with two queen beds, are quite adequate for a family. Another good choice for a family, particularly if you want to save money by cooking your own meals, are the one-bedroom villas at the South End. These are not inexpensive, but the guests who come back year after year seem to feel they're getting their money's worth.

A major draw at South Seas Plantation is the excellent tennis program. The resident pro and his teaching assistants give excellent instruction. Of the 21 courts, seven near the Tennis Center are lighted for night play, with the remaining 14 scattered about the property near villa accommodations. So, except for a lesson or clinic, guests don't have to go to the tennis complex to play a game.

The resort also has 18 swimming pools. Like the tennis courts, they are near the villas, and their varied locations contribute to the uncrowded ambience of the plantation. For those who love the beach, the beachside villas are the best choice. Water sports abound. Canoes, kayaks, sailboats, and power boats are all available for rentals.

'Tween Waters Inn

P.O. Box 249
Captiva Island, FL 33924
813-472-5161
800-223-5865
Fax: 813-472-0249

> *Informal
> old cottages and
> newer apartments
> for families*

General manager: Jeff Shuff. **Accommodations:** 125 rooms, apartments, and cottages. **Rates:** Rooms $80–$190, apartments $100–$240, cottages $100–$260. **Minimum stay:** 3 days on some holidays. **Added:** 9% tax; $15 extra person; $5 roll-away. **Payment:** MasterCard, Visa, Discover; personal check; cash. **Children:** Under 12 free in room with parents. **Pets:** Allowed with permission in some cottages at $8 per day.

You approach Captiva Island by its one main road, via the causeway from Sanibel. Beach Road then winds along Captiva under a canopy of pines. The Gulf of Mexico is shallow here, and the white sand lends the water a turquoise color. Where Beach Road bends to the east a little, a gray wooden sign announces the 'Tween Waters Inn. With Pine Island Sound on one side and the Gulf of Mexico on the other, the name is apt. Here you can watch the sun set over the sea in the evening and turn around the next morning to watch it rise over another beautiful body of water.

The inn is a collection of old cottages painted in shades of pink and salmon and newer apartment buildings constructed on supports with carports underneath. The inn started with just one cottage in 1926 and was operated by the same family until 1969. The atmosphere is nautical and beachy — very informal. Dress is a swimsuit or shorts and a shirt during the day, and casual dresses and pants for dinner.

Attractive paving stones and planters are at the entrance that leads to a small reception center. Sandy paths, boardwalks, and curved wooden bridges connect all the inn's buildings to the tennis courts and swimming pool complex, the marina, the conference meeting room, and the resort's popular restaurant and bar. 'Tween Waters has been added to for over 40 years, so there's a wide choice of accommodations for a place this small, with standard rooms, cottages, apartments, and efficiency rooms.

The old cottages are spacious and expensive, and some families have been coming to the same cottage for years. But they are not necessarily the best choice for everybody. Some of them are close to the road and restaurant and can be a bit noisy. The apartments in the inn's new buildings would be better for the average family or for vacationing friends. These have a modern, L-shaped kitchen, a spacious sitting area with a sofa bed, a bedroom with a double bed and a twin bed, and a screened-in balcony. The furniture is attractive and practical, with the cushions of the bentwood rattan sofas upholstered in heavy vinyl.

> The tennis courts, pool, and Oasis pool bar are tucked away in the middle of the property, where lush greenery and palm trees enhance the hideaway feeling of the place.

The smaller water-view rooms are good for families that don't want to do much cooking. These have one large room with two double beds, a mini-refrigerator, and a screened balcony that overlooks the water. All guests can opt for the inn's meal plan of a full breakfast and dinner served in the Old Captiva House dining room.

Two of the newer buildings have laundry facilities that are available to all guests. Rates include daily maid service, but people renting accommodations with kitchens must do their own dishes and kitchen clean-up. When making reservations, have the staff send you the inn's rate sheet, which has full descriptions and a map showing locations and water views.

Recreation includes shuffleboard, boating, tennis, and bicycling, as well as swimming in the inn's large free-form pool and soaking in the whirlpool.

Pelican's Roost, the marina store, sells everything from beer to sportswear to bait. The staff rents canoes, aquacycles, kayaks, sailboats, bicycles, tennis racquets, and fishing gear. They can arrange for fishing and sightseeing excursions and will provide supplies needed for shelling and information on bird watching.

The inn's Old Captiva House restaurant has been around for years, and is immensely popular with locals and guests. The Dining Room is open for breakfast and dinner and is best known for its local seafood, prime rib specials on Tuesdays and Saturdays, and brunch buffet on Sunday.

Behind the main dining room of the Old Captiva House is the Crow's Nest, a smaller dining room and lounge that serves lunch and dinner and has nightly entertainment. Behind that is the "Ding" Darling Room. J. N. Ding Darling was a conservationist and cartoonist who stayed at the inn for 30 years. His exuberant sketches and cartoons decorate the walls, and the wildlife refuge nearby is named for him.

It is understandable why 'Tween Waters has been so loved by so many. With luck and love, it will survive another 60 years.

CLEARWATER BEACH

Clearwater Beach Hotel

500 Mandalay Avenue
Clearwater Beach, FL 34630
800-292-2295
813-441-2425
Fax: 813-449-2083

> *A Clearwater Beach tradition*

General Manager: Wallace Lee. **Accommodations:** 157. **Rates:** Rooms $90–$140, suites $175–$195, kitchen suites $135–$195, efficiencies $90–$155; $8 for extra bed. **Minimum stay:** During some weekends or special events. **Added:** 10% tax. **Payment:** Major credit cards. **Children:** Welcome. **Smoking:** Allowed. **Open:** Year round.

The words "casual elegance" have been used in so many Florida and Caribbean resort brochures that they have become a cliché, but these words do epitomize the Clearwater Beach

Hotel. The original hotel was built in the early part of this century and was added to over the years to include beachside apartments and cottages and quarters for the hotel staff. Over the years, both luminaries and unknowns have stayed at the hotel. The wealthiest families from the North would arrive in winter by private railway car.

> With Clearwater's brass-studded lounge and restaurant and the beach out back, guests need not even leave the hotel grounds during their stay.

For many years, the hotel stood alone on the beach and was the only place to stay here. Then, as Clearwater Beach became more and more developed, the strip of highway along the beach became more and more commercialized and honky-tonk. The loyal clientele of the hotel aged, and young people stayed away from a hotel that was beginning to deteriorate. But today, the Clearwater Beach Hotel rises above the "strip" that is reminiscient of Ft. Lauderdale or Daytona. When guests enter the elegant hostelry they leave it all behind. There is both energy and graciousness here and a growing clientele mix of young couples, families, and retirees. If you call ahead, the hotel will even arrange to pick you up at the Tampa or Clearwater airport.

The main hotel building was razed a few years ago and replaced with a brand-new building that has the decor and ambience of the original — guests who aren't told think the place is at least 50 years old. In addition to the main building, the Clearwater has beachside efficiency apartments and the Gulf Court Building at the tennis courts. All the accommodations have pleasant views of the gulf, the bay, or the pool and gardens. Unless you need a great deal of space, a room in the main building is probably your best bet. These have wall-to-wall carpeting, a private balcony, small refrigerator, cable TV, and serviceable, attractive furniture.

The main building has some common rooms behind the reception area that wouldn't be found in a conventional modern hotel. There is a library for all guests to use and a banquet and function room called the Oval Room, which has an oval wall of windows at one end and is lushly decorated. The nearby Dining Room and Schooner Bar hark back to a gracious era, which means better service than the average South Florida hotel restaurant. The Dining Room serves all three meals and specializes in local fresh seafod. At poolside, there is also a casual bar for drinks and snacks.

The courteous staff can arrange for off-property water sports and fishing, although for most guests, the hotel's pool and private beach are the focal points of their stay. The Clearwater manages to make guests feel they can relax and "beach it" in elegant, Old-Florida surroundings.

GASPARILLA ISLAND

Gasparilla Inn

5th and Palm Streets
Boca Grande, Gasparilla Island,
    FL 33921
813-964-2201

*An Old-Florida inn
with a rich past*

General manager: Steven Seidensticker. **Accommodations:** 140 rooms and cottages. **Rates:** Rooms $110–$190, adjoining parlor $155–$254; off-season packages available; meal plans available. **Minimum stay:** Over some holidays and weekends. **Added:** 9% tax; $68–$78 extra person; $15 cribs; $12 per person daily service charge to cover gratuities. **Payment:** No credit cards; personal check. **Children:** Allowed. **Smoking:** Allowed. **Open:** Winter and spring.

The Gasparilla Inn has such a loyal following of retirees and others (85 percent repeat business) that it doesn't advertise. Consequently, not everybody knows about the inn, and lots of folks want to keep it that way.

To those who do know the island, Gasparilla is famous for tarpon fishing and a history of colorful pirates. The island and its namesake hostelry are named after the most famous of these, José Gaspar, an 18th-century Spanish courtier who made for the high seas when he got into trouble at court. Boca Grande, then called High Town, was his headquarters. He is reputed to have entertained his most beautiful captured women and — perhaps — to have buried treasure here.

The village of Boca Grande — the only town on the island — was exclusively a fishing port until the railroad came in at the turn of the century, after which it survived on phosphate shipping as well. By the 1920s, it was a winter enclave for industrialists, and even today, the DuPonts, Swifts, and Oscar Myers have winter homes here. But the inn staff and the villagers make little of this; an effort is made to protect the privacy of those who stay here.

> The island is a lovely place to stroll, particularly along the water, where sea oats grow on the sand dunes.

The inn has a history and character of its own. Built as the Boca Grande in 1912 by Barron Collier, who developed so much of the west coast, the inn was added to over the years. Its main building is a Greek Revival inn with yellow vinyl siding and white trim and a brick courtyard out front. Inside are common rooms furnished in wicker and chintz, and an old dining room in white and pale yellow with a white brick fireplace and wooden floors. All meals are prepared from scratch, even the ice cream.

Standard hotel rooms are available in the main inn building, but cottage accommodations are spread throughout the inn grounds and the town of Boca Grande. Rooms are motel-comfortable with ceiling fans, linoleum floors, and a mix of old wooden furniture, wicker, and formica. Bathrooms may have tubs only and some rooms come only with twin beds. Cottages are roomier, with kitchenettes and porches furnished with rockers. The homey yellow cottages have grassy front yards and are usually fenced.

The basic accommodations are a disappointment to those who envision luxurious resort suites. People come here for the creaky, Old-Florida ambience, the natural beauty of the island, and the funkiness of the little town of Boca Grand.

Although it calls itself an inn, the Gasparilla is also a resort. The 18-hole golf course is particularly nice, with a clubhouse built in 1926 that includes a handsome widow's walk. A split-rail fence encircles the course and pretty flower beds adjacent to the fence include oleander trees and bougainvillea. The Gasparilla Inn closes down in June for the summer, and the old course is groomed and improved upon each year.

The Beach and Tennis Club is located two blocks from the main inn building at the beach. The clubhouse is new, with gray wood siding and a shake roof. There are eight courts and a resident pro on hand to help guests improve their game. The facilities include two swimming pools, an exercise club with saunas, a restaurant and bar, and a Great Hall for parties and receptions.

Every April, the town of Boca Grande is taken over by a passion for sport fishing. The inn keeps a list of dozens of local fishing guides who take guests out for deep-sea excitement. April is also the best time for families to come to the Gasparilla Inn; the atmosphere is more festive and casual than it is in the winter, when the inn tends to have an older, wealthier crowd that is more sedate or, some might say, staid.

The town itself is fun to walk around in or bicycle through. The old railroad bed leading to Boca Grande from the mainland has been converted into a bicycle path, and the inn has bikes to rent. The bicycle path ends at the old depot. Now the Loose Caboose Restaurant and Ice Cream Shop, it's a whimsical place, with 1910 vacuum cleaners and other turn-of-the-century gadgets decorating the original matchstick paneled walls and a Lionel train zooming above patrons' heads on an overhead track.

KEEWAYDIN ISLAND

Keewaydin Island

260 Bay Road
Naples, Florida 33940
813-262-4149
Fax: 813-262-8235
800-688-1935

> *A rustic getaway accessible by the island's 1930s ferry*

General Manager: Tom Brumitt. **Accommodations:** 45 cottages. **Rates:** Private cottages $250–$325, suite cottages $250–$425, cottage room $230–$325. **Included:** 3 meals a day. **Minimum stay:** Some holidays. **Added:** 8%. **Payment:** Major credit cards. **Children:** Welcome. **Smoking:** Permitted only on porches. **Open:** Year round.

Founded as a camp and school and later operated as an exclusive Naples club, Keywaydin has been open to the public for only a few years. Many people from Naples who belong to the club or have simply heard about the great food make reservations for lunch or dinner and come over by boat — theirs or the resort's depression-era launch, *Kokomis*. Since the summer of 1993, Keewaydin has been open to those who simply want a restful vacation spot.

> No cars are allowed;
> guests walk or ride a golf
> cart along the shell paths
> to the lodge and cottages.
> The result is a real Old
> Florida, hideaway feeling.

A 60-acre barrier island a few minutes' boat ride from the coast of Naples, Keewaydin has become sought after because of its natural beauty and the ease with which people can get to the island — and yet feel many miles away from the rat race. The resort has a number of cottages for rent, a recreational area, and a superlative restaurant housed in a cypress and pine lodge. Overnight guests have a number of accommodation options: private cottages that stand alone, spacious suites in stilted cottages that have one to three other suites, and single rooms in cottages. When making reservations, be sure to ask questions about the water views, proximity to the lodge or pool, and the amount of privacy or neighborliness you wish. Also, bring some potent bug spray, for along with the beautiful waterfowl and Key deer, Keewaydin has some aggressive flying insects.

Ice is delivered daily for the tiny fridge, and guests can have their cottage stocked with snacks or bring their own from the mainland. Blissfully for all, there are no telephones or TVs in the cottages, though both are available at the lodge.

It would be nice if the cottages were sided with wood, but these buildings were constructed in the 1930s, when asbestos siding was popular and modern firefighting equipment wasn't available on small islands. Plantings around the front and sides of the cottages are minimal; shell paths connect the little cottages to trails to the lodge and gulf and the pool.

The Hilltop Cottage, which has some of the best water views, is popular with those celebrating their honeymoon or an anniversary. Hilltop has a small enclosed front porch furnished in white wicker that serves as a very pleasant sitting room. The bed is king size, the bath is modern, and the honey-colored original pine floors are covered with a green woven rug. A small back bedroom has twin beds. There's an outdoor shower with dual shower heads for those who wish to rinse off the sand in togetherness. The cottage has lots of windows and views of the gulf and palm trees.

All but three accommodations have water views, and these are in woodsy settings. When the present owners bought the island in 1989, they began ridding it of nutrient-robbing exotic plants that were not Florida natives and encouraged natural growth.

Here and there, hammocks are slung betwen trees. The official recreation area is Spoonbill, where there's a pool and patio with barbecue grill, a rustic cocktail lounge, and a thatched chikee hut that is popular for weddings. White lawn chairs and chaise longues rim the pool, which has a smashing view of the gulf. The lounge is housed in an informal shake-roofed builing. The bamboo and rattan chairs are a bit tired, but the mood is laid-back and convivial.

Another gathering spot for drinks is in the Sunset Lounge, in the lodge. The lounge seems to be all windows and affords wonderful views of the sun setting over the gulf. The dining rooms have ceilings of bamboo and handpainted murals of wildlife — interesting settings for food that is equally imaginative. A typical entree might be roast duck with jasmine rice, arugula and papaya mojo or gulf shrimp accompanied by malted watercress and Japanese eggplant. Herbs and garnishes come from the island's garden. Food here has been acclaimed by a number of restaurant critics, always earning a four- or five-star rating. Those who come over to the island for a meal pay about $20 per person for lunch and $37 for dinner with tip, but overnight guests enjoy the spectacular meals as part of the room rate.

After dinner, many guests go back to their cottages or walk along the beach, but a good many spend the rest of the evening in the lodge. The massive ceiling beams are of pecky cypress, and the floors are of native pine. The floor-to-ceiling stone fireplace has a simple pine mantle with a tarpon mounted above. Other rooms in the lodge include a library with a chess table and sitting rooms decorated with vintage photographs of the lodge, botanical and wildlife prints, and watercolors of the island. This has to be the "lodgiest"-looking lodge south of the Maine border.

It's no accident that the place looks this way, for Keewaydin started out as a southern version of the Kakoo (later Keewaydin) camps in Canada and Maine. The name comes from Longfellow's poem "Song of Hiawatha" and means "homeward bound wind."

LONGBOAT KEY

Colony Beach and Tennis Resort

1620 Gulf of Mexico Drive
Longboat Key, FL 34228
813-383-6464
800-282-1138 in Florida
800-237-9443 in U.S. and Canada
426-5669
Fax: 813-383-7549

*An island resort
for sports
and beachside
indolence*

General manager: Katie Moulton. **Accommodations:** 235 suites. **Rates:** 1-bedroom suites $210–$355, 2-bedroom suites $255–$475, clubhouse suites $415–$440, lanais and beach suites $440–$540, beachfront house $640–$870; holiday, weekend, and sports packages; special rates for month-long stays. **Minimum stay:** For some holidays and packages. **Added:** 9% tax; $15 one-time charge for crib or rollaway. **Payment:** Major credit cards. **Children:** Under 18 free in room with parents. **Smoking:** Allowed. **Open:** Year-round.

This resort really does have the feeling of a colony — an enclave of low-rise villas clustered together only a few hundred feet from the beach. And what a resort for tennis buffs. With five-star ratings from tennis magazines, this is one of the outstanding tennis resorts in Florida. There are 21 courts — 15 in Plexipave and six in soft Hydro surfaces, with two lit for night play. A professional staff of eight are on hand to teach; they also will play with guests whenever an appropriate match isn't possible. Court time is free for guests, although reservations are required. Special programs include Tiny Tots Tennis, for kids six and under; a Junior Clinic, hourly instruction for beginners and intermediates; and a four-day tennis package for adults. For guests traveling with someone who is on a higher or lower level, the Colony will find partners on the appropriate level.

The owner of the Colony, "Murf" Klauber, is a fitness buff, so this is an excellent resort for those who are health-conscious. The complimentary fitness center has a range of workout equipment and free weights. The health spa has a sauna, whirlpool, and steam room. The wide array of activities includes low-impact aerobics, "better back" classes, introductory weight training, walking races, and nature walks.

> On the beach, a short walk from the accommodations, the water sports center has sailboats, Windsurfers, and aqua bikes. Swimmers and sun worshipers can also enjoy the heated pool just a step away. After a swim, have a drink at Bamboo's or an ice cream cone at Jimmy Murfy's on the beach.

For a gourmet dinner overlooking the water, there's the Colony Restaurant. The awards this restaurant and its wine cellar have garnered over the years are well deserved. This is an excellent place for lunch as well as dinner, with some interesting hot entrées and imaginative salads and dressings. The crisp, flavorful vegetables are organically grown. Desserts are as sinful as one might expect at an award-wining restaurant. The staff is personable, fun, and efficient.

The other main restaurant, Windows, serves Floridian specialties and traditional American fare. Murfy's, a private dining room for up to 14 people, is ideal for small parties and family reunions. Tastebuds, a small grocery store, caters to those who cook in their suites and stocks pâtés, sandwiches, and salads made by the Colony Restaurant. Any of Tastebuds' offerings can be ordered ahead of time and delivered to your suite.

Shopping at the resort includes the Patio Shop for sundries, the Colony Beach Tennis Shop, and Le Tennique, with a selection of handcrafted gifts, antiques, and designer clothing. Most guests simply walk to the shops as well as to various activities. The resort is gated and has speed bumps and slow signs everywhere. Older kids can walk confidently from place to place.

The many amenities of the resort make it attractive to companies for corporate retreats and meetings. An expert conference staff helps corporate groups organize meetings of up to 250 people. Groups can opt for fitness breaks — several minutes of exercise and motivation scheduled in the middle of a conference — as well as the regularly scheduled activities at the fitness center. The conference center, recently redecorated, has a landscaped deck for breaks and outdoor buffets.

Some corporate groups rent the spacious beachfront executive houses or the adults-only lanais and clubhouse suites. These have many extras such as designer furniture, oversize marble bathrooms, cathedral ceilings, skylights, and oceanfront decks. Other suites popular with vacationing families are the standard one- and two-bedroom suites: they have a living room with twin Murphy beds or pull-out sofa, a fully equipped kitchen and dining area, an attractively decorated bedroom (or bedrooms), and a marble bathroom with a separate mirrored dressing room, a whirlpool bath, and a steam shower. Some of the suites have balconies with wonderful views of the gulf.

The Resort at Longboat Key Club

301 Gulf of Mexico Drive
Longboat Key, FL 34228
813-383-8821
800-237-8821

The Gulf of Mexico on one side, Sarasota Bay on the other

General manager: Gary K. Rogers.
Accommodations: 228 suites.
Rates: Club suites $135–$375, 2-bedroom suites $290–$575; packages available. **Minimum stay:** With some packages. **Payment:** Major credit cards. **Added:** 9% tax; $15 extra person. **Children:** Free in room with parents. **Smoking:** Allowed. **Open:** Year-round.

Longboat Key is an islet off the coast of Sarasota, accessible by the John Ringling Causeway. Longboat Key Club, like its neighbor just down the boulevard, the Colony, is indeed a club, with facilities open only to members, residents, and overnight guests. It's also a gated residential community and a wildlife sanctuary. Some first-time visitors are surprised to find that the club is so large and that accommodations open to the public are in high-rise condos. However, the rooms are very pleasant and command fantastic views of the gulf or the golf course and the Sarasota skyline. Even the parking lots are pretty, with landscaped barriers and arborlike carports.

At the club's 277-slip marina on Sarasota Bay, you can rent sailboats and arrange for group cruises, marine ecology wading trips, and fishing expeditions. If you're planning to arrive in your own boat, reserve dockage in advance.

Despite the club's high-rise look, there is surprising variety in accommodations: guest rooms with twin beds; club suites with a king-size bed, a kitchenette, and living/sleeping area; one-bedroom suites with king-size beds and a spacious living/dining room next to the kitchen; two-bedroom suites with a king-size bed in the master bedroom and twin beds in another; deluxe suites with two bedrooms, a kitchen, and a generous living/dining room.

All standard rooms have a washer and dryer and daily maid service, which includes dishwashing. All accommodations have balconies overlooking the gulf or Sarasota and the golf course lagoons. Bathrooms include a separate dressing area with a vanity and a makeup mirror.

Gastronomic needs — and temptations — are taken care of at the club's restaurants. The most formal of these is Orchids, serving excellent gourmet fare. Appetizers and salads are imaginative and fresh. A delicate lemon sherbet precedes the entrée. Seafood, chops, and steaks are expertly prepared and accented with cream, citrus, and wine sauces, or sautéed for a lower calorie count. Vegetables are lightly steamed or sautéed. Desserts include homemade pastries, hazelnut cheesecake, a fruit and cream tart, and fresh fruits. Service is efficiently carried out in teams but sometimes drags toward the end of the meal. The maitre d' is affable and gracious.

The casual Islandside Grille has indoor and outdoor dining,

and the lively Island House has a dance floor and live music. There are a number of excellent restaurants in Sarasota at St. Armand's Circle. The staff at the front desk will offer dining suggestions and directions. Recently, there have been complaints from guests that the staff at the desk are not as gracious as they could be.

Conference staff service is more praiseworthy. The resort has been a winner of the Successful Meetings Pinnacle Award. The Club's John Ringling Room covers 3,000 square feet and can be divided into two separate rooms for conferences or banquets. In addition, there are four smaller rooms that can accommodate 10 to 50 people. Anyone at Longboat Key Club for a conference or executive retreat can, of course, enjoy all that the resort has to offer.

For those who have heard about the club's championship courses, Longboat Key Club's most important offering is golf. The Islandside Course, for inn guests, was designed by Billy Mitchell, with views of the Gulf of Mexico and long, winding fairways situated among small lakes and lagoons. One of the delights of this course is the number of lagoons that are frequented by various species of waterfowl, who lounge along the banks. Tennis at Longboat Key Club is just as challenging, with 14 Har-Tru courts, six lit for night play, and a tennis center and pro shop.

In addition to golf and tennis, the resort has a number of activities organized by an activities coordinator: swimnastics, aerobics, arts and crafts, tennis and golf clinics, movies, shopping trips, and Ringling Museum tours. Special performing arts packages take advantage of Sarasota's concert series and theater productions.

Apart from fishing, golf, and tennis, most guests find that they can easily fill most of a day with beach activities. The resort offers a number of waterfront amenities, from snorkeling gear to sailboards to tandem bicycles to a double chaise longue with umbrella, all available for rent at the beach. Sailing lessons are also offered for a reasonable fee, and boats can be rented by the hour, half day, or full day. The waters of the Gulf of Mexico are warm, with gentle waves — especially good for children. The beach is famous for shelling, and sunsets over the gulf are impressive.

MARCO ISLAND

Marriott's Marco Island Resort

400 S. Collier Boulevard
Marco Island, FL 33937
813-394-2511
800-GET-HERE

> *A relaxed resort
> for people of
> many interests*

General manager: Bud Davis. **Accommodations:** 736 rooms. **Rates:** Rooms $130–$350, 1-bedroom suites $360–$580, 2-bedroom suites $550–$840, lanais $360–$640, villas $350–$595; packages available. **Minimum stay:** With packages and during holidays. **Added:** 8% tax; $10 for roll-away. **Payment:** Major credit cards; personal checks with credit card. **Children:** Free in room with parents. **Smoking:** Allowed. **Open:** Year-round.

Marco Island lies between Everglades City and Naples, accessible by bridge. One of the first things that strikes a visitor is how many people are outdoors: walking, jogging, bicycling, whacking tennis balls. It's no wonder, with an average year-round temperature of 74 degrees and miles and miles of gulf shoreline. Marriott's Marco Island is one of the friendliest places on the island. Even the people who work here seem to be having a good time.

Rooms and suites at the resort are some of the best in the Marriott chain. Amenities include a mini-bar, color cable TV, a small refrigerator, a coffeemaker, spacious closets, bath with two vanities and dressing area, and a little balcony overlooking the water. Rooms in the two high-rise towers offer king-size beds or two doubles. All rooms have a view of the water, with the best — and most expensive — directly on the beach.

Additional accommodations at Marco Island include six penthouse suites in the tower with wraparound balconies overlooking the gulf, 30 right on the beach, and eight private villas. Ask about special package rates.

Dining options include the Voyager seafood restaurant and lounge, offering such Florida delicacies as stone crabs and conch chowder. The Marco dining room is more formal, with an excellent wine list and delectable continental cuisine. Other offerings for food and drink are decidedly casual: Quinn's Beachfront

> **The sand is fine near the water and coarser and full of interesting shells near the walkway to the resort. Shell gathering is so popular here that there is a little shell-washing station with a sink and spigot at the edge of the beach.**

Bistro & Bar, Café del Sol (a good place for children), the poolside Tiki Bar & Grill, and the Ice Cream Parlor.

Shopping includes a number of boutiques off the lobby and a pro shop by the tennis courts. Amazingly for a resort, the shops have reasonable prices and even some sales.

The self-contained quality of the resort makes it popular for conventions. On the first floor, facilities include the large Promenade Ballroom and four boardrooms opening onto a triangular terrace. There are two conference rooms on the ground level and three more on the third floor. Corporations and professional groups usually choose this Marriott with the participants' families in mind. The well-supervised program for children aged five to thirteen includes storytelling, arts and crafts, swimming, sand castle building, video games, and scavenger hunts. Recreation for older children and adults includes three swimming pools, whirlpools, a pitch-and-putt course, a health club, tennis, volleyball, sailing, water skiing, and golf at the nearby Marco Shores Country Club.

If there were nothing else on Marco Island, it would be worth coming here just for the three and a half miles of beach in the resort's backyard. Sunsets are spectacular and are especially pleasant over a cool drink at the beachside Tiki Bar.

The hotel is beautifully landscaped and thoughtfully designed. Guests staying on the upper floors of the north and south towers can dress for swimming and take an elevator down to the pool on the first level, bypassing the second-level lobby. The atmosphere in the pool and recreation area between the hotel and the beach is relaxed, almost festive — there are massive flower beds everywhere. Convention groups often have colorful evening receptions and buffets on the patio.

The lobby has the same relaxed ambience despite its elegant decor — terrazzo floors, large planters of coral stone, and West Indies–style wicker and rattan furniture. But no one wants to take the elegance too seriously: a big green stuffed alligator holds court in the lobby.

NAPLES

Edgewater Beach Suite Hotel

1901 Gulf Shore Blvd. North
Naples, FL 33940
813-262-6511
800-821-0196 in U.S.
800-282-3766 in Florida
Fax: 813-262-1243

> *An all-suite
> beachside hotel with
> an American and
> European clientele*

Accommodations: 124 suites.
Rates: $115–$415; packages available. **Minimum stay:** 3 nights during holiday weekends. **Added:** 6% tax. **Payment:** MasterCard, Visa. **Children:** Under 18 free in room with parents. **Smoking:** Nonsmoking available. **Open:** Year-round.

The Edgewater Beach Hotel is on lovely Gulf Shore Drive. Once the playground of the wealthy, the Edgewater makes this beautiful location accessible to ordinary folks who want to splurge for a weekend or the winter season. Though some of the accommodations are expensive, the amenities of this all-suite hotel can make it a good value.

> **Later in the evening, when the kids have gone to bed, the patio walkway and softly lit garden are ideal for a romantic stroll.**

The atmosphere is unpretentious. Many retired people bring their grown children and grandchildren for part of their stay, coming here generation after generation; the Edgewater is not the enclave of any one age or economic group. Activities include an excellent children's program. The pleasant young staff is attentive and ready to arrange outings and golf excursions if you want more recreation than the hotel offers. And they are also sensitive to the fact that most people are here just to enjoy the beach and each other's company.

The Edgewater rests on a slight rise several yards back from Gulf Shore Boulevard. The facade is rather modern, with a crescent-shaped main building of about seven floors and two adjoining four-story wings. Inside, the lobby and adjacent Mistral's Lounge have marble floors of delicate ecru. The lounge is distinctively decorated with oversize wicker chairs and a huge wicker sofa. In the corner is a white grand piano, a favorite gathering place.

Just outside the lounge is the bilevel patio with bright flower beds, tropical plants, palm trees, a lovely fountain, and the swimming pool and patio where musicians play Caribbean music. Beyond that is Flippers, a poolside snack and beverage bar, and the walkway to the beach. The Naples beach is famous for its pink-peach sand and warm water. Although this is a public beach, the hotel is bordered on the north and south by other quiet hotels and condominiums and by expensive private residences, so there is rarely a problem with beer-swilling teenagers or loud radios.

The original hotel was built in the 1960s and had a multi-million-dollar renovation in 1985, which added 2,600 feet of executive conference space and turned the rooms on the upper floors into mammoth suites. Altogether, there are 124 one- and two-bedroom water-view suites and nine penthouse suites, some of which are occasionally used as conference rooms.

The suites are beautifully decorated and have a variety of bed sizes. Kitchens include a full-size refrigerator, good counter space, a microwave, and a double sink; some have a breakfast bar with padded stools. Daily dishwashing is included in the maid service.

In all the suites, one of the two sofas in the living room opens out into a bed. Two-bedroom suites are large enough to accommodate three generations if there are only one or two children in tow. All have gulf views from balconies or patios.

When the sun sets, the atmosphere at the Edgewater changes a bit. Young professionals from Naples and Fort Myers stop by for a sundowner in the Crystal Parrot. This sixth-floor lounge and award-winning restaurant is famous for its view of the gulf sunset — and, in Naples, watching the sun go down is an important ritual.

Inn by the Sea

287 Eleventh Avenue South
Naples, FL 33940
813-649-4124

*A real find —
the only B&B in
Olde Naples*

Innkeeper: Caitlin Maser. **Accommodations:** 3 rooms and 2 suites. **Rates:** Rooms $85–$130, suites $120. **Included:** Expanded Continental breakfast. **Added:** 6% tax. **Payment:** MasterCard, Visa. **Children:** Under 14 not allowed. **Smoking:** Prohibited. **Open:** Year-round.

On the corner of fashionable Third Street South and residential Eleventh Avenue, the Inn by the Sea couldn't be in a better spot in Naples. Guests are close to shopping and art galleries but are also in a quiet neighborhood. The house, built in 1937 of native yellow heart pine, is larger than it looks — from the street, one can see only a garden of ornamental grasses and flowers and an enclosed porch with a green and white awning.

Visitors enter the house through the screened-in front porch, furnished in wicker and a favorite spot for breakfast and reading. The comfortable living room has the original pine ceiling and a plaster fireplace. A braided rug, a plaid overstuffed chair, country collectibles, and stenciling give the room a country feel. In the dining room, a pot of coffee is always in the coffeemaker on the hutch; guests may help themselves.

One of the most interesting rooms is Captiva, with green-striped wallpaper and lacy linen pillows on the bed. The carved headboard was created from the doors of a 19th-century armoire, rubbed with a deep green stain. This room isn't for anyone who doesn't like green, but it is fun.

> Caitlin calls this a "tropical Continental" breakfast because of the emphasis on tropical fruits and freshly squeezed orange juice. There are also homemade breads and muffins, granola, and imported teas and coffees.

Sanibel is a quiet, restful room on the back of the house with Bahamian shades at the windows and a pine four-poster bed. The walls have been sponged in subtle brass and tan. The private bath is small but charming, with an original sink and tub and a tile floor. Some of the most unusual rooms in the house are bathrooms, with beribboned mirrors, rainbow-striped wallpaper, eyelet shower curtains, or handpainted walls.

Inn by the Sea has one room with twin beds that is ideal for older children traveling with their parents. There's also a suite, called Keewaydin, that has a quilted daybed and a queen-size bed, which is ideal for a family.

Breakfast is as outstanding as everything else at the inn. Guests can eat on the screened-in porch or the dining room, or have a "picnic breakfast" on the beach.

The inn has complimentary bikes for guests to use and folding chairs that can be taken to the gulf beach, just a block from the house. Naples is a wonderful town to explore — there are galleries and craft shops as well as expensive clothing stores. Restaurants are outstanding. Among the best are Truffles, great for salads or sandwiches at lunch or an informal dinner, and the Chef's Garden, a more formal restaurant that serves gourmet cuisine and light, creative desserts.

Naples Bath and Tennis Club

4995 Airport Road
Naples, FL 33942
813-261-5777
800-225-9692

> *A country club*
> *with rentals*
> *for vacationers*

Accommodations: 50 villas (number in rental pool varies). **Rates:** 1-bedroom villas $100–$120, 2-bedroom villas $125–$185, 3-bedroom villas $180–$250; tennis packages; special weekly, monthly, and group rates. **Included:** Club privileges. **Minimum stay:** 4 nights. **Added:** 8% tax. **Payment:** Major credit cards; personal check. **Children:** Under 18 free in room with parents. **Smoking:** Nonsmoking rooms available. **Open:** Year-round.

The "Bath" in Naples Bath and Tennis Club's name comes from the British. The organizers of the club could just as easily have used the word "Swim." But there is something proper and transatlantic about this resort and, after a few days here, "Bath" seems fitting enough. People are here simply to play a sport at a superlative facility and to enjoy the good life. Vacationers should remember that this is a private club, and overnight guests can feel shut out.

All the accommodations available are privately owned and rented out while the owners are away. Some of the units are quite elegant, while others are less than desirable. Some of the one-bedroom Bobolink Court villas have stained carpeting and tired-looking furniture in brown and mustard colors reminiscent of the 1970s. Query the reservationist closely to be sure you are getting a unit that has been newly refurbished or well-maintained. Accommodations are in one-, two-, and three-bedroom villas and a few three-bedroom houses. The larger villas and homes are some of the most beautiful in Florida, with luxurious appointments and furnishings, walk-in closets, spacious baths, modern kitchens (with a full set of pots and pans and service for eight), and screened-in porches with closeted washers and dryers. Accommodations overlook the tennis courts or a pool and the grounds; all have a view of one of the resort's manmade ponds and lakes.

> The 10 bass-filled lakes on the property are home to many exotic birds and several alligators who navigate the inter-connecting lakes. Small woodland birds swoop over or sing throatily on the fenceposts. Airplanes from Naples Airport buzz overhead, too, but they might as well be a million miles away.

The clubhouse is one of the oldest buildings on the property and has a venerable Florida country club look: yellow stucco, white shake roof, and floor-to-ceiling Palladian windows in the spacious rooms. The main dining room is especially pretty. White latticework gives an arboreal feeling that is enhanced by an arching ceiling painted with delicate birds and tropical vines and plants. Other amenities at the clubhouse include meeting space, a well-equipped health club, and a pro shop.

By the clubhouse is the patio with a junior Olympic-size pool, a children's wading pool, a Jacuzzi, and poolside refreshment service. On the other side are the racquetball courts and the tennis academy. Considered one of the best in the country, the All-American Sports Academy is run by pro Bill Beverly. Individual and group instruction for adults and children, round robins, and clinics make up a challenging curriculum, with 12 matches scheduled each week for all levels of play. The intensive program includes an introductory clinic and orientation, five hours of daily instruction, videotaping, and written evaluations.

There are more tennis courts directly across the street. Naples Bath and Tennis has 38 in all — 37 clay and one hard, with 14 lit for night play. They are beautifully maintained, and some have covered observation cabanas.

The grounds are landscaped with native and imported trees and a profusion of bright annuals and Florida perennials.

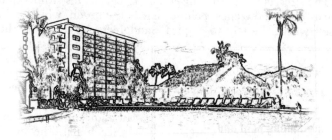

Naples Beach Hotel and Golf Club

851 Gulf Shore Boulevard North
Naples, FL 33940
813-261-2222
800-282-7601 in Florida
800-237-7600 in U.S.

A family-owned resort with a range of accommodations

Owners: The Watkins family.
Accommodations: 315 rooms, suites, and efficiencies. **Rates:** Rooms $100–$255, suites $125–$375; efficiencies add $30 per day high season; packages available; meal plans available in high season. **Included:** Children's program in high season. **Minimum stay:** With some packages. **Added:** 8% tax; $15 extra adult. **Payment:** Major credit cards. **Children:** Under 12 free in room with parents. **Smoking:** Nonsmoking available upon request. **Open:** Year-round.

The Naples Beach Hotel and Golf Club is for those who want the combination of golf and the beach — it is the only resort in Naples that has both right on the property. The staff is friendly and down to earth, and the grounds and accommodations are pleasant rather than slick. This is the sort of place where you see many three-generation families having lunch together after the adults have had a vigorous morning on the golf course and the kids have built sand castles on the beach.

The club's 18-hole, par championship course has large greens and tees and some challenging traps and water hazards. Many who play here have been coming back year after year since the course was bought and restored in 1946 by Henry B. Watkins, whose son is now the president of the club. The course was redesigned by Ron Garl in 1980 and completed in 1981.

The crescent-shaped Sunset Beach Bar serves drinks and salads and sandwiches. Behind that is the beach, which is in itself worth the trip to Naples. Sandpipers scurry along the water's edge, and gulls cry overhead. The white sand has the texture of sugar, and the water is a deep blue-green.

> **Naples Beach Hotel has recreational space right on the water that includes a swimming pool and facilities for water sports: pedal boats, Hobie Cats and Phantoms, paddle cruisers, and inflatable floats and rafts. A director of services can make arrangements for field trips and fishing off the property.**

In addition to the Sunset Beach Bar, the hotel has the Seagull, a casual dining room overlooking the water, and the Brasserie Café, overlooking the ninth green. The formal Everglades Dining Room is open in winter, serving traditional cuisine. Guests staying in efficiencies usually prepare some of their own meals. All guests can choose to take the hotel's meal plan at a cost of $30 a day.

There are many restaurants and trendy cafés in Old Naples for guests who wish to explore a little, and wonderful, if expensive, shopping on Third Avenue. The boutiques and internationally known stores are Mediterranean in style, and the immaculate streets and sidewalks are graced by palm trees and bright flowers. For those who want to get a sense of the natural environment here, there's the Naples Nature Center and nearby Corkscrew Swamp Sanctuary, operated by the National Audubon Society.

Lodgings are in six midrise buildings on the property. They include standard rooms, with wicker or bamboo furniture, color TVs, large closets, and attractive baths; deluxe suites, with one bedroom and a living room with bar and refrigerator; and efficiencies, with one bedroom and a kitchenette. The majority have striking views of the Gulf of Mexico or the golf course.

The Registry Resort

475 Seagate Drive
Naples, FL 33940
813-597-3232
800-247-9810 or 800-9-NAPLES
Fax: 813-597-3147

A luxury hotel near Vanderbilt Beach

Accommodations: 474 rooms and suites. **Rates:** Rooms $110–$355, suites $210–$750; packages available. **Minimum stay:** With packages. **Added:** 8% tax; $30 extra person. **Payment:** MasterCard, Visa. **Children:** Under 18 free in room with parents. **Smoking:** Allowed. **Open:** Year-round.

Seagate Drive cuts through a plush Naples development called Pelican's Bay, which includes a Tom Fazio golf course called the Pelican's Nest. The Registry, at the end of Seagate, has an atmosphere of informal luxury. There's courteous valet parking, as well as a convenient lot where you can park yourself. Most guests begin to unwind the minute they hear water flowing from the little manmade stream in a faux grotto at the entrance to the hotel.

Inside are floors of swirled Italian marble, hand-woven rugs from the Orient, and more water, this time from waterfalls tumbling over tiers of marble. The Registry fits in well with upscale Naples. The restaurants and lounges, frequented by Naples residents as well as hotel guests, are dramatically decorated with polished wood or marble.

The Registry is not right on the gulf, but guests can take a boardwalk across the nature preserve or hop on the open-air tram to get to the water. The resort's private beach club offers snorkeling, parasailing, sailing, and other water sports. The beach itself has fine, pale sand near the aqua water and a wide strip of shells at its edge.

The management and staff here are eager to take care of any minor glitch or inconvenience — no small achievement, since the hotel has become extremely busy in the last couple of years with both vacationers and executives. The management has worked hard to be true competition for the Ritz-Carlton in Naples; both hotels set a high standard for the area.

Lobby elevators whisk guests up to one of 474 rooms that overlook either the gulf or the canals and greenery of Naples from private balconies. Thick carpeting in the hallway is a foretaste of the decor in the rooms — no antiques here, just modern comfort. Standard guest rooms have queen or king beds, deep-pile carpeting, mini-bars, built-in desks, cable TV and movie channels, and luxury baths with a separate dressing room, makeup mirror, telephone, and hair dryer. The suites have similar appointments, along with Jacuzzis and large balconies.

The Registry has 50 tennis villas arranged in two clusters with Jacuzzis and patios off the bedrooms. The tennis center and courts are a draw for visitors from out of state who come to Naples to improve their game. Guests can also improve their aerobic capacity here. The Registry has its own health club with an exercise and aerobics room; sauna, steam, and massage rooms; tanning beds; and a whirlpool.

Two of the Registry's swimming pools are at the tennis center, the third behind the hotel tower. This is a fantastic free-form pool, with a grotto surrounded by tropical greenery and a waterfall. The rocks are fake, and the whole production is a little like Disney's Fantasyland, but kids love it.

Ritz-Carlton, Naples

280 Vanderbilt Beach Road
Naples, FL 33963
813-598-3300
800-241-3333

> *A palace hotel
> with superb
> service*

General manager: Joseph Freni, Jr.
Accommodations: 459 rooms, 28 suites. **Rates:** Rooms $130–$295, club rooms $310–$540, suites $550–$795; packages available. **Minimum stay:** With some packages. **Added:** 8% tax. **Payment:** Major credit cards. **Children:** 18 and under free in room with parents. **Smoking:** Nonsmoking available. **Open:** Year-round.

The sumptuous beauty of the Naples Ritz-Carlton makes some people feel guilty, even decadent, at first. But it takes only about five minutes to get used to the decadence.

The Ritz-Carlton is reminiscent of the palace hotels of the Riviera and of the resorts Flagler built in Florida in the 1920s. Set on 19 acres in upscale Pelican Bay, the Mediterranean-style hotel has a pale stucco exterior and spare, understated lines, almost austere in the Florida lushness. At the cobble-stoned, fountained entry, a bellman in top hat and blue tails greets you. Everywhere, service is attentive and concerned but unobtrusive. The ratio of employees to guests is almost two to one.

In the two-level lobby, guests are surrounded by beauty: deep-cushioned brocade sofas and chairs, English oil paintings, high ceilings and richly carved moldings, marble floors covered with fine Oriental rugs, and museum-quality antiques. It is especially pleasant in the afternoon, when tea and an array of pastries are served and the rays of a setting sun slant through the Palladian windows.

> The "playground" area behind the hotel has tennis courts, a Jacuzzi, a pool, and the beach. A long stretch of the Ritz's property fronts on Florida's "Platinum Coast." Here the sand is a pale peach, the shoreline ankle-deep in shells. The hotel has sailboats and Windsurfers, and the staff can arrange scuba diving, water skiing, and deep-sea fishing. There are covered cabanas on the beach, chaise longues, and beach towels for guests.

Between the beach and the large free-form swimming pool is a nature preserve of mangroves and other native trees set around a natural lagoon. This is real Florida jungle, with a resident alligator who, fortunately, is rather shy. A weathered boardwalk and two wooden bridges span the lagoon.

The patio around the heated pool and Jacuzzi is Italianate, with chairs and umbrella tables. There is even a large rose garden, a rarity in Florida.

Overlooking the rose garden is the aerobics room in the hotel's fitness center, with the very best in equipment. There are saunas and massage rooms in both the men's and women's locker rooms. The center also includes a game room with a pool table and a juice bar. "Ritzercise" classes are held several times a day.

The six tennis courts are excellent, with hard and clay surfaces and lights for night play. An arboreal covered pavilion overlooks the courts, where spectators can sit at tables and chairs to watch a game and sip drinks.

Golf is available at Pelican's Nest, a course designed by Tom Fazio, just 15 minutes from the hotel. Although the topography of Naples is as monotonous as anywhere in Florida, this course has manmade hills as high as 11 feet and an unusual combination of sand and grass bunkers. If you want a different challenge, golf can be arranged at nearby Bonita Bay, designed by Arthur Hills, and at the Eagle Creek links, designed by Ken Venturi.

The Ritz has a children's activity program, with swimming and outdoor games, sand castles on the beach, and movies in the afternoon and evening.

The Ritz is popular for conferences and corporate retreats. Meeting space includes a 10,000-square-foot ballroom, a second smaller ballroom, and 12 meeting rooms. All of these rooms are exquisitely appointed with beautiful carpets, mahogany-paneled walls, leather chairs, and museum-quality etchings and oil paintings. The facilities include teleconferencing, audiovisual equipment, and lighted lecterns. Secretarial service is also available.

The most popular accommodations for corporate groups are the Club Level guest rooms on the twelfth and fourteenth floors. Just off the elevator hallway is the Club itself, a large, private room with comfortable seating where guests can enjoy Continental breakfast, tea and pastries in the afternoon, and complimentary hors d'oeuvres in the evening. The Club floor deluxe rooms and suites have French provincial or fine mahogany furniture, botanical prints, hidden cable TV, a mini-bar and small refrigerator, and a separate dressing room.

All the suites and rooms at the Ritz have water views; most have a small terrace with European-style railings. The suites that view the gulf have a bedroom and sitting area separated by French doors, while royal suites have a large parlor and a separate bedroom. The two presidential suites are elegant and spacious, with working fireplaces. All accommodations have attractive bathrooms with marble floors, large shower-tubs with a marble surround, and thick marble sinktops. Twice-daily maid service includes turndown service, with chocolates and a rose on your pillow.

Though young waiters and waitresses may sometimes be a bit slow (as everywhere in Florida), the service is generally very good at the resort's three restaurants. In high season, there are 124 people on the kitchen staff alone.

The Dining Room, open for breakfast, lunch, and dinner, is the most formal of the three. Floor-to-ceiling French windows look out over the gulf. Cuisine here is nouvelle American and quite creative: duck foie gras, roast pheasant with lingonberries, lobster strudel, and loins of venison and lamb. The restaurant is also noted for its fresh Florida seafood: gulf shrimp, snapper, and pompano. Desserts are excellent here, with a particularly good key lime pie. The wine list is 20 pages long and has some outstanding offerings.

The Café, the most casual of the restaurants, serves breakfast, lunch, dinner, and midnight and afternoon snacks in its informal dining room, or on the terrace near the pool.

The Grill has a clubby atmosphere, with striped club chairs, bronze sculptures of hunting scenes, Honduran mahogany paneling, and an unusual carved fireplace. The specialties are Florida seafood, roasts, and grilled steaks and chops. A pianist plays softly at the Steinway grand and a fire roars in the grate, making this a special place for dinner.

World Tennis Center Resort and Club

4800 Airport Road
Naples, FL 33942
813-263-1900
800-292-6663
Fax: 813-649-7055

A tennis resort with a serious sporting attitude

Manager: Laura Legue. **Accommodations:** 148 villas. **Rates:** $85–$145; weekly and monthly rates. **Included:** Court time; club privileges; fishing privileges. **Minimum stay:** With packages. **Added:** 8% tax. **Payment:** MasterCard, Visa. **Children:** Two free in condo with parents; fee for each additional child. **Smoking:** Allowed. **Open:** Year-round. **Pets:** Allowed in some units at additional fee.

The World Tennis Center's brochure assures the visitor, "We're not just for tennis players." That's sorta true and sorta not. It's probably fair to say that most people staying are here for the tennis, with the exception of some families who want to stay in an accommodation near pricey Naples that allows them to cook some meals and to have spacious quarters for a reasonable rate. But a single person who is not a tennis player would find few people to cozy up to around the pool, although there is a convivial happy hour in the evening. Tennis is serious business here, and the atmosphere is a little cold, even at the reception center.

The tennis complex has 16 courts: 11 Har-Tru and five composite, and an impressive 2,500-seat stadium. The pro shop provides a number of services, and there is a small clubhouse. A full-time staff gives private and group lessons, camps for all ages and abilities, and clinics. Court time is free of charge for all guests. The center is several miles northeast of downtown Naples in an area that was once quite rural but is slowly being developed. Guests turn off the busy Airport Road onto a white-railed bridge over a little gulley. The road curves past a large fountain in front of the reception center, a white stucco Mediterranean building with bougainvillea draped over the doorway. Accommodations are in groups of two-story con- dominiums that are simi- lar in style to the recep- tion center. The idea was to create the look of a Greek village — condos are grouped near man- made lakes on the prop- erty, and the tennis facili- ties are centered at the reception area and club- house near the entrance to the resort.

> In the few years the World Tennis Center has been open, it has become a top choice for tennis buffs and the site for a number of tournaments and charitable events. The place can be quite crowded on tournament weekends.

Attractive subtropical landscaping accents the white stucco. The interiors of the condos are somewhat austere but efficient and roomy. Each condo has two bedrooms, one with twin beds, one with a king. The living/dining room has a TV, a sofa and easy chair, and a table and chairs near the kitchen. The kitchen has everything you could need for an extended stay. There's also a washer/dryer and generous cabinet and closet space. Second-floor accommodations have a balcony; first-floor units have a cement terrace.

Just a few minutes away are gulf beaches and the upscale town of Naples. Some good restaurants to try are the Third Street Café, Bayside, and Truffles/Chef's Garden. Old Naples is fun to stroll through, with brick courtyards and pretty fountains along Third Street. It's especially nice — and safe — at night. The clubhouse centers on tennis, but there is also a pool and patio with a whirlpool, where lots of non–ten- nis players and children spend the day. The clubhouse has men's and women's locker rooms and saunas, as well as aero- bics classes and various social activities. The clubhouse has an informal restaurant, where the food is acceptable and the staff is congenial. The resort also has several freshwater lakes stocked with bass for fishing.

PUNTA RASSA

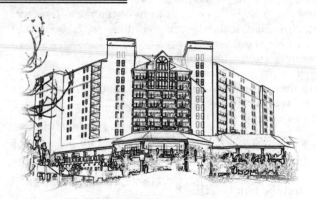

Sanibel Harbour Resort and Spa

17260 Harbour Pointe Drive
Ft. Myers, FL 33908
813-466-4000
800-767-7777
Fax: 813-466-2150

> *A secluded resort
> only 20 minutes
> from the airport*

General manager: Bob Moceri. **Accommodations:** 240 hotel rooms and suites; 80 2-bedroom condos. **Rates:** Rooms $105–$270, suites $150–$850, 2-bedroom condos $145–$505. **Included:** Water taxi and van shuttle to Sanibel Island; fishing privileges off resort dock. **Minimum stay:** With packages. **Added:** 9% tax; small charge for cribs. **Payment:** Major credit cards; personal check. **Children:** Under 18 free in room with parents (2 children maximum). **Smoking:** Nonsmoking available. **Open:** Year-round.

Sanibel Harbour Resort is located on Punta Rassa Peninsula in San Carlos Bay, an idyllic site. The resort overlooks several tiny outlying mangrove islands in the gulf as well as popular Sanibel Island, which is just a few minutes away via a causeway. Lately Sanibel Island has become a bit congested and, especially during the holidays, the causeway traffic at tollbooths can bottleneck. At this resort, guests have views of the island and the gulf but none of the congestion.

Primarily a tennis resort, Sanibel Harbour has a number of other amenities that make it popular with both locals and out-of-state vacationers and businesspeople. The spa is particularly impressive. Two floors in an attractively decorated facility just opposite the hotel and adjacent to the tennis center include exercise rooms, four racquetball courts, 10 whirlpools, a lap pool, hot and cold plunge pools, Swiss showers, sauna and steam rooms, a suspended Batar Bed with vibrating stereo speakers — the list goes on and on. Services include personal training sessions, aerobics classes, and a variety of beauty and health treatments. The unlimited usage fee is a modest $10.

Tennis facilities include 12 lighted courts, eight fast-dry clay courts, four Spin-flex courts, an

> **The recreational area behind the hotel is one of the most spectacular in Florida, with a three-tiered waterfall, a large pool with a cascading waterfall, and a thousand-foot beach overlooking the bay. One could easily spend every day of a vacation relaxing here.**

impressive tennis center, and a 5,500-seat stadium. Guests receive top-notch instruction from the pro staff, with private and group lessons, courtside video instruction, round robins, and clinics. Services include a player-matching service and re-stringing, a ball hopper, and ball machine rentals. The Sanibel's tennis getaway package includes unlimited court time, a day entrance to the spa, and a stadium stroke clinic.

Thatched chikee huts and canvas umbrellas set up on the beach offer shelter from the sun. A private dock provides fishing and water sport rentals. Staff at the dock can also arrange for more ambitious fishing charters off the property.

Like any large resort, Sanibel Harbour has restaurants that appeal to a range of tastes, and there are two lounges with nightly entertainment. Extensive meeting facilities include a grand ballroom, the smaller Caloosa ballroom, several conference rooms, and a full-service banquet kitchen.

Sanibel Harbour's one- and two-bedroom condominiums, in high-rises built several years ago, are particularly good for an extended stay. These are spacious, with full kitchens, living/dining areas, two bedrooms, and screened balconies overlooking barrier islands and the bay.

But the hotel, constructed on the site of a 19th-century inn, is the resort's showcase. The architecture is Old Florida, with a stucco exterior, white and green balconies, brackets and other Victorian embellishments, and a conical tin roof on the main lounge that overlooks the water.

The spacious rooms are attractively decorated with real wood furniture, mini-bars, color cable TV, a choice of king- or queen-size beds, quilted bedspreads and coordinating drapes, and wall-to-wall carpeting. All accommodations have balconies that provide spectacular views of the resort's 80 acres and the turquoise water of the San Carlos Bay.

The two-bedroom, two-bath condos have a washer and dryer, a king bed in the master bedroom, and a queen or two twins in the smaller bedroom. The master bedrom and the living room have sliding glass doors to the screened balcony. Each condominium group has its own pool and Jacuzzi.

SAFETY HARBOR

Safety Harbor Spa and Fitness Center

105 N. Bayshore Drive
Safety Harbor, FL 34695
813-726-1161
800-237-0155
Fax: 813-726-4268

A reasonably priced spa with plenty of pampering

Accommodations: 212 rooms.
Rates: 2-night weekend $188–$281 per person; also 5- or 8-day spa plans. **Included:** Meals with some spa plans. **Minimum**

stay: With spa packages. **Added:** 10% tax; 17% service charge; $10 for crib. **Payment:** Major credit cards; personal check with card. **Children:** Under 16 not permitted. **Smoking:** In restricted areas only. **Open:** Year-round.

In 1539, Hernando de Soto proclaimed the mineral springs along the subtropical shore of a New World bay to be the Fountain of Youth. For centuries, men and women have come to these mineral springs, insisting that the waters had rejuvenating and curative powers. In 1926, a high-domed pavilion was built over the main spring. Today, the New World territory is called Florida, the bay is called Old Tampa Bay, and the enclosure over the springs has been made into the dining room of the Safety Harbor Spa and Fitness Center. While not everyone would agree that the mineral water alone has rejuvenating powers, certainly the fitness program does.

> **A hot soak in one of the small elevated tubs that surround the oval indoor pool is a wonderful experience after a demanding exercise class.**

Once a spa that catered to retirees, Safety Harbor now has a clientele of fitness-minded men and women of all ages. And it's not just a place for the Beautiful People. This is the kind of spa where you can feel comfortable with a suburban wardrobe and generic jogging shoes. The staff are down-to-earth, low-key, and friendly.

A number of programs are available. The week-long "Total Fitness" plan is thorough, beginning with a fitness profile, blood chemistry analysis, and medical examination. It includes a prescribed number of facials, herbal wraps, a daily massage, a loofah scrub, a manicure, and a pedicure. Women get a Lancome makeover and a shampoo and blow-dry. Men get a scalp treatment and haircut. Other plans of shorter or longer duration may have a greater emphasis on exercise, with aerobics, dancercise, yoga, and water exercise.

The fitness center has recently added a second machine room and a third aerobics gym. Like the other two gymnasiums, it has Super-Gym aerobic flooring. All equipment is excellent, and there is everything you could want for a thorough workout, weight loss plan, or training program.

The mineral water that de Soto called *espiritu santo* (holy spirit) is used in all the water at the spa, and when heated, it does have a silky, refreshing quality. Besides indoor and outdoor swimming pools, there are men's and women's saunas and whirlpools and two Jacuzzis for coed groups.

All spa guests have access to Safety Harbor's shuffleboard courts, nine tennis courts, quarter-mile jogging track, and four-hole golf course and driving range, as well as the opportunity to participate in water volleyball and water basketball games.

Fueling all the hard work is a varied and healthy array of delicious food. A typical lunch is a salad of spinach and other greens, grilled or poached seafood, lightly cooked vegetables, and fresh fruits. Kosher and vegetarian menus are available. For snacks during the day there are raw vegetables and fruits and freshly squeezed fruit juices at the lobby juice bar.

Accommodations are in rooms and suites at the spa and in one-bedroom and studio apartments in Safety Harbor House, a low-rise apartment building. A Tampa Bay room is best for a couple. It includes a sitting area and large bathroom that has a dressing area, separate vanity, and two closets. Many of the spa guest rooms and suites have been recently redone and are quite attractive. Some have patios or balconies with views of the swimming pool or Old Tampa Bay, and the suites have kitchenettes. All are comfortable and have private bathrooms, telephones, and color TV.

The lobby and reception area of the spa has recently been refurbished, with new carpeting and new countertops and desks. The look is one of clean lines and efficiency, reflecting Safety Harbor's commitment to alter its image and attract more young fitness buffs.

ST. PETERSBURG

Mansion House Bed and Breakfast

105 Fifth Avenue, N.E.
St. Petersburg, FL 33701
813-821-9391
Fax: 813-821-9754

*Winner of a beauti-
fication award, a short
walk from the bay*

Innkeepers: Alan and Suzanne
Lucas. **Accommodations:** 6
rooms. **Rates:** $55–$65. **Included:** Full breakfast. **Minimum
stay:** None. **Added:** 10%tax. **Payment:** MasterCard and Visa.
Children: Older children preferred because of antiques. **Smoking:** Outside only. **Open:** Year-round.

Alan and Suzanne Lucas are originally from Wales, having
moved to Florida in 1991. They bought the Mansion House as
a rather dilapidated property in a run-down neighborhood.
Just down the street is the bay, a marina and city pier, a park,
and a spectacularly restored grand old resort, the Stouffer
Vinoy. Certain neighborhoods in old St. Pete are still derelict,
but this little area seems to have made a genuine recovery,
and the Mansion House is certainly contributing.

Reputedly the home of the first mayor of St. Petersburg,
this turn-of-the-century clapboard house was built in 1904.
With striped awnings that give it almost a jaunty look, the
place sits on the corner of two moderately busy city streets.
Inside is a sun room, an enclosed porch furnished in wicker,

and behind that, a large parlor with a tiled fireplace and comfortable sofas. One of the two dining rooms also serves as Alan's painting studio. The common rooms are furnished with antiques and comfortable sofas; some windows have leaded or stained glass.

> **In the morning, Suzanne serves a full English breakfast that is different every day. A favorite is Welsh pancakes, stuffed with blueberries and covered with a hot blueberry sauce. She enjoys having guests sample scone-like Welsh cake and English sausages called bangers.**

The Lucases spent almost a year renovating the house. All the guest rooms and the common rooms are immaculate, yet still have the at-home feel of an old house. The guest rooms all have traditional wallpapers and are furnished with period furniture. The private baths are modern but have some old-fashioned touches, like the claw-foot tub in the twin-bedded room called Caephilly. All the rooms are named after Welsh castles, with the exception of the Carriage Room. This suite is located above the garage and has a private stairway and roomy bath.

Stouffer Vinoy Resort

501 Fifth Avenue, N.E.
St. Petersburg, FL 33701-2644
813-894-1000
800-HOTELS-1
Fax: 813-822-2785
TDD for hearing impaired:
   813-821-7010

> *A recently restored grande dame*

Accommodations: 360 rooms and suites. **Rates:** Rooms $119–$229, suites vary according to season and night requested; special weekend rates and packages. **Included:** Meals and recreation with some packages. **Minimum stay:** With some packages. **Added:** 10% tax. **Payment:** Major credit cards. **Children:** Welcome. **Smoking:** Nonsmoking rooms available. **Open:** Year-round.

Residents of Tampa Bay have long awaited the completion of this fine old hotel. Mired in delays and financial complications, the hotel had a slow start but it is now taking off, to the delight of both residents and Tampa Bay visitors. This lovely place has helped to revitalize the whole neighborhood.

Guests enter the hotel and walk along an arched loggia-style reception area. Floors are the original European terra cotta tiles in variegated sizes with accents of figured tiles in primary colors. Chairs are upholstered in rich tapestries and ivory brocades with a deep silk fringe at the base. Pecky cypress beams above are stenciled with geometric figures and flowers. Vases of fresh tropical flowers and large pots planted with ginkgo trees create a gardenlike freshness.

> **The restoration of the Vinoy is one of the most meticulous ever done on a Florida hotel. What was preserved has been cleaned up and polished; what had to be replaced has been historically researched and duplicated with great concern for detail.**

Just beyond the arched loggia is the Grand Ballroom. Its ivory plaster walls are accented with a delicate gold, its Palladian windows are adorned with heavy, tassled drapes, and above are coffered ceilings. The Vinoy has more than 25,000 square feet of meeting space, including the Grand Ballroom and smaller Plaza Ballroom. The resort has an attractive boardroom and 11 breakout rooms for smaller meetings. There is also function space outside, and a white tent near the tennis courts can be transformed with tiny lights and flowers into an appealing space for parties and receptions. A professional convention services staff attends to all the details of catering and audiovisual needs.

At one end of the loggia is the main restaurant, really a lounge and two restaurants in one. The floors are of Brazilian cherry, and the wainscoting is mahogany. On one side of this large, long room is the Terrace Room, which serves three meals a day. On the other is Marchand's, for more formal evening dining. In the middle is the new bar, all polished wood and brass. Informal dining and imbibing are at the poolside Alfresco. Overlooking the resort's golf course on pretty Snell Island is the Clubhouse Restaurant, serving only dinner.

The golf course and clubhouse are worth the short trip

from the hotel. Snell Island, site of the resort's golf facilities, is an upscale residential area in St. Pete with many fine examples of early 20th-century architecture. The hacienda-like clubhouse has an ivory stucco exterior, barrel tile roof, and interesting little turrets and towers. The golf course is new, designed for the hotel by Ron Carl.

Tennis is perhaps more impressive. The Stouffer Vinoy's championship facility has been chosen as the official home of the Women's Tennis Association. The 16 courts have four different surfaces: Deco-Turf II, clay, Har-Tru, and grass. The pro shop is larger than most and carries fitness clothing as well as golf and tennis attire. Next to the shop is the fitness center, with excellent equipment in the exercise room, steam rooms, saunas, and spas, and an aerobics room.

Other recreation facilities at the Vinoy include a well-maintained croquet court and two swimming pools, one with a waterfall, and whirlpools. The main swimming pool is rather too contemporary in design for this old hotel: the tiles are cobalt blue and pistachio green, and a sheet of water tumbles down at the waterfall end.

Originally built in the early part of this century and called the Vinoy Park Hotel, the main hotel has 258 guest rooms, with 102 rooms in an adjoining new tower building. During the renovation, three rooms were made into two and bathrooms expanded so that even standard guest rooms are now quite spacious. In each room an armoire hides a TV; a second television is in the marble bathroom.

Most rooms have a sitting area and desk and chair. There are telephones at the desk, in the bathroom, and on the night table. First-floor rooms in the new tower have outdoor patio whirlpool tubs, while other rooms have small private balconies, many overlooking the bay and marina. Additional amenities include a hair dryer and double-sink vanity in the bathroom, a mini-bar, bathrobes, and complimentary newspaper and coffee with a Vinoy wake-up call. Except for the two dozen or so suites, the rooms are quite similar (and similar in price), so if a view of the bay and the resort's marina is important to you, be sure to ask for a bay-view room on a top floor. It's also worthwhile asking about the Vinoy's "Breakations" and other special packages, of which there are several. Some of these offer wonderful pampering for a special occasion. The honeymoon package is particularly lavish and includes a tower room with a patio spa, champagne and roses, and limousine service during your stay.

ST. PETERSBURG BEACH

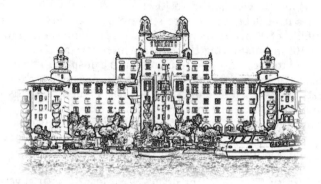

Don CeSar Beach Resort

3400 Gulf Boulevard
St. Petersburg Beach, FL 33706
813-360-1881
800-282-1116
Telex: 523496
Fax: 813-367-6952
Reservations: 800-637-7200

> *A landmark hotel
> where F. Scott and
> Zelda danced in
> the ballroom*

General manager: Larry Trainor. **Accommodations:** 277 rooms, suites, and penthouses. **Rates:** Rooms $140–$265, suites $220–$600, penthouses and packages available. **Included:** Shuttle service to golf course; KIDS Ltd. program. **Minimum stay:** With some packages. **Added:** 10% tax; $15 extra person; $15 roll-away. **Payment:** Major credit cards; personal checks. **Children:** Under 18 free in room with parents. **Smoking:** Nonsmoking available. **Open:** Year-round.

First-time visitors to the Don CeSar don't have to worry that they won't be able to find the hotel in the crowd of hotels and motels on St. Petersburg Beach. The grand pink palace is visible for miles. In fact, it's such a distinctive landmark that the National Maritime Association charts it on their maps as a navigational aid.

Opened in 1928, the Don CeSar hosted such celebrities as F. Scott Fitzgerald, Franklin D. Roosevelt, and Al Capone. When the banks failed in 1931, the founder of the resort,

Thomas Rowe, rallied his close-knit staff, and together they managed to survive the Depression, often working for half pay. When Rowe died in 1940, after having finally got the hotel out of debt, there were still troubles ahead. After the bombing of Pearl Harbor, the Don CeSar rented out fewer than 100 rooms during the entire winter season. The resort was sold to the Army and converted into a hospital. The penthouses became operating rooms, the third- and fourth-floor guest rooms dental clinics, and what is now the Bistro Restaurant served as a morgue.

After the war, the resort became an Air Force convalescent center, a hurricane shelter, and a Veterans Administration office, and whatever had thus far been preserved of the hotel's grandness was almost totally destroyed. Oriental rugs, expensive furniture, and elegant drapes were loaded onto government trucks and carted away. The walls were stripped of their bronze light fixtures and painted a drab green.

When the Veterans Administration moved out in 1967, there was talk of tearing the hotel down and building a public park. A "Save the Don" committee was formed, and the property was bought by hotelier William Bowman, Jr., who was determined to return the Don CeSar to its former glory. The hotel reopened at the end of 1973 and has been on the National Register of Historic Places since 1975. In 1988, during the 60th anniversary of the St. Petersburg Beach landmark, some of the old fixtures bought by St. Pete residents in the 1940s were returned to the hotel.

The Don's architecture is Mediterranean, with a red tile roof, white trim accenting the pink stucco exterior, bell towers, and archways on the gulf side that lead to terraces and curved white balustrades. A stately vehicular ramp has been built over the highway in front of the hotel, so guests can disembark at the elegant second-floor lobby entrance. Inside are pale marble floors, Axminster rugs, high ceilings, tall arched windows with fanlights, and tapestries, etchings, and original paintings.

All guest rooms have thick wall-to-wall carpeting and French country furniture kept scrupulously clean. There are arched doorways to many of the guest rooms and bathrooms. The walls in the guest rooms have interesting angles accented by brightly painted moldings. The bathrooms are of delicately veined Carrara marble, with fixtures of polished chrome.

The duplex penthouses are impressive, with spiral staircases and access to enormous rooftop terraces overlooking the gulf and St. Petersburg. The indoor-outdoor carpeting on the terraces is worn and a little buckled, but the penthouses are a fine place for a party or a corporate reception.

On the terrace, pink stucco shelters with arched doorways and tiled roofs provide guests with poolside drinks and light meals; you can almost see Fitzgerald sitting here in a white linen suit, ordering a drink.

The best restaurant is the King Charles, which has won awards including the Trans-Culinaire Five-Star. The presentation, service, and ambience are as outstanding as the food. Also at the Don is Le Jardin, is a more casual restaurant catering to those who love seafood. Le Bistro, in a gardenlike setting, is an informal café that doubles as a nightclub in the evening. Zelda's is a new restaurant at the Don that seeks to bring back the heady days of the Roaring Twenties.

> **Sunsets at the Don are legendary, largely because of the backdrop, an Italianate terrace set with tropical trees and bright flowers overlooking the water. Dramatic white balustrades curve from the terrace garden and pool to double stairways that ascend to the French doors of the lobby.**

Downstairs, in what was once the original lobby of the hotel, is an old-fashioned ice cream parlor and sundries store. The red broken-tile floors are the same that Zelda and F. Scott Fitzgerald trod when they visited. If you ask the staff behind the counter, they may show you the original staircase, now a storage area, that is hidden behind a door.

Though service has slipped a little recently, especially at the front desk, the overall performance is good. Particular attention is given to the children's program so that both parents and kids will enjoy themselves. A huge room in the basement is set up like a nursery school, and every kind of activity imaginable is offered. The program is headed by a former schoolteacher who constantly thinks up creative things to do.

Visitors who poke around the basement and the restored fifth floor will notice some of the hotel's eccentricities. In parts of the Don, there are funny angles and odd little platforms, many of them built to hide the heating and air conditioning ducts.

In the middle of the marble reception room off the ballroom is an unusual fountain, a touching remnant of the Don's past. Originally on the fifth floor, it was moved here to replace one that was apparently destroyed or carted away. At its base is a ring of monklike figures, their hands folded piously and water shooting out of their mouths in a most undignified way. This charming piece gives a taste of the humor, as well as the beauty, that still graces the Don.

Island's End Cottages

1 Passe-A-Grille Way
St. Petersburg Beach, FL 33706
813-360-5023
Fax: 813-367-7890

*A rustic group of
private cottages*

Hosts: Jone and Millard Gamble.
Accommodations: 6 cottages. **Rates:** 1-bedroom cottages $68–$99, 2-bedroom cottage $145, 3-bedroom cottage $160; weekly rates available except in 2- and 3-bedroom cottages. **Included:** Continental breakfast. **Added:** 10% tax; $8 extra person. **Minimum stay:** 10% surcharge for 1-night stay in 2- and 3-bedroom cottages. **Payment:** Major credit cards. **Children:** Welcome. **Smoking:** Allowed. **Open:** Year round.

Although the address of Island's End is St. Petersburg Beach, this island location is thought of by locals on the west coast as a separate, very special place. Passe-A-Grille is a historic town and has some preserved cottages from the early part of this century that residents are especially proud of. The town is on the southernmost tip of the peninsula that makes up St. Petersburg Beach, so you can stand at that tip and see the bay on one side and the gulf on the other. Island's End is on the southeast corner, more bay than gulf, but you can walk to the gulf's public beach. The beach is a free-wheeling place, with a mix of people — everyone from elderly widows taking a morning constitutional to gay couples sunbathing and picnicking. The area is not well known by tourists.

Like Passe-A-Grille, Island's End is a real find. The street side of the place looks like the back of a small motel. But tucked away behind the sub-tropical foliage are six hidden cottages, connected by weathered boardwalks and lattice porches. Each cottage in this rustic enclave is slightly different, with weathered gray vertical siding on the outside and knotty pine or plaster walls inside. Furnishings are contemporary, with a king, two twins, or queen bed in the bedroom and pull-out double or queen sofas. All have full kitchens, cable TV, and telephones. Laundry facilities and barbecue grills are available for everyone to use.

> **The boardwalk is punctuated by sandy flower beds and Florida greenery. Everything looks very natural and informal, but pretty.**

A special guest house, referred to in the office as "A," can be rented with either two or three of its bedrooms. There's also a queen-size sleep sofa in the living room. The well-equipped kitchen includes a dishwasher and microwave. The house has its own heated pool and an atrium. It's directly on the water; a wall of glass doors looks out over the gulf.

All the cottages have access to porches and decks of weathered wood and lattice. These are furnished with lawn chairs and tables. There's also a wood gazebo at the water's edge. Many guests enjoy the complimentary breakfast of orange juice and croissants on a covered porch or in the gazebo.

Most people staying here spend most of their time right here: in the sand and sunshine of the little beach or in the shade of the pavilionlike porches. But guests can also fish off the pier on the property, and there's the public beach adjacent and beaches all along the St. Pete coast. Along the bay side is a sea wall (where people also fish) and park benches that are pleasant to sit on in the evening. This end of St. Petersburg Beach seems to be safe and is quieter than the "strip" farther up on the peninsula at night. Most guests don't wander too far afield, however, since Island's End "backyard" is so pleasant. At night, the boardwalk and flower beds are softly lit, making the place look even more like a hideaway.

Trade Winds on St. Petersburg Beach

5500 Gulf Boulevard
St. Petersburg Beach, FL 33706
813-367-6461
Reservations: 800-237-0707

> *A beachside location
> and paddleboats*

General manager: Christopher Ezzo. **Accommodations:** 381 rooms. **Rates:** Rooms $110–$210, 1-bedroom suites $144–$310; packages available. **Minimum stay:** 2–5 nights with some packages. **Added:** 10% tax. **Payment:** Major credit cards. **Children:** Under 12 free in room with parents. **Smoking:** Allowed. **Open:** Year-round.

With paddleboats on the narrow waterways, railed verandahs, and white gazebos overlooking the beach, there is some romance to this busy resort. Yes, the little streams are man-made, and maybe it's all a bit much, but after a few hours it doesn't matter. Here you can leave your practical self behind.

> **There's paddleboating on the waterways that meander through the resort, and sailing and windsurfing on the beach.**

Trade Winds caters to families. Guests choose among hotel rooms, one-to three-bedroom suites, and penthouses. Guest rooms have a West Indian feel, with bamboo furniture and terra cotta tile floors. Amenities include TV, coffeemaker, toaster, wet bar, and, in the suites, full kitchens.

Trade Winds offers dining and dancing in the evening and live entertainment till late at night. The Palm Court, for intimate dining, is decorated with white open-work railings and potted palms. Silas Dent's restaurant across the street is more casual; you can sample alligator appetizers here. During the day, indulge in a refreshing drink at Reflections, the resort's waterside piano bar. You can also get a drink and a light meal at the Flying Bridge, which floats on the waterway along with the white ducks.

The chefs can create large buffets for groups, and Trade Winds is a popular meeting place. Its executive meeting center can handle up to 1,000 people, with a large conference hall and several meeting rooms that look out to a rectangular pool of gushing fountains.

A supervised children's activity program, play areas, and an electronic game room assure adults plenty of time to pursue their own activities,. There's tennis, paddle tennis, racquetball, croquet, and a putting green; golf is nearby. Deep-sea charter fishing can be arranged. Trade Winds has four pools, as well as beachfront whirlpools, a health center, and a sauna. Families can spend time together and apart.

Although the town of St. Petersburg Beach is a little tacky (and Trade Winds is on the main drag), the resort is worth visiting for its beachside location alone. Here, there is pale peach sand, millions of shells, and a warm, rolling surf.

SANIBEL ISLAND

Casa Ybel Resort

2255 W. Gulf Drive
P.O. Box 167
Sanibel Island, FL 33957
813-472-3145
Reservations:
813-481-3636
800-237-8906

> *A time-share resort that welcomes all*

General manager: Tom Britt. **Accommodations:** 114 villas. **Rates:** 1-bedroom suites $165–$260, 2-bedroom suites $199–

$320; weekly rates only during winter season; packages available. **Minimum stay:** In winter and with some packages. **Added:** 9% tax; $5–$10 extra adult; maid service $40 in 2-bedroom villas, free in 1-bedroom villas. **Payment:** Major credit cards. **Children:** Under 2 free in room with parents. **Smoking:** Allowed. **Open:** Year-round.

To get to Casa Ybel, guests take the causeway from Fort Myers to Sanibel Island. The entrance has a security gate and a bumpy wooden bridge beyond, which must be traversed slowly. The slowness is a good introduction to Casa Ybel. Here you can unwind and just lie on the beach, or you can play a sharp game of tennis — and then lie on the beach again.

> **Latticed gazebos and lighted barbecues invite old-fashioned community closeness.**

The resort was opened years ago as the Thistle Lodge, a Queen Anne–style house that was the island's first inn. The old inn is now a restaurant and lounge.

Accommodations are one- and two-bedroom villa suites in two-story Florida cottages with gray wooden siding and dormers. Like many homes in this region, the suites are built on stilts as a precaution against hurricanes. All the suites have kitchens, making them ideal for those who prefer to eat in. The two-bedroom villas have galley kitchens with a full-size refrigerator, stove, microwave, double metal sink, cutting board, coffeemaker, toaster, and a full set of dishes and pots. The master bedrooms have king-size beds, good wicker and oak furniture, and a private tile bath. The open living and dining area has a comfortable sofa and easy chairs, and a dining room table with four chairs. Upstairs is a bedroom with two twin beds and another bathroom. Bathrooms on both floors have a Roman tub and shower.

The one-bedroom villas are modest, with a small kitchen along one wall and a basic bath with tub and shower. The bedroom is large enough for two double beds and an ash bureau. There are some welcome touches here. All suites have screened-in porches that overlook the water and either wall-to-wall carpeting or ceramic tile.

Behind the villas is a patio with a poolside bar, a large swimming pool, a children's pool, and a whirlpool. Beyond is the beach and the emerald gulf. The tennis center, with several courts, is across the parking lot on Gulf Drive. It includes a pro shop and conference rooms.

Casa Ybel's gourmet restaurant is in the old Thistle Lodge, a re-creation of a Queen Anne cottage built by the original settler for one of his daughters. The lodge has a number of dining rooms on the first and second floors, each decorated differently. Many people have drinks overlooking the water at sunset and then have dinner in the attractive dining room with an intimate, turn-of-the-century setting.

A nature walk on the property runs past a lagoonlike fishing pond where an island gazebo is reached by a wooden bridge. Part of the grounds has been allowed to grow naturally, making a hospitable environment for waterfowl and other wildlife. A sign in the middle of the pond reads "Feeding Alligators Prohibited by Law." You know you're on a subtropical island.

Song of the Sea

863 East Gulf Dr.
Sanibel Island, FL 33957
800-231-1045,
813-472-2220
Fax: 813-472-8569

*A European-style
B&B overlooking
the gulf*

Innkeeper: Patricia Slater. **Accommodations:** 30 studios and suites. **Rates:** Studios $129–$259, beachfront suites $159–$289. **Included:** Continental breakfast, bicycles, beach chaises, club tennis. **Minimum stay:** With some packages. **Added:** 9% tax. **Payment:** Major credit cards. **Children:** Welcome. **Smoking:** Allowed. **Open:** Year-round.

Sanibel Island has become so popular that there are now a number of places to stay on the gulf. So many line Gulf Boulevard that it is difficult to choose. Song of the Sea is special in that its American informality is coupled with an eclectic Continental–West Indies decor and European sophistication. The result is a beach retreat where honeymooners, retirees, and young families all feel comfortable.

Song of the Sea was built by a Frenchman in 1969. Guests driving in first see a low-slung, pale pink stucco building with a barrel tile roof and a porte cochere. This is the lovely reception center where visitors register at a French country desk in the "living room." A lending library of best sellers and videotapes is arranged on bookshelves opposite the deeply cushioned sofa. A Continental breakfast buffet is set up here each morning.

Innkeeper Patricia Slater explains how to borrow books or bicycles, sign up for golf or tennis, use the laundry room and barbecue grills, or anything else about the island or the inn that guests need to know. The staff is unobtrusive but helpful so that visitors can have as much time on their own as they wish. Ms. Slater is qualified to marry guests or assist them in renewing their vows. Many couples come here for both honeymoons and anniversaries.

Just outside the French doors of the reception center is a brick-paved terrace with dark green iron lawn chairs and glass tables shaded by green and white striped umbrellas. Small Greek statuary pieces, white plaster urns filled with greenery, and clay pots of flowers are placed near the tables and at the little fountain in the center of the terrace. Citrus trees, palms, and other greenery screen the area, giving it privacy from the resort next door. During the day, guests can sun and read out on the terrace. In the morning, most people enjoy their breakfast here, which consists of croissants, cheese Danish, apple turnovers, bagels, fresh bread, and muffins. There's also yogurt and fruit.

Accommodations are in two-story stucco buildings painted light pink, with white trim and small green shutters. Each room has a European name, like Milano or Danzig. A water cooler provides spring water for those who find the taste of Sanibel water a bit sour. All accommodations have kitchenettes with a full-sized refrigerator, microwave, and small stovetop. The bathrooms are small but pretty, with hair dryer, single sink, and tub-shower.

Suites have a bedroom with a queen bed, TV, and small bureau. There is no closet in the bedroom, but there is good closet space in the entryway. The living–dining room has an armoire hiding a television and VCR, a small wood table with four chairs, and a queen-size sofa bed. Rollaways are available. A screened balcony or patio provides a view of poolside gardens and, in second-floor accommodatons, the gulf waters beyond.

> **A naturalist gives a talk on shells every Monday morning. The shell room behind the pool has a sorting table and a hot plate with a pot for boiling shells. Collectors often spread out their prizes on their patios and balconies to dry.**

Studio accommodations have two queen-size beds rather than a separate bedroom, but they are not too crowded. There is room for a kitchenette and small table in the entryway as well as a table and four chairs in the room itself. The studios have the same attractive balcony and carpeting. Fresh flowers are placed in the bedroom and the bath, and a bottle of wine sits on the little kitchen table, compliments of the innkeeper.

Cement sand dollar steps and paving bricks lead from the accommodations to the pool and Jacuzzi and a patio furnished with chaise longues. Beyond the patio is a lawn with barbecue grills, a shuffleboard court, a small shell room for washing and sorting seashells, and, at the end of the property nearest the beach, chaises and lawn chairs where guests can sit and watch the sun set over the gulf.

All the beaches on Sanibel Island are famous for excellent shelling, and most people on the beach in the morning have a bucket or plastic bag for collecting. The best time to look is in the early hours after a storm.

There are, of course, many other things to do here in addition to Sanibel's famous shelling. Guests can sign up for complimentary bicycles to ride into town or down to the lighthouse. Tennis is complimentary at the nearby Sundial Resort, and golf at the Dunes Country Club requires a moderate fee.

Then there is the beach, relatively uncrowded along this stretch, and the warm waters of the gulf. In town, there are a number of restaurants and boutiques, gourmet shops, and ice cream parlors along Periwinkle Way. For those who wish to do most of their own cooking, Jerry's is the place to stock up on groceries. This supermarket and shopping center is an event in itself, with a subtropical garden where a waterfall tumbles over fern-draped rocks and cockatoos and parrots squawk from their cages.

In spite of all the grumbling of locals about the onslaught of big city life, Sanibel Island remains one of the safest, most relaxing places to vacation in Florida.

Sundial Beach and Tennis Resort

1451 Middle Gulf Drive
Sanibel Island, FL 33957
813-472-4151

> *A large, happy, busy resort*

General Manager: Michael Peceri.
Accommodations: 265 suites.
Rates: Rooms $153–$383, suites $186–$435; packages available; special group rates. **Minimum stay:** With some packages. **Added:** 9% tax; $15–$20 extra person. **Payment:** Major credit cards. **Children:** Welcome. **Smoking:** Allowed. **Open:** Year-round.

Sundial is Sanibel Island's largest and most complete resort, with tennis and golf and extensive meeting facilities for large groups. For those who want a quiet retreat, this is not exactly it, though the Sundial may surprise visitors with its quiet side during spectacular sunsets in the evening and the peaceful waters of the gulf in early morning.

The resort has 10,000 square feet of meeting space, including two ballrooms and a number of conference rooms. The conference services staff has a reputation for excellent service no matter what the size of the meeting. Audiovisual equipment includes slide, movie, and overhead projectors, tape recorders, large-screen TV, VCRs, blackboards, flip charts, and sophisticated sound systems. Banquet catering for large functions seems to be quite professional. Children and spouses staying during a conference are well taken care of, with plenty to do day and night.

> **This is a place where everyone can successfully combine an appreciation of natural island beauty with vigorous activity and periods of relaxation.**

A recreation program called Smiles has activities for both children and adults conducted by recreational professionals. The resort has six clay and six hard tennis courts, with a matching service, pro clinics, lessons, and round robin tournaments. Golf privileges are at an 18-hole course at the Dunes Golf and Country Club. Boats and Windsurfers are also available, and deep-sea fishing can be arranged. In addition to swimming in the gulf, there's freshwater swimming at the five pools. The main pool is in a large patio area behind the reception center where there is also a ten-person Jacuzzi.

Near the patio restaurant is the Environmental Coastal Observatory Center, which acquaints kids and adults with the wildlife and vegetation of Florida. This little room has changing exhibits dealing with endangered species, mangrove forests, the predatory habits of various fish, and dangers to the saltwater environment. In the "touch tank," kids can actually hold some sea animals and watch as mollusks lay eggs or crabs crawl out of their shells. The center's aquarium holds various sea creatures from west coast waters that are frequently exchanged with new animals, so there is always something new to see during an extended vacation. An "adoption" program lets kids take home a hermit crab.

Kids and adults can, of course, learn a great deal about the environment by simply shelling on the beach. More than a dozen species are relatively easy to find, and there are so many thousands of individual specimens that people crunch on them everywhere. The gentle waves on the gulf make this an ideal place to wade with toddlers and help older children learn to swim. After the beach, guests can wash up in the patio bathroom, which has showers for those who don't want to track sand and seaweed into their room.

Accommodations are in condos in the resort's rental pool. They have a master bedroom with a king or two doubles, a twin-bedded room, two baths, a living room, dining area, and, in larger units, a den. Kitchens are equipped with full-sized appliances and dinnerware and cookware. Some units have two floors connected by a spiral staircase. All accommodations have access to a private swimming pool. Large, screened-in porches have views of the gulf or the pool and garden. The nicely landscaped lawn and garden areas include fountains at each accommodation cluster.

The Sundials has a lounge bar overlooking the gulf and two restaurants: Windows on the Water, specializing in gourmet seafood, and Hoopies, a Japanese seafood and steakhouse where chefs prepare the meal as guests watch. At the pool, there's Crocodile's, a bar and grill. The walls opposite Crocodile's are painted with mischievious crocodiles and bright green palm fronds. It's a whimsical touch that reminds people not to take anything too seriously at the Sundial.

SARASOTA

Half Moon Beach Club

2050 Ben Franklin Drive
Lido Beach, Sarasota, FL 34236
800-358-3245
813-388-3694
Fax: 813-388-1938

*An unpretentious
beachside resort*

General Manager: Shelley Lederman. **Accommodations:** 85 rooms and suites. **Rates:** Rooms $80–$225, suites $150–$225. **Included:** Complimentary breakfast with summer/fall packages. **Minimum stay:** During some holidays and special events. **Added:** 9% tax; $15 for extra person; roll-aways $15. **Payment:** Major credit cards. **Children:** 17 and under free in room with parents. **Smoking:** Smoking allowed. **Open:** Year-round.

The west coast of Florida is dotted with more than a thousand islands. The cluster of small islands or keys along Sarasota Bay are some of the loveliest. With the considerable cultural offerings of Sarasota just across the bridge, these islands are ideal for vacationers who want more than a beach. There is a chic quality to the area, especially along the boulevards and elegant shops of Armonds Circle.

Located at the lower end of the key, near a wooded beachside park, the Half Moon has a getaway feel. Although the word *club* in its name might sound as if this is one of the many private west coast resorts where overnight guests are just an afterthought, this is not the case. Part of the unassuming, friendly atmosphere is due to the staff, who are genuinely cordial and service-oriented.

Half Moon Beach Club is a host hotel for the Sarasota French Film Festival in November and the Sarasota Music Festival in June. It is also one of the sponsors of the Jazz Festival and the Winefest in April.

The exterior is of white stucco and glass bricks, a modern version of Florida Art Deco. Inside, green plants and tropical flower arrangements are set against the white stucco walls of the common rooms. Behind the crescent-shaped building are the pool and patio, landscaped in palms and tropical flowers and greenery. A short walk beyond is a beach deck, furnished with chaise longues and tables and chairs, and the beach itself, with powdery sand and gentle waves. There's also shuffleboard and beach volleyball, as well as golf and tennis off property that can be arranged by the staff.

All the rooms and suites were thoroughly refurbished in 1993. The deluxe beachfront rooms, with a king bed and kitchenette, are good for couples; so are the less expensive standard rooms, with a king bed and small refrigerator. Ideal for families are poolside accommodations with two queen beds or rooms in the Seaside building with two double beds or a king and sofa bed. These have kitchenettes with a stovetop, microwave oven, and small refrigerator. The one-bedroom suites are the most spacious for a family, with two queen beds, a living room with a sofa bed, and a kitchenette.

All accommodations have coffeemakers, direct-dial telephones, color TV, and a patio or balcony. Furnishings have a Caribbean flavor. The kitchenettes at the Half Moon Beach

Club are adequate for preparing simple menus, but most guests eat at least some of their meals in the restaurant.

There are also expensive but excellent restaurants and bistros at Armonds Circle. For regional theater that sometimes approaches the caliber of New York theater, ask the concierge about the Asolo Center for the Performing Arts. A popular outing is a visit to the Ringling museum.

TAMPA

Hyatt Regency Westshore

6200 Courtney Campbell
  Causeway
Tampa, FL 33607
813-874-1234
800-233-1234
Fax: 813-281-9168

> *One of Tampa's most appreciated business hotels*

Accommodations: 445 rooms. **Rates:** Rooms $105–$219; packages and weekend discounts available. **Minimum stay:** With special packages. **Added:** 10.5% tax; $10 roll-away. **Payment:** Discover, MasterCard, Visa. **Children:** Under 18 free in room with parents. **Smoking:** Nonsmoking available. **Open:** Year-round.

Just four minutes from the airport, and a few minutes' drive from downtown Tampa, the Hyatt Regency Westshore has much to recommend it. It is an ideal location for the business traveler, yet its 35-acre nature preserve and Old Tampa Bay location give it a relaxing, secluded ambience.

With two excellent restaurants, both on Tampa's Five Best Restaurants list, and the Casita Conference Center, the Hyatt is ideal for meetings. Although the hotel is in a section of the city that was for years a marshy territory of cheap honky-tonks and struggling businesses, Hyatt and other developers are doing their best to change that image. Tampa's recent surge in hotel construction has

> **Off-hours relaxation centers around the Hyatt's four lounges and three restaurants. The rooftop restaurant, Armani's, serves northern Italian cuisine, while Oystercatchers has mostly seafood. Both are frequented by discerning Tampa residents as well as hotel guests.**

resulted in some interesting high-rise architecture. The Hyatt Westshore has a serpentine design built of glass and concrete. Its 445 guest rooms and suites have some lovely views of the bay and the hotel's nature preserve. The grounds include the two-story whitewashed Casita Conference Center villas, with eight conference rooms and 40 guest rooms.

Both the villas and the hotel rooms are decorated in soothing pastels and French provincial or traditional furniture. The best rooms for business travelers are those on the Regency Club floor. These are quite spacious, well organized for work, and include 24-hour concierge service. A limousine to Tampa's business district is available for Regency Club guests.

There are two freshwater swimming pools on the property, as well as a health club, tennis courts, whirlpool spas, and sailing. Cruises and golf can be arranged through the hotel.

The Hyatt's lobby is another favorite gathering place. It is a pleasure simply to walk across the floors, which are made up of different kinds and colors of marble laid out in patterns and borders. Throughout are sitting areas of light French provincial chairs, and sofas upholstered in pastels. With massive pillars and archways and a trompe-l'oeil ceiling of leafy ferns, this lobby takes your breath away.

Sheraton Grand Hotel

4860 W. Kennedy Boulevard
Tampa, FL 33609
813-286-4400
800-325-3535
Fax: 813-286-4053

*A functional
and inspirational
place to work*

Accommodations: 325 rooms, 23 suites. **Rates:** Rooms $139–$159, suites $260; discounts available. **Minimum stay:** None. **Added:** 10.5% tax. **Payment:** Major credit cards; personal check. **Children:** Free in room with parents. **Smoking:** Nonsmoking available. **Open:** Year-round.

Connected to Tampa's Urban Centre offices by two 11-story atriums and only a few minutes' drive from downtown and the airport, the Sheraton Grand is an excellent convention and business hotel.

Convention and conference facilities are functional and beautiful, with a professional planning staff on hand. The 5,000-square-foot grand ballroom, which can be divided into three separate rooms, opens into a reception area with a spectacular view of one of the atriums. Other amenities are a theater with built-in audiovisual equipment, a boardroom, and eight executive meeting rooms.

The Sheraton is also an excellent place to unwind and play. The heated outdoor pool has a deck that overlooks Tampa Bay. Windows in the rooms and suites have double drapes to block out the sun on those mornings when you want to wake up late or slowly. Standard rooms include a desk, and the lighting is good; furniture is dark-stained bamboo or traditional. Suites have a comfortable, elegant parlor with deep-cushioned chairs and a sofa, ideal for a small conference or for relaxing.

Accommodations include a Grand Club Floor, which caters to the business traveler with extras like calculator telephones. The club room has a home-away-from-home ambience and elegant decor, with vases of orchids and other exotic flowers on the glass tables. A complimentary Continental breakfast is served here every morning, and cocktails are offered in the evening.

For unwinding in a lounge setting, the bar is intimate, with rich, dark woods, soft lighting, and welcoming armchairs.

Those who want a little more action and people-watching will find the lobby lounge a favorite spot, with piano music and the soothing rush of waterfalls and fountains from the gardenlike atrium.

The hotel's Courtyard Café has this same airy, garden feel, with a view of the fountains and green plants in the adjacent patio. French doors open for alfresco seating in balmy weather. The Sunday brunch here is popular with Tampa families. J. Fitzgerald's is an even bigger hit, especially with

> **A staff member is always on hand to give directions to downtown businesses, make arrangements for theater tickets, suggest places to eat downtown, and otherwise make a guest's stay hassle-free.**

local gourmands. It offers expensive and excellent international cuisine. Fresh seafood is a specialty, and the wine list is extensive.

Wyndham Harbour Island Hotel

725 S. Harbour Island Boulevard
Tampa, FL 33602
813-229-5000
800-822-4200
Fax: 813-229-5322

> *An excellent meeting place for business groups*

Accommodations: 300 rooms and suites. **Rates:** Rooms $179–$219; weekend and other discount rates available. **Minimum stay:** None. **Added:** 10.5% tax. **Payment:** Major credit cards. **Children:** Free in room with parents. **Smoking:** Allowed. **Open:** Year-round.

Harbour Island in Hillsborough Bay is a 177-acre complex of businesses, condominiums, restaurants, boutiques, a marina, and a luxury hotel — the Wyndham Harbour Island Hotel. But since Hillsborough Bay is right in the middle of Tampa/St. Pete, the island is essentially in downtown Tampa. Thus, views from the upper floors of the hotel are of both the city and the water.

Harbour Island is accessible by car or an air-cushioned launch called a people-mover. The complex has brick walkways, exuberant fountains, and a festive mix of boats, shops, and busy people. Just across the bridge from Harbour Island is the impressive Tampa Convention Center.

> **At the Market at Harbour Island, shoppers will find 70,000 square feet of boutiques, restaurants, and specialty shops.**

The hotel itself is beautifully furnished and decorated and has some outstanding amenities. The floors of the lobby are of dark green marble with deep-pile area rugs, furniture is upholstered in rich green wool or tapestry, and Oriental vases with dramatic flower arrangements accent the tables. The massive doors into the ballroom are of tiger maple, with distinctive brass handles. The design and craftsmanship are excellent, with interesting recessed areas, wooden moldings on the ceilings, and large wooden pillars.

The 300 guest rooms and executive suites are geared primarily toward businesspeople, though they are spacious enough for a family. A standard room has two double beds or a king-size bed, with traditional mahogany furniture, an armoire hiding the TV, substantial drapes, and wall-to-wall carpeting. Bathrooms have marble countertops and tile tub showers.

Executive suites have dark-stained traditional or Oriental furniture and a comfortable sofa and chairs. The bedroom and parlor are separated by double glass and louvered doors. Luxury suites are even more lavishly appointed and have a dining room table and chairs. The spacious bathrooms include hair dryers and a vase of fresh flowers. All suites have panoramic views of the waterfront, downtown Tampa, Davis Island, and the new convention center.

The restaurants at Wyndham Harbour Island Hotel have not been popular with Tampa residents in the past, but the Sunday brunch at Harbourview Room is now frequented by both locals and guests. With its spectacular views of the harbor, the Harbourview Room, which serves American cuisine, is also popular for breakfast meetings during the week. The atmosphere and dress code are casual — though sometimes the service is a little too casual.

Gourmet Continental and American cuisine is served in the more formal Island Room. The white china and linen is accented with brass and glass candlesticks, and guests are seated in comfortable black leather chairs. The food is good and the service attentive. For cocktails, Garrison's Bar is the favored meeting place. It has a tropical feel, with potted palms and terrific views of the water.

The Wyndham's large pool, surrounded by chaises longues and tables with umbrellas, overlooks the marina. For those who want more vigorous activity, the hotel has an affiliation with the Harbour Island Athletic Club. State-of-the-art facilities include lighted, all-weather tennis courts, racquetball and squash courts, Nautilus and Hydra Fitness weight training systems, and an aerobics studio.

These upscale attractions provide some enjoyable distractions, but the Harbour Island Hotel is also an excellent place to get business done. The attractively appointed ballroom can accommodate up to 500 people for banquets, or it can be subdivided into smaller meeting spaces. There are seven conference rooms connected by a spacious foyer. Services for conferences and small conventions include professional planning and catering.

TARPON SPRINGS

Innisbrook Resort

U.S. Highway 19 North
P.O. Drawer 1088
Tarpon Springs, FL 34688-1088
813-942-2000
800-456-2000 in U.S. and Canada
800 HILTON-1

A famous golf resort near a historic town

General manager: Richard Ferreira. **Accommodations:** 1,000 suites. **Rates:** Club suites $86–$187, 1-bedroom suites $121–$223, 2-bedroom suites $167–$364; packages available. **Minimum stay:** 2, 3, or 5 nights with some packages. **Added:** 10% tax. **Payment:** Major credit cards, personal checks. **Children:** 17 and under free in room with parents. **Smoking:** 10 nonsmoking rooms. **Open:** Year-round.

Although Hilton now operates Innisbrook Resort, it was operated for years by Golf Hosts, Inc., which indicates what the major focus has always been here. But excellent golf is accompanied by tennis and other recreation, as well as nice accommodations, food, and service. The lawns look like green velvet, and there are sweeping beds of brilliant flowers everywhere. The golf courses and tennis courts are well cared for, and the service is usually attentive but unintrusive.

> **At Innisbrook you can be dead serious about your golf game and devote many hours to it, or you can hit a leisurely round each day with a business associate or family member. The Innisbrook Golf Institute specializes in small-group instruction to enable all levels to improve.**

Innisbrook has won just about every golfing award that exists. Its Copperhead course ranks among the top 100 in the world, and it has often been ranked the number-one course in Florida. The Copperhead, par 71, is made up of three nines and totals 7,031 yards. The Sandpiper, 6,006 yards, is the shortest of the three championship courses. The 6,999-yard Island course, par 72, is fraught with bunkers and lake hazards and demands some long tee shots. All three are dotted with loblolly pines and other native trees and large free-form flowerbeds. Occasionally, there are unusual hazards: elegant — and slow-moving — blue herons who do not understand the frustrations of an impatient golfer.

Tennis hardly takes a back seat here. The 18 tennis courts include 11 of clay and seven of Laykold, with seven lighted for night games. Head pro Terry Addison and the instructors of the Australian Tennis Institute offer private and group lessons, a junior program for children of all ages and levels, and a videotape training center. The tennis center has four indoor racquetball courts, an observation deck, whirlpool spas, a pro shop, and a cocktail lounge and snack bar.

Innisbrook also has six swimming pools, a Parcourse jogging trail, bicycling, lakeside fishing, and a racketball and fitness center with saunas and whirlpools. There is plenty to see and do off the property, with Busch Gardens and Cypress Gardens nearby, and great deep-water fishing and sightseeing in the Greek fishing village of Old Tarpon Springs.

Innisbrook has had great success in organizing meeting/golf packages for corporate retreats. There are three conference centers here. The Carnelian Conference Center is the most impressive, with a spectacular ballroom that has a massive crystal chandelier hanging from a brass ceiling.

Innisbrook has four restaurants, serving fresh Florida seafood, northern Italian, American, and Continental fare. These are good restaurants, popular not only among corporate and vacationing guests at Innisbrook but also in the Tarpon Springs and North Tampa area. Packages at the resort include full and modified American plans. The restaurants are the only places at Innisbrook where tipping is allowed.

Accommodations are in low-rise stucco and wood villas, which blend nicely with the stands of tall loblolly pines along the fairways. Club suites have twin bedrooms separated from the spacious living and dining room by sliding doors, a well-equipped kitchen with a built-in bar, and a balcony or patio. One-bedroom suites have a living room, a separate bedroom, a kitchen with bar, and a balcony. Two-bedroom suites can sleep up to six, with a much larger living and dining room, a kitchen and built-in bar, and a balcony overlooking the fairways or landscaped grounds.

UPPER CAPTIVA ISLAND

Safety Harbour Club

c/o Upper Captiva Property
   Management
P.O. Box 476
Captiva Island, FL 33924
813-472-9223

A secluded resort on an island sanctuary

Rental manager: Lois Thorp. **Accommodations:** Number of villas available for rent varies. **Rates:** $800–$2,650 per week; 10% off for each day not used during a stay of three or more days. **Included:** All club facilities; golf carts with some rentals. **Minimum stay:** 3 nights. **Added:** 9% tax; $42 club fee. **Payment:** Personal checks. **Children:** Free in villa with parent. **Smoking:** Nonsmoking rooms available. **Open:** Year-round.

The journey to Pine Island and the launch for Upper Captiva Island is a journey through Old Florida. The back roads have names like Burnt Store and Stringfellow, and part of the trek is through a Florida fishing village called Matlatcha, where the scene hasn't changed much in the last 50 years. The road has expanses of pine woods and what can only be called palmetto fields. Finally, there's the bridge to the island and the tiny Pine Island post office, a curving stretch of road with a few houses and a religious retreat settlement, and the Pineland Marina, which offers a glimpse of the wildlife that thrives on Upper Captiva. So many pelicans roost in the mangroves at the marina that it looks as if the trees might collapse under their weight. Little fish and crabs dart in the shadows of the moored boats. Visitors park here for a few dollars a night and then take the launch to Upper Captiva (you *must* have reservations even in the off-season).

After the allotted passengers, luggage, and foodstuffs are loaded, the launch takes off, passing Useppa Island, Cabbage Key, and small mangrove islands. Several minutes later the boat arrives in small Safety Harbor, barely ruffling the feathers of the cormorants sunning on the dock and the ospreys nesting on the observation tower at the wharf.

No cars are allowed on the island. Some villas come with golf carts, and others are available for rent. Houses face either the Intracoastal Waterway and dock or the gulf. The best and most expensive houses are on the beach. Houses near the dock and the Intracoastal side of the island can be a little noisier because of the "traffic" from golf carts whisking by on the little sand paths.

Accommodations are all privately owned, mostly by members of the Safety Harbor Club, which owns 35 acres of land on the island. Rentals are handled by a variety of real estate companies, some on the mainland, some on the island. The agency most people call is Upper Captiva Property Management, which has an office by the docks. Whether you come on your own boat or take the marina launch, someone from the agency can greet you when your boat docks and guide you to your accommodation. A club office a few hundred feet from the dock has small maps of the enclave that will help you get oriented.

Accommodations are in two- or three-bedroom villas built on stilts that are contemporary or Old Florida in architecture. Carpeted stairs lead up to a second-floor living room with a dining room and fully equipped kitchen. Usually there's a bedroom with king bed and bath behind the living room and one or two bedrooms and a bathroom on the dormered second floor. All the villas have washer/dryers and plenty of extra towels. There's also generous closet space. Ceiling fans and screened-in porches make it possible to do without air conditioning for all but the hottest months of the year.

Most couples and families who come here stay for at least a long weekend, buying their own food at the supermarket near Pineland Marina. For years, both vacationers and island residents had to do their own cooking except for an occasional lunch at Barnacle Phil's restaurant, but now the

> **The woods are so dense and jungly in places that it's easy to see what the west coast of Florida must have looked like when DeSoto and other explorers hacked their way through.**

island has two fun new restaurants: Over the Waterfront and Grady's Island Café. Over the Waterfront is right on the dock and tiny, but it has some mighty seafood dishes and great desserts, among them a key lime pie made from island limes. Grady's Island Café is a little bigger, with natural clapboard siding, a tin roof, and wicker-furnished verandahs. Herbs growing in clay pots on the back porch attest to the freshness of the chef's ingredients.

Both restuarants have general stores that sell some food and sundries: juices, soda, sun screen, T-shirts, tennis balls, and, at Grady's, fresh cream and Haagen Dazs ice cream. They also stock insect repellent, which is a must at any time of year, for most of the island is state land and has remained wild. Safety Harbor feels like a wildlife sanctuary, with lots of birds winging across the perfect skies and tiny lizards darting across the sandy paths.

Those who have a golf cart can park it under their villa and in designated areas by the restaurants. Sandy golf cart paths lead to the club's recreational facilities: an attractive pool and patio, two well-maintained tennis courts, and a clubhouse with a lending library and a nifty observation deck overlooking forest, beachfront, and a small pond where herons fish. The narrow golf cart paths also lead to the beach, a peaceful expanse of sand and shells that the sandpipers love as much as kids and adults.

It's really more fun — and more in keeping with the slow pace of Upper Captiva — to dispense with the golf carts altogether. Walking also has the advantage of providing a closer kinship with the island's wildlife and plant life. Bougainvillea and other exotic plants have been planted around the villas, but elsewhere the natural vegetation still grows wild. One of the most beautiful plants on the island is a sea grape with yellow hibiscuslike flowers that turn orange and then red before cascading to the forest floor. Vines grow profusely. Small animals scurry under the palmetto leaves and fall silent when someone approaches.

There is so much wildlife and untamed flora on Upper Captiva because most of the 700-acre island is a sanctuary operated by the state of Florida. The rest is owned privately by Safety Harbor Club members and by other private landowners who have a great respect for wildlife and a desire for privacy.

USEPPA ISLAND

Useppa Island Club

P.O. Box 640
Bokeelia, FL 33922
813-283-1061

Some of the most spectacular scenery in Florida

General manager: Vincent Formosa. **Accommodations:** 23 duplexes and cottages. **Rates:** $126–$444. **Minimum stay:** 2 nights on weekends. **Added:** 9% tax. **Payment:** Major credit cards. **Children:** Free in room with parents. **Smoking:** Nonsmoking rooms available. **Open:** Year-round.

After a stay on Useppa Island, you might think back and wonder why it was so special. Was it the luxury of the accommodations or the beach or the fishing or the atmospheric old Collier club? Or is it really true that Useppa Island has a mysterious and indescribable aura?

Most overnight visitors would say it's all of these things. Useppa is an island several miles off the west coast of Florida that can be reached only by boat or seaplane. The island itself is unlike any other in Florida, perhaps because, for a time, the jungle vegetation was allowed to take over the buildings that had been constructed here in the early 20th century.

> **The island offers tennis, croquet, shuffleboard, saltwater and freshwater swimming, lawn chess, and fishing. There's even a small museum of island history.**

Today, the subtropical flora has been allowed to grow naturally — though it is restrained from completely taking over — and is profuse and almost primeval. Many of the palm trees leaning over the Old Florida–style homes are draped with long ribbons of cactus that look like green, spiny snakes. Ancient banyan trees form massive canopies over the pink shell walkway that links the clubhouse and residences. One of these banyans is so old and so enormous that the roots that flow from its limbs to the ground have spawned a miniature forest of middle-aged and baby banyans.

The tropical vegetation on Useppa Island is some of the oldest in Florida, and Useppa itself is the oldest continuously occupied land mass on the west coast. From about 3500 B.C., the Caloosa Indians fished its abundant waters. Some time in the 1700s the Indians disappeared and the history of the island became linked with the Spanish. Prominent among them was the pirate José Gaspar, who imprisoned his love, Joseffa de Mayorga, on the island. Because she spurned him, he had her killed, and her ghost supposedly haunted him until he later killed himself. Legend says she still haunts the island named after her, altered over the years by fishermen from Joseffa to "Useppa."

In the early 1900s, New York millionaire Barron Collier bought Useppa and built a mansion for himself and tin-roofed cottages for his friends. The main attractions were tarpon fishing and the beach. After Collier died in 1939, Useppa passed into neglect until the mid-1970s, when the island was bought by Garfield Beckstead. With his wife and partners, Beckstead brought it back to its former beauty. Buried under ten feet of vegetation he found a winding pink pathway of crushed conch shells and cement that links the cottages to Collier's mansion, now the clubhouse and dining room.

The old cottages were restored and new ones built. Today, Useppa is a private club and residential community of mostly winter homes, with several cottages available for rent by a limited number of outside visitors. The interiors are attractively decorated and well laid out, with modern bathrooms and kitchens. All have screened-in porches. Houses are scattered throughout the island, but all must conform to strict design guidelines — ten pages of them. Their architecture follows the 1920s Old Florida style of the original Collier bungalows: crimped tin or gray asphalt roofs, large porches, latticework, and, usually, clapboard siding that is stained or painted gray or white.

In 1994, Gasparilla Cottage, an original building constructed by Collier's craftsmen, was converted into B&B-style accommodations for visitors here for a short stay. The old two-story, clapboard cottage has appealing features such as a stained glass window on the second floor and a wide front porch. Four rooms and suites have been furnished in period antiques. Plans call for additional hotel suites to be created above the dining rooms in the Collier mansion. Three meals a day will be available to guests at both Gasparilla Cottage and the mansion.

No automobiles are allowed on Useppa except for a few trucks used by the island maintenance crew. Most people get around by walking, bicycling, or driving a golf cart. Club activity is centered around the mansion, with its well-proportioned rooms converted into conference space, a lounge that feels like the living room of a summer cottage, an informal bar, and an elegant dining room. Food is good here, with a nouvelle cuisine menu, excellent service, and a great key lime pie.

At the Tarpon Inn Restaurant and Island Market, near the marina boat dock, a casual bar serves continental breakfast, light snacks and sandwiches, and drinks. The market sells some canned goods and other staples as well as the morning newspaper. The place has a summer camp atmosphere — friendly and unpretentious. Kitchen staff, corporate millionaires, and boatmen talk and joke easily together.

Useppa is only half a mile long and a third of a mile wide, so many of the paths and trails have views of water to east and west. In many of the cottages, you can see Pineland Sound from living room windows or a porch on one side of the house and the Gulf of Mexico from the bedroom on the other. The island's marina overlooks Pine Island Sound, part of the Intracoastal Waterway. The beach on the gulf side has fine, light sand that the maintenance crew rake almost every morning. The surf is gentle and warm. This is a very peaceful beach for sunning, strolling, or making sand castles.

VENICE

Banyan House

519 South Harbor Drive
Venice, FL 34285
813-484-1385
Fax: 813-484-8032

> *B&B rooms and apartments hosted by cordial innkeepers*

Innkeepers: Susan and Chuck McCormick. **Accommodations:** 1 room, 3 efficiencies, 5 apartments. **Rates:** Room $59–$79, efficiencies $79–$99, apartments $395–$595/week; $15 for extra adult. **Included:** Expanded Continental breakfast. **Minimum stay:** 2 nights on weekends; one week in some accommodations. **Added:** 9% tax. **Payment:** Personal checks. **Children:** Under 8 not allowed. **Smoking:** Only on patio. **Open:** Year-round.

Venice, Florida, offers just what one might hope from its name: warm waters and sunshine, Mediterranean homes and charming shops, palm trees and tropical flowers. The group that had the vision to create Venice, Florida, in the 1920s was the Brotherhood of Locomotive Engineers. One member of that group, Robert Marvin, had a beautiful Mediterranean-style house built for himself that, happily, is now the Banyan House.

To get to residential South Harbor Drive, visitors drive over a bridge to the historic section of Venice, called "the island," part of the city that was originally planned by the Brotherhood in the 1920s. The stucco Banyan House is one of the most distinctive homes in the area, with a brick drive and subtropical landscaping accenting the Spanish architecture. It's easy to find the place; just keep an eye out for the trees — huge, spreading banyan trees. The one at the end of the drive is a wonder. In the back of the house there's another amazing tree, a Cuban laurel, which hangs picturesquely above a bilevel patio.

Adjacent to the patio is a tree-shaded whirlpool and swimming pool, the first one constructed in Venice. Closer to the house is a terrace that leads to a solarium. This is where guests enjoy a breakfast that is modestly referred to as Continental: one day it's crêpes, another day it's French toast stuffed with cream cheese and strawberries. There's always a generous offering of homemade muffins or bread, fresh fruit, and steaming coffee. It's as filling as any "full" breakfast.

Behind the solarium is the living room, furnished in Victorian antiques, with elaborate valances above the windows. At one end of the room is a piano. Above is a beamed cypress ceiling. Guest rooms are upstairs. The Palm Room, the original master bedroom, has a king-size bed. Decorated in shades of pink, it has hardwood floors and area rugs and a fine fireplace and mantle. This room has a kitchenette and an original bathroom, which has a special step up to the tub, built for the former lady of the house, who was only four feet seven. The Laurel Room has a queen-size bed and a detached private bathroom. Compared to many of the B&Bs that have recently opened in Florida, the furnishings are fairly pedestrian. Drapes are polyester, and furniture is apt to be department-store French provincial or woven bamboo — it isn't up to the standard of the Victorian furnishings in the living room.

Accommodations include five apartments with private baths and kitchens next door and in a carriage house in the back, overlooking the patio. These are usually rented out by the week or month and are perfect for a family. Chuck and Susan constantly upgrade these, doing much of the work themselves. The ranch house next door has a newly refurbished apartment with a living room, a kitchen–dining area, a separate bedroom with king-size bed, and a tile bath with Jacuzzi. Floors are of ceramic tile or carpeted, and the furniture is a mix of contemporary and Mediterannean. The screened-in porch is furnished with a small table and chairs and a chaise. There is off-street parking for two cars.

> One of the best things about breakfast at the Banyan Tree is dining in the solarium, overlooking the back garden and the big laurel tree; the McCormicks encourage guests to linger over coffee and talk with other guests.

Apartment number 3, on the second floor of the carriage house, has a balcony from which guests have a wonderful view of the sunset while they barbecue on the grill. They can also look out over the Banyan House patio and pool The apartment has a dining room with a parquet floor, a kitchenette with a full-size stove and refrigerator, and a bedroom that can be outfitted with two twins or a king. A roll-away bed is also available. The tile and marble bathroom is bilevel — a sink and vanity on the first level and a large tub shower and toilet on the second. The living room is furnished with contemporary bamboo furniture and a round marble coffee table. Ceilings are a little low here, so someone six feet two might be happier in one of the other rooms or apartments. All guests at the Banyan House have access to coin-operated laundry facilities.

Guests say that the best thing about the Banyan House is the McCormicks themselves — their ideas and their hospitality. They do a number of small things that make people feel like guests in their home, like providing chilled fruit drinks in your kitchenette fridge or leaving a hand-lettered welcoming card from "Chuck and Susan" on the table. They leave post cards of the Banyan House in your room for you to use — already stamped, so you can send them off to friends without even stopping at the post office. Then more people can come here to sleep late and take in the charm of Old Venice, or soak in the whirlpool under the banyan trees.

WESLEY CHAPEL

Saddlebrook Golf and Tennis Resort

100 Saddlebrook Way
Wesley Chapel, FL 34249
813-973-1111
800-237-7519

*A walking village,
with spacious villa
accommodations*

Accommodations: 700 rooms and
suites. **Rates:** $90–$325; packages
available. **Minimum stay:** With packages. **Added:** 10.5% tax;
$20 extra person. **Payment:** Major credit cards; personal
check. **Children:** Under 12 free in room with parents. **Smoking:** Allowed. **Open:** Year-round.

There is a sense of community at Saddlebrook, even if one is
at the resort for a short stay. This, no doubt, is due to the fact
that vacationers and conference participants walk nearly
everywhere.

Saddlebrook has earned its reputation as a mecca for golf
enthusiasts and is the world headquarters of the Arnold
Palmer Golf Academy. Staff and management insure that
golfers want for nothing. Rather than simply having soft-
drink machines at shelters on the courses, a snack cart makes
daily rounds for those with a mid-game thirst. The two golf
courses have been ranked among Florida's best for years. Designed by Arnold Palmer, with cypress trees and lagoons a
part of the beauty and challenge, the Saddlebrook and the
Palmer provide hours of excitement. Special putting greens, a
practice range, and an excellent pro shop complete the picture.

The resort's reputation for tennis is largely derived from its
stature as the home base of the Harry Hopman International
Tennis Academy. This program has trained thousands of
young athletes and touring professionals from all over the
world, including many Davis Cup winners. Instruction in-
volves well-focused clinics, individual and private lessons,
round robins, and amateur tournaments. The courts themselves — 27 Har-Tru and 10 Laykold, with five lighted at
night — are immaculate and are in a beautiful setting. Small
islands between the courts are sheltered by awnings and have
tables and chairs for spectators. At Centre Court, there is

seating for up to 150. The tennis center includes a well-equipped pro shop and match services.

Golf and tennis are often incorporated into conference activities at Saddlebrook. Apart from this temptation, Saddlebrook is popular for meetings because of its impressive facilities and services: two ballrooms, several seminar and board rooms, catering, and a professional conference-planning staff. Meeting space includes the Lagoon Pavilion, accessible by a wooden bridge over a lagoon and worth seeing even for nonconventioneers. The pavilion's unusual design won awards for its architects. It can be used as an open-air facility or enclosed. The pavilion has lovely views of the lagoon and the tropical waterfowl who winter here or reside year-round.

Saddlebrook's 480 acres have so many species of wildlife and vegetation — including mysterious and beautiful cypress swamps — that it could be designated as a wildlife sanctuary. But, accommodations are a good deal more luxurious than the usual state-park digs. The hotel rooms and suites are all privately owned and rented out by the resort. Both the rooms and one- and two-bedroom villas feature kitchens, combination or separate living and dining rooms, and balconies. The bathrooms have mirrored closets and tile or marble shower baths. Luxury extras include terry robes.

The Jockey Club is equipped with a large exercise room and men's and women's spas, with whirlpools, saunas, steam rooms, and massage rooms. Guests can have fitness programs set up for the duration of their stay. The spa has a health bar and a unisex hair salon. As everywhere at Saddlebrook, the staff are friendly, knowledgeable, and concerned.

Rooms are decorated with Oriental artwork, and brass chandeliers hang over the dining room tables. For the most part, the low-rise villas are well constructed, with extras like marble window sills. In some of the rooms, however, the soundproofing is weak, and guests can hear creaking and muffled noises from the upstairs floors. Light sleepers might prefer a top floor or an end room.

Most guests stay in Saddlebrook's "walking village" accommodations, but there are also weekly, monthly, and annual rentals available in Lakeside Village. This development includes the resort's presidential suite, with a sunken living room, a spiral staircase, three bedrooms, three and a half baths, a private swimming pool and whirlpool just outside the door, and spectacular views of the pond and the golf course. The villa facades are buff-colored stucco with Tahitian-style shake roofs.

The reception center is the site of the resort's "superpool," a huge, lagoonlike pool that holds half a million gallons of water, has 25-meter racing lanes, and hosts water basketball and volleyball games. Adjacent are two whirlpools, a swim shop, and a children's wading pool and playground. During summer and the holidays, Saddlebrook has a well-supervised children's program.

For those as interested in good food and wine as in staying fit, the Cypress Room has an impressive gourmet menu. The Cypress Room is large enough to be used for banquets, but room dividers lend intimacy. A row of windows overlooks cypress trees draped with Spanish moss that emerge from a lake. Adjacent is the three-level Polo Lounge. With polished brass railings, soft candlelight, and a fireplace, this is clubby in the early evening and lively later on, when the band gets going.

Other spots for dining and convivial libation are the Little Club, a greenhouse-style lounge and dining room; the alfresco Little Club Patio, for light meals and drinks; the Gourmet Room, an elegant oak and brass dining room open Tuesday through Friday for small groups; and the Snack Shack and Halfway House on the golf course, serving light refreshments.

All the major facilities blend in with the scenery of Saddlebrook, rather than compete with it. Much use has been made of fieldstones in construction. Wherever possible, wood has been used for bridges and walkways. Native and imported trees and plants have been allowed to grow naturally. The cypress trees, with their Spanish moss dangling over lake and swamp waters, are the most impressive. But there are also several varieties of palm and oleanders, and small evergreens originally imported from China that now thrive in Florida.

Recommended Guidebooks

These books are excellent sources of information for fishing, camping, sightseeing, and restaurant suggestions.

Birnbaum's Walt Disney World. Edited by Stephen Birnbaum, Avon Books, 1994, 256 pages, paper, $10.95. This is the official guide to Walt Disney World, and the emphasis is on information rather than a more critical appraisal of each ride and attraction. Copious information is provided in this easy-to-read large-format book. The sheer volume of up-to-date information on every nook and cranny of this delightful place makes this guide well worth the price, even though ratings of many attractions are unclear. The maps are excellent in this annually updated guide.

Camper's Guide to Florida Parks, Trails, Rivers, and Beaches. Mickey Little, Gulf Publishing, 1987, 156 pages, paper, $12.95. Regionally organized and comprehensive in its coverage, this camping guide provides the essential details on camping sites, as well as maps showing campsites, trails, parking, and so on. Special features and riding and hiking trails are clearly marked.

Canoeing and Kayaking Guide to the Streams of Florida, Volume I: North Florida. Elizabeth F. Carter and John L. Pearce, Menasha Ridge Press, 1985, 190 pages, paper, $12.95. **Canoeing and Kayaking Guide to the Streams of Florida, Volume II: Central and South Florida.** Lou Glaros and Doug Sphar, Menasha Ridge Press, 1987, 136 pages, paper, $11.95. These solid guides to canoeing and kayaking opportunities provide all the detailed information needed to plan enjoyable, safe day trips or longer camping trips.

Cruising Guide to the Florida Keys. Frank Papy, Great Outdoors Publishing, 240 pages, paper, $16.95. Although a bit cluttered with ads, this book contains a lot of information on places to go, things to see, weather, marinas, and more, as well as several aerial satellite photos. Numerous charts (an "artist's sketch, not for navigation") are provided to orient travelers. The book is updated every two to three years.

Diver's Guide to Florida and the Florida Keys. Jim Stachowicz, Windward Publishing, 1991, 64 pages, paper, $4.95. This is a very useful collection of the best diving and snorkeling spots along the Florida coast, complete with charts, rules, and laws to consider, and a review of hazardous marine life to keep an eye on.

Diving and Snorkeling Guide to Florida's East Coast. Greg Johnston, PBC International, 1987, 96 pages, paper, $9.95. This guide, part of the Pisces series, is marvelously done, containing beautiful photos and information on the best areas, safety tips, and more. It provides the information you need for planning and experiencing the perfect diving and snorkeling vacation.

Fish Florida: Saltwater. Boris Arnov, Gulf Publishing, 1991, 232 pages, paper, $12.95. A top-notch guide that tells you where, when, and how to catch Florida's abundant marine fishes. It includes maps, tips on lures, baits, and riggings, and illustrations of fish species.

Florida Island Exploring: 57 Tropic Islands and the Keys. Joan Scalpone, Great Outdoors Publishing, 1987, 64 pages, paper, $4.95. This book contains myriad day-trip ideas. Also authored by Joan Scalpone are the *Let's Go Somewhere* booklets for South West, North West, and Tampa to Big Bend, Florida, published by the same publisher.

The Florida Keys, From Key Largo to Key West: A History and Guide. Joy Williams, Random House, 1992, 240 pages, paper, $12.00. An irreverant but loving look at the Keys' checkered past and ecologically endangered present. It includes maps and descriptions of worthwhile attractions as well as a few restaurant reviews.

Florida Off the Beaten Path: A Guide to Unique Places. Bill and Diana Gleasner, Globe Pequot Press, 1990, 136 pages, paper, $8.95. Full of unusual and delightful things to see and do, this guide takes you to some of those wonderful, less-discovered spots that most tourists just don't know about. Included are good descriptions, directions, general location maps, and other helpful details.

The Florida One-Day Trip Book: 52 Offbeat Excursions In and Around Orlando. Edward Hayes and Betty Ann Weber, EPM Publications, 152 pages, paper, $7.95. This is part of a well-done series on one-day trips in the Orlando area. Tours include history, sightseeing, shopping, festivals, galleries, music, dance, and just about anything else you could hope to do. There are lots of good ideas here. Most titles are updated regularly, and all the practical facts, including good driving directions, are included.

Florida Parks: A Guide to Camping in Nature. Gerald

Grow, Long Leaf Publications, 1987 (3rd ed.), 255 pages, paper, $11.50. This is an excellent guide to the vast selection of parks in Florida. It is arranged regionally, with each park nicely described and camping options and other important facts discussed. The latest updates are added to the back of each regional section. A clear emphasis on the environment and man's impact on it make this a particularly good guide for natives and visitors alike.

Florida's Historic Restaurants and Their Recipes. Dawn O'Brien and Becky Roper Matkov, John F. Blair Publisher, 1987, 204 pages, cloth, $12.95. This is a fantastic series of inexpensive hardback books combining the best recipes of the historic restaurants of each state with informative descriptions and reviews, including the practical details. Of course, the emphasis is on the recipes, so some of the titles are a bit old to be absolutely reliable on the current state of affairs at any particular restaurant. Nonetheless, they are a good way to start the selection process. For those who like to look over the recipes before they choose their restaurant, this series is just plain great.

Florida's Sandy Beaches: An Access Guide. University Presses of Florida, 1985, 221 pages, paper, $14.95. The options of beachgoers in Florida are many, and this is just the guide for those who need help making decisions. A large-format book, it gives a bit of history for each coastal county, as well as interesting anecdotes from the past. However, it mainly provides a comprehensive listing of beaches, location maps, and descriptions on how to get there and what to expect. This is a superb resource to the land where the beach is king, but bear in mind that severe weather and other realities can change a beach location in various ways.

Fodor's Disney World and Orlando Area. Fodor's Travel Publications/Random House, 1994, 146 pages, paper, $9.00. Solid information on tours, sporting activities, and sightseeing is included in this up-to-date guide.

A Gunkholer's Cruising Guide to Florida's West Coast. Tom Lenfestey, Great Outdoors Publishing, 1991 (8th ed.), 158 pages, paper, $17.95. This excellent large-format book covers in great detail all the specifics of sailing/cruising the waters of Florida's west coast from the Everglades to Pensacola. The charts are exact and usable for navigational purposes. The text is specific as to routes, anchorages, fuel, food, and every other need. This title is updated every one to two years.

Insight Guide: Florida. Houghton Mifflin Company, 1994, 396 pages, paper, $19.95. This is part of the excellent Insight Guide series. Produced by a Singapore company, these books weave an interesting text through a potpourri of spectacular photographs. There is a vast amount of information inside as well. The book devotes a good, meaty 50 pages or so to the history, geography, and people of the state. Then it takes the reader on a guided tour of all the major areas — the backcountry too — as well as providing special features on areas of unusual interest, parks, and so on. The "guide in brief" at the back does a commendable job with practical details, including respectable lists of lodging and accommodations. In general, these guides seem to be updated every two or three years, so information is quite current.

What's What

A cross-reference of accommodations by type and special interest.

Dockage Available with Advance Notice

Big Pine Key
  Bahia Honda Bayside Cabins, 305
Boca Raton
  Boca Raton Resort & Club, 232
Captiva
  South Seas Plantation, 375
  'Tween Waters Inn, 379
Destin
  Sandestin Beach Resort, 133
Fort Lauderdale
  Fort Lauderdale Marriott Hotel & Marina, 246
  Riverside Hotel, 252
Gasparilla Island
  Gasparilla Inn (limited), 383
Grenelefe
  Grenelefe Resort & Conference Center, 171
Howey-in-the-Hills
  Mission Inn Golf & Tennis Resort, 174
Hutchison Island
  Indian River Plantation Resort & Marina, 60
Islamorada
  Pelican Cove Resort (limited), 313
Lake Buena Vista
  The Grand Floridian, 186
Key Largo
  Marina Del Mar, 315
  Sheraton Key Largo Resort (limited), 317
Key West
  Hyatt Key West, 330
  Ocean Key House Resort & Marina, 344
Longboat Key
  Resort at Longboat Key Club, 390
Marathon
  Faro Blanco Marine Resort, 358

Hawk's Cay Resort & Marina, 360
Miami
Fisher Island, 241
The Spa at Turnberry Isle Yacht & Country Club, 229
New Smyrna Beach
Riverview Hotel, 75
Niceville
Bluewater Bay, 137
Orlando
Hyatt Regency Grand Cypress, 206
Palm Coast
Sheraton Palm Coast Resort, 81
Panama City Beach
Marriott's Bay Point Resort, 139
Punta Rassa
Sanibel Harbour Resort, 410
St. Petersburg
Stouffer Vinoy Resort, 416
Stuart
HarborFront Inn, 115
Tampa
Wyndham Harbour Island Hotel, 436
Upper Captiva Island
Safety Harbor Club, 441
Useppa Island
Useppa Island Club, 444

Fishing

Amelia Island
Amelia Island Plantation, 33
Big Pine Key
Bed and Breakfast on the Ocean: Casa Grande, 303
Bahia Honda Bayside Cabins, 305
Boca Raton
Boca Raton Resort & Country Club, 232
Captiva
'Tween Waters Inn, 379
Daytona Beach
Indigo Lakes Golf & Tennis Resort, 52
Destin
Sandestin Beach Resort, 133

Fort Lauderdale
  Lago Mar Resort, 248
Grenelefe
  Grenelefe Resort & Conference Center, 171
Hutchinson Island
  Indian River Plantation Resort, 60
Innisbrook
  Innisbrook Resort & Golf Club, 439
Islamorada
  Cheeca Lodge, 308
  Chesapeake Resort, 311
  Pelican Cove Resort, 313
Jupiter
  Comfort Suites-Intercoastal Marina, 70
Key Largo
  Largo Lodge, 314
  Marina Del Mar, 315
Key West
  Hyatt Key West, 330
  La Mer Hotel, 336
  Marriott's Casa Marina, 341
  Ocean Key House Resort & Marina, 344
  South Beach Oceanfront Motel, 351
  Southernmost Motel, 352
Lake Buena Vista
  Walt Disney World Resort, 181
Marathon
  Faro Blanco Marine Resort, 358
  Hawk's Cay Resort & Marina, 360
Niceville
  Bluewater Bay, 137
Palm Beach Gardens
  PGA National Resort, 288
Palm Coast
  Sheraton Palm Coast Resort, 81
Panama City Beach
  Marriott's Bay Point Resort, 139
Ponte Vedra Beach
  Ponte Vedra Inn & Club, 87
Punta Rassa
  Sanibel Harbour Resort & Spa, 410
St. Petersburg Beach
  Don CeSar Beach Resort, 419

Island's End Cottages (at sea wall), 422
Stuart
HarborFront Inn, 115
Upper Captiva Island
Safety Harbor Club, 441
Useppa Island
Useppa Island Club, 444

Golf

Amelia Island
Amelia Island Plantation, 33
Ritz-Carlton, Amelia Island, 45
Boca Raton
Boca Raton Resort & Country Club, 232
Captiva
South Seas Plantation, 375
Coral Gables
The Biltmore Hotel, 235
Daytona Beach
Indigo Lakes Golf and Tennis, 52
Destin
Sandestin Beach Resort, 133
Fort Lauderdale
Bonaventure Resort & Spa, 244
Gasparilla Island
Gasparilla Inn, 383
Grenelefe
Grenelefe Resort & Conference Center, 171
Howey-in-the-Hills
Mission Inn Golf & Tennis Resort, 174
Hutchinson Island
Indian River Plantation Resort, 60
Innisbrook
Innisbrook Resort & Golf Club, 439
Islamorada
Cheeca Lodge, 308
Jupiter
Jupiter Beach Resort, 73
Lake Buena Vista
Walt Disney World Resort, 181
Longboat Key
Colony Beach and Tennis Resort, 388
Resort at Longboat Key Club, 390

Miami
 Doral Saturnia International Spa Resort, 256
 Fisher Island, 241
 The Spa at Turnberry Isle Yacht & Country Club, 229
Naples
 Naples Beach Hotel and Golf Club, 401
Niceville
 Bluewater Bay, 137
Orlando
 Hyatt Regency Grand Cypress, 206
Palm Beach
 The Breakers, 278
Palm Beach Gardens
 PGA National Resort & Spa, 288
Palm Coast
 Sheraton Palm Coast Resort, 81
Panama City Beach
 Marriott's Bay Point Resort, 139
Pompano Beach
 Palm-Aire Spa Resort, 289
Ponte Vedra Beach
 Marriott at Sawgrass Resort, 85
 Ponte Vedra Inn & Club, 87
Port St. Lucie
 Club Med-Sandpiper, 89
St. Petersburg
 Stouffer Vinoy Resort, 416
Wesley Chapel
 Saddlebrook Golf and Tennis Resort, 450
West Palm Beach
 Palm Beach Polo & Country Club, 291

Nonsmoking Rooms Available or Smoking Prohibited

Amelia Island
 Amelia Island Plantation, 33
 Elizabeth Pointe Lodge, 36
 Florida House Inn, 39
 Phoenix' Nest, 42
 1735 House, 47

Apalachicola
   Gibson Inn, 131
Big Pine Key
   Bed and Breakfast on the Ocean: Casa Grande, 303
Boca Raton
   Boca Raton Resort & Country Club, 232
Captiva
   South Seas Plantation Resort, 375
Coral Gables
   The Biltmore Hotel, 235
   Hotel Place St. Michel, 237
   Omni Colonnade Hotel, 239
Daytona Beach
   Coquina Inn, 50
   Indigo Lakes Hilton Golf &Tennis Resort, 52
   Live Oak Inn, 54
Fort Lauderdale
   Bonaventure Resort & Spa, 244
   Riverside Hotel, 252
Gainesville
   Magnolia Plantation, 168
Grenelefe
   Grenelefe Resort & Conference Center, 171
Howey-in-the-Hills
   Mission Inn Golf & Tennis Resort, 174
Hutchinson Island
   Indian River Plantation Resort, 60
Innisbrook
   Innisbrook Resort & Golf Club, 439
Islamorada
   Cheeca Lodge, 308
Jacksonville
   House on Cherry Street, 64
   Plantation Manor Inn, 68
Jupiter
   Comfort Suites-Intercoastal Marina, 70
   Jupiter Beach Resort, 73
Key Largo
   Marina Del Mar, 315
Key West
   The Artist House, 320
   Eden House, 326
   Heron House, 328
   Pier House Resort & Caribbean Spa, 346

Lake Buena Vista
  Walt Disney World Resort, 181
Lake Helen
  Clauser's B&B, 188
Maitland
  Thurston House, 194
Miami
  Doral Saturnia, 256
  Grand Bay Hotel, 260
  Hotel Inter-Continental Miami, 262
  Mayfair House, 266
  The Spa at Turnberry Isle Yacht & Country Club, 229
Naples
  Inn by the Sea, 397
  Naples Bath & Tennis Club,399
  Naples Beach Hotel & Golf Club, 401
New Smyrna Beach
  Riverview Hotel, 75
  Safety Harbor Club, 441
Niceville
  Bluewater Bay, 137
Ocala
  Seven Sisters Inn, 199
Orange Park
  The Club Continental, 77
Orlando
  Peabody Orlando, 210
Palm Beach
  Brazilian Court, 277
  The Breakers, 278
  The Chesterfield, 281
  The Ocean Grand, 282
  Palm Beach Historic Inn, 284
Pensacola
  Leichty's Homestead Inn, 143
  Pensacola Grand Hotel, 146
Pompano Beach
  Palm-Aire Spa Resort, 289
Ponte Vedra Beach
  Lodge & Bath Club at Ponte Vedra Beach, 82
  Marriott at Sawgrass Resort, 85
Safety Harbor
  Safety Harbor Spa, 412

St. Augustine
  Carriage Way B&B, 92
  Casa de la Paz, 94
  Casa de Solana, 96
  Castle Garden B&B, 99
  Kenwood Inn, 100
  Old City House Inn & Restaurant, 103
  Old Powder House Inn, 105
  St. Francis Inn, 107
  Southern Wind, 109
  Victorian House, 111
  Westcott House, 113
St. Petersburg
  Mansion House B&B, 415
St. Petersburg Beach
  Don CeSar Beach Resort, 419
Sanford
  Higgins House, 215
Seaside
  Seaside, 148
Stuart
  HarborFront Inn, 115
  The Homeplace, 118
Tallahassee
  Cabot Lodge, 152
  Governors Inn, 154
Venice
  Banyan House, 447
Winter Park
  Fortnightly Inn, 217
  Park Plaza, 219
Useppa Island
  Useppa Island Club, 444
Wakulla Springs
  Wakulla Springs Lodge, 156

Pets Allowed with Fee and Advance Notice

Amelia Island
  Amelia Island Lodging System (some rentals), 47
Apalachicola
  Gibson Inn, 131

Captiva
'Tween Waters Inn, 379
Lake Wales
Chalet Suzanne, 190
Marathon
Faro Blanco Marine Resort, 358
Naples
World Tennis Center, 408

Tennis

Amelia Island
Amelia Island Plantation Resort, 33
Boca Raton
Boca Raton Resort & Country Club, 232
Captiva
South Seas Plantation, 375
'Tween Waters Inn, 379
Coral Gables
The Biltmore Hotel, 235
Daytona Beach
Indigo Lakes Golf and Tennis, 52
Destin
Sandestin Beach Resort, 133
Fort Lauderdale
Bonaventure Resort & Spa, 244
Fort Lauderdale Marriott Hotel & Marina, 246
Lago Mar Resort, 248
Marriott's Harbor Beach Resort, 250
Gasparilla Island
Gasparilla Inn, 383
Grenelefe
Grenelefe Resort and Conference Center, 171
Howey-in-the-Hills
Mission Inn Golf and Tennis Resort, 174
Hutchinson Island
Indian River Plantation Resort, 60
Innisbrook
Innisbrook Resort & Golf Club, 439
Islamorada
Cheeca Lodge, 308
Chesapeake Resort, 311
Pelican Cove Resort, 313

Jupiter
   Jupiter Beach Resort, 73
Key Biscayne
   Sonesta Beach Hotel, 254
Key Largo
   Marina Del Mar, 315
   Sheraton Key Largo Resort, 317
Key West
   Marriott's Casa Marina, 341
Lake Buena Vista
   Vistana Resort, 179
   Walt Disney World Resort, 181
Longboat Key
   Colony Beach and Tennis Resort, 388
   Resort at Longboat Key Club, 390
Marathon
   Hawk's Cay Resort & Marina, 360
Marco Island
   Marriott's Marco Island Resort, 393
Miami
   Doral Saturnia International Spa Resort, 256
   Fisher Island, 241
   The Spa at Turnberry Isle Yacht & Country Club, 229
Naples
   Naples Bath and Tennis Club, 399
   Registry Resort, 403
   World Tennis Center, 408
Niceville
   Bluewater Bay, 137
Orange Park
   The Club Continental, 77
Orlando
   Hyatt Regency Grand Cypress, 206
   Peabody Orlando, 210
   Sonesta Villa Resort Orlando, 212
Palm Beach
   The Breakers, 278
   Four Seasons Ocean Grand, 282
   Palm Beach Polo & Country Club, 291
Palm Beach Gardens
   PGA National Resort and Spa, 288
Palm Coast
   Sheraton Palm Coast Resort, 81

Panama City Beach
Marriott's Bay Point Resort, 139
Pompano Beach
Palm-Aire Spa Resort, 289
Ponte Vedra Beach
Lodge & Bath Club at Ponte Vendra Beach, 82
Marriott at Sawgrass Resort, 85
Ponte Vedra Inn & Club, 87
Port St. Lucie
Club Med-Sandpiper, 89
Punta Rassa
Sanibel Harbour Resort and Spa, 410
Safety Harbor
Safety Harbor Spa, 412
St. Petersburg
Stouffer Vinoy Resort, 416
St. Petersburg Beach
Don CeSar Beach Resort, 419
Trade Winds on St. Petersburg Beach, 424
Sanibel
Casa Ybel, 425
Sundial Beach and Tennis Resort, 430
Seaside
Seaside, 148
Tampa
Hyatt Regency Westshore, 434
Wyndham Harbour Island Hotel, 436
Upper Captiva Island
Safety Harbor Club, 441
Useppa Island
Useppa Island Club, 444
Wesley Chapel
Saddlebrook Golf & Tennis Resort, 450

Index

The Alexander, 268
Amelia Island Lodging Systems, 47
Amelia Island Plantation, 33
The Art Deco Hotels, 270
The Artist House, 320

Bahia Honda Bayside Cabins, 305
Banyan House, 447
The Banyan Resort, 322
The Beach Club, 183
Bed & Breakfast on the Ocean: Casa Grande, 303
Betsy Ross Hotel, 272
The Biltmore Hotel, 235
Bluewater Bay, 137
Boca Raton Resort & Country Club, 232
Bonaventure Resort and Spa, 244
Brazilian Court, 277
The Breakers, 278

Cabot Lodge, 152
The Caribbean Beach Resort, 184
Carriage Way B & B, 92
Casa de la Paz, 94
Casa de Solana, 96
Casa Ybel Resort, 425
Castle Garden, 99
The Cavalier, 270
Chalet Suzanne, 190
Cheeca Lodge, 308
Chesapeake Resort, 311
The Chesterfield, 281

Clauser's Bed and Breakfast, 188
Clearwater Beach Hotel, 381
The Club Continental on the St. Johns, 77
Club Med-Sandpiper, 89
Colony Beach and Tennis Resort, 388
Colony Hotel, 274
Comfort Suites–Intercoastal Marina, 70
The Contemporary Resort, 184
Coquina Inn B&B, 50
Courtyard at Lake Lucerne, 202

Disney Vacation Club, 185
Disney Village Resort, 185
Dixie Landings Resort, 187
The Dolphin, 178
Don CeSar Beach Resort, 419
Doral Saturnia International Spa Resort, 256
Driftwood Inn, 136
The Driftwood Resort, 121
Duval House, 324

Eden House, 326
Edgewater Beach Suite Hotel, 395
Elizabeth Pointe Lodge, 36
Essex House Hotel, 275

Faro Blanco Marine Resort, 358
Fisher Island, 241

Florida House Inn, 39
Ft. Lauderdale Marriott Hotel & Marina, 246
Fort Wilderness Campground, 186
The Fortnightly Inn, 217
Four Seasons Ocean Grand, 282

Gasparilla Inn, 383
Gibson Inn, 131
Governors Inn, 154
Grand Bay Hotel, 260
The Grand Floridian, 186
Grenelefe Resort & Conference Center, 171

Half Moon Beach Club, 432
HarborFront Inn B&B, 115
Hawk's Cay Resort and Marina, 360
The Herlong Mansion, 196
Heron House, 328
The Higgins House, 215
The Homeplace, 118
Hotel Inter-Continental Miami, 262
Hotel Place St. Michel, 237
House on Cherry Street, 64
Hyatt Key West, 330
Hyatt Regency Grand Cypress, 206
Hyatt Regency Miami, 264
Hyatt Regency Westshore, 434

Indian River Plantation, 60
Indigo Lakes Golf & Tennis, 52
Inn by the Sea, 397
Innisbrook Resort & Golf Club, 439
Island City House, 333
Island's End Cottages, 422

Jupiter Beach Resort, 73
Keewaydin Island, 385
The Kenwood Inn, 100

La Mer Hotel, 336
La Pensione, 334
Lago Mar Resort, 248
Largo Lodge Motel, 314
Leichty's Homestead Inn, 143
Little Palm Island, 354
Live Oak Inn and Restaurant, 54
The Lodge and Bath Club at Ponte Vedra Beach, 82

The Magnolia Plantation, 168
Mansion House Bed and Breakfast, 415
Marina Del Mar, 315
The Marquesa Hotel, 338
Marriott at Sawgrass Resort, 85
Marriott Reach Resort, 348
Marriott's Bay Point Resort, 139
Marriott's Casa Marina, 341
Marriott's Harbor Beach Resort, 250
Marriott's Marco Island Resort, 393
Mayfair House, 266
Mission Inn Golf & Tennis Resort, 174

Naples Bath & Tennis Club, 399
Naples Beach Hotel & Golf Club, 401
New World Inn, 145

Ocean Key House Resort & Marina, 344

Old City House Inn & Restaurant, 103
Old Powder House Inn, 105
Omni Colonnade Hotel, 239
Omni Jacksonville Hotel, 66
Omni Orlando Hotel at Centroplex, 208

Palm Beach Historic Inn, 284
Palm Beach Polo & Country Club, 291
Palm Island Resort, 373
Palm-Aire Spa Resort, 289
Park Plaza, 219
Peabody Orlando, 210
Pelican Cove Resort, 313
The Pensacola Grand Hotel, 146
Perry's Ocean-Edge, 56
PGA National Resort, 288
Phoenix' Nest, 42
Pier House Resort & Caribbean Spa, 346
Plantation Manor Inn, 68
Polynesian Village, 186
Ponte Vedra Inn & Club, 87
Port Orleans Resort, 187

The Registry Resort, 403
The Resort at Longboat Key Club, 390
Ritz-Carlton, Amelia Island, 45
Ritz-Carlton, Naples, 405
Ritz-Carlton, Palm Beach, 284
Riverside Hotel, 252
Riverview Hotel, 75

Saddlebrook Golf & Tennis Resort, 450
Safety Harbour Club, 441
Safety Harbor Spa & Fitness Center, 412

St. Francis Inn, 107
Sandestin Beach Resort, 133
Sanibel Harbour Resort and Spa, 410
Seaside, 148
Seven Sisters Inn, 199
1735 House, 47
Sheraton Grand Hotel, 436
Sheraton Key Largo Resort, 317
Sheraton Palm Coast Resort, 81
Simonton Court, 349
Sonesta Beach Hotel, 254
Sonesta Villa Resort Orlando, 212
Song of the Sea, 427
South Beach Oceanfront Motel, 351
South Seas Plantation, 375
Southern Wind, 109
Southernmost Motel, 352
Spa at Turnberry Isle Yacht & Country Club, 229
Stouffer Vinoy Resort, 416
Sundial Beach and Tennis Resort, 430
Sunny Shore Motel, 59
The Swan, 177

Thurston House, 194
Trade Winds on St. Petersburg Beach, 424
'Tween Waters Inn, 379

Useppa Island Club, 444

Victorian House, 111
Vistana Resort, 179

Wakulla Springs Lodge and Conference Center, 156

The Walt Disney World Resorts, 181
Westcott House, 113
World Tennis Center, 408
Wyndham Harbour Island Hotel, 436

Wynfield Inn–Main Gate East, 176
Wynfield Inn–Westwood, 214

The Yacht Club, 183